MIND TRIPS

Ulric Neisser shows how John Dean's Watergate testimony illustrates the complex relationship between memory and reality . . .

Maya Pines discusses how the healthy psyche handles stress . . .

Carol Gilligan explores whether the thoughts and feelings of men and women are fundamentally different . , .

Stanley Milgram illumines the dilemma of obedience . . .

Abraham Maslow offers his views on individual growth toward maximum psychological potential . . .

David D. Burns tells of the perils of perfectionism

Jerome D. Frank examines how and why a sane mind might launch an insane nuclear holocaust . . .

Discovering all this and far more are among—

THE PLEASURES
OF PSYCHOLOGY

DANIEL GOLEMAN, Ph.D., is a former editor at *Psychology Today*, and currently writes on psychology for *The New York Times*. He is the author of *Vital Lies, Simple Truths*. DAVID HELLER, Ph.D., is the author of *Power in Psychotherapeutic Practice* and *The Children's God*.

THE PLEASURES OF PSYCHOLOGY

Edited by

Daniel Goleman, Ph.D.
and
David Heller, Ph.D.

A MENTOR BOOK

NEW AMERICAN LIBRARY

NEW YORK AND SCARBOROUGH, ONTARIO

Library of Congress Catalog Card Number: 86-60521

ACKNOWLEDGMENTS

Singer, Dorothy G. "Piglet, Pooh and Piaget" reprinted from *Psychology Today*, June 1972, page 71. Copyright © 1972 by American Psychological Association.

Skolnick, Arlene. "The Myth of the Vulnerable Child" reprinted from *Psychology Today*, February 1978, page 56. Copyright © 1978 by American Psychological Association.

Heller, David. "The Children's God" reprinted from *Psychology Today*, December 1985, page 22. Copyright © 1985 by American Psychological Association.

Gilligan, Carol. "Why Should a Woman Be More Like a Man?" Excerpt from IN A DIFFERENT VOICE by Carol Gilligan by permission of Harvard University Press. Copyright © 1982 by Carol Gilligan.

Garfinkel, Perry. "Mentors: Bridging the Gap" reprinted from IN A MAN'S WORLD, pages 52–57 by permission of New American Library. Copyright © 1985 by Perry Garfinkel.

Neisser, Ulric. "John Dean's Memory: A Case Study" reprinted from MEMORY OBSERVED, pages 139–159, by permission of W. H. Freeman and Company. Copyright © 1982 by Ulric Neisser.

Norman, Donald A. "Answering Questions" reprinted from LEARNING AND MEMORY, edited by V. Neisser, pages 28–32, by permission of W. H. Freeman and Company. Copyright © 1982 by Donald A. Norman.

Norman, Donald A. "Post-Freudian Slips" reprinted from *Psychology Today*, April 1980, page 43. Copyright © 1980 by American Psychological Association.

Zajonc, Robert B. "Dumber by the Dozen" reprinted from *Psychology Today*, November 1975, page 37. Copyright © 1975 by American Psychological Association.

Rosenberg, Albert. "Creative Contradictions" reprinted from *Psychology Today*, June 1979, page 54. Copyright © 1979 by American Psychological Association.

Gaylin, Willard. "Feeling Good" reprinted from FEELINGS: OUR VITAL SIGNS, pages 204–216, by permission of Harper and Row. Copyright © 1979

Keen, Sam. "The Boredom Epidemic" reprinted from WHAT TO DO WHEN YOU'RE BORED AND BLUE (Wyden Books), pages 3–15, by permission of Sam Keen. Copyright © 1980 by Sam Keen.

(The following pages constitute an extension of this copyright page.)

SIGNET, SIGNET CLASSIC, MENTOR, PLUME, MERIDIAN AND NAL BOOKS
are published *in the United States* by New American Library,
1633 Broadway, New York, New York 10019,
in Canada by The New American Library of Canada Limited,
81 Mack Avenue, Scarborough, Ontario M1L 1M9

First Printing, July, 1986

1 2 3 4 5 6 7 8 9

PRINTED IN THE UNITED STATES OF AMERICA

CONTENTS

VII. GROUPS

Introduction

The philosopher's injunction, "Know thyself," has been responded to in the modern age not by philosophy, but by psychology. Psychology, the study of the psyche, is that science which seeks to reveal man to himself. For modern man, *psyche* has come to mean not *soul,* as the ancients interpreted it, but *mind.* It is through studying the mind that psychology seeks its answers.

There have been two major streams by which modern psychology has sought to fulfill its mission: the clinical and the experimental. Freud, the grand innovator of the therapist's art, showed the way for an exploration of the psyche that is practiced today by thousands of psychotherapists. Their method is the clinical approach: careful explorations with a client of his inner life and of his past and how it effects the present.

The experimentalists, on the other hand, seek to plumb the psyche through methods like those of the other sciences: experimental observations that can be repeated, verified, and refined through other experiments. The therapist seeks a truth that illuminates a single life: the patient's. The experimentalist seeks a truth that applies to all of us in equal measure.

Both these approaches to truth have much to reveal about our inner lives, and each can help us to know ourselves more fully. That process of self-discovery is one of the principal pleasures of psychology.

There are others, to be sure. One variety of pleasure to be found in plumbing the psyche is in the delight of insight, in gaining a new sense of why it is we do what we do. And another source of pleasure in psychology is in gaining those insights through the reading of engaging writing.

In seeking to bring together a collection that could be called *The Pleasures of Psychology*, there are two rules of thumb we have followed. We have sought readings that offer the pleasure of a new understanding of the human animal, and which do so with a liveliness that reflects the excitement of the field.

Because the human animal is so complex, psychology accommodates many, many approaches, from the therapist's insight to the neuroscientist's mapping of the brain. We offer here a cross section of these approaches, a sampling of pleasures from each.

We start with the growing child, looking at the stages of life through which we all are fated to pass, from infancy to old age. To begin, there is a foray into the work of Jean Piaget, who mapped the stages of children's cognitive growth; we see how Piaget's stages are exemplified by everyone's childhood favorite, Winnie-the-Pooh.

There are many dimensions to growth and development, and we touch on several of the major ones. The child is father to the man: Children's ideas about God, for example, shift as they grow, and the seeds of adult religious outlook are to be found in these early notions. And a look at the influence of childhood trauma and difficulty on how children adjust has a hopeful message: Children from extremely troubled homes can emerge not just unscathed but strengthened.

Psychological growth continues through adulthood, and at later stages of life new issues emerge. One set of issues has to do with gender: The identity and outlook of each sex take uniquely different turns and twists, as a study of the bases of moral judgments in men and women shows.

In thinking about thinking, psychologists include memory and perception as well under the topic, since these mental processes are intricately interwoven with the web of thought. It is enlightening to consider the biases that we build into our mental life: a look at John Dean's testimony during the Watergate hearings shows just how slanted our memories can be. And something as mundane as how we go about answering questions, or the dumb mistakes we sometimes make in, say, a slip of the tongue, offer the psychologist rich clues about thought and memory. When it comes to the thinking that bears fruit in creativity, more complex matters of the mind are concerned, among them the paradoxical usefulness of holding in mind two apparently contradictory ideas.

The flow of thought is a more placid subject than is feelings, the next topic of this collection. Our feelings are at the heart of our inner self; they put us at our most vulnerable—or our most self-confident. We consider here a range of the feelings that sweep over us: feeling good, feeling bored, feeling jealous or angry. And that grandest of feelings: love. All are ripe topics for examination by the psychologist, and all are an intimate part of our experience.

When it comes to understanding how thoughts and feelings come about, many psychologists turn to the brain to seek the physiological roots of mental life. It is in the exquisite links between mind and body, psychologists tell us, that we can find keys to understanding how it is, for example, that some hardy people thrive on the rigors of a pressured life while others wilt. One bit of brain lore that has become common knowledge—the difference in mental talents between the left and right brains—turns out to be wrong; a leading researcher in the area here sets us straight.

When it comes to facing the ups and downs of life, psychology has much insight to offer. The perfectionist, for example, is a prisoner of his own habits of thought and of an unthinking allegiance to impossible standards: He is doomed to set goals he will never achieve. All of us are vulnerable to some universal tendencies that make adjustment less easy: We handily miscalculate the actual risk to ourselves of all manner of threats, from household accidents to nuclear disaster; we each harbor a talent for

self-deception that can crop up to sabatoge us. The antidotes to these dangers are one and the same: a dose of
insight.

As for more serious problems in life, the answer is not
always so simple. Depression, for example, is a more
extreme form of mental trap, similar to those the perfectionist suffers, but the way out is not easy without help.
The understanding of mental illness requires multiple perspectives: biological, developmental, sociological, even linguistic. All of these are brought to bear here.

And finally, when it comes to group life, to the subtle
and not so subtle interactions between us, psychology
looks at such oddities of the human animal as the fact that
most of us think we are better than average—a statistical
impossibility, but perhaps a helpful illusion.

Psychology also deals with the darker side of group life:
the propensity to obey, even when obedience and conscience do not agree, and the tendency to agree in order to
fit in with a group, even when we know the group is
off-base. And, in the widest of arenas, the world stage,
psychologists point out how the foibles of the person and
the group operate, too, among world leaders, putting us all
at peril in this nuclear age.

We offer you the readings here assembled as a rich and
varied set of vantage points on the human beast—on each
and every one of us. We hope you will find much that is
enlightening, and that all of it will be of interest—and a
pleasure.

—D. G., D. H.

I.

GROWING

Piglet, Pooh & Piaget

by Dorothy G. Singer

Psychology and literature share a natural relationship because each is concerned with the inner world, with personality, and with human development. This is particularly true for child development and children's literature, where the motifs of childhood are expressed through theory and story respectively. In this sense, the developmental psychologist is a storyteller of nonfiction; the children's writer is a wise psychologist. Each plays an important role in helping us understand children and the child in all of us.

With "Piglet, Pooh & Piaget," developmental psychologist Dorothy Singer brings together influential figures from each of these realms. She uses "Winnie-the-Pooh," a story read and revered by thousands of children for the last sixty years, to illustrate the theories of the Swiss developmental psychologist Jean Piaget. Besides Freud, Piaget has probably had more influence on the psychology of childhood than anyone. In her enjoyable integration, Singer shows that fairy tale and psychological observation are two sides of a single coin.

A. A. MILNE published *Winnie-the-Pooh* in 1926, three years after Jean Piaget wrote *The Language and Thought of the Child.* I am sure that neither had heard of the other's work, yet Milne's story exemplifies the concepts that Piaget had developed through his experimental and observational work in Geneva. In the make-believe world of Christopher

Robin we find instances of egocentrism, time confusion, animism, ludic (playful) symbolism, immanent justice, artificialism, realism, centering, adaptation, preoperational logic, conservation, and collective monologue. From the moment we are introduced to Edward Bear to the final pages when Christopher Robin leads his imaginary play-mate up the stairs to bed, Milne provides an enchanting picture of how a child uses logic, language and fantasy.

Fantasy. Where did Milne find his insight into children? He was a mathematics student at Cambridge between 1900 and 1903. Psychology in England then was devoted mainly to studies of learning, practice and fatigue. Piaget did not start his work until 1920. By then, Milne was writing essays, plays, and humorous pieces for *Punch*. His first adventure into children's literature came at the request of a friend who was starting a children's magazine. Milne responded with a poem. "The Dormouse and the Doctor," then followed that with a book of verse, *When We Were Very Young*. This was the first of the four books that have since become classics in children's literature. They are favorites because they so accurately reflect the child's fantasy world. Milne commented on the success of his books in his autobiography:

"Whether I have added to technique that 'wonderful insight into a child's mind' of which publishers' advertisements talk so airily, I wouldn't know. I am not inordinately fond of or interested in children; their appeal to me is a physical appeal such as the young of other animals make. I have never felt in the least sentimental about them, or no more sentimental than one becomes for a moment over a puppy or a kitten. In as far as I understand their minds, the understanding is based on the observation, casual enough and mostly unconscious, which I give to people generally: on memories of my own childhood: and on the imagination which every writer must bring to memory and observation."

In the 1920s Piaget worked at the Jean Jacques Rousseau Institute of Psychology where he developed systematic methods of observing children at play. He designed experiments that would provide data about the child's logic, his view of the world, and his development of language and concept formation. Piaget's first work *The Language and Thought of the Child* deals with the notion of egocentrism—the idea that the child views the world subjectively. The child believes that the world was created for him, that everyone thinks as he does, and that everyone shares his feelings and wishes. The child cannot distinguish between what is self and what is outside world.

The concept of egocentrism is at the core of *Winnie-the-Pooh*. Milne states in his autobiography:

"Heaven, that is, does really appear to lie about the child in its infancy, as it does not lie about even the most attractive kitten. But with this outstanding physical quality there is a natural lack of moral quality, which expresses itself, as Nature always insists on expressing herself, in an egotism entirely ruthless. . . . A pen-picture of a child which showed it as loving, grateful and full of thought for others would be false to the truth; but equally false would be a picture which insisted on the brutal egotism of the child, and ignored the physical beauty which softens it."

Milne cites many examples in his poetry that reflect the child's egotism. Christopher wants to know after he has watched them changing guard at Buckingham Palace, "Do you think the King knows all about me?" In "Disobedience" James James Morrison Morrison, the child whose mother has died, tells his other relations "not to go blaming *him*."

Piaget felt that the growth of intellect freed the child from egocentrism. He outlined four periods of cognitive development. I do not intend to present Piaget's theory in detail in this article, but the four periods may be summarized as follows:

1) The sensorimotor period (birth to age two): the infant first displays intelligence in the use of his senses (vision, hearing, taste and smell), and in his motor activities (reaching, grasping, crawling, walking and running). He internalizes his perceptions and activities to create his private view of the world. The infant begins to develop language, and to use symbolic imagery.

2) Preoperational period (ages two to seven): the child

begins to use language more fully and he begins to conceptualize. He may not make distinctions within classes (all cats or dogs have the same name as the child's own cat or dog). The child can express his view of the world through drawings, language, or dreams. Prelogical reasoning appears in the intuitive stage of this period from ages four to seven. The child may play with imaginary companions or engage in compensatory play (doing in make-believe what he is forbidden in reality).

3) Concrete-operational period (ages seven to 11): the child's thinking becomes logical and reversible. He understands the logic of classes. He has learned to conserve, to see that objects or quantities remain the same despite changes made in their appearance. Play is more social and has strict rules.

4) Formal-operational period (age 11 to adulthood): the child now understands the logic of propositions and hypotheses. He can think about theories such as space, motion, time. He develops a value system, and a sense of morality.

Stairs. *Winnie-the-Pooh* focuses on the world of the child in the preoperational period and more specifically, the period of intuitive thought (ages four to seven).

We first meet Edward Bear as he is being dragged down the stairs on the back of his head. "It is, as far as he knows, the only way of coming downstairs." This example of *egocentrism* sets the tone for the rest of the book. The narrator informs us that Edward's name is Winnie-the-Pooh. When asked if Winnie is not a girl's name, Christopher replies with a second example of egocentric reasoning. "He's Winnie-ther-Pooh. Don't you know what 'ther' means?" Again, an example of *egocentrism*. Christopher knows, so no further explanation is necessary, or forthcoming.

Christopher Robin wants a story, and his father obliges him, incidentally demonstrating the child's *conception of time*.

"Once upon a time, a very long time ago now, *about last Friday*." Piaget suggests that the child's sense of time is dependent on the order of succession of events and on the duration of intervals. The young child often confuses

present and past events. Minutes may seem like hours as
he waits for the promised trip to a friend's house.

Pooh's first monologue is another example of egocentric
thinking. Sitting in the forest, he muses: "That buzzing-
noise means something. You don't get a buzzing-noise like
that, just buzzing and buzzing without its meaning something. If there is a buzzing-noise, somebody's making a
buzzing-noise, and the only reason for making a buzzing-
noise that *I* know of is because you're a bee . . . and the
only reason for being a bee that *I* know of is for making
honey . . . and the only reason for making honey is so as *I*
can eat it," and in the chapter where the great flood
comes, Pooh discovers a note in a bottle floating past his
house. On the note is a message from Piglet: "Help Piglet
(me)" and on the other side "It's Me Piglet, Help, Help."

Piglet, an egocentric friend of Pooh, is sure that everyone must know where he is in his distress. But Pooh is just
as egocentric when he interprets the note. Pooh only recognizes the letter "P" and each "P" convinces him further that " 'P' means 'Pooh' so it's a very important
Missage to *me*."

In a later chapter Pooh eats a jar of honey that he had
intended to give to Eeyore on his birthday. In perfect
form, Pooh rationalizes his gluttony and decides to give
Eeyore the empty jar: after all, "It's a very nice pot,
Eeyore could keep things in it."

Toys. Piaget has shown that children in the preoperational
stage attribute life to inanimate objects; he calls this tendency *animism*. Milne recognized this process in his own
son, Christopher. All of the characters in *Winnie-the-Pooh*
(except for Rabbit and Owl) are based on toys from Christopher's nursery. They all have distinct personalities.

Pooh, the teddy bear of "little brain," is always in
search of honey and adventure; Piglet, a weak and timid
pig, is Pooh's best friend. Eeyore, the donkey, is a cynic
and pessimist; Kanga, the kangaroo, is the bossy, practical
image of motherhood; Owl, the expert on spelling, is
all-wise and knowing; and Rabbit, who attempts to be
clever, is sometimes a bit mean.

Each of these imaginary characters displays a talent for

animism. In the first chapter, Pooh evolves an elaborate plan to steal some honey from a bee's nest. He will disguise himself as a cloud in a blue sky. He rolls over and over in the mud until he is as dark as a thundercloud. He borrows a sky-blue balloon from Christopher and floats off into the sky. As Winnie-the-Pooh approaches the bee's nest, he sings:

"How sweet to be a Cloud
Floating in the Blue!
Every little cloud
Always sings aloud."

Pony. The singing cloud is an example of *animism* and it is also an example of *ludic symbolism*—the symbolism of child's games. Sometimes, for a child, a broom becomes a pony. For Pooh, the balloon becomes the sky. Pooh, feeling very proud and happy with his deception, calls down to Christopher: "What do I look like?"

Christopher, who always serves to bring fantasy back to reality, replies, "You look like a bear holding on to a balloon."

Poor Pooh replies, "Not like a small black cloud in a blue sky?"

"Not very much," says Christopher.

Pooh persists. He says: "Ah well, perhaps from up here it looks different."

Pooh reasons intuitively; he bases his reasoning on perceptual appearances. He urges Christopher to walk below him with an umbrella, saying loudly: "Tut, tut, it looks like rain."

Pooh is certain that if the bees see the blue sky *and* an *umbrella* they will surely be fooled by "the little dark cloud."

Honey. Piaget has shown that the child believes that justice is built into the natural order of things. Matches burn children who play with them when they have been forbidden to do so. This notion of *immanent justice* is evident in the same honey-and-bee adventure. Pooh falls down into a gorse bush, where he is covered with prickles. In true Piaget fashion he believes his punishment comes "of *liking* honey so much."

Later in the book, Pooh pays Rabbit a visit, hoping to
be fed in the bargain. Rabbit plays the kind host and Pooh
eats so much that he cannot get back out the way he came
in. He becomes stuck and blames it on the narrowness of
the door. Rabbit sternly advises: "It all comes of eating
too much."

Pooh is punished now, and can't get out. Christopher
Robin comes to the rescue and declares that the only way
for the bear to get out of the hole is to get thin.

"How long does getting thin take?" asks Pooh.

"About a week," Christopher Robin replies.

Here again Milne uses time as a child might experience
it. Christopher settles down to read to the bear who indeed
becomes thin, and then is pulled out of the hole.

Magic. Piaget suggests that the child is confused about
the physical world as well as the temporal world. The
child believes in artificialism, or the notion that human
beings have created mountains, lakes, trees, etc. The young
child believes too that his chants and songs can in some
magical way control the elements. ("Rain, rain, go away,
come again another day.") The child in the intuitive period cannot easily recognize a familiar scene if he looks at
it from a different angle. The tree he sees from his window
is not the same tree he sees from the garden below.

This difficulty with physical space is shown in the chapter called "Pooh and Piglet Go Hunting and Nearly Catch
a Woozle." While the two friends are out hunting they
walk in circles and cross each other's tracks in the snow,
not realizing that they have made the extra footprints they
see. They believe that "woozles or strange animals are
about." Piglet suddenly remembers some things that he
must do immediately. He checks the time with Pooh, finds
out that it is about 12:00, and excuses himself from the
hunt: "It isn't the sort of thing you can do in the afternoon, it's a very particular morning thing, that has to be
done in the morning . . . between as I was saying, the
hours of 12:00 and 12:05. So, really, dear old Pooh, if you
will excuse me." Eventually Christopher appears and explains the whole thing to Pooh—the two friends had made
the tracks themselves.

Pole. Piaget states that the young child has a tolerant belief in the *realism* of words, pictures, dreams and objects. Everything is credible. If an adult mentions the North Pole, it must exist. The child associates things without making logical connections between them. Things just seem to go together. Names exist as parts of the things named. The sun is always the sun, and gets its name from someplace in the sky. Rabbit says the North Pole is "sure to be a pole because of calling it a pole, and if it's a pole, well, I should think it would be sticking in the ground, shouldn't you, because there'd be nowhere else to stick it."

Christopher plans an expedition to discover the North Pole. When Pooh asks him, "What *is* the North Pole?" Christopher replies, "It's just a thing you discover." During the expedition to the North Pole, Roo, the baby kangaroo, manages to fall into some water. Pooh saves Roo with a long pole that he happens to find. After the rescue, Christopher looks at Pooh and says quite solemnly, "The Expedition is over. You have found the North Pole." Christopher, who knows about the South Pole, believes that there must be an East Pole and West Pole, "though people don't like talking about them."

Clay. *Conservation* is probably the most familiar of Piaget's concepts, and the one most readily adapted to research. Piaget defines conservation as the ability to see that objects or quantities remain the same despite changes in appearance. Piaget believes that children learn to conserve substance, weight and volume, in that order, and that they cannot truly conserve until age seven. In one experiment Piaget presents to a child two *identical* balls of clay, one of which is elongated or flattened or cut into pieces. He then asks the child if there is still as much clay in the one as in the other. The child below the age of seven generally sees the elongated clay as having more clay than the ball of clay. The child believes that the experimenter has actually produced *more* clay by changing the shape or container.

Milne's story of Eeyore's birthday illustrates this inability to conserve. Piglet plans to give Eeyore a large red balloon. On the way, Piglet catches his foot in a rabbit's hole, and falls down. When he recovers he discovers to his dismay that the balloon has burst. All that he has left is a "small piece of damp rag." Nevertheless, Piglet is determined to give a present to Eeyore. When he finally reaches Eeyore, the conversation goes like this:

" 'Eeyore, I brought you a balloon.' 'Balloon?' said Eeyore, . . . 'one of those big coloured things you blow up? Gaiety, song-and-dance, here we are and there we are?'

'Yes . . . but I fell down . . . and I burst the balloon.'

'My birthday balloon?'

'Yes, Eeyore,' said Piglet, sniffing a little. 'Here it is. With—with many happy returns of the day.'

'My present?'

Piglet nodded again.

'The balloon?'

'Yes.'

'Thank you, Piglet,' said Eeyore, 'you don't mind my asking,' he went on, 'but what color was this balloon when it—when it *was* a balloon?' " Poor Eeyore cannot understand that red remains red even when the balloon is small and no longer round or full.

Tail. Eeyore is the victim of centering, another of Piaget's concepts, in a later chapter. Piaget has shown that a child will focus on the most compelling feature of what he sees, while excluding all other aspects. Eeyore's most compelling feature is his tail, but he loses it. Pooh promises to help look for the missing tail. Visiting Owl, Pooh notices that the bell-rope on Owl's front door looks rather familiar to him. " 'Handsome bell-rope, isn't it?' said Owl. Pooh nodded and said, 'It reminds me of something, where did you get it?' "

Owl describes how he found it hanging over a bush. Owl thought someone must live in the bush and he rang it but nothing happened. He rang it again and it came off in his hands. Since nobody wanted the bell-rope, Owl took it home and hung it on his door. For Owl, a tail without Eeyore attached to it is not a tail. Hanging over a bush, it becomes a bell-rope, waiting to be pulled.

Pooh tells Owl that the bell-rope is Eeyore's tail, and the story ends happily with Christopher Robin nailing it back onto Eeyore.

Lesson. The child constantly learns how to adapt to his environment. Piaget described how his own children learned to explore empty boxes and to seek out toys hidden under pillows. They repeated their motor acts until they understood and mastered a situation. Roo learns that he cannot eat and talk at the same time or he chokes and gets the hiccups. Pooh presents an empty honey jar to Eeyore who discovers that it's a good thing to put things into and take things out of. He repeats the act until he learns the lesson.

Pooh discovers that a bottle with a cork stopper can float on water. It becomes a suitable boat for him. Later he learns that an inverted umbrella makes a bigger boat that can accommodate two adventurers.

These characters are participating in what Piaget calls *assimilation* and *accommodation*. Both are necessary for the child to adapt to his environment. The child must organize the data from his senses into his conceptual framework. Milne presents several episodes that show how Christopher and his friends use play to assimilate the customs, manners and values of middle-class English society into their experience. The little girl who plays house and the boy who plays fireman learn about their world through symbolic play, just as Christopher, the explorer, learns about his.

Songs. Language in its beginning stages is primarily egocentric. A child talks for himself and not for the point of view of the listener. Echolalia—repeating phrases—gives him much pleasure. Certainly, Pooh's songs are repetitive.

"How sweet to be a child" or "Sing Ho for the life of a Bear" are themes repeated over and over in two separate little songs.

The child also uses *onomatopoeia*—words that sound like the noises the objects make. For example, many children say "choo-choo," before learning the word "train," or "bow-wow" before learning the word "dog." After the bee-and-cloud adventure, Pooh's arms were so stiff from holding on to the balloon that whenever a fly landed on his nose, Pooh had to blow it off: "Pooh."

"That is why he's called Pooh," says Christopher Robin.

Sign. Children use language in concrete ways during the preoperational stage. For example, Pooh lived in the forest all by himself "under the name 'Sanders.' " Christopher interprets this to mean that a sign must be hanging *above* the door with the name "Sanders" printed in gold letters.

Piglet has a broken sign with the words "Trespassers W" on it. Piglet explains to Christopher that this was his grandfather's name. When Christopher takes issue with this, Piglet says that this sign is short for "Trespassers Will," which is short for "Trespassers William," and his grandfather had had two names in case he lost one . . . "Trespassers" after an uncle, and "William" after "Trespassers."

"I've got two names," said Christopher Robin, carelessly.

"Well, there you are, that proves it," said Piglet.

Neither recognizes the partial meaning of the sign (Trespassers Will Be Prosecuted), a typical fault in the logic of children.

A conversation between Owl and Pooh exemplifies other linguistic tricks that are peculiar to children. Owl tells Pooh that the "customary procedure in such cases is as follows": "What does Crustimoney Proseedcake mean?" said Pooh, "for I am a bear of Very Little Brain and long words bother me." Again, when Pooh calls the expedition an "Expotition," Christopher corrects him, "Expedition, silly old Bear. It's got an 'x' in it."

Parallel. One of the delightful aspects of preoperational language is *collective monologue*—the conversation of the child who does not try to understand or even listen to the point of view of another person. The other person is mainly a stimulus for the child. Children sit alongside each other in a sand box busily playing, but they are completely absorbed in their own fantasies and conversations. Piaget calls this *parallel play*. The child pays little attention to questions posed by playmates; he gives answers that are unrelated to specific questions. And yet, the child would be distressed if his friend left his side.

Milne demonstrates this notion of *collective monologue* in his final chapter of *Winnie-the-Pooh*.

Pencils. Christopher Robin gives a party for Pooh and invites all the forest animals. Several conversations are taking place at once around the festive table. Owl tries to tell Christopher about an accident that nearly happened to his friend; Roo is steadily hiccuping; Kanga is preoccupied with scolding Roo; Eeyore is making a long-winded, senseless speech; and finally, Christopher is attempting to praise Pooh for his past heroics. All are happy to be together at the party, but each egocentric animal is involved with his own thoughts and conversation.

Finally, Christopher presents to Pooh a Pencil Case with "Blue Pencils, and Red Pencils, and Green Pencils for saying special things in blue, and red, and green." Christopher Robin believes that words have special meanings when they are written in special colors. He endows the little gift with one more of Piaget's notions—that of *physiognomic properties*. Inanimate objects can take on the emotions of human beings. If Jean Piaget opened the pages of *Winnie-the-Pooh*, he would discover, as I have, how A. A. Milne intuitively uses psychological insight to give life and meaning to a story about an imaginary forest, peopled with animals from the nursery. But instead, Piaget has collaborated with Etienne Delessert on a tale about a mouse to demonstrate how children of five and six view the world. It remains to be seen whether Piaget's effort will ever match the popularity of *Winnie-the-Pooh* among children and adults.

The Myth of the Vulnerable Child

by Arlene Skolnick

We hear in all sorts of ways that parents have great and lasting impact on children. The movie *Kramer vs. Kramer* told us that fathering—and mothering—after divorce was crucial to the well-being of the child. Television shows such as *The Cosby Show* subtly convey that children in normal circumstances still require great wisdom and humor from their parents to make it through the rigors of growing up. Psychologists, too, have been a source of streams of advice to parents on how children should be cared for, and why they need that care. The overall message has been that parents bear considerable, if not exclusive, responsibility for the welfare of their children. But are parents so exclusively responsible?

Arlene Skolnick observes that we have exaggerated the impact of parents on the child and underemphasized the effects of the child on the parent. She argues that children are not quite as vulnerable and brittle as we sometimes fear, and that thankfully, they often manage to find their own way. Skolnick advises anxious parents to relax. Despite what the culture and what psychologists have often urged, parents do not always have "make-or-break" power over their children's lives.

AMERICANS HAVE LONG been considered the most child-centered people in the world. In the 20th century, this traditional American obsession with children has generated

19

new kinds of child-rearing experts—psychologists and psychiatrists, clothed in the authority of modern science, who issue prescriptions for child-rearing. Most child-care advice assumes that if the parents administer the proper prescriptions, the child will develop as planned. It places exaggerated faith not only in the perfectibility of the children and their parents, but in the infallibility of the particular child-rearing technique as well. But increasing evidence suggests that parents simply do not have that much control over their children's development; too many other factors are influencing it.

Popular and professional knowledge does not seem to have made parenting easier. On the contrary, the insights and guidelines provided by the experts seem to have made parents more anxious. Since modern child-rearing literature asserts that parents can do irreparable harm to their children's social and emotional development, modern parents must examine their words and actions for a significance that parents in the past had never imagined. Besides, psychological experts disagree among themselves. Not only have they been divided into competing schools, but they also have repeatedly shifted their emphasis from one developmental goal to another, from one technique to another.

TWO MODELS OF PARENTING

Two basic models of parental influence emerge from all this competition and variety, however. One, loosely based on Freudian ideas, has presented an image of the vulnerable child: children are sensitive beings, easily damaged not only by traumatic events and emotional stress, but also by overdoses of affection. The second model is that of the behaviorists, whose intellectual ancestors, the empiricist philosophers, described the child's mind as a *tabula rasa*, or blank slate. The behaviorist model of child-rearing is based on the view that the child is malleable, and parents are therefore cast in the role of Pygmalions who can shape their children however they wish. "Give me a dozen healthy infants, well-formed, and my own specified world to bring them up in," wrote J. B. Watson, the father of modern behaviorism, "and I'll guarantee to take any one at random and train him to be any type of specialist I might—doctor, lawyer, artist, merchant, chief, and yes, even beggar man and thief!"

The image of the vulnerable child calls for gentle parents who are sensitive to their child's innermost thoughts and feelings in order to protect him from trauma. The image of the malleable child requires stern parents who coolly follow the dictates of their own explicit training procedures: only the early eradication of bad habits in eating, sleeping, crying, can fend off permanent maladjustments.

Despite their disagreements, both models grant parents an omnipotent role in child development. Both stress that (1) only if parents do the right things at the right time will their children turn out to be happy, successful adults; (2) parents can raise superior beings, free of the mental frailities of previous generations; and (3) if something goes wrong with their child, the parents have only themselves to blame.

Contemporary research increasingly suggests, however, that both models greatly exaggerate the power of the parents and the passivity of the child. In fact, the children's own needs, their developing mental and physical qualities, influence the way they perceive and interpret external events. This is not to say that parents exercise no influence on their children's development. Like all myths, that of parental determinism contains a kernel of truth. But there is an important difference between influence and control. Finally, both models also fail to consider that parent-child relations do not occur in a social vacuum, but in the complex world of daily life.

Traditionally, child-study researchers have assumed that influence in the parent-child relationship flowed only one way, from active parent to passive child. For example, a large number of studies tested the assumption, derived from Freudian theory, that the decisive events of early childhood centered around feeding, weaning, and toilet-training. It is now generally conceded that such practices in themselves have few demonstrable effects on later development. Such studies may have erred because they assumed that children must experience and react to parental behavior in the same ways.

Even when studies *do* find connections between the behavior of the parents and the child, cause and effect are by no means clear. Psychologist Richard Bell argues that many studies claiming to show the effects of parents on children can just as well be interpreted as showing children's effects on parents. For instance, a study finding a correlation between severe punishment and children's aggressiveness is often taken to show that harsh discipline produces aggressive children; yet it could show instead that aggressive children evoke harsh child-rearing methods in their parents.

A METHODOLOGICAL FLAW

The image of a troubled adult scarred for life by an early trauma such as the loss of a parent, lack of love, or family tension has passed from the clinical literature to become a cliché of the popular media. The idea that childhood stress must inevitably result in psychological damage is a conclusion that rests on a methodological flaw inherent in the clinical literature: instead of studying development through time, these studies start with adult problems and trace them back to possible causes.

It's true that when researchers investigate the backgrounds of delinquents, mental patients, or psychiatric referrals from military service, they find that a large number come from "broken" or troubled homes, have overpossessive, domineering, or rejecting mothers, or have inadequate or violent fathers. The usual argument is that these circumstances cause maladjustments in the offspring. But most children who experience disorder and early sorrow grow up to be adequate adults. Further, studies sampling "normal" or "superior" people—college students, business executives, professionals, creative artists, and scientists—find such "pathological" conditions in similar or greater proportions. Thus, many studies trying to document the effects of early pathological and traumatic conditions have failed to demonstrate more than a weak link between them and later development.

The striking differences between retrospective studies that start with adult misfits and look back to childhood conditions, and longitudinal studies that start with children and follow them through time, were shown in a study at the University of California's Institute of Human Development, under the direction of Jean Macfarlane. Approximately 200 children were studied intensively from infancy through adolescence, and then were seen again at age 30. The researchers predicted that children from troubled homes would be troubled adults and, conversely, that those who had had happy, successful childhoods would be happy adults. They were wrong in two-thirds of their predictions. Not only had they overestimated the traumatic effects of stressful family situations, but even more surprisingly, they also had not anticipated that many of those who grew up under the best circumstances would turn out to be unhappy, strained, or immature adults (a pattern that seemed especially strong for boys who had been athletic leaders and girls who had been beautiful and popular in high school).

Psychologist Norman Garmezy's work on "invulnerability" offers more recent evidence that children can thrive in spite of genetic disadvantages and environmental deprivations. Garmezy began by studying adult schizophrenics and trying to trace the sources of their problems. Later, he turned to developmental studies of children who were judged high risks to develop schizophrenia and other disorders at a later age. When such children were studied over time, only 10 or 12 percent of the high-risk group became schizophrenic, while the majority did not.

OTHER SOURCES OF LOVE

The term "invulnerables" is misleading. It suggests an imperviousness to pain. Yet, the ability to cope does not mean the child doesn't suffer. One woman, who successfully overcame a childhood marked by the death of her beloved but alcoholic and abusive father, and rejection by her mother and stepmother, put it this way: "We suffer, but we don't let it destroy us."

The term also seems to imply that the ability to cope is a trait, something internal to the child. One often finds in the case histories of those who have coped with their problems successfully that external supports softened the impact of the traumatic event. Often something in the child's environment provides alternative sources of love and gratification—one parent compensating for the inadequacy of the other, a loving sibling or grandparent, an understanding teacher, a hobby or strong interest, a pet, recreational opportunities, and so on.

Indeed, the local community may play an important role in modulating the effects of home environments. Erik Erikson, who worked on the study at the Institute of Human Development, was asked at a seminar, "How is it that so many of the people studied overcame the effects of truly awful homes?" He answered that it might have been the active street life in those days, which enabled children to enjoy the support of peers when parent-child relations got too difficult.

Psychologist Martin Seligman's learned-helplessness theory provides a further clue to what makes a child vulnerable to stress. Summarizing a vast array of data, including animal experiments, clinical studies, and reports from prisoner-of-war camps, Seligman proposes that people give up in despair not because of the actual severity of their situation, but because they feel they can have little or no effect in changing it. The feeling of helplessness is learned by actually experiencing events we cannot control, or by being led to believe that we have no control.

Seligman's theory helps to explain two puzzling phenomena: the biographies of eminent people that often reveal stressful family relations, and Macfarlane's findings that many children who did come from "ideal" homes failed to live up to their seeming potential. The theory of learned helplessness suggests that controllable stress may be better for a child's ego development than good things that happen without any effort on the child's part. Self-esteem and a sense of competence may not depend on whether we experience good or bad events, but rather on whether we perceive some control over what happens to us.

PARENTS CAN'T BE PYGMALIONS

Many of the same reasons that limit the effect of events on children also limit the ability of parents to shape their children according to behavioral prescription. The facts of cognition and environmental complexity get in the way of best-laid parental plans. There is no guarantee, for example, that children will interpret parental behavior accurately. Psychologist Jane Loevinger gives the example of a mother trying to discipline her five-year-old son for hitting his younger sister: if she spanks him, she may discourage the hitting, or she may be demonstrating that hitting is okay; if she reasons with the child, he may accept her view of hitting as bad, or he may conclude that hitting is something you can get away with and not be punished for.

Other factors, interacting with the child's cognitive processes and sense of self, limit the parents' ability to shape their children. Perhaps the most basic is that parents have their own temperamental qualities that may modify the message they convey to their children. One recurrent finding in the research literature, for example, is that parental warmth is important to a child's development. Yet warmth and acceptance cannot be created by following behavioral prescriptions, since they are spontaneous feelings.

Further, the parent-child relationship does not exist apart from other social contexts. A study of child-rearing in six cultures, directed by Harvard anthropologists John Whiting and Beatrice Whiting, found that parents' behavior toward children is based not so much on beliefs and principles as on a "horde of apparently irrelevant considerations": work pressures, the household work load, the availability of other adults to help with household tasks and child care, the design of houses and neighborhoods, the social structure of the community. All these influences, over which parents usually have little control, affect the resources of time, energy, attention, and affection they have for their children.

The effects of social class may also be very hard to overcome, even if the parent tries. Psychiatrist Robert Coles has written about poor and minority children who often come to learn from their families that they are persons of worth—only to have this belief shattered when they encounter the devaluing attitudes of the outside world. Conversely, middle-class children from troubled homes may take psychological nourishment from the social power and esteem that are enjoyed by their families in the community.

SCIENCE AND THE FAMILY: HISTORICAL ROOTS

Given the lack of evidence for the parental-determinism model of child-rearing, why has it been so persistent? Why have we continued to believe that science can provide infallible prescriptions for raising happy, successful people and curing social problems?

As psychologist Sheldon White has recently observed, psychology's existence as a field of scientific research has rested upon "promissory notes" laid down at the turn of the century. The beginnings of modern academic psychology were closely tied to education and the growth of large public expenditures for the socialization of children. The first psychologists moved from philosophy departments to the newly forming education schools, expecting to provide scientific methods of education and child-rearing. The founding fathers of American psychology—J. B. Watson, G. S. Hall, L. M. Terman, and others—accepted the challenge. Thus, learning has always been a central focus of psychologists, even though the rat eventually came to compete with the child as the favored experimental animal.

If the behaviorists' social prescriptions conjure up images of *Brave New World* or *1984*, a more humane promise was implicit in Freudian theory. The earliest generations of Freudians encouraged the belief that if the new knowledge derived from psychoanalysis was applied to the upbringing of children, it would be possible to eliminate anxiety, conflict, and neurosis. The medical miracles achieved in the 19th and early 20th centuries gave the medical experts immense prestige in the eyes of parents. There seemed little reason to doubt that science could have as far-reaching effects on mental health as it had on physical health. Furthermore, as parents were becoming more certain of their children's physical survival, children's social futures were becoming less certain. When the family was no longer an economic unit, it could no longer initiate children directly into work. Middle-class parents had to educate their children to find their way in a complex job market. The coming of urban industrial society also changed women's roles. Women were removed from the world of work, and motherhood came to be defined as a separate task for women, the primary focus of their lives. Psychological ideas became an intrinsic part of the domestic-science movement that arose around the end of the 19th century; this ideology taught that scientific household management would result in perfected human relationships within the home, as well as in the improvement of the larger society.

THE LIMITS OF PERFECTIBILITY

As we approach the 1980s, Americans are coming to reject the idea that science and technology can guarantee limitless progress and solve all problems. Just as we have come to accept that there are limits to growth and to our natural resources, it is time we lowered our expectations about the perfectibility of family life. Instead of trying to rear perfectly happy, adjusted, creative, and successful children, we should recognize that few, if any, such people exist, and even if they did, it would be impossible to produce such a person by following a behavioral formula.

Far from harming family relations, lowered expectations could greatly benefit them.

What is more, the belief in parental determinism has had an unfortunate influence on social policy. It has encouraged the hope that major social problems can be eradicated without major changes in society and its institutions. For example, we have in the past preferred to view the poor as victims of faulty child-rearing rather than of unemployment, inadequate income, or miserable housing. Ironically, while we have been obsessed with producing ideal child-rearing environments in our own homes, we have permitted millions of American children to suffer basic deprivations. A seemingly endless series of governmental and private commissions has documented the sorry statistics on infant mortality, child malnutrition, unattended health needs, and so on, but the problems persist. In short, the standards of perfection that have been applied to child-rearing and the family in this century have not only created guilt and anxiety in those who try to live up to them, but have also contributed to the neglect of children on a national scale.

The Children's God

by David Heller

Ever since Freud theorized that God was an illusion, the relationship between psychology and religion has been uneasy. The Freudian premise that man has a psychological need to create a god as a kind of grandiose father figure has found many followers among psychologists. But even strict devotees of psychoanalysis sometimes depart from Freud on this issue.

Most psychologists who study it consider religious beliefs of adults, paying little attention to children's beliefs. "The Children's God," based on a recent book with the same title (Heller, David, University of Chicago Press, Chicago, Ill., 1986), is one of the first studies on children's religious views. In this article David Heller asks, "What do children actually imagine when they say the word God?"

"God is with me when I round second base," claims one young follower of baseball's Detroit Tigers. The spontaneous responses of the forty children in this study are frequently humorous and graphic, including such lively characters as "God, the Friendly Ghost" and "Dr. God, the Therapist."

But this is not to suggest that the children's words and images are necessarily simple and mundane. On the contrary, there are clear theological perspectives presented here, often in fresh and unpredictable language. Children have their own kind of style and grace; perhaps after you read the following article, you may feel that they convey a religious sense of "grace" as well.

EVERY AMERICAN SCHOOLCHILD is familiar with God, having pledged allegiance again and again to a flag and nation "under God." God's presence has never been confined to our churches; God is in our schools, on our currency, in our casual prayers (God forbid), and in our other than casual damnations. Every day many times over we send messages to our children about the existence of this abstraction called God, and we tend to assume that God means the same thing to them as it does to us. But does it? What ideas and images of God do our children form as a result of God's large cultural presence?

I became captivated by this subject several years ago and became involved in an extensive study of God—God, that is, as imagined by forty young theologians, ages four to twelve. I wanted to study normal religious development, to explore how children conceive of God and how those conceptions change along with normal intellectual growth. The result was a baptism into the mysteries of childhood creativity and spirituality, and an intriguing exploration into the human quest for God.

The children I studied were recruited by local teachers in Ann Arbor, Michigan, who, according to my request, included children whose parents were affiliated with one of four major religions: Judaism, Catholicism, Protestantism (Baptists), and Hinduism (American-born Hindus). They were also equally divided by sex and age, so that I could look for any differences in boys' and girls' developing notions of the deity.

I wanted to be careful not to influence the children's ideas with my own, so at the project's outset I asked each child this question: "What word or idea best describes for you the most important thing that you can think of?" The variety of responses was rich: Jesus, Baba, HaShem (Hebrew), and My Friend God are just a few of the names the children used. Whatever the child's choice, I then focused the interview on that name and notion, gently leading each child through a series of uninterrupted, recorded exercises. I asked them to write "Dear God" letters, had them express their visions of the deity through drawings and doll-play exercises. In addition, each child offered an original story about his or her choice of God and, finally, answered a sequence of questions.

The interview questions were designed to capture the nature and strength of the child's beliefs. Is God a physical presence for them? Does he live somewhere? Does God have a sex? What does God do? Is God involved in people's everyday lives? Is God associated with fun? With trouble and pain?

I found some most interesting socialized differences among the children, depending on their formal religious training, their age, sex, and personality.

When compared by religion, for example, the Catholic children—perhaps owing to their interpretations of Church policy—indicated that God played an active role in marriage and divorce. In doll play, God might bring a male and a female doll together or advise mother and father dolls "to stick out the marriage for the kids' sake." Child dolls, bystanders in this heavenly marriage counseling, were often ambivalent about what was best for them. As Chris, a nine-year-old girl, narrated, "The girl doll—her name is Christie—knows that divorce is wrong. But she doesn't want God to allow her parents to keep fighting, either. Maybe God should ask the pope what he thinks."

The God of the Catholic children was actively and prominently involved in family decisions and family tensions. The deity would quietly intervene, helping to sort out problems and reminding parents of the Church's opposition to divorce. While the children expressed great trepidation about a parental breakup, they also intimated an underlying desire for the forbidden separation to occur. To resolve this formidable conflict, the children employ God in a "popelike" role as the holy arbiter and symbol of family cohesion. The deity image thus helps to alleviate family-related fears and maintain the family unit intact. In his well-known book, *The American Catholic* (1977), Andrew Greeley also commented upon family concerns as a prevailing motif of Catholic children and suggested that the children express this theme with greater obligation or delight than do Protestant or Jewish children.

One of the most compelling religious differences I found

concerned the children's preferred form of prayer or spiritual exercise. While Baptist children typically report that they are quite comfortable with silent public devotion, Catholic children emphasize the importance of dialogue. Eight-year-old Mark, a Catholic, reports: "I realize what I believe about God by these talks I have with my dad." Jewish children show a similar inclination, though they more often equate devotion with ritualistic practices as well as informal conversation. American-born Hindu children voiced their own special preference: chanting. As one erudite six-year-old explained to his naive interviewer, "Group chanting is really important because it gives us the feeling we are all part of one big community." Such descriptive distinctions in religious style may bear important implications for social policy; too often we falsely assume that all children find meaningful religious experience in the same form of devotion, notably conventional silent prayer.

Such an assumption is adult-centered and troublesome when one takes into account the children's displeasures with formal, conventional practices. Across religious groups, the children initially expressed positive associations to their respective religious heritages. Yet these favorable inclinations were qualified by discontent, particularly in regard to practices that the children perceived as obsessive routines; silent prayer was among the rituals most commonly mentioned, even if it was not the preferred form of worship for a child's religious group or family.

All of the children I studied seemed to weave their most pressing emotional concerns into the fabric of their God creations, and as a result, their deities undergo important changes as the children age. The four- to six-year-olds, for example, associate God very closely with generalized play and gaiety. In order to preserve such a happy state, however, the youngest children tend to create two coexisting Gods, one all good and the other all bad. Four-year-old Marcie, for example, had this to say about God's home: "God lives in a big castle . . . like our church. God also probably has a choir. I think he probably has Christmas parties too." Not realizing that very young children strongly connect God with all that is pleasant in the world, we adults tend to dismiss their benign, concrete imagery as simplistic. Of course, children must deal with unpleasantness in life as well, so there often emerges a second figure, a ''bad God who lives in a much darker, not-so-nice castle,'' as four-year-old Marcie later explained.

Occasionally, in those moments when a young child is trying to make sense of the mixed nature of things, episodes of rare creativity and humor take place. One boy was bothered by the disturbing image of the Crucifixion, and so tried to gain some distance by imagining a cheerier version: He replaced Jesus with Bugs Bunny.

The older children also imprint their own emotions on God, including the worries and yearnings that come with growing up. While an eight-year-old might become absorbed in being ''special'' in God's eyes, a twelve-year-old typically becomes immersed in ''afterlife things''—a symbolic harbinger of adolescence and its pending biological and psychological changes. In each individual the God figure changes slightly to suit the phenomenological needs of the child.

These needs are somewhat different for boys and girls, as might be expected. While both boys and girls in my study had been socialized to imagine a masculine God, the girls subliminally included more aesthetic and classically feminine qualities as well. A typical compromise for a girl was to imagine a male figure surrounded by flowers, dancing figures, or musical accompaniment. Seven-year-old Jeri, for example, reports that she always thinks of God when listening to Roberta Flack songs. The boys, in contrast, showed no interest in allying God with the arts, instead emphasizing the size of the deity and his rational, imposing demeanor.

The boys' predilections were well illustrated by twelve-year-old Tom, who described God as ''a real gigantic thinking man who can hold the world in his hands.'' Later, Tom wrote in his letter to this herculean deity:

> Dear God,
>   How is it in heaven up there? How is it being the Big Cheese?
>   Tom

Of considerable contemporary interest were the children's responses to the question: "What if God were the opposite sex?" Almost without exception the boys showed unquestionable signs of agitation concerning the prospect of a female God. As if some all-encompassing feminine force were about to descend on them, they were reluctant even to entertain the question. Here, for example, is my discussion with nine-year-old Arthur on this issue:

A: "God is a man, for sure."

DH: "But could you make believe that God was the other sex?"

A: "But God is a man!"

DH: "But could you play what-if?"

A: "If God was a . . . huh! (*look of astonishment*) Well, I don't know. (*nervous laughter*) Well, I couldn't even imagine God being a lady. No, sir. Boy, that would change the whole world."

Arthur demonstrates in his vociferous reaction a strong need to reject any thought of a female deity. Whether his fears and those of his male peers represent a reaction against girls, apprehension concerning their own feminine qualities, or anxiety about the mystery of motherhood, their responses were memorable and thought-provoking. My own impression is that the boys intimated an undercurrent of love and fear of femininity and that these conflicts were most difficult to cope with.

Girls, in contrast, used the same questions about God's sex as an opportunity to express their budding political views.

Eleven year-old Becky Sue asserted that she "didn't see why a girl couldn't be God, or at least president of a country." Similarly, twelve-year-old Tamara suggested that if God were a woman, "There would be less violence in the world."

Both boys and girls in the study showed differences in God imagery that appeared to reflect individual personality types. One popular conception can aptly be described as

"God, the Friendly Ghost." This type of deity appears as a congenial spirit that befriends the child and engages in peerlike activities. While such imagery is created by children of all ages, it appears most frequently with the youngest group of children. The deity resembles an imaginary playmate who just happens to possess some very extraordinary powers. Thus, in one seven-year-old's doll play God plays a board game with family members; in keeping with God's stature, however, it is not Trivial Pursuit® they play but the game of Life®.

Children of the Friendly God yearn for an inner world of harmony and peace, but the deity figure seems to arise partly out of loneliness. God provides for a happy world and serves to protect against conflict, which is considered flagrantly noxious to the child. God makes sure things go "okay" even if (or because) family or school events seem to go awry in real life. Fun and pleasure may prevail in the child's waking thoughts, but their exclusive appearance limits the child's perspective and inhibits his drive for novelty and complexity.

In contrast, other children describe a much more intense and influential deity, which might be called "God, the Lover in Heaven." In this guise God emerges in highly romanticized fashion as a mate or spouse. God has greater physicality than the image engendered by the New Testament bridgroom parable; instead, this deity has all of the qualities of Sir Lancelot and Casanova. God is the object and fountain of considerable yearning, but the child's growing sexual feelings cause much reluctance and confusion. The Lover in Heaven child suggests a pronounced, emotional affiliation with the deity, as well as a substantial fear of its attraction. Nine-year-old Carin talks of a "handsome gentleman who gives me presents." Later she acknowledges, "I love Him so much, it is hard to say in words." At the interview's conclusion she offers, "I get scared sometimes by how much I feel about God. I feel like I'd like to be in a palace in heaven with him but not just yet."

A third common deity type is one I have come to call "Dr. God, the Therapist." This is a healing God, a nurturing figure who cures all the ills of the family and the

world. The core quality of this God is the ability to mend
injury, both physical and psychological, though God's role
in the healing process is not always clear to the child.

The "Dear God" letter of twelve-year-old James, dis-
traught over the vicissitudes of fifth grade, provides a good
illustration:

> Dear God,
>   I have a problem about school. We had exams this
> week and I am nerverse [nervous] about what I got on
> them. I hope I did good. I know you really can't help
> me since there [they're] all done . . . Or maybe you
> could? I want you to know that I am scared about
> it. . . . Tell Mary I said hi.
>   I will talk to you later.
>   James.

Despite the differences that I found associated with age,
sex, religion and personality, all forty children also demonstrated some similar processes in their expression of
religious ideas. Family imagery, for example, strongly
influenced the deity imagery. Family members interpret
scripture and stricture for the children and act as the most
influential socializers, so it is not surprising that God is
closely associated with fathers, mothers, and even grand-
parents.

The familial connection is not always an easy one for the
children; a parent's anger or depression has the potential to
blacken the image of God and trigger great religious doubt.
An important real-life task, then, is for the child to sort out
the parents' attitudes and emotions from what is ultimately
defined as a nonparental, nonhuman God.

At the same time that family dynamics are foremost in
the child's life, the mass media—especially television—
are also having an influence. God imagery can be colored
and distorted by association with TV fantasy, especially its
numerable superheroes. Nine-year-old Ted tells us, for
example, that God is like the star of *Knight Rider*, because
"both work against crime and evil." And ten-year-old
Scott offered that divine communication can get a bit

"weird"—"like when God talked through the burning bush to the guy in *The Ten Commandments*." These screen versions of omnipotence sometimes compete with the views of God offered by parents or the Church. Particularly when anxious or confused, children seem to rely upon accessible, popular renditions, perhaps at the expense of their creativity and search for belief.

Ultimately the children in this study revealed a powerful yearning to have their own very private and personal insights accepted. A seven-year-old Jewish girl tells the Biblical story of Joseph, and then, as if violating some age-old taboo, adds nervously, "Is it okay if I tell one of my own now?" A six-year-old Catholic boy, carefully arranging a set of family dolls, asks politely, "Is it all right if I don't have them in Church praying?" And an eight-year-old Jewish boy describes his feeling for God this way: "I don't know if this is what you're asking. But I feel closest to God, like after I'm rounding second base after I hit a double."

The children's doubts and affirmations seem to suggest that religion is above all else a spontaneous phenomenon of the heart. Whether through their drawings, storytelling, or one boy's baseball recap, the children tell us that this is where God exists for them on a day-to-day basis.

One question that inspired the study was whether or not there exists a common God, a central theme to all of the children's Gods. To the extent that we can unravel clearly socialized conceptions from more original notions, we can begin to gain a glimpse of some collectively held image. The closest thing to a universal God in my small sample was a God who weaves its work through human intimacy and the interconnectedness of lives. Repeatedly, the children made reference to "a feeling of closeness" and the belief "that we are all related, even if I doubt sometimes." All forty children also envisioned a deity involved in self-change and growth, transformations that make the world fresh, alive, and meaningful. The relationship between God and the wish for transformation was movingly illustrated by nine-year-old Carin's plaintive question: "How do you get to be an angel, God?"

Indeed, the children collectively attribute tremendous and expansive power to God. They really believe that this is the God of creation—one who can order floods, rainbows, and lasting sunshine. Yet each child showed considerable anxiety in the face of such power, and it was not the normal anxiety associated with performance worries or personal limitations; it was pervasive and global anxiety, as nine-year-old Arthur's commentary makes clear: "It must be a complicated God. It's often hard to make sense of . . . (*pause, then cautiously*) Sometimes, when I think about death in the world and God, I can't even stay thinking about it."

How do children resolve this anxiety? Well, they seem to believe that God's power is qualified, that divine power depends upon men and women, and, of course, upon boys and girls too. As twelve-year-old Gerald explained to me during doll play, "God is inside the boy. This is how the boy learns to love and make a difference in the world."

Closely associated with the common themes of godliness was the imagery of light. As the child is socialized, light may emerge as an instrument of God or as a symbol of the divine presence; it might also be seen as a means of communication. Occasionally, however, light imagery referred to a special quality of the child. Nine-year-old Ted was most articulate on this point: "I don't know what to call it exactly, but it's sort of like there is a little light inside you. . . . Even when something goes wrong, like when my sister died [in a car accident], it can still shine. I can't say I feel it all the time. But when I feel it, I feel it very strong (*a look of enchantment*)."

The common themes suggest that the God image finds its way into the children's deeper thoughts and feelings. Eventually, children indicate a growing, if not glowing, sense of identity—as individual thinkers who are beginning to leave behind facile interpretations of religious experiences. They even seem to have moments of great faith. These moments carry with them a special quality. The children speak with an air of conviction and authority and communicate a greater tranquillity about the world and about themselves. No longer do they see God, as theologian Hans Küng is fond of saying, as "that distant thing in the sky" (Küng, 1979). No longer do the children see themselves as small marionettes in an adult religious drama. They believe in their own efficacy and take into the world a natural appetite for meaning and love for exploration.

Through their ideas and images of God these children teach us a great deal about the world as they perceive it. It is a world characterized by contradictions, where joy and confusion, belief and doubt, are in constant flux. And through their lively and creative expression they seem to say, "If there is a God, and we think there is, then it could well be the children's God."

Why Should a Woman Be More Like a Man?

Carol Gilligan

Most theories of human development—such as Freud's—
have been conceived by men. In these models of how a
person grows from childhood to adulthood, women sometimes seem to fall short of men. The question is whether this
is due to the theories or to the problems of women. The
answer seems to be that some theories are gender-biased,
as psychologist Carol Gilligan suggests in "Why Should a
Woman Be More Like a Man?"

Gilligan, a professor at the Harvard Graduate School of
Education, previously worked with Lawrence Kohlberg, whose
theory of moral development she challenges. "The conflict
between self and other," she has written, "constitutes the
central moral problem for women"—a difficulty that does not
dominate the moral lives of men. Gilligan contends that men
are more likely to emphasize separation throughout the life
cycle, while women stress attachment. Above all, she co-
gently argues that there is more than one path to the development of health, and that each sex has its own route.

"It is obvious," Virginia Woolf says in *A Room of One's
Own*, "that the values of women differ very often from the
values which have been made by the other sex." Yet, she
adds, "it is the masculine values that prevail." As a
result, women come to question the normality of their
feelings and to alter their judgments in deference to the
opinions of others. In 19th-century novels written by women,

Woolf sees at work "a mind which was slightly pulled from the straight and made to alter its clear vision in deference to external authority."

The same deference to the values and opinions of others can be seen in the judgments of 20th-century women. The difficulty that women experience in finding or speaking in their own voices emerges repeatedly in the form of qualification and self-doubt, and also in intimations of a divided judgment—a public and a private assessment that are fundamentally at odds.

Yet the deference and confusion that Woolf criticizes in women stem from the values she sees as their strength. Women's deference is rooted not only in their social subordination, but also in the substance of their moral concern. Sensitivity to the needs of others and the assumption of responsibility for taking care lead women to listen to the voices of others and to include in their judgment points of view other than their own. Women's moral weakness, seen in an apparent diffusion and confusion of judgment, is thus inseparable from women's moral strength, which is an overriding concern with relationships and responsibilities.

Women not only define themselves in a context of human relationships, but judge themselves in terms of their ability to care. Woman's place in man's life cycle has been that of nurturer, caretaker, and helpmate, the weaver of those networks of relationships on which she, in turn, relies. But while women have thus taken care of men, it is equally true that men in their theories of psychological development, as in their economic arrangements, have tended to devalue that care. The theories of Lawrence Kohlberg, Daniel Levinson, and George Vaillant, derived from research on men, identify the process by which they become separate, autonomous individuals and, in the case of Vaillant's and Levinson's work, achieve career success. When maturity is thus equated with personal autonomy, concern with relationships appears as a weakness of women rather than a human strength.

I first became aware of this bias while teaching with Kohlberg in an undergraduate course at Harvard on moral and political choice. Observing that more women than men were dropping Kohlberg's course, I suggested interviewing several of the female dropouts in depth. When I read the transcripts, I was puzzled by what I found. These women were experiencing moral conflicts that simply could not be understood within Kohlberg's framework.

Dissatisfied with existing measures of identity and moral growth, I undertook with Michael Murphy a systematic study of 144 male and female subjects of different ages in the Boston area. What I wanted to do in these interviews was to find a new structure that could describe the apparent differences in moral development between the two sexes.

At midlife, men suddenly discover the value of intimacy, relationships, and care, the importance of which women have known from the beginning. However, because that knowledge in women has been considered "intuitive" or "instinctive," psychologists have neglected to describe its development. Choosing, like Virgil, to "sing of arms and the man," psychologists describing adulthood have focused on the development of self and work. The distance separating women from this view of adulthood is nowhere clearer than in the studies on sex-role stereotypes reported by psychologist Inge Broverman and colleagues in 1972. The repeated finding of these studies is that the qualities considered necessary for adulthood—autonomous thinking, sharp decision-making, and responsible action— are associated with masculinity and are considered undesirable as feminine attributes.

The sexual stereotypes suggest a splitting of love and work. Expressive capacities are assigned to women, instrumental abilities to men. Yet these stereotypes show an adulthood that is out of balance, favoring separateness over connection, and leaning more toward an autonomous life of work than toward the interdependence of love and care.

Daniel Levinson, of Yale, despite his evident distress about the exclusion of women from his necessarily small sample, set out on the basis of an all-male study "to create an overarching conception of development that could encompass the diverse biological, psychological, and social changes occurring in adult life." [See "Growing Up With the Dream," *Psychology Today*, January 1978.] Levinson's conception is informed by the idea of "the Dream," which orders the seasons of a man's life in the same way that Jupiter's prophecy of a glorious destiny steers the course of Aeneas's journey. Levinson's Dream is also a vision of glorious achievement whose realization or modification will shape the character and life of the man. In the important relationships in Levinson's analysis, the "mentor" furthers the realization of the Dream, while the "special woman" is the helpmate who encourages the hero to shape and live out his vision.

The significant relationships of early adulthood are thus construed as the means to an end—individual achievement—and these "transitional figures" must be cast off or reconstructed following success. If in the process they become an impediment to the fulfillment of the Dream, then the relationship must be renounced, "to allow the developmental process" to continue. Levinson explains this process: "Throughout the life cycle, but especially in the key transition periods . . . the developmental process of individuation is going on."

If in the course of "becoming one's own man," this structure is found to be flawed and threatens the great expectations of the Dream, then in order to avert "serious failure or decline," the man must "break out" to salvage his Dream. The act of breaking out is consummated by a "market event" of separation, such as "leaving his wife, quitting his job, or moving to another region." Thus the road to midlife salvation runs through either achievement or separation.

Levinson's male subjects steady their lives by their devotion to realizing their Dream, measuring their progress in terms of their distance from the shores of its promised success. In the stories that Levinson recounts, relationships, whatever their particular intensity, play a relatively subordinate role in the individual drama of adult development.

The focus on work is also apparent in George Vaillant's account of adaptation to life—based on a longitudinal study of Harvard men. [See "The Climb to Maturity: How the Best and Brightest Came of Age,'' *Psychology Today*, September 1977.] Filling in what he sees as ''an uncharted period of development'' that Erik Erikson left ''between the 20s and 40s,'' Vaillant describes the 30s as the age of ''career consolidation.'' The continuity of intimacy and generativity is interrupted by a stage of further individuation and achievement, which is realized by work and consummated by success.

Erikson's notion of generativity, however, is changed in the process of this recasting. Conceiving generativity as ''the concern in establishing and guiding the next generation,'' Erikson took the productivity and creativity of parenthood to be a metaphor for an adulthood based on relationships and devoted to the activity of taking care. In Erikson's account, generativity is the central stage of adult development, encompassing ''man's relationship to his production as well as to his progeny.'' In Vaillant's data, this relationship is relegated to midlife.

Asserting that generativity is ''not just a stage for making little things grow,'' Vaillant argues against Erikson's metaphor of parenthood by cautioning that ''the world is filled with irresponsible mothers who are marvelous at bearing and loving children up to the age of 2 and then despair of taking the process further.'' Generativity, in order to exclude such women, is redefined as ''responsibility for the growth, leadership, and well-being of one's fellow creatures, not just raising crops or children.'' The breadth of Erikson's conception, then, is narrowed to development in midadulthood and is made more restrictive in its definition of care.

Vaillant emphasizes the relation of self to society and minimizes attachment to others. In an interview about work, health, stress, death, and a variety of family relationships, Vaillant says to the men in his study that ''the hardest question'' he will ask is, ''Can you describe your wife?'' This prefatory caution presumably arose from his experience with this particular sample of men, but it points to the limits of their adaptation, or perhaps to its psychological expense.

Vaillant's ''models for a healthy life cycle'' are men

who seem distant in their relationships and find it difficult to describe their wives, whose importance in their lives they nevertheless acknowledge. The same sense of distance between self and others is evident in Levinson's conclusion that "in our interviews, friendship was largely noticeable by its absence. As a tentative generalization we would say that close friendship with a man or a woman is rarely experienced by American men."

Though both Vaillant and Levinson argue that separation leads to attachment, and individuation to mutuality, rarely do the case histories offer support. In all of these accounts, the women are silent. There are no descriptions of interdependence; the reality of connection is lost.

The conception of development that emerges from this work casts a familiar shadow on women's lives. It suggests that women's separation from others is somehow incomplete, and portrays them as mired in relationships. For women, however, separation and attachment are not discrete stages that they go through in adolescence and adulthood, but are fused. This fusion leaves them at risk in a society that rewards separation.

The problem of interpretation posed by the differences observed in women's development is illustrated by the moral judgments of two 11-year-old sixth-graders, a boy and a girl, who participated in the study designed to explore different conceptions of morality and self. The children were asked to resolve Kohlberg's famous dilemma as to whether a man named Heinz should steal an overpriced drug that he cannot afford in order to save his wife's life. [Kohlberg's dilemmas are designed to present a conflict between moral norms and to assess the level of moral sophistication in the reasoning used to resolve them.)

Eleven-year-old Jake is convinced from the outset that Heinz should steal the drug. Constructing the dilemma, as Kohlberg did, as a conflict between the values of property and life, he discerns *the logical priority* of life and uses that logic to justify his choice. "For one thing, a human life is worth more than money, and if the druggist only makes $1,000 he is still going to live, but if Heinz doesn't

steal the drug his wife is going to die. . . . The druggist
can get $1,000 later from rich people with cancer, but
Heinz can't get his wife again.''

Fascinated by the power of logic, Jake considers the
moral dilemma to be ''sort of like a math problem with
humans.'' He sets it up as an equation and proceeds to
work out the solution. Since his solution is rationally
derived, he assumes that anyone following reason will
arrive at the same conclusion.

In contrast, Amy's response to the dilemma conveys an
image of development stunted by a failure of logic, an
inability to think for herself. Asked whether Heinz should
steal the drug, she replies in a way that seems evasive and
unsure: ''Well, I don't think so. I think there might be
other ways besides stealing it, like if he could borrow the
money or make a loan or something, but he really shouldn't
steal the drug—but his wife shouldn't die either.''

Seeing in the dilemma not a math problem with humans
but a narrative of relationships that extends over time,
Amy envisions the wife's continuing need for her husband
and the husband's continuing need for her, and seeks to
respond to the druggist's need in a way that would sustain
rather than sever connection.

When considered in the light of Kohlberg's definition of
the stages and sequences of moral development, Amy's
judgments appear to be a full stage lower than Jake's on
moral maturity. Her reliance on relationships seems to
reveal dependence and vulnerability, and her belief in
communication as the mode through which to resolve moral
dilemmas appears naïve and immature.

To the question ''What does he see that she does not?''
Kohlberg's theory provides a ready response. To the question ''What does she see that he does not?'' Kohlberg's
theory has nothing to say. Since most of Amy's responses
fall through the sieve of Kohlberg's scoring system, they
appear from his perspective to lie outside the moral domain.

The same differences emerged in the college-student
study of identity and moral development in the early adult
years: Once again the women's responses lay outside current maps of human growth. At age 27, the five women in

the study were all actively pursuing careers—two in medicine, one in law, one in graduate study, and one as an organizer of labor unions. In the five years following their graduation from college, three had married and one had had a child. When they were asked, "How would you describe yourself to yourself?" Claire said: "This sounds sort of strange, but I think maternal, with all its connotations. I see myself in a nurturing role. . . . It's hard for me to think of myself without thinking about the other people around me that I'm giving to."

Leslie's response was similar: "I am fairly hardworking, fairly thorough, and fairly responsible. In terms of weaknesses, I am sometimes hesitant about making decisions and unsure of myself and afraid of doing things and taking responsibility, and I think maybe that is one of the biggest conflicts I have had. The other very important aspect of my life is my husband and trying to make his life easier and trying to help him out."

Measuring their strength in terms of attachment ("giving to," "helping out," "being kind," "not hurting"), these successful women do not once mention their academic and professional distinctions when describing themselves as women. If anything, they regard their professional lives as jeopardizing their sense of themselves, and the conflict that they encounter between achievement and care leaves them either divided in judgment or feeling betrayed.

While in all of the women's descriptions, identity is defined in a context of relationship and judged by a standard of responsibility and care, for the men the tone of identity is clearer, more direct, and sharper-edged. Replacing the women's verbs of attachment are adjectives of separation—"intelligent," "logical," "imaginative,' "honest," sometimes even "arrogant" and "cocky." The male "I" is defined in separation, although the men speak of having "real contacts" and "deep emotions," or wishing for them. One man, an architect, described himself this way: "Logical, compromising, outwardly calm. If it seems like my statements are short and abrupt, it is because of my background and training. Architectural statements have to be concise. Accepting. Those are all on an emotional level. I consider myself educated, reasonably intelligent.''

Another man described himself as ''well developed intellectually and emotionally. Relatively narrow circle of friends, acquaintances, persons with whom I have real contacts as opposed to professional contacts or community contacts. And relatively proud of the intellectual skills and development, content with the emotional development as such, as a not very actively pursued goal. Desiring to broaden that one, the emotional aspect.''

For men, intimacy becomes the critical experience that brings the self back into connection with others and makes it possible to see both sides—to discover the effects of actions on others as well as the cost of distance to the self. For men, intimacy brings an end to isolation, and for this reason is the transformative experience through which adolescent identity turns into the generativity of adult love and work. In the process, as Erikson observed, the knowledge gained through intimacy changes the ideological morality of adolescence into the adult ethic of taking care.

Since women, however, define their identity through intimacy and care, the moral problems they encounter involve issues of a different sort. When relationships are formed by masking desire, and conflict is avoided by equivocation, confusion arises about the locus of responsibility and truth, and the critical experience becomes that of choice.

Thus, in the transition from adolescence to adulthood, the dilemma itself is the same for both sexes, a conflict between integrity and care. But two different moral ideologies exist, since separation is justified by an ethic of rights, while attachment is supported by an ethic of care.

My interviews with college students demonstrated the changes in moral understanding that occur between the ages of 21 and 26. Though both sexes move away from absolutes, the absolutes themselves differ. In women's development, the absolute of care, defined initially as not hurting others, becomes complicated through the recognition of the need for personal integrity. This gives rise to the claim for equality, embodied in the concept of rights, which changes the understanding of relationships and transforms the definition of care. For men, the absolutes of truth and fairness are called into question by experiences that reveal differences between self and others. This new awareness of multiple truths gives rise to an ethnic of generosity and care.

Starting from very different points, the men and women in the study thus come to a greater understanding of both points of view and to a greater convergence in judgment. Justice and care, they now realize, exist side by side. Moral judgment depends on the way in which the moral problem is framed.

The difference in framing is manifested in women's vision of maturity. David McClelland, a professor of psychology at Harvard, observes that "women are more concerned than men with both sides of an interdependent relationship" and are "quicker to recognize their own interdependence." This focus on interdependence is apparent in fantasies that equate power with giving and care. McClelland reports that while men represent powerful activity as assertion and aggression, women portray acts of nurturance as acts of strength.

Jean Baker Miller, a psychoanalyst, agrees with McClelland. Focusing on relationships of dominance and subordination, she finds that the woman's role in these relationships provides "a crucial key to understanding the psychological order."

Miller calls for a new psychology of women that recognizes the different starting point for women's development, the fact "that women stay with, build on, and develop in a context of attachment and affiliation with others. . . . Women's sense of self becomes very much organized around being able to make, and then to maintain, affiliations and relationships . . . [and] eventually, for many women, the threat of disruption of an affiliation is perceived not just as a loss of a relationship but as something closer to a total loss of self."

The implication of these differences is evident in considering the circumstance of women at midlife. The middle years for women have been portrayed as a time of return to

the unfinished business of adolescence. This interpretation
has been particularly compelling, since life-cycle descriptions, based primarily on studies of men, have made women
appear deficient in their development. Female development has been especially marked off in the adolescent
years when girls appear to confuse identity with intimacy
by defining themselves through relationships with others.
Thus defined, the female self is considered to be vulnerable to the issues of separation that arise at midlife.

This construction reveals the limitations of measuring
female development against a male standard. The observation that women's embeddedness in lines of relationships,
their awareness of interdependence, and their subordination of achievement to care leave them personally at risk in
midlife seems more a commentary on society than a problem in women's development.

To see midlife in adolescent terms, as a similar crisis of
identity and separation, is to ignore the reality of what has
happened in the years between; and it trivializes the history
of love and work. For generativity to begin at midlife, as
Vaillant's data on men suggest, seems from a woman's
perspective too late for both sexes, since the bearing and
raising of children have already taken place. Similarly, the
image of women as arriving at midlife childlike and dependent on others is belied by the activity of their care in
nurturing and sustaining family relationships.

Because women's sense of integrity appears to be en-
twined with an ethic of care, the major transitions in
women's lives involve changes in the understanding and
activities of nurturance. Certainly the shift from childhood
to adulthood calls for a major redefinition. When the
distinction between helping and pleasing frees the activity
of taking care from the wish for approval by others, responsibility can become a self-chosen anchor of personal
integrity and strength.

But at the same time, the events of midlife—menopause
and changes in family and work—can alter a woman's
activities of care in ways that affect her sense of herself. If
midlife brings an end to relationships, to the sense of

connection on which she relies, as well as to the activities of care through which she judges her worth, then the mourning that accompanies all life transitions can give way to self-deprecation and despair.

When a distinction is made between neurotic and real conflict—between the reluctance to choose and the reality of having no choice—then it becomes possible to see more clearly how woman's experience provides a key to understanding central truths of adult life. Rather than viewing her anatomy as destined to leave her with a scar of inferiority, as Freud suggested, one can see, instead, how it gives rise to experiences that illuminate a reality common to both of the sexes: the fact that in life you never see it all, that there is more than one path to gratification, and that the boundaries between self and others are less than they sometimes seem.

Mentors: Bridging the Gap

by Perry Garfinkel

In finding one's path through life, there are many, many people who help along the way. When the time comes to establish an identity at work, the one who helps most directly is a mentor, a person a bit further along in his or her career than oneself, but advanced enough to be able to teach some of the ropes. In the following article Perry Garfinkel describes the role of the mentor in a man's life (things are not much different for a woman with her mentor).

The mentor believes in the abilities of his protégé, and so gives him a vote of confidence, just as he is trying to prove himself. This boost is of critical importance at that stage of life in which, as Erik Erikson has observed, the main psychological task is to establish one's own separate identity. And once that identity is firmly established, the protégé must finally put his mentor behind him, passing on to the point where he himself can, in turn, become a mentor.

YOUNG BOYS BEGIN to look outside the family circle for male role models—especially if they have been disappointed by fathers they could not depend on, look up to, or believe in. In this turn outward, boys are looking primarily for training and development in specific skills; reinforcement, approval, and acceptance as individuals; and entree

52

into the world of grown-up men. These desires were echoed
by men I interviewed, with comments like these:

> "What I needed was someone who'd show me the
> ropes."
>
> "I was looking for a man I could talk to, who
> *listened* to me, who appreciated me for who I am and
> what I could become."
>
> "I wanted someone who would take me under his
> wing."

Enter the mentor. He is a man who fills in those gaps in
a young man's education by teaching him the nuts and
bolts of a chosen field of interest; by encouraging and
simply paying attention to an apprentice's development;
and by serving as a stepping stone to the next level to
which the younger man aspires. Such men pass through a
boy's or man's life as teachers, coaches, or instructors; as
mechanics, grocers, or the guy down the street; as supervisors, department heads, or bosses.

The mentor is usually a half generation older, from eight
to fifteen years—too old to suggest competitive peership
and not old enough to invite comparisons to one's father.
He is a transitional figure, embodying equal parts peer and
parent and serving as a bridge between them for the protegé.
A man's mentor is almost always male, according to my
research and that of others, a fact that reconfirms to me
men's belief that power (in this case skills, knowledge,
and access) comes through a male hierarchy.

Most relationships with mentors are encounters that may
last several years. A mentor may be someone a man meets
only briefly but who leaves a lasting impression. Or he
may be someone he never meets but who remains an
inspirational male model to emulate (sports heroes, for
example, or movie or rock stars, writers, politicians, war
heroes). And then there is the actual teacher with whom a
man interacts for a number of years.

Throughout history and across cultures, mentors have
held a highly regarded place in a man's world. The Japanese might call him *sensei* or "the person born before," or

"older"; it is one of the highest forms of address that can
be bestowed on a person in that culture. In the Hindu
tradition he is a *guru*, "venerable one." The Latin word
mentor means "advisor" or "wise man." In Greek my-
thology, Mentor was a trusted friend, a consultant to
Odysseus, and later a guide to Odysseus's son Telemachus.

Plato expressed the strong emotional bond a protegé
feels for his mentor as he sat beside Socrates, who was
about to take the poison hemlock:

> And we waited, talking and thinking of the greatness of
> our sorrow; he was like a father of whom we were
> being bereaved, and we were about to pass the rest of
> our lives as orphans. Hitherto most of us had been able
> to control our sorrow but we could no longer forbear
> and in spite of myself my own tears were flowing fast
> (so that I covered my face and wept over myself) for
> certainly I was not weeping over him, but at the thought
> of my own calamity in having lost such a companion.

Though the relationship of Socrates and Plato became a
model for almost all mentors thereafter, scholars say one
would have to hunt and peck through volumes of Plato's
writings for passages revealing the nature of that relationship. In fact, almost no one analyzed the mentor-protegé
relationship until 1978 when Yale psychologist Daniel
Levinson stumbled onto it in the course of researching his
book *The Seasons of a Man's Life*. Looking at the stages
of adult male development, he called the relationship with
a mentor "one of the most complex, and developmentally
important a man can have in early adulthood."

Yet, as important as mentors appear to be, surprisingly
few men in my study or Levinson's could identify actual
men in their lives whom they would describe as mentors.
Most recite the names of heroes from history or film: from
John F. Kennedy, to John Wayne. Why do male figures
like these loom larger in men's lives than real-life people?
Are there so few men worth emulating? Despite their own
understanding of the need to find such mentors, are men

simply afraid of seeking out and making contact with potential mentors?

One explanation may be that men define the mentor in such idealistic and heroic terms that finding *any* man who could live up to the expectations in the first place would be difficult. Levinson described the "functions" of a mentor this way:

> He may act as a teacher to enhance the young man's skills and intellectual development. Serving as a sponsor, he may use his influence to facilitate the young man's entry and advancement. He may be a host and guide, welcoming the initiate into a new occupational social world and acquainting him with its values, customs, resources and cast of characters. Through his own virtues, achievements and way of living, the mentor may be an exemplar that the protegé can admire and seek to emulate. He may provide counsel and moral support in times of stress.

Observe first that Levinson applies a *functional* index to the definition, making it seem like a list of accomplishments one checks off. Also note the order in which he lists them, with skills first and emotional support last, and even that only "in time of stress."

Another clue to the reason for a relative scarcity of real-live mentors came out in my interviews. Men responded to questions about mentors with descriptions of what they referred to as "heroes" and "father figures." The repetition of these terms forced a comparison to our father/heroes. Were these so-called "father figures" based on real father models or mythical archetypes? If men are looking for mentors who resemble their fathers—or their ideas of what their fathers should be—it would be reasonable to expect them to have trouble relating to the outsiders they actually encountered, given the proscriptions against intimate father-son interaction. In the search for "fatherly" mentors, men are inevitably bound to come face to face as protegés with the same issues, patterns, and stages they encountered as sons.

In cases where the mentor-protegé relationships are established, men often hope to gain companionships free of the emotional complexities they found with their fathers or sons. In fact, the emotions in this relationship run very high, setting up the familiar reverence and revolt stages as seen between father and son. Reconciliation is often less noticeable simply because the relationship is so short-lived. Here is a closer look at the stages.

Reverence

A mentor earns much of the reverence he is paid by a younger man simply by demonstrating a belief in the latter's skills and abilities. The mentor sees promise in the protegé and often gives a vote of confidence just when the young man is trying to prove himself to his own father.

A Maine potter, age thirty-five, told me about his "male hero":

His name was Bill Foster, an older guy, my father's age. I grew up down the street from him in suburban Rochester, New York. I had worked for him since I was young. I cut his lawn, painted his house. He started building a houseboat in his backyard and I helped him on that. And I loved him; he was a wonderful guy. I guess he was the closest thing for me to a "good guy" father figure. My own father used to scare the shit out of me—when he wasn't working. But Bill—he related to me as a person. We'd talk for long periods while he worked; he'd tell me stories about when he was a kid. It was very important for me to see other males acting like regular people. He was a warm kind of guy—and it was through him that I knew such a feeling was possible between men.

Without all the complexities, Oedipal and otherwise, inherent in the father-son relationship—a matter of being *too* close, too emotionally involved and egotistically invested—the young man can share his hopes and dreams, his fears and insecurities with the mentor without fear of reproval and rejection. The young and the older man usually share an interest in a subject, a sport, a car or machine; they have a common language in its jargon and technicalities. Here is a universe in which the two can interact, where the standards are objective and the criteria for excellence mutually understood—as contrasted directly with the domain of a father and son.

Growing up in a working class district of Pittsburgh, a forty-four-year-old man recalled treasured friendships with older men who took the time his father could not:

After school I would go to the local bus garage. And I met a guy there, Hugh McDonald, and he taught me all about how to deal with machinery. Every day I used to go help him fix the buses. It went on for years from the time I was seven. He'd expect me to come and I really enjoyed going there, seeing how excited he was to see me. He'd give me a cup of tea. . . . I was thinking recently that my "male learning" came from men like that, passing figures, rather than my father. There was another guy who ran a little two-acre farm nearby and every weekend for four or five years I'd go hang out with him. I'd help him tend the cows and sheep and plow the fields and plant vegetables. So during the week I'd be with one guy and on weekends with the other. More than anybody else, these two guys taught me the skills of being alive in the world. I learned about mechanics and I learned about the earth—powerful elemental tools.

Where a father is likely to challenge his son's chosen interests, weighing them for value against his own or against his own aspirations for the boy, the mentor accepts the boy's interest as a given, sharing what he knows and even justifying the boy's interest by holding it himself.

Revolt

Slowly things begin to turn. Just as in the father-son relationship, the young man who had felt respect, admiration, commonality, gratitude, and even love for—and from—

his mentor now reaches a point in his growth where he needs once again to declare his independence, as he did with his father. He needs to assert his position and authority—to be autonomous. Now he feels hemmed in by the mentor: patronized, unappreciated, and resentful. He views his mentor's ideology and methodology as old-fashioned, uninventive, and unbending. Having attained some stature of his own in the world into which he was ushered by the older man, the protegé sees the limits of the mentor—and he sees something for himself beyond his mentor. He begins to feel that in the world of grown-up men his mentor is not such a big deal after all. And in order to become a big deal himself he must put his mentor behind him. Of this phase Levinson wrote:

> The mentor he formerly loved and admired is now experienced as destructively critical and demanding, or as seeking to make one over in his own image rather than fostering one's individuality and independence. The mentor who only yesterday was regarded as an enabling teacher and friend has become a tyrannic father and smothering mother. The mentor, for his part, finds the young man inexplicably touchy, unreceptive to even the best counsel, irrationally rebellious and ungrateful. By the time they are through, there is generally some validity in each one's criticism of the other.

The break is often bitter and hostile. But it is essential for the young man if he is ever to feel fully empowered. The mentor as well grieves at losing a special relationship. It is a tribute to the intensity of the relationship that it takes a while for feelings to settle. After the break, the two may never see each other again or they may establish a much cooler and cordial working relationship.

Reconciliation

Once the protegé feels that his power is his own and that he is recognized for it, he can usually acknowledge freely the important role the mentor played in his life. As time heals wounds, each is more able to understand the effect of their meeting and their influence on the other. Whether they reconcile their differences with each other in spoken words or not (though, true to most man-to-man relationships, they probably will not) the protegé will reconcile with his mentor in one of the most important ways—by making the mentor a more intrinsic part of himself, his philosophy, and his style, by incorporating into himself aspects of the older man he admires and even some of those he does not. Just as the son who later realizes he *has* followed in his father's footsteps or picked up his father's values, attitudes, and even physical mannerisms, so too does the young man come to terms with the imprint of his mentor on himself. Nonetheless it may take a lifetime for some men to acknowledge the influence of their mentors—if they even can claim to have found one.

BEING A MENTOR

It would appear that most of the value of the mentor-protegé relationship is gained by the protegé. What is in it for the older man?

My interviews and the literature suggest that being a mentor is as important a developmental stage as *having* a mentor. To step into the mentor role is to acknowledge a man has accumulated enough knowledge, skill, and expertise to graduate from student to teacher. That in itself is enough reward for many men continuously yearning to be looked up to by other men, after being looked down upon for many years.

Men in their twenties and thirties become mentors to younger men but it is not until they reach their forties that their full potential is realized. A mentor of forty would be passing through a phase of adult maturation Levinson termed the "mid-life transition." Beginning as a man leaves his early adulthood behind and enters his middle adulthood (forty to sixty) this transition is marked by awareness of physical decline, career solidification, family stabilization, and generally greater responsibility as an adult. A man's relationship with his parents changes; roles reverse. His children, if he has them, are becoming independent. Psychoanalyst Erik Erikson identified an important aspect of middle adulthood as the concern for the nurturance of future generations. He termed this natural inclination to assume responsibility for the education and indoctrination of the next line of adults as "generativity." A man acts on this drive as a father, Cub Scout leader, teacher, supervisor, or mentor.

For a man of this age, finding a protegé to whom he can transmit knowledge can be a deeply satisfying way to fulfill the urge toward generativity. The mentor's own meaning is justified by the new knowledge that part of himself will be projected into the future via the younger man.

At the same time it makes him feel connected to the future, the mentor role connects a man with his own youth, which he sees quickly fading. Contact with young men—working with them, planning, directing, socializing—recharges the middle-aged man's own youthful energies and reminds him of the continuity of the life process as he comes to terms with the inevitability of his own death.

But there is a negative side as well. Being a mentor can be an awkward and heavy burden to carry. I learned this first hand on a visit to an editor who had been an important professional and personal influence in my life. When I started out as a freelance writer he had given me several key assignments for major magazines that helped both my career and my self-confidence. More than that, though, I admired the humanistic touch he retained while wielding power and ideas in a big way. In the library of his Princeton, New Jersey, home I finally got up the courage to declare my debt, respect, and thanks.

The first thing I learned, as I tripped over my own words, was how difficult it was to take the leap into feelings. His response did not help matters. He quickly deflected the compliment and my awkward expression of gratitude:

Mentor? That always troubles me as a way to be thinking about relationships. Ultimately, it's the language I dislike. It implies dominance by one over the other. I don't know of a mentor-protegé situation in which both aren't gaining something. It's not a one-way thing. There has to be a fundamental exchange going on.

He seemed to have jumped so quickly from the personal to the general that the emotion of the moment I had built myself up for was lost.

"What I wanted to say to you was that I really appreciate our friendship beyond all that," I said.

"So do I," he said and then went on:

I know it doesn't work unless there's a parity. I benefitted as much from the things you've written as you have, in a purely commercial sense. I needed somebody to do a story that nobody else could do and you did it. Part of my stock in trade is to be able to have access to writers like you. That's what editors get paid for. So the books are balanced at the end of the day in those terms.

This all sounded hard-boiled and out of character from a man with whom I had had long talks about magazines and human nature. But what I realized was that in all that time we had never broached the subject about our feelings for each other. They were understood. There was mutual admiration and respect, personally and professionally. When it came to talking about it, however, my mentor became curiously impersonal.

"Does it make you uncomfortable knowing that you're such a strong role model for me?" I finally asked.

"Well, it does bother me," he admitted. "I get scared of it. Am I deserving of it? I wonder. But I don't take it seriously. I know you won't be blinded; you see my weaknesses and flaws. If I do take on 'protegés' they are usually of the sort that I know are too independent to buy my model entirely."

It took me a long time to realize that in giving vent to my feelings for him I had stepped outside the bounds of our structured relationship into the never-never-land of feelings. That was all that was needed to make him close up and back off—just as he was undoubtedly trained to do by his father and perhaps his own mentor as well.

SIGMUND FREUD/CARL JUNG

The competition for power, the lack of personal exchange about intimate feelings, the great need for approval and confidence—all dynamics seen in the father-son relationship—are clear in the relationship of Sigmund Freud, known as the "father" of psychoanalysis, and Carl Jung, Freud's leading disciple. Though the two men saw each other in person but a few times during a seven-year period, they maintained close contact through letters. *The Freud-Jung Letters* is a collection of 360 letters written from 1906 to 1913. This correspondence is "the record of a friendship, a spiritual father-son relationship between two unique and ultimately irreconcilable talents," according to the book's editor, William McGuire. Though there are pages and pages of letters exploring the evolving theories and practices of this new field of research and practice, only here and there—and sometimes only between the lines—do these two lift the professional veils to focus on the interpersonal relationship between them. When they do, one of the things they reveal is that their relationship was at least as important as their exchange of ideas. For students of psychiatry, this relationship carries special meaning as well; these were, after all, the founding father and the heir-apparent of psychoanalysis.

In the first stage of their interaction, the reverence and respect they exhibit is mutual. Each had the effect of building the other's confidence, though for different reasons.

"You have inspired me with confidence for the future," Freud wrote to Jung after the young man had written to the older telling him how much he admired his theories and wanted to be his student. "I now realize that I am as replaceable as everyone else and that I could hope for no one better than yourself . . . to continue and complete my work."

"I only fear that you overestimate me and my powers," Jung wrote back, confessing his lack of self-confidence, especially in the shadow of his hero.

Freud understated the point when he wrote Jung: "I hope you will gain the recognition you desire and deserve . . . it means a great deal to me too." Finding an able second in Jung ensured Freud's own desire to gain recognition.

In the early years of their relationship Jung continued to put Freud on the hero's pedestal. "My veneration for you has something of the character of a 'religious' crush." Ironically, the issue of religion and its place in analysis would eventually cause their schism.

At one point in their correspondence, Jung suggested a form by which they continue their interpersonal liaison: "Let me enjoy your friendship not as one between equals but as that of father and son. This distance appears to me fitting and natural. It strikes a note that would prevent misunderstanding and enable two hard-headed people to exist alongside one another in an easy unrestrained relationship."

Distance? Prevent misunderstanding? Unrestrained? Surely this student of psychoanalysis was not inviting them into what they both knew was the briar patch of human relationships.

Inevitably their friendship began to turn. Differences began to surface. Jung wanted to explore parapsychology and precognition; Freud rejected these pursuits as nonsense. One evening, while they talked together in one of their few personal encounters, a loud noise sounded in a bookcase. At once, Jung predicted it would happen again—and it did. But Freud would have none of his friend's claim to psychic power. "That evening freed me inwardly from the oppressive sense of your paternal authority," Jung wrote. Freud replied that he indulged in Jung's interest in what he called the "spook complex" with the interest "one accords a charming delusion in which one does not participate oneself."

New differences arose around such theories as incest and libido. Jung's letters began to contain a tension: He

chomped at the bit of theoretic discovery while Freud tried
to tame his impatience. Freud wrote back to Jung: "Rest
easy, dear son Alexander, I will leave you more to conquer
than I myself have managed." The reference to Alexander
is an allusion to the ancient lineage of mentors and their
protegés—from Socrates to Plato to Aristotle to Alexander
the Great. Jung, however, would not be satisfied with
Freud's leftovers, and he invoked these lines from Nietzche's
Zarathustra: "One repays a teacher badly if one remains
only a pupil. And why, then, should you not pluck at my
laurels? Now I bid you lose me and find yourselves; and
only when you have all denied me will I return to you."

If only every mentor had that enlightened attitude. Now,
in order to find himself, Jung had to revolt fully from his
mentor. He realized "how different I am from you—enough
to effect a radical change in my whole attitude." He felt
Freud "underestimates my work by a very wide margin."
He lashed out at Freud, suggesting, "Look at your bit of
neurosis—but you could not submit to analysis, 'without
losing your authority.' " Later he added this critical
appraisal:

> Your technique of treating your pupils like patients is a
> blunder. You produce either slavish sons or impudent
> puppies. . . . You remain on top, as the father, sitting
> pretty. . . . If ever you should rid yourself entirely of
> your complexes and stop playing father to your sons
> and instead of continuously aiming at their weak spots
> took a good look at your own for a change, then I will
> mend my ways and at one stroke uproot the vice of
> being of two minds about you.

At first Freud, emotionally tongue-tied, could only mus-
ter a brief, terse reply. Then he wrote again: "I propose
we abandon our personal relation entirely. I shall lose
nothing by it for my own emotional tie with you has long
been a thin thread—the lingering effects of past disappoint-
ments—take your full freedom." He added, "We are
agreed a man should subordinate his personal feelings to
the general interest of his branch of endeavor."

Following that there are only stilted letters back and forth. Jung eventually resigned from the editorship of the publication of the psychoanalytic society Freud started with Jung's help. Then Jung resigned the presidency of the organization. Freud barely mentioned Jung's name after that while Jung, though crediting Freud as his teacher and founder of the field of psychoanalysis, never contacted his mentor again. Their eventual reconciliation was only an obligatory payment of obeisance to each other.

Whether one's mentor is Freud or Freddie the Fireman, the importance of his contribution to a young man's development is the same. He serves as a bridge from the inner circle of the family to the wide-open outside world. He supplies the polishing phase of the young man's training, one in which objective criteria, not the father's subjective standards, are made explicit, and then applied. In a sense, when a young man has found a mentor, learned from him what he can, and then surpassed him, he is truly a man for better or worse. No longer merely a son, a grandson, a student, or protegé, the young man has earned his autonomy as a full-fledged man in a man's world: the embodiment of a special culture transmitted to him by now-receding figures of fathers, grandfathers, and mentors.

Nonetheless, there is one role a man plays forever in his life, and it is one that apparently changes very little over the course of development: He'll always be a brother.

II.

THINKING

John Dean's Memory: A Case Study

by Ulric Neisser

NIXON RESIGNS. So read the nation's newspaper headlines some twelve years ago as the country's most agonizing political drama reached its culmination. The Senate Watergate hearings that preceded President Nixon's resignation are the focal point of Ulric Neisser's article: "John Dean's Memory: A Case Study" because issues of information access and memory were crucial. Senator Howard Baker's recurring question concerning Richard Nixon's awareness of illegal events was: "What did the President know and when did he know it?"

Perhaps the most dramatic testimony came from John Dean, a presidential adviser, whose amazingly detailed recollections were as noteworthy as his clearly blind ambitions. Dean's memories of the Watergate-related events were pivotal in Nixon's downfall. At the same time, the interview transcripts are important because of the classic psychological principles they illustrate. Neisser took advantage of a bizarre circumstance: Dean did not know, when others testified, that all the conversations he described had been secretly taped.

In his article Neisser applies his keen observational acumen to the record of Dean's testimony about the eyewitness account of White House machinations. Neisser's discussion points out that memory is essentially reconstructive and is therefore prone to mistakes. Especially when a great deal is at stake, a witness's memory can be highly fallible, though it may bear some semblance of the truth. When John Dean

70 THINKING

was wrong about a precise conversation, he often provided
a reasonably accurate account of the facts lying behind the
conversation. In this way he could reproduce the gist of
events, though not their specifics—a kind of reconstruction—
which, Neisser says, is true of all our memories.

"HAVE YOU ALWAYS had a facility for recalling the details
of conversations which took place many months ago?"
Senator Inouye of Hawaii asked this question of John Dean
with more than a trace of disbelief. Dean, the former
counsel to President Richard M. Nixon, was testifying
before the "Watergate" Committee of the United States
Senate in June 1973. His testimony had opened with a
245-page statement, in which he described literally dozens
of meetings that he had attended over a period of several
years. The meetings were with John Mitchell, Robert
Haldeman, Charles Colson, Gordon Liddy, and others whose
names became American household words as the Watergate
scandal brought down the Nixon Administration. Some
were with Nixon himself. Dean's testimony seemed to
confirm what many already suspected: that these high
officials were engaged in a "cover-up" of White House
involvement in the original Watergate burglary. But was
he telling the truth? How much did he really remember?
  For some of Dean's testimony it is now possible to
compare what he said with a factual record—the *Presidential Transcripts*. This comparison will enable us to assess
the accuracy of his memory rather precisely. In addition, it
may clarify our theoretical conceptions of memory itself.
  When Dean first testified, his "facility for recalling
details" seemed so impressive that some writers called
him "the human tape recorder." Ironically, a very real
tape recorder had been tuned in to some of the same
"details." Not long after its interrogation of Dean, the
Senate Committee discovered that all conversations in Nixon's Oval Office were routinely (but secretly) recorded.
The result of this discovery was a sharp legal struggle for
possession of the tapes. When the President realized that
he would not be able to keep the tapes out of the hands of
the prosecutors indefinitely, he decided to transcribe some

of them and release the transcripts himself. Although he did this reluctantly, he also thought it possible that they might actually help his cause. The published version of the *Presidential Transcripts* (1974) includes a lengthy fore-word reiterating Nixon's claim that he knew nothing of the cover-up. (It does admit that there are ". . . possible ambiguities that . . . someone with a motive to discredit the President could take out of context and distort to suit his own purposes" [p. 5].) The foreword explicitly insists that the transcripts discredit Dean's testimony. Dean him-self, however, saw them as substantiating *his* side of the story. In his autobiography (Dean, 1976) he describes himself as "ecstatic" (p. 332) to learn of the tapes' exis-tence, because they would prove he had told the truth.

The testimony and the transcripts are now in the public domain. I propose to treat them as data, as if they had resulted from a deliberately conducted memory experi-ment. If history has ever proven anything, it surely proves that Dean remembered those conversations and told the truth about them. I will not quarrel with that assessment here, but we shall see that "truth," "accuracy," and "memory" are not simple notions. Dean's testimony was by no means always accurate. Yet even when he was wrong, there was a sense in which he was telling the truth; even when he was right, it was not necessarily because he remembered a particular conversation well.

Verbatim recall is word-for-word reproduction. It is not something that we expect of ourselves in everyday life. Dean did not claim to be able to recall conversations verbatim, and indeed he could not. Memory for gist, on the other hand, occurs when we recall the "sense" of an original text in different words. To remember the gist of a story or a conversation is to be roughly faithful to the argument, the story line, the underlying sequence of ideas.

Analysis of Dean's testimony does indeed reveal some instances of memory for the gist of what was said on a particular occasion. Elsewhere in his testimony, however, there is surprisingly little correspondence between the course of a conversation and his account of it. Even in those cases, however, there is usually a deeper level at which he is right. Psychology is unaccustomed to analyzing the truthfulness of memory at this level, because we usually work with laboratory material that has no reference beyond itself. One of my purposes in analyzing John Dean's testimony is to call attention to this level of memory, and perhaps to devise ways in which it can be studied.

DEAN'S OWN ACCOUNT OF HIS MEMORY

The two conversations we will examine are those of September 15, 1972 and March 21, 1973. These two meetings with the President were crucial for the Senate Committee, which was trying to determine the extent of Nixon's involvement in the Watergate cover-up. Accordingly, Dean was cross-examined about both of them at length. He had already described each conversation in his long opening statement to the Committee: it was that statement which aroused Senator Inouye's incredulity. The interchange between Dean and Inouye is interesting in its own right: it may be the only discussion of mnemonics and metamemory in the Congressional Record.

Senator Inouye: Your 245-page statement is remarkable for the detail with which it recounts events and conversations occurring over a period of many months. It is particularly remarkable in view of the fact that you indicated that it was prepared without benefit of note or daily diary. Would you describe what documents were available to you in addition to those which have been identified as exhibits?

Mr. Dean: What I did in preparing this statement, I had kept a newspaper clipping file from roughly June 17 [*June 17, 1972 was the date of the Watergate break-in*], up until about the time these hearings started when I stopped doing any clipping with any regularity. It was by going through every single newspaper article outlining what had happened and then placing myself in what I had done in a given sequence in time, I was aware of all the principal activities I had been involved in, the dealings I had had with others in relationship to those activities. Many times things were in response to press activities or press stories that would result in further activities. I had a good memory of most of the high-lights of things that had occurred, and it was through this process, and being extremely careful in my recol-lection, particularly of the meetings with the President (*Hearings*, pp. 1432–1433).

Note that Dean has spontaneously invented the temporal equivalent of an ancient mnemonic device: the famous "method of loci." In that method, one mentally moves through a familiar series of places in order to recall images that were previously assigned to them. Dean apparently used newspaper clippings in a similar way, to pinpoint moments in time rather than loci in space; then he tried to recall what he had been doing at those moments.

Later Inouye asks Dean to say more about his memory:

Senator Inouye: Have you always had a facility for recalling the details of conversations which took place many months ago?

Dean responds with examples of things he would certainly never forget, beginning with conversations in the Oval Office:

Mr. Dean: Well, I would like to start with the President of the United States. It was not a regular activity for me to go in and visit with the President. For most of the members of the White House staff it is not a daily activity. When you meet with the President of the United States it is a very momentous occasion, and you tend to remember what the President of the United States says when you have a conversation with him. [*Dean goes on to mention several other salient events that he remembers well, and concludes*] . . . So I would say that I have an ability to recall not specific words necessarily but certainly the tenor of a conversation and the gist of a conversation (*Ibid.*, pp. 1433–1434).

We shall see later that Dean recalls the "gist" of some conversations and not of others; the determinants of memory are more complicated than he believes them to be. In particular, he did *not* remember what the President said in their first prolonged and "momentous" meeting. But there is no doubt about his confidence in his own testimony: at the end of the exchange with Inouye, he expresses it again:

> *Mr. Dean*: I cannot repeat the very words he [*the President*] used, no, Sir. As I explained to Senator Gurney, my mind is not a tape recorder, but it certainly receives the message that is being given (*Ibid.*).

The Meeting of September 15

On June 17, 1972, five men were arrested in the offices of the Democratic National Committee in the Watergate Office Building. They had planned to tap the Committee's telephones as part of an illegal "political intelligence" operation, mounted on President Nixon's behalf in the 1972 presidential elections. High White House officials then began a major effort to conceal their involvement in the affair, even to the point of paying "hush money" to some of those who had been arrested. John Dean was centrally involved in the cover-up. His chief task was to "contain" the legal investigation of the Watergate break-in, concealing every link between the underlings already caught and the White House. On September 15 this aim seemed achieved, because on that day the Grand Jury handed down indictments against only seven men: the five burglars plus Howard Hunt and Gordon Liddy. Since Hunt and Liddy were "small fish," and the Justice Department said it had no evidence to indict anyone else, Dean felt victorious. When the President summoned him to the Oval Office that afternoon, he expected to be praised.

The transcript indicates that the meeting lasted 50 minutes. It begins with the following interchange among the President [*P*], Dean [*D*], and Robert Haldeman [*H*], Nixon's "Chief of Staff." Note that Dean and Haldeman are both obviously pleased by the events of the day, while the President has little to say about them:

P: Hi, how are you? You had quite a day today, didn't you? You got Watergate on the way, didn't you?

D: We tried.

H: How did it all end up?

D: Ah, I think we can say well, at this point. The press is playing it just as we expected.

H: Whitewash?

D: No, not yet—the story right now—

P: It is a big story.

H: Five indicted plus the WH former guy and all that.

D: Plus two White House fellows.

H: That is good; that takes the edge off whitewash, really. That was the thing Mitchell kept saying, that to people in the country Liddy and Hunt were big men. Maybe that is good.

P: How did MacGregor handle himself?

D: I think very well. He had a good statement, which said that the Grand Jury had met and that it was now time to realize that some apologies may be due.

H: Fat chance.

D: Get the damn (inaudible)

H: We can't do that.

P: Just remember, all the trouble we're taking, we'll have a chance to get back one day. How are you doing on your other investigation? (*Presidential Transcripts*, p. 32)

The next few exchanges are about other details of the Watergate "bugs" (telephone taps), and then about the scope of the investigations being conducted. It all seemed "silly" to them, expecially since they believed that "bugging" was common in politics:

P: Yes (expletive deleted). Goldwater put it in context when he said "(expletive deleted) everybody bugs everybody else. You know that."

D: That was priceless.

P: It happens to be totally true. We were bugged in '68 on the plane and even in '62 running for Governor—(expletive deleted) thing you ever saw.

D: It is a shame that evidence to the fact that that happened in '68 was never around. I understand that only the former director [*J. Edgar Hoover, former head of the FBI*] had that information.
H: No, that is not true.
D: There was evidence of it?
H: There are others who have information (*Ibid.*, p. 34).

This interchange about "bugging" is noteworthy not only because of the light it sheds on the attitudes of the participants, but also because it stuck in Dean's mind. It is one of the few parts of the conversation which will be recognizable in his testimony nine months later.

The conversation continues from this point with more talk about "bugging," plans for action against White House enemies, questions about another pending legal action. It is interrupted briefly when Nixon takes a phone call. As soon as he hangs up, Dean speaks. He wants to point out how well things are going:

D: Three months ago I would have had trouble predicting there would be a day when this would be forgotten, but I think I can say that 54 days from now [*i.e., on election day in November*] nothing is going to come crashing down to our surprise.
P: That what?
D: Nothing is going to come crashing down to our surprise (*Ibid.*, p. 36).

He finally gets a bit of Presidential praise in return:

P: Oh well, this is a can of worms as you know, a lot of this stuff that went on. And the people who worked this way are awfully embarrassed. But the way you have handled all this seems to me has been very skillful, putting your fingers in the leaks that have sprung here and sprung there. The Grand Jury is dismissed now?
D: That is correct . . . (*Ibid.*).

Dean's Testimony About September 15

Nine months later, Dean devoted about two pages of his prepared statement to the September 15 meeting. The first paragraph purports to describe the way the meeting began. It is an important bit of testimony because the remarks Dean ascribes to Nixon would indicate full knowledge (and approval) of the cover-up. This is his account:

> On September 15 the Justice Department announced the handing down of the seven indictments by the Federal Grand Jury investigating the Watergate. Late that afternoon I received a call requesting me to come to the President's Oval Office. When I arrived at the Oval Office I found Haldeman and the President. The President asked me to sit down. Both men appeared to be in very good spirits and my reception was very warm and cordial. The President then told me that Bob—referring to Haldeman—had kept him posted on my handling of the Watergate case. The President told me I had done a good job and he appreciated how difficult a task it had been and the President was pleased that the case had stopped with Liddy. I responded that I could not take credit because others had done much more difficult things than I had done. As the President discussed the present status of the situation I told him that all I had been able to do was to contain the case and assist in keeping it out of the White House. I also told him there was a long way to go before this matter would end and that I certainly could make no assurances that the day would not come when this matter would start to unravel (*Hearings*, p. 957).

Comparison with the transcript shows that hardly a word of Dean's account is true. Nixon did not say *any* of the things attributed to him here: He didn't ask Dean to sit down, he didn't say Haldeman had kept him posted, he didn't say Dean had done a good job (at least not in that part of the conversation), he didn't say anything about Liddy or the indictments. Nor had Dean himself said the things he later describes himself as saying: that he couldn't take credit, that the matter might unravel some day, etc. (Indeed, he said just the opposite later on: "Nothing is going to come crashing down.") His account is plausible, but entirely incorrect. In this early part of the conversation Nixon did not offer him any praise at all, unless "You had quite a day, didn't you" was intended as a compliment. Dean cannot be said to have reported the "gist" of the opening remarks.

Was he simply lying to the Senators? I do not think so. The transcript makes it quite clear that Nixon *is* fully aware of the coverup: Haldeman and Dean discuss it freely in front of him, and while he occasionally asks questions he never seems surprised. Later on he even praises Dean for "putting his fingers in the leaks." Because the real conversation is just as incriminating as the one Dean described, it seems unlikely that he was remembering one thing and saying another. His responses to Senator Baker during cross-examination (see below) also indicate that he was doing his best to be honest. Mary McCarthy's assessment of Dean has stood the test of time: she wrote in 1973 of her overpowering impression ". . . not so much of a truthful person as of someone resolved to tell the truth about this particular set of events because his intelligence has warned him to do so" (McCarthy, 1975, pp. 40–41).

If Dean was trying to tell the truth, where did his erroneous account of the September 15 meeting come from? Some of it might be explained by the currently popular notion that everyone knows certain "scripts" for common events and that these scripts are used in the course of recall (Bower, Black, and Turner, 1979). Dean's recollection of the very beginning of the meeting may have been constructed on the basis of an "entering-the-room script." People do often ask their guests to sit down, though Nixon apparently did not ask Dean. It is also possible, however, that Dean's recollection of such a request is a case of nonverbal gist recall rather than a script-based construction. Perhaps Nixon *did* ask Dean to sit down, but with a gesture rather than a word—a brief wave of a commanding presidential hand. To recall such a gesture as if it had been a verbal request would not be much of an error. Current theoretical interest in the recall of written texts should not blind us to the nonverbal components of real conversation.

Although familiar scripts and nonverbal cues explain a few of Dean's errors, most of them seem to have deeper roots. They follow, I believe, from Dean's own character and especially from his self-centered assessment of events at the White House. What his testimony really describes is not the September 15 meeting itself but his fantasy of it: the meeting as it should have been, so to speak. In his mind Nixon *should* have been glad that the indictments stopped with Liddy, Haldeman *should* have been telling Nixon what a great job Dean was doing; most of all, praising him *should* have been the first order of business. In addition, Dean *should* have told Nixon that the cover-up might unravel, as it eventually did, instead of telling him it was a great success.

Almost. But Dean was not really as confident of his recollection as the tone of his statement suggested; not as sure of himself as he claimed in the exchange with Senator Inouye. This becomes clear in a very sharp interrogation by Senator Baker:

> *Senator Baker*: I am going to try now to focus entirely on the meeting of September 15.
> *Mr. Dean*: Right.
> *Senator Baker*: And I have an ambition to focus sharply on it in order to disclose as much information as possible about the September 15 meeting. What I want to do is to test, once again, not the credibility of your testimony but the quality of the evidence, that is, is it direct evidence.
> *Mr. Dean*: I understand (*Hearings*, p. 1474).

The Meeting of March 21

The cover-up was only temporarily successful. Although Nixon was reelected overwhelmingly in November of 1972, Dean's problems increased steadily. There were more black-

mail demands by the indicted Watergate defendants and
more investigations moving closer to the White House.
Dean met frequently with Nixon, Haldeman, and the others, but their strategems were unsuccessful. Dean began to
realize that he and the others were engaging in a crime
("obstruction of justice"), and might eventually go to
prison for it. He was not sure whether Nixon understood
the gravity of the situation. Finally he resolved to ask the
President for a private meeting at which he could lay out
all the facts. This meeting took place on March 21, 1973.

Dean's autobiography (1976) relates an incident that
occurred on the day before the critical meeting. When he
was trying to describe the relentlessly increasing complexity of the Watergate affair to Richard Moore, another
White House aide, Moore compared it to the growth of a
tumor. The metaphor attracted Dean, and he resolved to
use it in his report the next day: to tell Nixon that there
was a "cancer" growing on the presidency. The transcript
of the meeting shows that he did so. After a few minutes
of conversation about the day's events, Dean and the
President continue as follows:

> *D*: The reason I thought we ought to talk this morning
> is because in our conversations I have the impression
> that you don't know everything I know, and it makes it
> very difficult for you to make judgments that only you
> can make on some of these targets, and I thought that—
> *P*: In other words, I have to know why you feel that we
> shouldn't unravel something?
> *D*: Let me give you my overall first.
> *P*: In other words, your judgment as to where it stands,
> and where we will go.
> *D*: I think there is no doubt about the seriousness of the
> problem we've got. We have a cancer within, close to
> the presidency, that is growing. It is growing daily. It's
> compounded, growing geometrically now because it
> compounds itself. That will be clear if I, you know,
> explain some of the details of why it is. Basically it is
> because (1) we are being blackmailed; (2) people are
> going to start perjuring themselves very quickly that

have not had to perjure themselves to protect other people in the line. And there is no assurance—

P: That that won't bust?

D: That that won't bust (*Presidential Transcripts*, pp. 98–99).

In this first part of the March 21 meeting, Dean was alone with the President. They remained alone for about an hour, and then Haldeman came in to join the discussion for another 45 minutes or so. Haldeman's entrance proved to be a critical turning point in Dean's later memory of that morning: he forgot the rest of the conversation almost completely. What he said about the first hour, in contrast, was quite accurate. Comparison of the transcript with Dean's subsequent testimony shows clear recall of the gist of what was said. One's admiration for his memory is somewhat diminished, however, by the realization that the March 21 meeting was less a conversation than the delivery of a well-prepared report. Dean did most of the talking, taking 20 minutes to describe the events before the break-in and 40 more for the cover-up. Although Nixon interjected occasional remarks, questions, or expletives, the hour stayed quite close to the script Dean had prepared for it in advance.

The difference between this meeting and that of September 15 is instructive. This one fulfilled Dean's hopes as the earlier one had not: he really did give a personal lecture to the President of the United States, talking while Nixon listened. His testimony, too long to reproduce here, highlights the meetings' didactic quality. Almost every statement begins with "I told him . . . ," "I proceeded to tell him . . . ," "I informed the President . . ." or some similar phrase. He was remembering a report that he had rehearsed ahead of time, presented as planned, and probably continued to rehearse afterwards. It became John Dean's own story; March 21 had merely been his first opportunity to tell it.

IMPLICATIONS FOR THE PSYCHOLOGY
OF MEMORY

Are we all like this? Is everyone's memory constructed, staged, self-centered? And do we all have access to certain invariant facts nevertheless? My own guess—and it is only a guess—is that reconstruction played an exaggerated part in Dean's testimony. The circumstances and the man conspired to favor exaggeration. The events *were* important; his testimony *was* critical; its effect *was* historic. Dean was too intelligent not to know what he was doing, and too ambitious and egocentric to remain unaffected by it. His ambition reorganized his recollections: even when he tries to tell the truth, he can't help emphasizing his own role in every event. A different man in the same position might have observed more dispassionately, reflected on his experiences more thoughtfully, and reported them more accurately.

What have we learned about testimony by comparing "the human tape recorder" with a real one? We are hardly surprised to find that memory is constructive or that confident witnesses may be wrong. William Stern studied the psychology of testimony at the turn of the century and warned us not to trust memory even under oath; Bartlett was doing experiments on "constructive" memory fifty years ago. I believe, however, that John Dean's testimony can do more than remind us of their work. For one thing, his constructed memories were not altogether wrong. On the contrary, there is a sense in which he was altogether right; a level at which he was telling the truth about the Nixon White House. And sometimes—as in his testimony about March 21—he was more specifically right as well.

Dean's task as he testified before the Senate Committee was to recall specific well-defined conversations, ". . . conversations which took place months ago." This is what witnesses are always instructed to do: stick to the facts, avoid inferences and generalizations. Such recall is what Tulving (1972) called *episodic*; it involves the retrieval of particular autobiographical moments, individual episodes of one's life. Dean believes that he is recalling one conversation at a time, that his memory is "episodic" in Tulving's sense, but he is mistaken.

He is not alone in making this mistake. I believe that this aspect of Dean's testimony illustrates a very common process. The single clear memories that we recollect so vividly actually stand for something else; they are "screen memories," a little like those Freud discussed long ago. Often their real basis is a set of repeated experiences, a sequence of related events that the single recollection merely typifies or represents. Dean is not remembering the "gist" of a single episode by itself, but the common characteristics of a whole series of events.

This notion may help us to interpret the paradoxical sense in which Dean was accurate throughout his testimony. Give the numerous errors in his reports of conversations, what did he tell the truth about? I think that he extracted the common themes that remained invariant across many conversations and many experiences, and then incorporated those themes in his testimony. There were certain consistent and repeated elements in all those meetings; they had a theme that expressed itself in different ways on different occasions. Nixon wanted the cover-up to succeed; he was pleased when it went well; he was troubled when it began to unravel; he was perfectly willing to consider illegal activities if they would extend his power or confound his enemies. John Dean did not misrepresent this theme in his testimony; he just dramatized it. In memory experiments, subjects often recall the gist of a sentence but express it in different words. Dean's consistency was deeper; he recalled the theme of a whole series of conversations and expressed it in different events. Nixon hoped that the transcripts would undermine Dean's testimony by showing that he had been wrong. They did not have this effect because he was wrong only in terms of isolated episodes. Episodes are not the only kinds of facts. Except where the significance of his own role was at stake, Dean was right about what had really been going on in the White House. What he later told the Senators was fairly close to the mark: his mind was not a tape recorder, but it certainly received the message that was being given.

Answering Questions

by Donald Norman

Who was your first-grade teacher? And what color are your mother's eyes? Memory seems simple, but is quite complex in its workings. In "Answering Questions," Donald Norman examines what goes on in the mind when we answer the simplest questions—or the hardest ones. When we answer a question, we are oblivious to the intricate workings of the mind that finally allows us to offer the answer.

Norman offers us a glimpse into the behind-the-scenes mental operations that go on during conversation. The overall picture is of an entire "information processing system"—an assembly line of perception, memory storage, and retrieval that helps us function in everyday discourse. Occasionally, when we pause to respond because we are uncertain of what to say, there is a slight glitch in an otherwise superbly designed mental system.

What was the telephone number of the composer Ludwig van Beethoven?

As you entered the front door of the house you lived in three houses ago, was the doorknob on the left or the right?

THOSE TWO QUESTIONS are favorites of mine. Most people are much faster at answering the first. There is a feeling of immediate recognition that the answer is not known and never was known, followed quickly by the realization that there is no answer—the telephone was invented after Beethoven's death. With the second question, the feeling is that the answer was once readily available, but that now it is either forgotten or, if still present, is bound to take a lot of effort to get to, more effort than the result seems to be worth.

Your reactions to the questions reveal knowledge about the contents and workings of the memory system, knowledge about knowledge, or metaknowledge. Note that the knowledge of your lack of knowledge of Beethoven's telephone number comes rapidly, and it is likely that your introspections reflect what happened after the memory system reported the absence of information.

When we psychologists examine questions of this form, we are studying secondary memory—the human knowledge system. We need to know how information is represented, how it is retrieved, how it is used. We must ask about mental strategies and procedures. Sensory memory is automatic—there is little or nothing that affects its operations. Primary memory allows for a little control, especially for rehearsal and for selective retention and elaboration of the contents. Secondary memory also has its mixture. On the one hand, we can start and stop processes or go off and look for things here or there, using what we find to direct the search to some other spot in memory. On the other hand, when we retrieve from one spot in memory, we may trigger some interesting things, and off we go, following that line of thought, even if it is irrelevant to the original question we were following. Sometimes a process we thought we had terminated keeps functioning and suddenly reports some result that diverts our attention once again.

Simple questions often shed light on mental strategies and procedures. Consider *mgdptzy*. What does it mean? As a word it is nonsense, and its rejection is immediate. *Mgdptzy* cannot be pronounced, it does not fit the rules of orthography, and it has no meaning. With such a peculiar combination of letters it is impossible to start the search of memory—there is no way to begin. This is an important datum. Before a search can be performed, the query must be put into the form proper for the type of information sought.

Note the ease with which we all decide whether or not we know something. Even combinations of letters that look like English words (but aren't)—*mantiness* or *tralidity*—seem to be rejected immediately. How? According to some simple schemes of memory we would need to examine all the words that are known to see that these were not among them. That doesn't seem practicable, but how else could we do the job? The only answer seems to be that we have a content-addressable storage system—a system in which the route that must be taken to find the relevant information is given by the information itself. We look where "mantiness" ought to be and find nothing there.

Consider the series:

pt&*z	Not the correct symbols for a word.
mgdptzy	Correct symbols, but not a legitimate spelling.
mantiness	Legitimate word form, but no meaning is stored.
mansuetude	Legitimate word form and an actual word, but most people have never encountered it.
happiness	Legitimate word, meanings can be retrieved.

If I were to do an experiment along these lines, I would have to control for all the possible contaminants. Each query would have to be carefully presented, items randomized to avoid problems with ordering, and many different examples of each query tested to avoid accidents of peculiar letter combinations or peculiar associations. Different people would have to be presented with different orderings of items to avoid contamination from learning or boredom or other irrelevant effects. Although the experiment has not yet been done, I don't really have much doubt about its outcome. I feel certain I would find that the amount of time taken to respond to *pt&*z* would be the shortest, and that *mantiness* and *mansuetude* would take the most time, and that the positive response to *happiness* would occur more quickly than responses to the prior two items.

Here is a different set of examples. The basic paradigm for this memory query is a search for a telephone number, and the mental operations that ensue depend critically on what number is being sought.

Query: As fast as possible, give the telephone number of each of the following:

Charles Dickens (the novelist)

the White House

your favorite local restaurant

the local fire department

your telephone of five years ago (or two telephones ago)

a friend

your current home telephone

As before, the queries take different amounts of time to be answered or rejected. Is the input a name or a place? Might it logically have a telephone? Is there any reason to suppose that you might know the number? Different amounts of information from memory are involved in each query.

Again, I expect the middle items to take the longest. "Charles Dickens" should be rejected immediately. The time for the next three items will depend on how frequently you have been exposed to them. They could take several minutes. To recall the telephone number you had five years or two telephones ago requires the prior step of determining where you lived then. Considerable effort could be required for the next step—retrieval—despite the fact that this is a number you presumably once knew well.

The two different examples of memory retrieval—identifying words and remembering telephone numbers—demonstrate some of the varied properties of memory.

In reading and listening, we can usually interpret each word within tenths of a second of its arrival at the sensory system. The recognition and retrieval of linguistic information—part of speech, tense, number, meaning, and so on—happens so rapidly that we are usually quite unaware of its operation. It is only by throwing in the very rare word or the fake word of nonsensical characters that psychologists can get some glimmer of the complexity of the operations that must be taking place. For normal words, going from sound or sight to recognition and retrieval of meaning is a fast, smooth, effortless process.

The situation changes with the converse operation: going from meaning to item. Access is now more difficult. We can search for hours or days for a word that has a particular meaning. The attempt to recollect one of your telephone numbers from the past was meant to illustrate this kind of searching. Rigorous memory search can be involved, requiring mental effort, deliberate strategies, rejection of offered possibilities, and sometimes reconstruction of what the answer must be.

Again I turn to the answering of questions to illustrate a point. Some questions can be answered directly. If I ask whether a canary has wings, you might search for that fact directly. Alternatively you might create a mental image of a relevant scene and derive the answer by examining the image. It is also possible that information required may not be directly available but can be derived from other facts that are known. Did the dodo have wings? A dodo was a bird, all birds have wings; therefore a dodo had wings. Those three different ways of answering a question suggest three different types of memory use:

1. Questions that seem to be answered by searching memory for information:
   a. Is a porpoise a mammal or a fish?
   b. How old are you?
   c. What is the capital of New South Wales?
2. Questions that seem to be answered by examining a mental image:
   a. If you fly from Madrid to Berlin, what countries will you pass over?

    b. Does Lincoln's profile on the penny face to the right or left? (Substitute any currency you wish that has a face on it.)

    c. How many windows are there in the place where you live?

3. Questions that seem to be answered by inference:

    a. Does a male whale have a penis?

    b. Are there more piano tuners in New York City or in Tokyo?

    c. Does an elephant eat more food in a day than a lion?

Thus, we have three separate categories of questions, and three different types of memory use. These three uses are not independent or exhaustive. However, most people use several search methods in seeking answers for the nine questions and most will be similar to the three types of memory use I have described.

Post-Freudian Slips

by Donald Norman

If a friend repeating a slogan for bread says to you, "Wonder*bed* builds strong minds and bodies!" would you call it a "Freudian slip"? It was Freud, of course, who first took such slips seriously, proposing that they always had hidden meaning. Such slips, he said, signified unconscious wishes that push their way, rather elegantly, to consciousness.

But a new interpretation of why slips occur suggests that Freud had only part of the story. Many slips, it holds, are innocent mistakes.

In "Post-Freudian Slips," Donald Norman argues that many accidents of language and behavior are a consequence of simple breakdowns in normal routines; in other words, mindlessness. For example, if a man dressing for dinner starts putting on his pajamas, this is a sign that the computer of the human mind has temporarily gone awry. In presenting his view, Norman also offers a categorization of slips, ranging from description errors to "capture errors," which result from long-standing habits of behavior taking over when they should not. He also has a suggestion for catching slips as they threaten to emerge: Pay attention to what you are doing.

"I WAS IN A HOTEL RESTAURANT *when the check came. I signed my name to it, but couldn't remember the number of my hotel room. So I looked at my watch.*"

A friend reported that she got into her automobile, started the engine, and then noticed that the windshield was dirty. She turned on the wipers and squirted water on the windshield. When the windows were clean, she intended to turn off the wipers, but turned off the ignition.

THESE EXAMPLES ILLUSTRATE two typical slips of action among the more than 200 that I have collected in the past two years. Slips are amusing, a sure way of starting conversations. Slips happen to all of us, and except when they lead to embarrassment, usually seem like harmless oddities. But slips that can occur in the conduct of certain tasks can be dangerous.

An air-traffic controller once told an aircraft to taxi to the left runway when he really meant the right one. The slip of interchanging "left" for "right" is the most common of verbal confusions, but in this case it could have led to tragedy (fortunately, it did not). Forgetting to turn on headlights when driving a car at night is also common and potentially dangerous. The slip is usually caught before an accident occurs, but not always. Today, human error is one of the largest causes of accidents in the large-scale technologies I have examined.

Freud analyzed errors primarily to discover a person's true beliefs or intentions. One case he examined involved the president of the lower house of the Austrian parliament, who opened a meeting by declaring it closed. The act does seem to reveal hidden motives: as Freud noted, "the president secretly wished he was already in a position to close the sitting, from which little good was to be expected."

But I believe that the human mind is an exceedingly complex computer, and that slips can also occur when stray information throws off human information-processing systems. Slips can have many causes, often all operating simultaneously. Yes, there are hidden motives, but tiny miscues from the situations we are in can also cause errors. Even in the case of Freud's president, the hidden intent needed a quite precise opportunity to reveal itself.

Consider verbal slips such as saying "canpakes" for "pancakes" or interchanging sounds among several words, as in "the sweeter hitch" instead of "the heater switch." The actual word selection is influenced by a combination of syntactical considerations, possible meanings, and the set of possible words with similar sounds, as well as possible underlying motives and plans. Individually, none of these things would suffice; it takes the whole ensemble.

I think that Freud made important contributions. But during Freud's era, the science of computation, information-processing, and control was primitive, and Freud was not led to think about the nature of a human processing system that could contribute to errors. I interpret Freud in modern terms as saying that slips result from competition and intermixing among underlying mental-processing mechanisms, often working parallel to one another. What about the pilot who lands a plane with the wheels still up? What about the F-111 pilots who, in preparing for landing, intend to pull back on the throttle and push foward the control that extends the wings, but then pull back on both? Do these pilots have a hidden wish to kill themselves? It's possible, but simpler explanations are possible, too.

A THEORY OF ACTIONS

Whenever I observe a slip, I immediately write down what happened and usually ask whoever made the slip to provide additional information, such as what they were thinking, and, if they themselves noticed the error, how they came to notice it and what their explanation is. (I do not necessarily believe their explanation.) I have enlisted my students and colleagues to help collect examples, and in addition to my own collection, I have examined nearly 1,000 slips collected by other people, including various academic students of error.

I study slips because I feel they provide insight into the workings of the mind. As a theoretical psychologist, I wish to develop formal models of human information-processing structures. These models have useful applications, however, for if we know how errors occur, it may be possible to prevent them. Overall, the goal is to design machines that might work to complement human abilities, rather than thwart them.

Wiggle the second finger of your right hand. Now wiggle the third finger. What did you do differently? Introspection is of little use. The difference is noticeable only in the intention: the actual selection of muscles was carried out at a level not subject to conscious inspection. Most actions, I propose, are carried out in a similar way, by subconscious mechanisms. At our conscious level we prepare only the general selection of the act: that is, we will an action, and the lower-level components of that action complete the story—to a large extent, without further need for conscious intervention, except at critical choice points. The intention, once specified, releases control processes that then lead to the exquisitely timed complex motor actions involved in manipulation of the body, limbs, fingers, eyes, and voice. How specific the selection or "plan" is depends on how many of its subcomponents already exist. The less skilled we are at the needed sequence or the more novel the sequence is, the more specific the plan must be.

These subconscious components of our acts, I think, are independent, structured assemblages of control processes, or "schemas." They get switched into readiness or "activated" in various ways: sometimes by our current short-term memory of the steps that have served us well in similar situations, sometimes by motives, sometimes by sudden cues from the situation we are in—including the grammar of a sentence we may be in the middle of speaking. Schemas in readiness then are triggered by particular instructions—but many schemas may be active at any given moment, and they all compete for control. The same aspects of this system that allow for its power and flexibility also leave it wide open to the potential for making errors.

When I drive home from work, the appropriate schemas are activated and triggered by previous actions, by the environment, by my perceptions. I need not plan the details. I simply decide to drive home. If I want to deviate from the normal route, however, I must set up a new schema that will be activated and triggered by some appropriate conditions along the way.

Do I wish to detour to the fish store? I must have "fish store" actively in mind at the time I pass the critical choice point between home and the store. If I wish to go to a place I have not been to before, I have to exert much more conscious specification, for I must construct the appropriate schemas: "When I get to the light at 4th Street, I must turn right, not left." If the relevant schemas for the deviation are not sufficiently active at the critical time, they are apt to be missed—and the normal plan will get executed by default. Let "fish store" lapse from my memory at the critical junction, and I am apt to find myself at home shortly thereafter, fishless.

KINDS OF SLIPS

My analysis suggests that in different slips, different parts of the information-processing sequence go awry. For purposes of convenience, I categorize them according to which part of the human machinery is involved. Some of the categories are described below.

Description Errors. Given a choice of plans, sometimes we describe the wrong one to ourselves. Consider the following incident:

> A chartered airliner flying from Houston to Montreal crashed exactly on the border between the United States and Canada. A major political issue developed over the following question: In which country should the survivors be buried?

Most people puzzle over the choice of country. In fact, the story was made up to trap the unwary: it is the casualties who should be buried, not the survivors.

I believe that in understanding, we use previous experiences as a guide as much as possible. We process new information only enough to figure out where it fits into the structure of previous knowledge. This is done, in part, by forming a description of the information, a description that characterizes things at as high a level of abstraction as possible, because that form of abstraction takes less mental effort.

Survivors and casualties share a common high-level description: the ones left over after an accident. The story sets us up to expect the critical leftovers to be the dead ones, so we don't need to process the word "survivors" deeply: the meaning is in the structure, and that structure is too abstract to describe the necessary next step.

Such mental laziness usually is beneficial, because it allows us to save mental resources for more important things (such as reaching the answer to the question). But shortcuts also lead to the tendency to see what we expect to happen rather than what has actually happened. This tendency, coupled with similar distortions of memory, often makes eyewitness testimony unreliable (see "Eyewitless News," *Psychology Today*, March 1980); in a different form, it can make people overestimate or underestimate hazards and risks.

In day-to-day activities, selection errors are similarly common. For instance:

> *Two sales clerks in a catalog order department were both at the same counter, each talking on different phones with customers and filling out different forms for charge-card purchases. One of the clerks had to pass behind the other in order to get a form, and so the clerks changed positions. When the first clerk finished her telephone call, she hung up the phone, but hung it up on the wrong instrument, thereby cutting off her coworker's conversation.*

Here again, the mental description of the desired act was too abstract. Such inadvertent ambiguity can also lead to eating your friend's sandwich from a plate that looks like yours, or to putting the top of the sugar bowl on top of a coffee mug of the same size. We all know of people who put letters into the wrong envelopes. Other variations on the theme culled from my collection include:

> One of my graduate students returned to his home after a track workout, pulled off his sweaty T-shirt, and neatly tossed it into the toilet. It was not an aiming error—the laundry basket, his intended target, was in another room.

> A colleague left home early in the morning and noticed that he had forgotten his briefcase. He returned home, turned off the ignition of the car, and unbuckled his wristwatch instead of his seat belt.

> In getting ready for a party, one person carefully prepared a cake and a salad, then put the cake in the refrigerator and the salad in the oven.

Activation and Triggering Errors. Once an intention is selected, executing it can easily misfire. We can, for example, forget the initial intention while some of the schemas it ordered run their course. One colleague reported that before starting work at his desk at home he headed for his bedroom, only to realize after getting there that he'd forgotten why he had gone there. "I kept going," he reported, "hoping that something in the bedroom would remind me." Nothing did. He finally went to his desk, realized that his glasses were dirty, and with a great sense of relief, returned to the bedroom for the handkerchief he needed to wipe them off with.

Components of actions can also get misblended, usually when two or more activated schemas are triggered simultaneously. Sometimes such triggering starts with a brief uncertainty, such as when indecision about whether to say "momentary" or "instantaneous" produces "momentaneous."

On other occasions, a schema can simply be skipped; for instance, when we fill an electric coffeepot with water and plug it in but forget to add the coffee. Sometimes a sequence is completed, but is restarted at some earlier stage. In the collection of James T. Reason, the British psychologist who has performed a number of interesting studies of slips, is the story of someone who reported:

> *"As I was leaving the bathroom this morning, it suddenly struck me that I couldn't remember whether or not I had shaved. I had to feel my chin to establish that I had."*

Capture Errors. William James, in his classic textbook on psychology published in 1890, reported that "very absentminded persons in going to their bedrooms to dress for dinner have been known to take off one garment after another and finally to get into bed, merely because that was the habitual issue of the first few movements when performed at a later hour."

Such errors, called "capture errors," constitute one of the most fascinating subcategories in the field of error. They involve a simple principle: pass too near a well-formed habit and it will capture your behavior. Strong habits are easily provoked. If a habit is strong enough, even cues that only partially match the situation it usually fits are apt to activate it, and once those cues activated, the habit can get triggered. As one student said:

> *"I was using a copying machine, and I was counting the pages. I found myself counting 1, 2, 3, 4, 5, 6, 7, 8, 9, 10, Jack, Queen, King. (I had been playing cards recently.)"*

Reason notes several similar cases, including the person who reported:

> *"I meant to get my car out, but as I passed through the back porch on my way to the garage I stopped to put on my Wellington boots and gardening jacket, as if to work in the garden."*

CATCHING SLIPS

Although slips happen frequently, their perpetrators catch most of them before they lead to harm. Slips seem to be caught in two ways: with various processes that we constantly use to monitor our behavior (checking to make sure what was done matches what we intended); or when the slip causes something to happen that then serves to bring the errors to our attention.

Monitoring goes on constantly, for reasons that range from catching errors to keeping our movements accurate to enabling our conscious selves to keep track of things our subconscious sets forth. Thus, when I talk, although I may consciously direct the flow of conversation, I am usually quite unaware of the particular words that I select until I have said them aloud. You might say that I am like the writer who once asked, "How do I know what I think until I see what I say?" I monitor my speech in part to know what I am saying.

But the information-processing involved in monitoring behavior is prone to slips, too. Consider the following incident:

> *"I was driving and noticed that the rear-view mirror on the passenger side was not adjusted properly. I asked my passenger to correct it, but instead of asking him to adjust the mirror, I said, 'Please adjust the window.' The passenger was confused, and asked, 'What should I do, what do you want?' So I repeated the request: 'Adjust the window for me.' We went through this sequence several times. Believing the problem was that I was not speaking loudly and clearly enough over the noise of the car, I kept repeating the erroneous request over and over again, each time more loudly and with greater frustration."*

This example includes two problems: realizing that an error has been made and determining exactly what it was. For the first job, one part of the system has to know something that another part does not. If I knew enough to listen to my speech and detect an error of some kind, why didn't I know enough not to have made it in the first place? The answer is that the "I" making the error and the "I" detecting it are different, each reflecting knowledge from a different part of the complex information-processing structures within me. Beyond that, the selection of monitoring processes was somehow at the wrong level, set to monitor failure in word enunciation, not word selection. In the case of the salesperson who hung up the wrong telephone, one level of monitoring was probably necessary to make sure the telephone did indeed move properly to a cradle, but a deeper level would have been required to detect that the act was done properly, but on the wrong cradle.

Another way to consider the complexities of monitoring is to ask how I might monitor a wish to stop at the post office on the way to my office. What part of my action do I monitor? Looking at myself, I see only that I am moving my hands and feet in the way required to drive my car. To know whether I am actually on the way to the post office, I must interpret the actions I take in terms of the overall route. Similarly, when I speak, the meaning gets spoken as a stream of sounds: an error can be in the pronunciation or enunciation of the sounds, in the selection of words, in the meaning of the utterance, or in a confusion of one intended hearer with another.

Errors are much easier to detect, of course, when they have obvious consequences. Sometimes the consequence materializes several minutes after the event: when you start the coffeepot in the morning and forget the coffee, you learn of your slip when you start to pour. Sometimes the payoff is immediate: when you forget to unbuckle a seat belt and try to get out of the car, or replace the top of the sugar container on the coffee cup and try to drink the coffee.

My analysis of slips reveals two kinds of consequences, which I call *side effects* and *forcing functions*. Suppose I wish to enter a room, and must open a door. The main effect is going through the door, but a side effect is that the door is open. Usually, it's no big deal (except to those of us who spend much of our lives trying to teach children to shut the door behind them).

If the door is opaque, I am less likely to make the slip of failing to open it first: the sight of the door is a forcing function, forcing a correction and prohibiting further action until the right step has been taken. Glass doors and screen doors are another story—people can and do walk into them when they fail to see them. Even if I fail to notice the door, I get another forceful reminder when I bang into it.

Suppose you encounter daytime fog and turn on the lights of your automobile to make it visible to approaching cars. The side effect is that the lights are on. When you get to your destination and leave the car, will you remember to take care of that side effect? The number of incidents I have observed in which people do not remember indicates that this is a frequent slip. (At night, of course, the sight of the lights is a forcing function to turn off the switch.) Similarly, another frequent slip is to put a car in gear and drive off before releasing the emergency brake. This slip is usually detected immediately because it is simply not possible to drive most automobiles without first releasing the brake: the mechanics of the car itself serves as a forcing function for the right action.

Why am I making such a fuss over components that may seem obvious? Consider a situation in which innocent side effects can have serious consequences: nuclear power plants. The control panels in these complex systems may be 100 feet long. With 3,000 instruments and controls, supervision is taxing. For testing or servicing, operators temporarily disconnect subsystems. Shutting the disconnecting valve sets up a side effect: when the test is over, the valve is closed. Since there is no immediate forcing function to reopen the valve, a person must remember to do so at the completion of the tests, which places the burden entirely on the memory of people who are often distracted.

The accident at Three Mile Island was intensified by just such a side-effect slip. Two valves had been closed in the auxiliary feedwater system to allow servicing. They were not reopened, and it took the operators eight minutes to discover the fact, a critical eight minutes at the very start of the incident.

It seems obvious that potential side-effect conditions should be blocked by the development of forcing functions that insist on their clean-up. This strategy is much easier to propose than to implement, but, clearly, forcing functions are worth more effort than we have put in so far. And they are likely to be worth more still as technology itself becomes an increasingly frequent cause of catastrophic events.

In industrial, aircraft, and nuclear accidents, my analyses indicate that the system is most often at fault, not the operator. People make errors as a fundamental byproduct of the same information-processing mechanisms that produce their great creativity and flexibility. Yet systems designers ignore both human strengths and weaknesses, and today's systems sometimes seem designed to cause the very errors that they should be set up to prevent.

The design of control panels for nuclear power plants is particularly negligent, but think of what a salesperson must do in a modern department store. Even for a simple purchase, a huge array of numbers must be entered into the computer cash register. The numbers are supposed to make the accounting system work smoothly, but the priorities are backward. Instead of forcing people to act like machines for the benefit of machines, why not make the machines so that they let us act like people? Machines can be made to do the translation into whatever hidden, laborious codes they require. In this case, the cash register would "know" automatically which department it is located in. The salesperson would simply have to punch a button for "shirt"; if the computer needed to know more it could present specific alternatives about questions of style and size, for example, that the salesperson could pick by punching other buttons on the cash register.

The prevalence of human error increases when there is stress. In the wake of the Three Mile Island incident, the Nuclear Regulatory Commission is requiring, among other things, that by January 1, 1981 all reactors have a safety officer, in a separate room away from the hustle and bustle of the operating room, who can make calm, long-range decisions to alter the course of any accident. This change is beneficial, and will surely reduce the number of further errors once an accident has started. However, it does not get at the basis of the difficulty of controlling reactors, which is simply poor systems design.

Modern systems of all sorts are inconsiderate of human beings. In my research laboratory, my colleagues and assistants are attempting to understand the basic properties of human information-processing, with emphasis on how skilled people select and guide their actions—and make their slips.

Although the basic thrust of the research is theoretical, we share an important subgoal: to give designers guidelines for designing systems that work with people, not against them. The development of forcing functions (and of related concepts such as "cuing" and "blocking") is only one aspect of this work. We hope not only to eliminate the disastrous effects of error, but also to make human interaction with machines pleasurable, efficient, and creative.

Dumber by the Dozen?

by Robert Zajonc

Robert Zajonc, of the University of Michigan, asks the question: "Is there any significant relationship between birth order and intelligence?" Does it pay off intellectually to be born first, middle, or last?

To answer the questions, Zajonc summarizes the research on birth order, including an unparalleled Dutch study in which a huge number of people—nearly four hundred thousand—was included. In overview, Zajonc finds that families that have few children and have them born far apart produce the most intelligent offspring. Thus, the brightest children come from the smallest families. Yet, whatever the family size, the children who come along earlier tend to have the highest IQs.

Zajonc's findings are important not only in terms of birth order (as well as promoting sibling rivalry!), but because of possible implications for the study of race and IQ—a most controversial and hotly debated sociological and psychological problem. Birth-order researchers usually ignore race differences, and race researchers have neglected the impact of birth order and birth interval. Zajonc's findings suggest that the two may be related, easily reason enough to bring the two lines of research together.

PARENTS AND PSYCHOLOGISTS have always regarded first-born children as different or special. We have known for decades that first-borns are more likely to be high achievers and intellectual stars in the manner of Galileo, Pascal and Newton, although they tend to be fearful in strange situations. A spate of studies tried to find relationships between birth order and the most extraordinary things: creativity, tolerance of pain, marital adjustment, eyesight, even ESP.

Then this promising line of research slowed and faltered. Researchers weren't getting consistent results, one study contradicted another, and the whole matter became one of the most frustrating areas of psychology. Some researchers began to argue that birth order, like handwriting analysis, inkblot tests and astrology, is a quagmire unlikely to yield more than muddy feet and a fevered brain. But now it appears that birth order is related reliably to at least one very important human trait: intelligence.

Intelligence, of course, is influenced in some degree by heredity, by the quality of education one gets, by styles of child-rearing. But now a number of studies show that, such factors aside, intelligence is also a product of how many brothers and sisters you have, and of your seniority in the family. Intelligence declines with family size; the fewer children in your family, the smarter you are likely to be. Intelligence also declines with birth order; the fewer older brothers or sisters you have, the brighter you are likely to be.

The best evidence for these effects came from a remarkable study by Lillian Belmont and Francis A. Marolla, who examined birth order and intelligence scores of 386,114 Dutchmen. These data, taken from the Dutch military examinations, represented almost the entire population of 19-year-old men in the Netherlands born between 1944 and 1947. Studies on birth order ordinarily involve small samples, and cannot, therefore, control for some important factors. However, with their large data set, Belmont and Marolla were able to examine family size and socioeconomic status. To classify the men, the Dutch military had used the Raven Progressive Matrices, a nonverbal intelligence test that is relatively free of cultural bias. This means that it should show less favoritism to the upper socioeconomic classes who may have an advantage on verbal tests.

The Brightest and Earliest. Many studies of birth order lump all first-born children together, regardless of their respective family sizes, and compare them with all second-born children, all third-born children, etc. Belmont and Marolla's contribution was to account for the interaction of birth order and family size. That is, they computed the average Raven scores for the first-born in a family of two, the second-born in a family of two, the first in a family of three, the second in a family of three, and so forth. They found a clear effect of family size on IQ, and an effect of birth order within a given family size. The brightest children came from the smallest families, and within a given family size, the brightest children were those who came along early. The first child in a family of two, for example, got the highest scores, while the last child in a family of nine produced the lowest scores.

But the fact that brighter children come from smaller families could be explained in other ways. Perhaps brighter parents are more likely to limit family size, and thereby have the time and money to create a more favorable intellectual environment for their children. Perhaps the higher scores of their children simply reflect the influence of heredity. To test these hypotheses, Belmont and Marolla computed the average Raven scores separately for each of three occupational groups. It turned out that children whose fathers were professional or white-collar workers scored higher than the children of manual workers, who in turn scored higher than those who came from farm backgrounds. But within each occupational group, the relationship between intelligence and family size remained.

Belmont and Marolla also recalculated the average Raven scores for each occupational level to see if the birth-order effect continued to hold up. The relationship between birth order and intelligence proved independent of social class, with the exception that among farm children the disadvantage of being born late is less pronounced.

Belmont and Marolla admit that they are puzzled by their data. There is no known biological reason why larger families should produce less intelligent children within a given social class, and it is even more baffling why last-borns should have lower IQs than first-borns. It is possible that with each successive child, the uterus deteriorates, thus producing increasingly inferior children, but this notion is speculative at best. And there is no reason to suspect that children born later inherit inferior genes.

I believe I have a good explanation for Belmont and Marolla's findings. As an only child myself, I was well aware that my family experiences were far different from those of my friends who had many siblings—siblings they could fight with, study with, or teach mischief and math to. Many psychologists, in their haste to study the effects of parents on the growing child, forget that brothers and sisters are an important part of a child's early environment. A child who is the oldest of six has adventures and problems that differ from those of a last-born of six, and a child who is the first of two grows up in a different milieu from one who is the fifth of nine.

Pool of Intellectual Capacity. Greg Markus and I examined the influence of siblings on IQ by constructing a mathematical model for Belmont and Marolla's data. We began by arbitrarily setting the parents' intellectual level at 100, and the newborns' at near zero. Then we used theoretical growth curves to estimate the intellect of a child at a given time, and to describe the intellectual level of any family. I want to emphasize here that these figures are not IQ scores. An IQ score shows a person's intelligence corrected for his age, whereas our estimates are absolute and vary with age. They refer to the total absolute "quantity" of intellect at the person's disposal: his knowledge, wisdom, skills and abilities.

For example, a couple without children has an average intellectual environment of $\left(\dfrac{100 + 100}{2} = 100 \right)$

When they have their first child the family's average environment changes. Now there are two adults, each contributing their maximum to the intellectual environment, and one child whose intellect is near zero. The average of the three is 200/3, or 67. The family environment—the pool of intellectual capacity—is now about 67 percent of what it was before the child arrived. If a second child is born to our hypothetical parents after two years, the family intellect drops again. After two years the first child has about four percent of his adult intellect, so the second child enters an environment of 100 plus 100 plus four plus zero, for an average level of 51. The second child enters a less intelligent atmosphere.

If a third child is born in another two years, the family level sinks still further. The eldest child is four years old and up to a whopping 15 percent of adult intelligence, while the second child is at four percent; the family average falls to 44. Note that we consider that the individual's intellectual environment consists not only of the intellectual levels of those around him, but of his own level as well.

With each additional child, the family's intellectual environment depreciates, because a child's intellectual growth is partly controlled by the overall intellectual climate of his household. Children who grow up surrounded by people with higher intellectual levels have a better chance to achieve their maximum intellectual powers than children who develop in intellectually impoverished milieus. Thus, children from large families, who spend more time in a world of child-sized minds, should develop more slowly and therefore attain lower IQs than children from small families, who have more contacts with grown-up minds.

According to our model of sibling influence, another variable that ought to affect intelligence is the length of time between the births of the children. The longer the gaps, the more time the older children have to develop, hence to raise the family's intellectual level.

Twins and Triplets. For example, suppose our hypothetical couple has a child each year instead of every two years. As before, the first child's environment is 67. After one year he has achieved about one percent of adult intelligence, and the second child brings the family level to 50. A year later, the third child is born. By now, the first child is functioning at about four percent of adult intelligence, while the second is near one percent. The third child enters an environment with an overall value of 41. When the gaps between children were two years, the third child entered an environment of 44. These differences are small, but if our model is accurate, the differences will be larger for each successive child. With one-year intervals, the ninth child will enter an intellectual environment of about 33, while with two-year intervals the level is nearly 57. With very large gaps the negative effects of birth order can even be reversed. If the second birth occurs when the first child already has 80 percent of adult intelligence, the second-born enters an environment of 100 plus 100 plus 80 plus zero, or an average level of 70. He is thus better off than the only child, whose level is 67.

Information on the intervals between children was too scanty for us to test our predictions about gaps directly. However, we can answer this question indirectly by looking at the research on twins and triplets, who, if our model is accurate, should receive lower IQ scores than children born singly. Several studies reveal that they do. R. G. Record, Thomas McKeown, and J. H. Edwards, for instance, found an average verbal reasoning score of 95.7 for 2,164 twins and 91.6 for 33 triplets; a group of children born singly averaged 100.1 Other factors may influence the intellectual attainment of multiple-birth children, but these findings are consistent with our theory of sibling influence. If the first offspring of a couple are twins, their intellectual environment is 50 percent of the adult level. For nontwin siblings, the level at the birth of the first child is 67 and, if the second is born one year later, the level drops to 50. Thus, on the average, singles do better than multiples.

The Chance to Teach. One apparent flaw in our theory is that only children are not the highest scorers. If our mathematical estimates of intellectual environment are accurate, then only children should be the smartest of the lot; they have only their parents to provide their intellectual environment. Instead, their attainment is almost identical to the first-born in a family of four.

Those of us who are only children know quite well that we are not only first-borns but also last-borns. Last-borns and only children share a common disadvantage; they have no younger siblings whom they can instruct in the fine arts of kite flying, puzzle solving, and the meaning of words. The chance to teach, I suggest, is an important boost to intellectual development. Older children have such opportunities; sometimes by proximity in age and room sharing. Assistant-parenthood gives older children much experience in solving intellectual problems that their younger siblings want solved.

To see whether the youngest child in fact misses something because he has no one to teach, we further analyzed the data. The last child *does* show a greater decline in his Raven score than his predecessors. This is even true in the larger families, where the scores of later-born children begin to rise. As the first-borns get older and smarter, the intellectual level of the family improves; thus, the last child in a family of seven, eight or nine ought to score as well as or better than his nearest sibling. Yet he does worse. Apparently there's a handicap to being the baby of the family, even if he or she is the spoiled darling.

Our model fits the data on birth order and family size remarkably well. It predicts that it is better to have a younger sibling you can show the world to than an older one who shows it off to you. It predicts that it is better to be a lonely only than one of a crowd. If the intellectual growth of your children is important to you, the model predicts that you should have no more than two. The first will have the greatest benefit as teacher. Perhaps you can find a neighbor's younger child for the second child to tutor.

But stop at two. Intelligence decreases with family size because the larger the family, the lower the overall level of intellectual functioning. Children, after all, may have a negative effect on the intellectual level of their parents. Ask kindergarten teachers, who often complain that they must regress to the verbal level of their charges. Parents who interact frequently with large numbers of intellectually immature children may suffer a similar fate. An unexpected and sorry consequence of overpopulation may be the dilution of our children's intellectual ability—and our own.

But our theory offers more than just bleak prospects, for it follows that if you switch from your present intellectual environment to a superior one, your intelligence will increase. And if you do this whenever you reach the level of your current surroundings, your intelligence may keep on growing indefinitely.

Creative Contradictions

by Albert Rosenberg

Some of the most remarkable creative achievements begin with the awareness of a tension between opposites. The creative person feels some inner conflict, a personal "tug-of-war," which finds its ultimate resolution through the creative act. That scenario, says Albert Rosenberg, was as true for Albert Einstein as it was for Eugene O'Neill. But are these and other famous creative thinkers and artists aware of the process as it unfolds?

According to Rosenberg, the intense personal tension caused by contradictions is resolved through a highly *conscious* process—contrary to the popular image of the impulsive, loosely inspirational artist. Rosenberg, a psychiatrist, has studied the nature of creativity for well over a decade, documenting his observations with several empirical studies as well as interviews with writers, artists, and scientists. Here he explains "janusian thinking," named after the Roman god Janus, who, like the artist, could look in two directions at the same time. Janusian thinking is what allows the creative genius to live with his struggle.

WHILE WORKING ON an essay for the *Yearbook of Radioactivity and Electronics* in 1907, Albert Einstein had what he called "the happiest thought of my life." Einstein's happy thought was the key to the most far-reaching scientific breakthrough of the 20th century: the general theory of relativity. The unusual circumstances surrounding it were revealed for the first time in another essay, unpublished and discovered only recently, entitled, "Fundamental Ideas and Methods of Relativity Theory, Presented in Their Development."

Einstein had already developed the special theory of relativity, which holds that since the speed of light is constant for all frames of reference, perceptions of time and motion depend upon the relative position of the observer. He had been forced to postulate the theory, he said, to explain the seeming contradictions in electromagnetic phenomena; that "one is dealing here with two fundamentally different cases was, for me, unbearable." Einstein was trying to modify Newton's classical theory of gravitation so that it could be encompassed within a broad relativity principle. And here, again, it seemed that what was lacking was a physical basis for bringing together Newton's theory and his own special theory.

Pondering those seemingly irreconcilable constructs, Einstein reached a startling conception: "For an observer in free fall from the roof of a house," he realized, "there exists, during his fall, no gravitational field . . . in his immediate vicinity. If the observer releases any objects, they will remain, relative to him, in a state of rest. The [falling] observer is therefore justified in considering his state as one of 'rest.' "

The general theory itself is highly complex, and the points of connection to Einstein's "happiest thought" are not simple to explicate or trace. But the specific structure of the key step is clear: Einstein had concluded that a person falling from the roof of a house was both in motion and at rest *at the same time*. The hypothesis was illogical and contradictory in structure, but it possessed a superior logic and salience that brought Newtonian physics and his own into the same overall conceptual scheme.

I describe this cognitive process as "janusian thinking," after Janus, the Roman god of doorways and beginnings, whose faces (he is variously portrayed as having two, four, and even six of them) look in different directions at the same time. Janusian thinking lies at the heart of the most striking creative breakthroughs. Contrary to the romantic notion that creativity grows largely out of inspiration, the "primary process" thinking of dreams, or some unconscious source, I have found janusian thinking—a major element of the creative process—to be a fully conscious, intentional, rational process.

In janusian thinking, two or more opposites or antitheses are conceived *simultaneously*, either as existing side by side, or as equally operative, valid, or true. In an apparent defiance of logic or of physical possibility, the creative person consciously formulates the simultaneous operation of antithetical elements and develops those into integrated entities and creations. It is a leap that transcends ordinary logic. What emerges is no mere combination or blending of elements: the conception does not only contain different entities, it contains opposing and antagonistic elements, which are understood as coexistent. As a self-contradictory structure, the janusian formulation is surprising when seriously posited in naked form. Though it usually appears modified and transformed in the final product, it leaves the mark of implicit unexpectedness and paradox on the work.

Janusian thinking operates in diverse types of creativity—in the visual arts, literature, and music, as well as in science and philosophy. I discovered the mode after a number of different studies of the creative process, over the past 15 years, which included efforts to collect data on creative thinking in the work and testimony of people like Einstein, O'Neill, Conrad, Mozart, and Picasso, and through intensive interviews with 54 highly creative artists and scientists living in the United States and England.

Most of the living subjects were chosen because they were nominated to me by their peers and had won major recognition: a Nobel Prize, a National Book Award, a Pulitzer Prize, or membership in societies like the National Academy of Science, the American Academy of Science, the American Academy of Arts and Letters, or the Royal Society of London. Moreover, I selected a number of highly rated but less-known subjects who were also recommended by peers and colleagues in their fields. I similarly interviewed an unusual group of controls who were matched in age, sex, and social status to the writers—

successful but not creative persons, as assessed by their employers, counselors, and peers. To study their approach to a creative task, I asked each of the controls to embark on writing a piece of imaginative literature. Some wrote a poem; others, a short story.

In all, I have carried out 1,690 hours of interviewing to date. The sessions are weekly or biweekly, and the subjects have been assured of confidentiality. Rather than reporting on their personal history, they talk about their current work and the thoughts, dreams, and emotions connected with it. Before the sessions start, they give me material from their current projects, which forms the focus of our discussions. We talk extensively about general themes as well as specific details, such as what revisions take place as the work unfolds, and we attempt to trace the generating psychological factors throughout the entire period of creation—in most cases, over months and even years.

Janusian thinking seldom appears in the final artistic product, but it occurs at crucial points in the generation and development of the work. In the initial phases of interviews with some of the writers, they reported using numerous opposite ideas, images, and concepts, but there were usually no clues at that point to the importance of those ideas. Their plays, novels, and poems showed elements of conflict, irony, tragic tension, and ambiguity as major elements, but there was no reason to believe that those elements derived from a factor like janusian thinking, or that such thinking played any major role in key creative conceptions. It was generally only after weeks or months of interviewing, and the development of some confidence and rapport, that the research subjects revealed the precise—and self-contradictory—nature of the critical ideas in their creations.

For instance, a Pulitzer Prize-winning novelist told me, after we had discussed for some months the novel he was working on, that he had developed the key idea as he sat in a lawn chair reading Erik Erikson's book on Martin Luther's rebellion. He thought of constructing a novel about another rebel, a revolutionary hero, who, he said, "was responsible for the deaths of hundreds of people, but he himself would kill only one person with his own hand—and this was the one person who had been very kind to him and the one person he loved." In another case, a major American playwright told me he had come up with the specific idea for a play while traveling through Germany: "Driving on the autobahn, I suddenly felt amazed and overwhelmed at how beautiful Germany had become." He then thought of writing a play that would simultaneously express both the beauty of modern Germany and Hitler's destructiveness. "And then, I remembered a story I'd been told about a sacrifice made by an Austrian nobleman for a Jew in a Nazi official's waiting room." Later, the playwright incorporated the sacrifice into his play.

Two poets described initial conceptions that were only implicitly present in their finished poems. Because I had been conducting regular interviews with them during the writing of the poems, I knew that their recall of circumstances and thoughts was quite exact. One said that he had been walking on a beach and became interested in the quality of some rocks along the sand. As he touched the surface of the rocks, he noted that they seemed to feel like human skin. But they were also hard, heavy objects—violent weapons. The idea that the rocks were at once sensual objects and weapons led to a conception of the simultaneous operation of sex and violence in the world, and the writer elaborated those aspects separately in the final version of the poem.

On another occasion, this poet was sitting at his desk and he thought of a poetic line connoting rest and motion as operating simultaneously in the action of long-distance running. The thought led him to write a poignant poem about marathon racing, and the ravages of time and age, which elaborated on, and modified, the initial line.

The other poet, also sitting at his desk, had been thinking about an incident in which a horse had appeared at a lonely desert site, when it occurred to him that horses are animals who "renounce their own kind in order to live our lives." The idea that horses live human lives, that they are both beast and not-beast simultaneously, generated a vibrant poem with a central image and theme of a happy and intense relationship between a young person and a horse, followed by a sad, resigned separation.

When, after a year's interviewing, I directed one novelist to the earliest idea for his book, he referred to a line in it indicating that love and hate were the same. The phrase had also guided the novel's whole construction. Similarly, a poet said her first idea for a certain poem was the line, "Cream of celery soup has a soul of its own." She had been thinking, she recalled, about the simultaneously formed and unformed qualities of both soul and soup. And a playwright said that the earliest formulations in one of his works grew out of ideas and phrases that came to him while imagining that the white knight in a TV commercial was a black man.

A novelist-poet told me that he was doing his morning exercises when he thought of a series of lines that, as he described them, would use the last word of each line as the first word for the next—a juxtaposition that sets one word to opposite functions, both ending and beginning a poetic thought. In the end, his poem implicitly retained that structure.

Janusian thinking appeared and reappeared throughout the interviews and studies of creative people. But the controls never displayed it in their thoughts or in any aspects of the writing assignment they were asked to do.

Those subjects approached the writing in various ways: constructing a story outline, trying to think of a good ending, or merely trying to write out every thought that came to them. As with the creative group, I discussed with them the general themes and detailed revisions they made during the course of writing from week to week. Some persevered to complete an imaginative work, but many gave up. Though some occasionally wrote interesting lines and found fairly interesting themes, their earliest conceptions, and those along the way, were devoid of simultaneous antithesis. And no new or fresh creation appeared from their labors.

Because creativity is defined as something that "stands the test of time," I used another empirical method to study it in great works of the past. This involved doing statistical assessments of patterns of revisions in manuscripts by Eugene O'Neill, Maxwell Anderson, and Stephen Vincent Benét, developing specific hypotheses and predictions about their behavior in the course of writing the works, and then interviewing surviving family members to assess the predictions.

I first identified janusian thinking through reconstructing O'Neill's work on *The Iceman Cometh*. After examining all manuscript versions of the play, as well as the final work, and performing a special statistical type of content analysis, I discovered evidence for the author's persistent preoccupation with a simultaneous antithesis in an event whose meaning he had come to understand only years after it happened: a friend and roommate of his youth committed suicide because he was distressed over his wife's infidelity—but also because he had wanted her to be unfaithful to him. The idea produced the focus on infidelity, both religious and sexual, in the substance and title of the play.

Similarly, Maxwell Anderson created the prizewinning play *High Tor* with the idea of presenting characters who were both alive and dead at the same time. The characters were not merely ghosts but lost persons struggling to survive, to understand what had happened to them. Much of the action in the play turns on the dual nature of their existence as survivors of a Dutch explorer's ship who interact with modern inhabitants of the Hudson River Palisades.

Conceiving the important novel *Nostromo*, Joseph Conrad followed a janusian sequence, which he described in the preface. Conrad was struck by a story he had heard about an "unmitigated rascal" who had stolen a large quantity of silver somewhere on the seaboard of South America during a revolution. "I did not see anything at first in the mere story," he recalled. Then: "it dawned upon me that the purloiner of the treasure need not necessarily be a confirmed rogue, that he could even be a man of character." This key idea of the criminal as both rogue and man of character was elaborated in the story of a land that was both good and evil simultaneously. As Conrad reported, "It was only then that I had the first vision of a twilight country . . . with . . . its high, shadowy sierra and its misty campo for mute witnesses of events flowing from the passions of men short-sighted in good and evil. Such are in very truth the obscure origins of *Nostromo*—the book. From that moment, I supppose, it had to be."

We can trace janusian thinking in some of the most profound creations in music and the visual arts, as well. Successive sketches for Picasso's mural *Guernica*, for instance, reveal that the painter initially conceived of a female figure oriented spatially in opposite directions. In the first sketch, Picaasso represented the figure (who is holding a torch in the completed mural) as both looking into a room and looking out to a courtyard at the same time. In successive sketches, he made this feature of the figure less obvious. However, the entire mural portrays human carnage both inside a room and without at the same time.

Other artists, among them Leonardo da Vinci, Vincent van Gogh, and John Constable, as well as members of the modern schools, have provided descriptions of similar formulations. The celebrated British sculptor Henry Moore said: "To know one thing, you must know the opposite . . . just as much, else you don't know that one thing. So that, quite often, one does the opposite as an expression of the positive." And the late Josef Albers, the influential painter of the "hard edge" school, described his own approach: "I start from experiences and read . . . always between polarities . . . loud and not-loud . . . young and old . . . spring and winter. . . . If I can make black and white behave together instead of shooting at each other only, I feel proud. . . ."

Recently, in a brilliant series of Harvard lectures on music, Leonard Bernstein described the simultaneous operation of the antithetical factors of diatonicism (the tone relationships among the notes within the traditional scales) and chromaticism (relationship among the various keys) in the construction of virtually all types of music. Using a

Mozart piece to make his point, Bernstein demonstrated such conceptualization in Mozart's creative process and left little doubt that it is an important aspect of his own work.

Finally, another outstanding scientific achievement of the 20th century reveals, on close inspection, the clear imprint of janusian thinking. In discovering the double-helical structure of DNA and the key to genetic replication, James Watson and Francis Crick made possible an enormous acceleration of knowledge of natural processes in the field of microbiology. Describing the events leading up to the discovery in *The Double Helix*, Watson recounted a long and arduous series of trials and errors, and collation of the work of others. One day, he was trying to construct a large-scale model of a DNA molecule, as he and others had been doing for some time. He was briefly interrupted by a colleague who entered the lab, but he went back to thinking about the problem, shifting segments of the molecule with his hands, and considering various ways in which they might fit together. He realized that, instead of a structure based on the pairing of like-with-like segments, the molecule could consist of *identical but spatially opposed chains*.

"Suddenly," Watson said, "I became aware . . . that both pairs could be flip-flopped over and still have their . . . bonds facing in the same direction." Unhesitatingly, he concluded: "It strongly suggested that the backbones of the two chains run in opposite directions."

To make that discovery, Watson had to conceive of opposites operating simultaneously, a conception none of the many colleagues searching for the same answer were able to do at the time. Like Einstein, he was fully conscious, aware, and logical at that moment—but in that creative leap, he was able to transcend the bounds of ordinary logic and cognition.

Characteristically, as in the Einstein and Conrad examples, janusian concepts occur early in the creative process. They do not, of course, account for the entire creation: they are key steps, often initial formulations, that are later elaborated and transformed. Einstein's enormous intellect and capacity for both inductive and deductive logic certainly played a major role in the development of his theory. So did his ability to combine separate symbols, his intense concentration, his profound understanding of the categories of science and mathematics, and, in a special way, his use of mental imagery. Conrad's facility with language, his personal experience with sailing and exotic lands, his dual identity as an Englishman and the son of Polish intellectual gentry, all entered into the arduous creation of *Nostromo*.

Commonly, in the final product or creation—the scientific theory or crucial experiment, the poem, play, musical composition, or work of architecture—there is little overt sign of the janusian constructs that have occurred along the way. Several of the world's religions, however, have achieved integrations that retain a clear simultaneity, and tension, between opposite or anithetical factors.

In Taoism, the yin and the yang are two opposite and universal moral principles operating together as a single force. In Buddhism, nirvana, the end of the cycle of rebirth, is opposed to and unified with samsara, the endless series of incarnations and reincarnations of living things. And nirvana itself is both nonlife and nondeath. Some Western theology postulates a similar tension in the opposing powers of God and the devil.

In philosophy, simultaneous opposition and antithesis are manifest in the pre-Socratic conceptions of being and becoming, in Neitzsche's Dionysian and Apollonian principles, in Kierkegaard's belief by virtue of the absurd, and in Sartre's representation of being and nothingness. In psychology, there are Freud's formulation of the conscious operating together with the unconscious, the theory of the dually functioning but opposed instincts of sex and aggression, and Jung's animus and anima.

Janusian thinking differs from the types of creative cognition that other writers have hypothesized. In the Einstein example, the scientist could not have come to his theory merely by associating two incompatible elements, as Arthur Koestler proposes. It was by consciously formulating

the givens in a different way, by conceiving the incon-
ceivable—attributing the possibility of rest to the state of
falling—that Einstein was able to see the larger context of
relativity. That is not merely association, in which any
number of alternatives could fit the definition. In janusian
thinking, the creative person is fully rational and intentional at the time he selects particular opposites and juxta-
poses them.

Clearly, bringing together any opposites at all won't do.
It matters very much which opposites are selected, and
how the janusian formulation is elaborated in a particular
work. In artistic fields, the creator chooses and develops
those opposites and antitheses that most meaningfully crys-
tallize and express personal as well as universal values,
experiences, and feelings. The scientist also selects and
elaborates the context to some extent, but he has the
specific task of determining which opposites derived from
the world of natural events are significant at a particular
point in the evolution and growth of theory and knowledge.

The action of janusian thinking in creative processes
helps to explain, among other things, some of the sense of
newness and surprise when reactions first appear. Always
surprising is the discovery that the opposite of a previously
held idea, concept, or belief is operative or true. Even
more surprising is this: not only is the opposite true but
both the opposite and the previously held idea are operative or true. Nothing could jar our expectations more.

III.

III.

FEELINGS

Feeling Good

by Willard Gaylin, M.D.

We all try to feel good about the world and about ourselves. But when it comes to finding happiness, psychiatrist
Willard Gaylin presents a most provocative argument. Contrary to what we might expect, Gaylin tells us that difficult
feelings, like anxiety and guilt, are not necessarily our worst
enemies. In fact, these very experiences can help us be
happy if we learn to make sense of them: We can become more fully human if we can learn to read and trust our
feelings.

The road to a good life, Dr. Gaylin tells us, is through
responsible attention to our inner world. Feelings represent
a kind of warning system for our spiritual desires and needs.
When we disregard these feelings, we do so at our own risk.

THERE COMES A moment—often transitory at first—when a
patient who has been mired in depression begins to emerge
from the disease. With the alleviation of that oppressive
sense of alive deadness that is called depression, the patient once again simply, but exultantly, "feels good." As
a psychiatrist struggling to help patients with depression, I
can recognize the moment when it happens before the
patient has said a word, often before he is aware of what is
happening, in a fleeting moment on catching sight of the
patient—his facial expression, his body tone, his movement and posture.

What is that feeling of goodness? It is not just the relief that the depression is lifting. It is not just the absence of the pain that preceded it. Some believe that—with drug treatment, particularly   it is the emotional feeling which begins to cause the despair to lift. At any rate, the emotional feeling and the lifting of despair occur so simultaneously that the patient cannot distinguish one from the other. The patient feels the relief, joy, and optimism related to the sense of having won a battle, a joust with his sickness, and also the wonder of that non-specific "feeling good" again, after not having felt so for weeks.

"Feeling good" is generic and vague. Whenever questioned, any individual will find "reasons" why he feels good, but the emotion itself eludes specific cause and specific description. Lightness, buoyancy, aliveness, enthusiasm, optimism, peace, relaxation, hope, involvement—all are words that have been used to amplify the specific feeling of feeling good. All of us know that feeling good can be independent of a right to feel so, and can irrationally occur in the midst of problems. A day dawns like any other and we wake up "feeling good."

In one sense, feeling good is the opposite of despair; in another sense, it is the opposite of feeling upset. The major ingredients of feeling good are the antitheses and antidotes of those negative feelings. To feel good is to have a sense of hope, mastery, self-confidence, and self-esteem.

Part of the difficulty in defining or describing what the feeling is lies in our general ignorance in detailing the mechanisms of pleasure. Psychiatry, of course, has always been more successful in dealing with pain than pleasure, sickness than health. I suspect that in most fields of scholarship it is easier to analyze what has gone wrong than what went right. Failure is analyzed, while success is merely enjoyed. Rightness is therefore understood in terms of the absence of things gone wrong.

But there is a positive sense of pleasure. And surely there must be some concept that relates one form of pleasure to another—that defines the entity. We can feel different forms of pleasure in relationship to different kinds of stimuli. Still there must be something of the nature of pleasure that binds the individual experiences together. And whatever that is must define the generic sensation of feeling good.

It is with reluctance that I begin an analysis of pleasure. Almost inevitably, like an analysis of humor, it is heavy-handed work. Some things are meant to be experienced, relished, without analysis—indeed without cognition of any sort. Distress ought to be analyzed. The mere intellectual exercise reduces the distress. But to try to say why a joke is funny or why fun is fun almost ordains a certain resentment against the analyst. In the practice of psychoanalysis we know better. We rarely, if ever, analyze success for our patients. Health is its own excuse for being, and is accepted gratefully by both the parties.

Joy stems from an altered sense of self and, in turn, alters our view of our world and the way we are viewed. In the following quotation, Flush, a cocker spaniel, with some amazement and not a little jealousy, observes the transforming impact of a strange man on his ailing and unhappy mistress:

> Flush lay with his eyes wide open, listening. Though he could make no sense of the little words . . . he could detect with terrible accuracy that the tone of the words was changing. Miss Barrett's voice had been forced and unnaturally lively at first. Now it had gained a warmth and an ease that he had never heard in it before. And every time the man came, some new sound came into their voices.

The change Flush first senses only in his mistress's tone will eventually transform her perceptions, her behavior, and the world she inhabits.

> If Flush had changed, so had Miss Barrett. It was not merely that she called herself Mrs. Browning now; that she flashed the gold ring on her hand in the sun; she was changed, as much as Flush was changed. Flush heard her say, "Robert," "my husband," fifty times a

day, and always with a ring of pride that made his
hackles rise and his heart jump. But it was not her
language only that had changed. She was a different
person altogether. Now, for instance, instead of sipping
a thimbleful of port and complaining of the headache,
she tossed off a tumbler of Chianti and slept the sounder.
There was a flowering branch of oranges on the dinner-
table instead of one denuded sour, yellow fruit. Then
instead of driving in a barouche landau to Regent's Park
she pulled on her thick boots and scrambled over rocks.
Instead of sitting in a carriage and rumbling along
Oxford Street, they rattled off in a ramshackle fly to the
borders of a lake and looked at mountains; and when
she tired she did not hail another cab; she sat on a stone
and watched the lizards. She delighted in the sun; she
delighted in the cold.

If there is a common ingredient to the various sources
and forms of pleasure, the only one that I can identify is
that they all seem to contribute to an enhanced sense of
self. Pleasurable events either intensify our sense of ourselves or enlarge our view of ourselves. We tend to stretch
to our limits, and satiation and easy gratification ultimately
destroy pleasure. Samuel Johnson recognized this when he
said:

> . . . [The Pyramid] seems to have been erected only
> in compliance with *that hunger of imagination which
> preys incessantly upon life*. . . . Those who have al-
> ready all that they can enjoy, must enlarge their desires.
> He that has built for use, till use is supplied, must begin
> to build for vanity. . . . *I consider this mighty structure
> as a monument to the insufficiency of human enjoyments*.

A second category of pleasures—beyond particularly
physical sensation, invoking our total self as person—is
discovery. I have already discussed the sheer joy of the
child on finding something new; observe his pleasure even
in the pursuit of the unknown—in poking, examining, and
exploring. Discovery takes us beyond mere stimulation. It

allows us by using our distance perceptors, combined with our intelligence, to produce a form of pleasure that fuses the sensate with the intellectual.

Discovery can even abandon sensation and still produce pleasure. There is the form of pure discovery in the intellectual world. To those who have not experienced the pleasure of immersion in the world of knowledge and ideas, the phenomenon will be as impossible to communicate as to explain music to the deaf. There are people who have never developed intellectual pleasure. Obviously, an author is reasonably secure in the knowledge that the mere fact someone is reading his book means that whether the reader is getting pleasure in this specific book or not, he has an awareness of intellectual pleasure. There is something in the learning experience, independent of usefulness, that seems to give us joy. And it is again the concept of the enlargement of self. Our intellect extends our horizons. It frees us from the limits of our own experience. It allows us to transcend our own world, our own time, and our own identity.

> The whole book of Canticles used to be pleasant to me, and I used to be much in reading it . . . and found, from time to time, an inward sweetness that would carry me away in my contemplations. This I know not how to express otherwise than by a calm, sweet abstraction of soul from all the concerns of this world. . . . The sense I had of divine things would often of a sudden kindle up, as it were, a sweet burning in my heart; an ardor of soul, that I know not how to express.

All individuals originally have joy in discovery. It is part of the common developmental experience. Discovery is an essential ingredient in the separation process which leads a child away from the protection of the maternal environment into the large world. The two-year-old is a bundle of intellectual curiosity. He is explorer, adventurer, philosopher, and scientist. What in heaven's name happens to this questing creature? How is it that as our sensate pleasures expand through adolescence, so many of us lose this other source of joy? Surely they need not be alternative sources. Is there a natural attrition of pleasure in discovery—particularly intellectual discovery—with aging, or is it some dreadful artifact of our educational and cultural system? I suspect that the latter must play some part. To have delivered to an educational system such an incredibly curious creature as the average five-year-old, and to have delivered back to us, after twelve years of education, the average seventeen-year-old, seems to imply certain complicity in the educational process. Even allowing that there may be a natural attrition in delight in life (necessitated by our eventual need to abandon existence), seventeen seems too early an age for the processes to have started!

I do believe that the capacity for all pleasure diminishes with age, and that diminution serves a purpose. The acceptance of death, intolerable as it now is, would be too unbearable if we carried into our seventies the intensity and passion of sixteen or seventeen. It would be too much to ask that we give up a food so nourishing. But later, when much of the experience of life is tinged with pain, when we are left with the dry residue of unfulfilled hopes and the remembrance of powers that are lost, friends that are gone, and sensations that are no longer—an end can at least be contemplated if not accepted.

A third category of pleasure, closely related to discovery, is the concept of expansion and mastery. We enjoy the sense of growth, of improvement. There is incredible pleasure in the smooth, unhurried, perfectly timed backhand passing shot, when it is executed. There is an elation in any athletic endeavor when one has the sense of one's body having done well. A thrill can be experienced merely by the sense of our own muscles, sinew and tendon perfectly timed and perfectly executing an action. The fact that it comes so rarely to most of us only enlarges the pleasure of mastery.

Mastery also occurs with mental processes. Mastery is the capacity to say, "I did it," with pride. The intellectual aspects of pleasure then go well beyond just discovery. Think of the joy of using your mind, independent of any useful purposes or accretion of knowledge. Think of problem-solving. There is a delight for many in mathematics, in logical reasoning, or in the efforts of the kind of thinking associated with solving puzzles. It is a mental exercise. What we enjoy is the nimbleness of our mind. It is the pleasure of sensing our minds in operation. It is in every way an enhancement of the sense of self, if only the intellectual self.

Obviously, we do many things perfectly which we do not comment about. We are all master breathers, and the mechanics of breathing is intricate and magnificent. The moving of the diaphragm, which creates a negative vacuum, which allows for the influx of air; the stretching of the intercostal muscles between the ribs, which allows for the expansion of the rib cage and the dilatation of the lungs and the biological and chemical transactions across the lung membrane—all exercised so beautifully many times a minute, yet producing no pride or pleasure. Pleasure comes with the *sense* of enlargement or enrichment, and it must involve awareness of change from other conditions.

One of the real confusions about pleasure is the assumption that it is the opposite of pain. This confusion can be best resolved by considering mastery. In this category we can readily see that most things that involve great pleasure also involve pain. Here, without the pain, there would be no pleasure. The "I did it" phenomenon is significant only when there is the sense that what was done was difficult to do. Otherwise, where is the achievement? There is pleasure in attending a beautiful play. There has to be infinitely greater pleasure in having written one. The pleasure of seeing a superbly executed piece of cabinetry is far exceeded by the creativity of having made it. Part of the joy to the woodworker involves the hundreds of hours of painstaking, boring, painful sanding and finishing necessary to produce the perfection of fit and finish that goes into a beautiful cabinet. It is only because of the awareness of the sweat, toil, perseverance, and agony involved that the words "I did it!" have so rewarding a quality. The implication is: "It was not easy; and having done it, I have proved something about myself and my nature."

The cabinetmaking is, in fact, an example of a fourth category of pleasure that follows closely on mastery—and is simply an extension of it. That is creativity. The fact of having done something well is expanded in joy when it is more than a graceful turn on the ski slope, but actually a production of something of worth.

To make something, to be a maker of things, is a worthy pursuit. In that pursuit we often experience a fifth form of pleasure—immersion. To be totally immersed in something, to have lost the sense of time, perception, and seemingly sense of self, is obviously a joyous experience. This at first may seem contrary to the principle of expansion of self. I think not. The immersion of ourselves in an activity allows us to transcend our awareness of bodily needs, pain, trivial sensate pleasure. Immersion is profound involvement of thing with self. It allows us to sense ourselves in a new environment like floating in water; the environment of the activity allows for a new awareness of ourselves through a new surrounding medium.

Closely related to the idea of immersion in things is the idea of fusion with people—our sixth category. What does one make of the pleasure that is achieved by playing in an ensemble or orchestra, singing in a choir, being a part of team activity? Here the individual's effort is not isolatable from the effect of the total group. This is the distinction between the soloist with the choir and the choir singer. Surely this, then, beyond immersion may be seen as a denial of self. But here again I think not. Rather than disappearing into the crowd, we are allowed by the pleasure of fusion to enlarge ourselves in identifying with the larger body. That we—knowing the limitations of our own voice—are part of that glorious sound emerging from the chorus is awesome and thrilling. We have found a form of enlargement through joining with our fellows. We are not lost in the group, intimidated by the mass, as when we are part of an inchoate crowd. That mighty sound of the chorus is *our* voice. We are the group. This is the thrill one gets in all cooperative effort. It is the excitement of sitting in a scull, pulling together, where your own back-breaking effort is indistinguishable from those fore and aft of you. The sense of power and motion is compounded by the fact that you are pulling all together, and at times the whole scull seems to be moving by your own individual effort. Fusion activities of all sorts are profound delights.

Fusion is a bridge in helping us understand our seventh category of pleasurable experience. For want of a better word, I will call it the transcendental experience. The transcendental experience is that sense of feeling lifted out of oneself. In the same way that immersion in an activity or fusion with a group allows us to expand the limits of self by including the activity or the others in our sense of self, the transcendent feeling allows for an even larger attachment beyond groups, things, people, world. When we are moved by some transcendental experience, we are reminded that we are a part of something even larger than the course and activities of our life. It is our sense of continuity beyond existence. To be a part of the cosmos, to affirm our place in the larger order of things, excites us. It is for this reason that confrontation with nature is the most common source of this experience.

My categories of pleasure are undoubtedly incomplete. Each individual may have unique sources of pleasure unto himself, and each will dictate different sets of categorization. In every list will be discovered, however, that enlargement of self which goes into feeling good. Was it chance that I uncovered seven? Or was it the magic of the number intruding on the unconscious of a hedonist and an optimist? It is nice to balance the seven deadly sins and the seven cardinal virtues with seven sources of pleasure.

There are specific qualities of feeling good, however, that are unrelated to pleasure. There is a form of feeling good related to the alleviation of distress. There is the feeling good that follows reassurance. In this sense, the feeling of goodness is related not to pleasure but to the removal of a threat. We feel good, independent of what pleasure there may be in our life, when we are told that the sickness from which we are still suffering is not the cancer we suspected. This is feeling good even while in a state of misery.

All feeling good, therefore, does not necessarily tie to pleasure—even in its broadest sense. The term is too vague. A sense of well-being may come into play with a removal of pain or a revival of hope.

Then, beyond all rationality, there is the pure and existential feeling good simply related to being alive. Considering the impact of existentialism on our society, and the amount of thought devoted to existential anxiety, it is incredible how little thinking has been devoted to existential pleasure. Directly analyzing existential pleasure is uncommon, because we usually believe that despair is close to an antithesis of feeling good. All feeling is a reminder that we exist, and all good is defined in the existence of ourselves and our species.

When we "feel good," we carry the feeling so tightly to our senses that we are often unaware of its existence. Like the fluid movements of a healthy body, we most often accept the value of feeling good without acknowledging its existence. But that sense of good feeling, whether exploited for other purposes or enjoyed directly, is the sole support of the value of living in this world. It is, at any rate, good "to feel good."

The Boredom Epidemic

by Sam Keen

What do you do when you're bored and blue? That's the question that Sam Keen poses as he looks at the problem of boredom in contemporary society. Heart disease is dramatic and its impact apparent; depression is unmistakable. But boredom is less readily recognized, perhaps because, like a shadow, it is always lurking in the background. In "The Boredom Epidemic," Keen asks us to take a serious, thoughtful look at a major, but little discussed, dilemma.

In treating boredom as the common cold of the psyche, Keen suggests that boredom is a much deeper problem than the visible yawn—that, in fact, boredom is symptomatic of the way we think about our entire existence. Too often, Keen observes, we try to rid ourselves of the "blahs" by escaping into some menial task or mindless diversion. This is not a useful resolution, he argues, and it exacerbates our predicament. Instead, he recommends that we confront our sense of ennui directly, by experiencing it and then coming to terms with its origins—not just for the present but for good.

BOREDOM IS OUR number-one social disease. It's growing in epidemic proportions. The closer we get to the brave new prepackaged world in 1984, the more we are engulfed by psychic smog.

Unfortunately, boredom is not dramatic like cancer. It appears to be a minor league demon, gray and anonymous.

Congress doesn't mount a war against boredom or announce a five-year program for conquering ennui. There is no Anti-Boredom Week, no Boredom Liberation movement, no Crusade Against Tedium, no Boredom Anonymous, no Foundation for the Elimination of Monotony. But the amorphous blob creeps over our land like a giant fungus in a grade B science fiction movie. It devours our innocent enthusiasms and destroys our dreams. It insinuates itself into any ho-hum corner of our lives which has been prepared by fatigue. And the plague is mostly invisible because it paralyzes our powers of perception even as it invades our psyches. So many of us suffer from it that we consider it normal, part of the inevitable atmosphere of modern life.

The fish doesn't know it is swimming in water. We have learned to accept tedious jobs, depressing cities, deadly bureaucracies, the television wasteland, and hopeless politics as just the way things are. Lively people, full of sap and sass, content with simplicity and few things, are rare as Shaker furniture. Wisdom has become an antique virtue, to be studied in the tintypes of great men and women of former ages. And wonder, which ancient philosophers celebrated as the aim and reward of a good human life, never makes the cover of *Rolling Stone* or *Newsweek*.

The blahs have us. The Sisyphus strain. The disease from inner space. Some vampire is quietly sucking away the lifeblood of our enthusiasm (from the Greek *entheos*, "inspired by a god") and hope—that spirit which former ages called "the soul." Most frightening, we allow our vitality to ebb away with scarcely a protest. Boredom may become such a natural part of modern technological society that we don't notice our dis-ease, or accept it passively. And die with both a bang and a whimper.

How is it with you?

Perhaps you wake up one morning, and for no particular reason it is February in your soul. Blue Monday. The tide out. Nothing is visible except mud flats. There isn't much pain, just a great and aching emptiness. And restlessness. The excitement has ebbed away from your life. Only a littered line of memories is left along the shore to mark the receding tide of your passion. You think about your job, your marriage, the vacation you are going to take in August—everything seems stale and tasteless. Nothing matters much. You have no burning dreams or lively hopes. Not even outrage. You go through the day automatically, by the numbers, without feeling. Same old rat race.

When did you lose it? It is hard to remember.

Or maybe the boredom began the week after you retired or the children left for college and, suddenly, nobody needed you anymore. You tried to fill your days with hobbies but time hung heavy. You did make-work around the house, joined a club, played golf three days a week. But when you weren't busy, that nameless sadness came over you and the future seemed to stretch before you like a sterile desert.

Or maybe you work at Electric Hose and Rubber Company, the three-to-eleven shift. You've been there seven years and have some seniority, but you are still young. Lately the monotony has been getting you down. After cutting and bundling 12,000 Chevrolet heater hoses, or watching an extruder squeeze out an endless ribbon of polyvinyl chloride pipe, your spirit feels deadened. Maybe it's just job fatigue. But then why do you feel so depressed, so much at a dead end?

Or maybe you are in teenage limbo. At school it's the same old thing every day. Like a prison. Eight 45-minute periods—including lunch and study hall. A curriculum and teachers tell you what you must learn for your own good. And after school, there is not much to do. So you hang out and smoke a joint or two.

Or maybe you are unemployed. You know it's not your fault but you can't help feeling low about yourself. The day stretches ahead. What will you do? Read the paper. Maybe something good will turn up in the classifieds. Then wait till noon for the phone call from the contractor who just might have a job. In the afternoon you walk downtown and try to look busy. You resist the impulse to have a drink or look at TV until after dark. You are not going to sink to that.

If you are like most Americans you will ignore your boredom and hope it will go away. Or take up a hobby. Or have an affair. Or get divorced. Or start a new business. Or keep busy. Or eat to fill up the void. When none of these works you will fall into depression and wonder what's the matter with you. (Think of boredom as the common cold of the psyche and depression as pneumonia.) If you can afford it and aren't afraid of introspection you will seek psychiatric help. If you can't, you will get your physician to prescribe tranquilizers or mood elevators. Or you will drink. Or try to tough it out.

And you will feel alone. But you are not. If the 1950s were the age of anxiety, the 1970s and 80s are the Age of Melancholy and Boredom. Accurate statistics are hard to come by, but we can estimate from the dramatic increase in suicide attempts and sales of antidepressant drugs that boredom and depression will likely strike half of the population at some time in their lives. Psychiatrists report that most patients nowadays arrive in their consulting rooms not with raw pain but with a severe case of emptiness. "Doctor, I just don't feel anything. Something is missing and I don't know what it is. There must be more to life than this."

Modern literature warned us of the spiritual malaise long before psychiatric clinics were inundated with depressed patients. In 1936, Georges Bernanos in *Diary of the Country Priest* warned:

> The word is eaten up by boredom (ennui). To perceive this needs a little preliminary thought: you can't see it all at once. It is like dust. You go about and never notice it, you breathe it in, you eat and drink it. It is sifted so fine, it doesn't even grit on your teeth. But stand still for an instant and there it is, coating your face and hands. To shake off this drizzle of ashes you must be forever on the go. . . . I wonder if man has ever before experienced this contagion, this leprosy of boredom, an aborted despair, a shameful form of despair in some way like the fermentation of a Christianity in decay. . . . If ever our species is to perish it will

die of boredom, of stale disgust. (As for instance the world wars of today, which would seem to show such prodigious human activity, are in fact indictments of a growing apathy of humanity. In the end, at certain stated periods, they will lead huge flocks of resigned sheep to be slaughtered.)

T. S. Eliot sketched the outline of the modern wasteland and showed us in J. Alfred Prufrock a man whose enthusiasm has fled:

I have seen them all already
The mornings, evenings, afternoons.
I have measured out my life in coffee spoons.

Hemingway provided the litany for a world where the experiences of the void replaced both hope and satisfaction. In "A Clean, Well-Lighted Place" he tells the story of an old man who has failed at everything, even suicide. He sits in a well-lit café for a moment before going out again into the night and his life is summed up in a refrain that is a parody of the ancient prayer: "Our *nada* [Spanish for "nothing"] who art in *nada, nada* by thy name. . . ."

Samuel Beckett showed us the absurdity in *Waiting for Godot*. One bum asks the other: "Do you believe in the life to come?" "Mine always was," he replies. Paddy Chayevsky gave us an unforgettable vignette in *Marty* where two young men, hanging out on a Saturday night with nothing to do, keep asking each other:

What do you want to do, Marty?
I don't know. What do you want to do, Angie?
I don't know, Marty. What do you want to do?

Boredom is doubly difficult to diagnose and cure because it is a closet disease. We are ashamed of it. Like guilt or shame we hide it behind a curtain of silence and denial. I found in conducting interviews for this book that most people protest too much: "I'm *never* bored." As if I had suggested they enjoyed incest! I asked one beautiful young mother if she was ever bored. "Never." she replied, "I'm always doing something. I don't have time." A week later she called me and asked if we could talk again. "When you first asked me if I was ever bored I denied it," she said. "But when I thought about it I realized I was bored all the time but I felt too embarrassed to admit it. I feel guilty. What right do I have to feel bored? I have everything, a beautiful house, a child. I travel to exotic places. I could take a job if I wanted, or even have an affair. I don't have any excuse for being bored. I have no restrictions. But I don't really enjoy my life. I'm ashamed of myself. Here is all the beauty and preciousness of life and I'm not appreciating it! I feel lifeless. I just don't have enthusiasm for anything."

Americans are particularly phobic about boredom. We see ourselves as go-getters and the right to the pursuit of happiness is guaranteed us by law. By industry and imagination we have created a society richer in things than any past society. Most of us live in material luxury which medieval kings would have envied. In fact we have democratized the dis-ease of kings. Everyone now can afford ennui.

To get a true picture of how much our lives are shaped by boredom we have to look at its secondary effects—all the ways we spend our substance in trying to escape from this monster we deny is chasing us. The frenzy of our flight (and the strategies we use to avoid the void) give us a true index of how much we fear what the early Christian monks referred to as "the demon of noontide." What price do we pay to maintain our false self-image as robust, never-bored-a-day-in-our-lives, on-top-of-it-all extroverts? What is the hidden cost of denying our boredom? Here are some of our substitutes, our favorite ways of dodging boredom:

Keeping busy. (The devil finds work for idle hands.) Stay on the go. Keep moving. Work and produce. We are what we do. If you are retired or find yourself with leisure, get a "hobby."

Speed. Americans are caught in perpetual motion. Our favorite drugs are caffeine and sugar. Never let the body, the psyche, or the economy slow down. Stimulate. We are addicted to our own adrenaline. Speed freaks.

Consume. Eat. Fill the void. If any desire arises, satiate it with instant food, sex, or the latest gadget.

Keep entertained. Fill up your time. Plug your nervous system into a radio or TV.

And what are the *results* of our flight from boredom? What price our denial of our dis-ease?

Fatigue. We are always tired. Our nervous systems and economy are exhausted by a diet of artificial stimulants. Speed freaks wear out young. We are suffering from a massive energy crisis. At the psychological level it is called depression. At the economic-political level it is called recession, stagnation, readjustment. But a depression by any other name smells just the same. And our addiction to stimulation as a way of life binds us to our drugs and blinds us to the possible joys of a slower "steady-state" way of life. All our anxieties are focused on maintaining our "energy" sources. The manic-depressive cycle *is* the American way of life. Psychic, spiritual, economic exhaustion is the flip side of the drive for unbroken intensity, progress, "growth." The rule we follow is Satchel Paige's: "Don't never look back, 'cause something might be gaining on you."

Violence. Our love affair with violence springs from our desperate need to make our exhausted systems feel something. We would rather smash things and people than face our boredom.

Violence comes in many forms:

1. Divorce. We tear the fabric of the family. Nearly half of us have cut and run rather than continue to till the soil of fallow marriages. We have no faith that we must wait through the sterile winter before new life will appear. We demand that our relationships always be "interesting," "exciting," "growing."

2. Drugs stimulate the deadened psyche and imagination. Grass to make green the fields of imagination burned out by "education" and work. Amphetamines and "uppers" elevate the moods of those who cannot stand the depths. Alcohol deadens the pain of the loss of passion and puts our conscience to troubled sleep.

3. Juvenile delinquents horrify us because they practice what the media preach—violence pays. Why should we be surprised that after watching 25,000 murders and an equal number of miscellaneous crimes on TV our young people get hooked on violence? Here is what the playwright Arthur Miller says about it in an article, "The Bored and the Violent" (*Harper's*, No. 62, November 1962):

> No one knows what "causes" delinquency. Having spent some months in the streets with boys of an American gang, I came away with . . . a single, overwhelming conviction—that the problem underneath is boredom. . . . People no longer seem to know why they are alive; existence is simply a string of near-experiences marked off by periods of stupefying spiritual and psychological stasis, and the good life is basically an amused one. . . . The delinquent is stuck with his boredom, stuck inside, stuck to it, until for two or three minutes he "lives"; he goes on a raid around the corner and feels the thrill of risking his skin or his life as he smashes a bottle filled with gasoline on some other kid's head. In a sense, it is his trip to Miami. It makes his day. It is his shopping tour. It gives him something to talk about for a week. It is life. Standing around with nothing coming up is as close to dying as you can get. Unless one grasps the power of boredom, the threat of it to one's existence, it is impossible to "place" the delinquent as a member of the human race.

And deliquency is only Little League violence, not even big enough for the NFL. In big league violence the play-off is between suicide and war.

4. Suicide is violence for the introvert; war is violence for the extrovert. The suicide rate among teenagers, the

unemployed, and the retired is soaring. We murder the self because of disgust at our unlived lives. When our capacity for hope has been exhausted some of us prefer to die all at once rather than by inches. Without work or worth life is empty. Better to take the "only way out" than face the void. Certain phrases keep popping up in suicide notes: "I'm tired." "I can't go on." "I've lost my nerve." "There is nothing left to live for." "This is the only thing left that I can do." "I just want to rest." "My soul is dead." "I have felt myself slipping."

5. War is the final distraction from boredom. Nations regularly sacrifice their blood for "adventure" disguised as honor. Violence makes us feel alive. War gives us an occasion for heroism and intensity. When we get too secure boredom creeps in; we want the excitement that war gives us. (The rate of individual suicides drops in wartime.) Warfare is relief from tedium.

> Reflecting on the exaltation of the Vienna crowds in August 1914, Trotsky later wrote, "The people whose lives day in and day out pass in a monotony of hopelessness are many: they are the mainstay of modern society. The alarm of mobilizations breaks into their lives like a promise; the familiar and long-hated is overthrown, and the new and unusual reigns in its place. Changes still more incredible are in store for them in the future. For better or worse? For better of course—what can seem worse . . . than normal conditions."
>
> —Elwin Powell, *The Design of Discord,*
> Oxford University Press, 1970, p. 172.

6. Illness. How much sickness is escape from boredom? Every hypochondriac knows it is better to suffer than face the void. One of Faulkner's characters says: "Between nothingness and grief, I will choose grief." Illness is a break in the routine.

Some specialists in psychosomatic medicine have lately suggested that cancer and other life-threatening diseases

may sometimes be ways for novelty to be introduced into
stuck lives. The disease provokes a crisis: change or die!

Certainly we all recognize how much we do daily violence to ourselves. We worry, fill ourselves with constant
anxiety. It is the unusual person who can tolerate happiness for more than three days at a time.

Why do we have this love affair with suffering? What is
worse than pain? Nothingness perhaps. We court stress
and dis-ease rather than risk contentment. Why are we so
threatened by psychological, spiritual, physical health?

When we begin to tally the cost of our "normal" efforts
to escape boredom, it is clear that it is time to bring our
dis-ease out of the closet. Bertrand Russell said, "Boredom is a vital problem for the moralist, since at least half
of the sins of mankind are caused by the fear of it" (*The
Conquest of Happiness*, New York: The Book League of
America, 1930, p. 60). Perhaps, if we dare to look this
demon square in the eye, we may be able to tame it rather
than destroy ourselves in futile attempts to escape. It is
even remotely possible that if we sit quietly with our
boredom and meditate on the void that underlies our manic
pursuits and distraction we may find that the monster we
have feared for a lifetime is an angel in disguise. By
tracing our way through the labyrinth of our dis-ease, we
may find the path to health.

In the last century there was a common saying among
doctors: "If you know syphilis, you know medicine"
(because syphilis could manifest itself through such a wide
variety of symptoms). The same might be said about boredom. Boredom is an element in all disease. Neurosis is
boring yourself, psychosis is scaring yourself to death.
Know your boredom, know yourself.

As we move more deeply into night country, into the
heart of boredom, we will encounter all the major themes
of psychology: guilt and shame, freedom and compulsion,
will, imagination, feeling, sensation. By studying your
boredom you may come to understand what motivates you,
what values you hold, and what risks you must take to
remain truly alive for all of your days.

The basic strategy this book suggests for dealing with boredom is: embrace it. Don't run. Don't avoid it. Don't try positive thinking. A fundamental rule of the psyche is: *whatever you resist will persist*. Those who run from boredom and depression will spend a lifetime running. Surrender. Go into it. Study your dis-ease and it will lead you to health. Memorize your neurotic cycles and you can run through them in minutes rather than weeks. Dealing with boredom (or any "negative" emotion) is like running the rapids in the Grand Canyon. In the turbulent Colorado River the greatest danger is getting thrown out of the boat and getting caught in a whirlpool or roller that sucks you down. If you struggle prematurely to get to the surface you will likely drown. But if you go deeper, the action of the water will spit you out twenty feet downstream on the surface.

The philosophical and psychological view on which the diagnosis and prescriptions of this book are based is that boredom and depression are dis-eases by which the psyche is trying to heal itself. They are invitations to descend into your depths and be reborn. The awareness of boredom is the gateway to the hero's journey. Pay attention to the creeping paralysis and deadness of boredom and you may embark on a journey from which you may emerge more virile and wonder-ful. Blue is the color of melancholy and eternity. Go deep and find the wild blue yonder.

The Social Psychology of Jealousy

by Elaine Hatfield and G. William Walster

Much as it embarrasses and perplexes us, we have all known jealousy in our lives. We experience it as a small brush fire that we just cannot put out; soon it spreads to threaten our vital preserves. With roots in our earliest experiences of sibling rivalry or infant attachment to a mother, jealousy retains its full power in adulthood.

We frequently think of jealousy as the fear of losing something possessed. It is in this context that the authors offer this piece on jealousy in a larger social context. Jealousy, they say, involves socially shaped beliefs that help us to interpret our feelings. These feelings are physiological in nature; hence jealousy involves both mind and body.

The Walsters' view may help to explain why a given set of circumstances will trigger jealousy in one person but not in another. The social meaning of events is different for each of us, and this makes jealousy a highly personalized affair.

jealous/'jel-əs/*adj* (ME *jelous*, fr. OF, fr. (assumed) VL *zelosus*, fr. LL *zelus* zeal—more at ZEAL) 1 a: intolerant of rivalry or unfaithfulness b: disposed to suspect rivalry or unfaithfulness: apprehensive of the loss of another's exclusive devotion 2: hostile toward a rival or one believed to enjoy an advantage 3: vigilant in guarding a possession 4: distrustfully watchful: SUSPICIOUS *syn* see ENVIOUS—

Webster (1963)

WE BEGIN THE section on "Sexual Jealousy" in our Human Sexuality classes with a simple question: What would you most like to know about jealousy? Students' answers are surprisingly redundant. They ask: "What is jealousy?" and—whatever it is—"How can you get rid of it?" A scattering of anthropologists, sociologists, and psychologists—as well as a tidal wave of novelists—*have* addressed these two questions. Unfortunately, their answers are unnervingly inconsistent.

WHAT IS THIS THING CALLED JEALOUSY?

Since Aristotle's time, theorists have been unable to agree as to what jealousy "really" is. They have insisted that jealousy should really be equated with "love/hate," "a perverse kind of pleasure," "shock," "uncertainty," "confusion," "suspicion," "fear of loss," "hurt pride," "rivalry,'" "sorrow," "shame," "humiliation," "anger," "despair," "depression," or "a desire for vengeance."

Probably most theorists can agree that jealousy possesses two basic components: (1) a feeling of bruised pride, and (2) a feeling that one's property rights have been violated.

According to such analysts as Bohm (1967), Fenichel (1955), Freud (1922), Lagache (1947), Langfeldt (1961), Mairet (1908), or Mead (1960), jealousy is "really" little more than wounded pride. For example, Margaret Mead contends that the more shaky one's self-esteem, the more vulnerable one is to jealousy's pangs:

> Jealousy is not a barometer by which the depth of love can be read. It merely records the degree of the lover's insecurity. . . . It is a negative miserable state of feeling having its origin in the sense of insecurity and inferiority.

According to such analysts as Davis (1936) and Gottschalk (1936), jealousy is "really" little more than one's fear that he may lose his property. For example, Davis claims:

. . . In every case it [jealousy] is apparently a fear . . .
or rage reaction to a threatened appropriation of one's
own, or what is desired as one's own property.

At this point, however, theorists' descriptions of jealousy begin to diverge.

The man on the street shows similar confusion as to
what jealousy "really" is. For example, Ankles (1939)
asked university graduates:

What are the emotions and feelings involved in jealous
behavior? (Cross out those which do not apply)

(1) Anger	(8) Narcissism or self-love
(2) Fear	(9) Antagonism
(3) Ridicule	(10) Pleasure
(4) Joy	(11) Stupidity
(5) Cruelty	(12) Respect
(6) Hate	(13) Elation
(7) Self-feeling	(14) Shame

To Ankles' surprise, he found that at least a few of his
respondents insisted that jealousy was associated with *all*
of the preceding emotions. In a more recent study, Davitz
(1969) interviewed 50 people and secured 50 different
descriptions of jealousy.

CAN WE CONTROL JEALOUSY?

If we know what a social commentator thinks society
should be like, we can pretty well predict whether s/he
thinks jealousy is "bred in the bone" or can easily be
stimulated—or extinguished.

Jealousy Is "Bred in the Bone"

Traditionalists insist that marriage should be both permanent and exclusive. Thus, *they* naturally prefer to believe that jealousy is a natural emotion.

Traditionalists generally begin their spirited defenses of jealousy by pointing out that even animals are jealous. They cite the "jealous" courtship battles of stags, antelopes, wild pigs, seals, kangaroos, howler monkeys, and so on (See Bohm 1967). They go on to mention that even Kinsey and his associates (1948:411) believed that male jealousy had a mammalian basis:

> While cultural traditions may account for some of the human male's behavior, his jealousies so closely parallel those of the lower species that one is forced to conclude that his mammalian heritage may be partly responsible for his attitudes.

Generally they end their defense by reminding us that many societies simply take it for granted that jealousy is a basic emotion. (For example, in some societies, if a man catches his mate and his rival *in flagrante delicto*, he is allowed to kill them.)

Jealousy Should Be, And Can Be, Extinguished

Radical reformers such as Beecher and Beecher (1971) or O'Neill and O'Neill (1972) see things differently. They are convinced that people could evolve more loving personal lives, and more creative and productive professional lives, if they felt free to love all mankind—or at least a larger subset of it. Thus, *they* naturally prefer to believe that society has the power to arouse, or to temper, jealousy as it chooses.

Radical reformers generally begin their spirited attacks on jealousy by pointing out that not all men are jealous. They note that in most societies men are allowed to have more than one partner. Ford and Beach (1951) report that 84% of the 185 societies they studied allowed men to have more than one wife. Only 1% of the societies permittted women to have more than one husband. Most societies also look more tolerantly on "wife lending" or "mate swapping" and on extramarital sex than does our own. For example, Ford and Beach (1951) report that when Chukchee men (Siberia) travel to distant communities, they often engage in sexual liaisons with their hosts' mates. They reciprocate in kind when their hosts visit their community.

Radical reformers point out that, traditionally, our own society has strongly fostered marital permanence, exclusivity—and jealousy. Yet, in spite of the fact that our society tells men they *should* be jealous of their mates, many are not. For example, Kinsey and his associates (1953) found that if a husband learned about his wife's extramarital relations, his discovery caused "serious difficulty" only 42% of the time; 42% of the time it caused "no difficulty at all."

THE SOCIAL-PSYCHOLOGICAL PERSPECTIVE

What does social psychology have to say about these questions? Can we add to the existing confusion? Certainly.

Currently, Schachter's (1964) theory of emotion is probably the most popular social-psychological theory of human emotional response. Schachter argues that both one's mind and one's body must be engaged if s/he is to have a true emotional experience.

Mind: A person must feel that it is appropriate to interpret his/her feelings in emotional terms. A person learns—from society, parents, friends, and from his or her own experience—what emotions it is "appropriate" to feel in various settings. We know that we feel "joyous excitement" when a friend comes to visit, and "anxiety" when an enemy swaggers into town. The untutored may well experience the very same feeling on both occasions (a sort of anxious excitement). Schachter argues that a person will experience an emotion only if s/he interprets his or her "feelings" in emotional terms.

Body: A person must be physiologically aroused.
Schachter argues that a person can experience an emotion
only if s/he *has* some "feelings." Schachter argues that—*by
themselves*—neither appropriate cognitions nor physiological arousal constitute a complete emotional experience.

Schachter tested his two-component theory in an ingenious series of experiments.

Manipulating Physiological Arousal

Schachter's first step was to manipulate the first component of emotion—physiological arousal. In one now classic experiment, Schachter gave half of his participants
(those in the *Unaroused* groups) a placebo. He gave the
remaining participants (those in the *Aroused* groups) an
arousing drug—epinephrine. Epinephrine is an ideal drug
for producing a "high." Its effects mimic the discharge of
the sympathetic nervous system. Shortly after a person
receives an epinephrine injection, s/he experiences palpitations, tremor, flushes, and accelerated breathing. In short,
s/he experiences the same physiological reactions which
accompany a variety of natural emotional states.

Manipulating "Appropriate" Cognitions

Schachter's second step was to manipulate the second
component of emotion—the participants' cognitions. In the
Non-Emotional Attribution Groups, Schachter wished to
lead volunteers to attribute their feelings to a non-emotional
cause—the injection. In the Emotional Attribution Groups,
Schachter tried to lead volunteers to attribute their tranquil
(or stirred up) feelings to an emotional cause.

Non-Emotional Attribution Groups. In these groups, Non-
Aroused volunteers (who should have no reaction to the
placebo shot) were given no information about how the
shot would affect them. The Aroused volunteers were
given a complete description of the shot's effects; they
were warned that in a very few minutes they would experience palpitations, tremors, flushing, and accelerated
breathing.

Emotional Attribution Groups. In these groups, Schachter tried to lead volunteers to attribute their tranquil or aroused feelings to an emotional cause. For example, in some groups, Schachter arranged things so that, at the time the shot took effect, volunteers were caught up in a wild, abandoned, happy social interaction. In this setting, Schachter hoped that when the Aroused subjects felt the effects of the shot, and asked themselves, "What's happening to me?" they would answer, "I'm having fun— that's what."

In other groups, Schachter arranged things so that, at the time the shot took effect, volunteers were involved in a tense, explosive, angry interaction. In this setting, Schachter hoped that when Aroused subjects felt the effects of the shot, and asked themselves, "What's happening to me?" they would answer, "I'm mad . . . mad as hell—that's what."

Schachter found support for his hypothesis. He found that *both* appropriate cognitions and physiological arousal *are* indispensable components of a complete emotional experience. Additional support for the two-component theory of emotion comes from Schachter and Wheeler (1962) and Hohmann (1962).

This, then, in brief, is the Schachterian emotion paradigm. Can this social-psychological perspective give us some new insights into the complex and confusing nature of jealousy? Let us see how a Schachterian would answer the two questions with which we began.

What Is Jealousy?

Interestingly enough, Schachter's "revolutionary" theory of emotion generates an equally revolutionary view as to the nature of jealousy.

From Aristotle to Schachter, almost all analysts simply assumed that emotions such as jealousy are somehow built into the organism. They took for granted that all persons, at all times, "really" experience the same thing. It was *their* job to ferret out the essential elements of those emotions. The fact that individuals' emotional descriptions were unnervingly inconsistent—the fact that some "jealous" persons insisted they felt "joyous anticipation of revenge" while others insisted they felt "depressed" and "lethargic" *or* the fact that some claimed they were suffering unbearably, while others stoutly insisted they felt perfectly content—was simply chalked up to the fact that human beings possess poor powers of observation and often deceive themselves.

The Schachterians would insist that a person's confidences should be treated with more respect. For the Schachterians, one's mind, as well as one's body, contributes to emotional experiences. One's beliefs about what a jealous person *should* be feeling, and what s/he *must* be feeling, should have a potent impact on what s/he *does* feel. If society's sub-groups have radically different ideas about the essential nature of jealousy—and they do—our labeling will necessarily reflect these differences. Thus Schachterians would argue that jealousy is "really" a vastly different experience for different people.

Can Jealousy Be Controlled?

According to Schachter's two-component theory, society has the ability to shape *all* of our emotional experiences. If society wanted to do so, it could suppress jealousy in either of two ways: (1) Society could try to persuade people to *label* their feelings in a somewhat different way; or (2) society could try to arrange things so that the realization that we must share our "possessions" with others would arouse a far less intense physiological reaction.

Altering Labeling. Societies vary from considering jealousy to be a natural human response to considering it to be an entirely illegitimate one. If our society wishes, it could change from one which encourages marital permanence and exclusivity—and jealousy—to one which insists that people should not, and must not, be jealous. Surely, the wily citizen would be clever enough to come up with a host of new, more acceptable, labels for his or her feelings. Social reformers would naturally hope that the once-jealous individual could be persuaded to re-label his or her feelings in positive, or at least neutral, terms (i.e., to label "jealous" feelings as "sexual curiosity," "pride that others value one's mate," etc.). Unfortunately for potential reformers, it is probably at least as likely that the persons would come up with alternative *negative* labels for their feelings (i.e., "chagrin at my mate's poor taste," "anger," or "depression at her neglect," etc.). From the reformer's point of view, such changes would really constitute no change at all.

According to the Schachterians, there is a second way society can eliminate jealousy: It can reduce the "jealous" person's physiological arousal—and this is a distinctly harder task.

Reducing Physiological Arousal. If society works at it, it should be able to affect *some* reduction in the intensity of people's jealous feelings.

Currently, it is believed that one's value depends on the faithfulness of one's spouse, and on his/her possession of people and things, which accounts for some of jealousy's sting. Society *could* teach its citizens that self-worth depends on what one is and does—not on how many people one can control. If the association between "pride" and "a partner's exclusive possession" were reduced, jealous feelings should be less intense.

Unfortunately, society would have a harder time eradicating many of the links between "a mate's loss" and "physiological arousal." Currently the person who loses his or her mate is confronted with an enormity of practical problems. S/he loses the partner's love. S/he may have to endure the loss of friends—and worse yet, the loss of his or her children. One's daily life is disrupted in a thousand different ways. It is likely, then, that society might be able to make the jealous person's feelings somewhat less intense, but they are unlikely to be able to eliminate one's physiological arousal altogether.

"Jealousy"—by any other name, even at a reduced intensity—may still remain a painfully devastating experience.

The Anatomy of Anger

by Carol Tavris

Anger is one of the less pleasant emotions, but Carol Tavris has made a major contribution to helping unravel its mysteries. Even an emotion as potentially destructive as anger, she says, can have a positive side if we can understand its origins and harness its energy.

We have barely begun to know the angry heart—the full extent of anger's effects on the body are yet to be determined. This is the starting point of Carol Tavris's article, and she links her observations on anger to some of the very foundations on which the study of psychology was begun: turn-of-the-century studies of physiology and emotion.

Tavris, reporting on the present state of affairs in anger research, suggests that it is not bouts of anger per se, but rather chronic, intense anger that is bad for our health. To the extent that anger can be a responsible and rational tool for communication, then it may open the way for greater pleasures.

WHEN YOU GET angry, what happens to your body? How do you feel? Try to recall a recent incident and compare your reactions to these symptoms: muscle tension, scowling, flushing, paling, goose bumps, chills and shudders, numbness, choking, twitching, feeling hot, feeling cold.

These are a few of the items from the first modern, scientific effort to study anger. In 1894, psychologist G. Stanley Hall asked people to provide examples of their angriest episodes—what provoked them, what they did, how they felt later, and physical and mental changes. One of his most curious results was the physical variation in people's experiences of anger. Some said that anger made them feel good, and others that it made them feel sick. And some reported their reactions depended on circumstance: "When angry I feel all of a sudden burning hot, stifled and compelled to make a noise. Sometimes I grow icy cold and feel like blancmange inside."

Such findings go against an assumption that most of us share: that each emotion has its own distinctive physiology. Researchers have often acted as if each feeling had its own trigger somewhere in the body. Push one neurological button and you get fear; another, and a laugh results.

But the best evidence now suggests that this view is misguided. In the first place, what happens to my body when I am angry may be very different from what happens to yours. And our emotions are not physically distinct from each other, either. An angry body can go through the same changes as a joyful one. Anger, in short, is not a simple reflex, like a sneeze or a hiccup.

Some children and adults *do* suffer tantrums or rage attacks that seem uncontrollable, almost like seizures. And these extreme cases may have a physical cause, like allergies to a specific food or a whole range of brain disorders, from encephalitis to epilepsy. But such abnormal rage may tell us little about normal anger—the anger of people who do not suffer brain disease, but who suffer life.

Many scientists now argue that people have different thresholds of responsiveness. Those who have very low anger thresholds are easily provoked and as quick to calm as they are to rage. Others are placid: You could come up behind them, yell "boo!" and their reflexes would barely ripple.

Genetic differences may help account for these temperamental styles. Andrew Sostek and Richard J. Wyatt of the National Institute of Mental Health have found that one enzyme in the blood and the brain—monoamine oxidase (MAO)—mirrors the behavior of newborns. Babies born with low levels of MAO tend to be more excitable than babies with high levels.

No one is suggesting that individuals are born with an ''anger'' gene (or lack thereof). But genes may affect the amount of energy a person summons during an emotional response. How we channel that energy, however, depends on what we learn as children. As psychologist L. Alan Sroufe once put it, ''A child who has a rapid tempo may be seething with anger. . . . But a child who has a rapid tempo also may be eager, spirited, effective and a pleasure to others.'' It's the world, not our genes, that decides which way we go.

THE FUEL OF EMOTION

Even if you're slow to anger, a rage, when it happens, can feel like it's taking over your body. You may feel almost compelled to yell, pace, slam a door. You're physically aroused, no question about it. But your body isn't telling you that you're angry: Your situation is making you interpret your body's signals that way. Change your thinking, and you can change your feelings as well.

In the early 1950s, psychologist Albert Ax conducted a series of clever experiments at Boston Psychiatric Hospital to compare the symptoms of people who were first made afraid and later made angry (or vice versa). He concluded that the symptoms of fear resembled the effects of adrenaline, while anger reflected a mixture of adrenaline and noradrenaline, hormones of the adrenal glands.

But if we look more closely at the study, we see that the differences between fear and anger that Dr. Ax thought he found were actually minimal. The same bodily response occurred in fear as in anger, differing only in degree.

Today more accurate tests show that adrenaline is not just ''the anger hormone,'' but an all-purpose fuel. It is the energy behind most of our emotions: fear and anger, but also excitement, anxiety, jealousy, even joy. Adrenaline and, to a varying extent, noradrenaline provide the *feeling* of a feeling: that tingle, arousal, excitement, energy. They act throughout the body, stimulating the heart, dilating coronary vessels, constricting blood vessels in the intestines and shutting off digestion. This is why, when you are excited, scared, furious, or wildly in love, you don't want to eat.

Adrenaline and noradrenaline set the stage for strong emotions, whose content, however, will depend largely on your background and the situation. Some people learn to associate physiological excitement with the positive sensations of risk, fun and power; for others, a rush of adrenaline signifies fear, danger and powerlessness. Without psychological perceptions, arousal has no content; it's that sinking feeling in your gut or the nervous palpitations of your heart. Are you angry or anxious? Are you sick or just in love? Your body alone won't tell you.

For example: One afternoon, as I was leaving the subway at rush hour, trudging wearily up the stairs, I felt a hand brush my rear. It was an ambiguous gesture, but by the time I'd climbed the stairs, I had convinced myself that a pervert was behind me. The hand struck again—this time unmistakably a pinch. In a fury, I spun around, umbrella poised to strike a blow for womanhood and self-respect . . . and stared face-to-face at my husband. The realization— "This man is a friend with a rotten sense of humor, not a pervert"—transformed my anger and apprehension into delight.

Because the same hormones can fuel different feelings, our emotions tend to occur in bunches, like bananas. We rarely feel one emotion or another, but one emotion *and* another. Our language discriminates between these feelings, implying that each exists by itself. In some African languages, by contrast, one word represents both anger and sadness—which may be closer to emotional truth.

CIVILITY CAN BE HEALTHY

A major misconception is that anger is a thing that we must get out of the body or else it will fester and make us sick. ("I don't get angry," Woody Allen tells Diane Keaton in *Manhattan.* "I grow a tumor instead.") "Suppressed anger" has been unjustifiably blamed for a host of ills, including ulcers, hypertension, back pain and cancer.

These psychosomatic theories have brought on a fad for the "honest," if hostile, ventilation of emotion. One man I know rationalizes his 12-year-old son's temper tantrums by saying they will ward off ulcers and heart attacks later on (he assumes the boy will make it unscathed to manhood). In fact, there is no good evidence that stifling the impulse to scream is physically harmful, any more than is holding back the urge to laugh.

Now I'm not arguing that persistent anger is good for you. Any chronic condition—anger, anxiety, stress—that pumps out high levels of adrenaline and noradrenaline without relief is unhealthy in the long run. For example, according to Dr. Charles Spielberger, anger can increase the risk of coronary heart disease; but it doesn't matter whether you let anger out or suppress it. What's bad for your health is chronic, intense anger.

Suppressing anger is not desirable if you mutter curses to yourself and keep your hormones pumping. But simply ventilating anger won't help either, any more than scratching an itch will cure the eczema that's causing it. Because anger is a social response to a stressful situation or a personal problem, it's your circumstances, not your biology, that determine what you "should" do about it.

I take all this as good news. We can decide to accept our anger as an instrument, a tool of rational and responsible behavior. We may learn to transform the energy of anger into directed effort, physical work, the healing mood of humor. Finally, if we are not helpless hostages to our biology, it means we can take responsibility for our emotions and how we act on them. We can't plead that the devil (or Henry) made us do it.

The Measure of Love

by Robert Sternberg

"Suddenly you're in love" goes a popular song, which proclaimed that love just happens and is a great mystery. Love has been, for the most part, as elusive in the study of psychology as the song says. Psychologists have had a most frustrating time trying to capture a phenomenon that popular lore tells us may be uncategorizable.

On one hand, some researchers have focused on what attracts people to each other. This approach has sometimes been so tightly systematic that it lost sight of the true splendor of love. On the other hand, researchers who have focused on the experiences of love have been vague and diffuse.

Few psychologists have been successful in balancing these diverse perspectives. Robert Sternberg's work is one of those, though, that comes the closest to that balance. In his effort to take a measure of love, Sternberg captures the essence of the actual experience of love—not just of the passionate sort but of all kinds.

LOVE IS ONE of the most important things in life. People have been known to lie, cheat, steal and kill for it. Even in the most materialistic of societies, it remains one of the few things that cannot be bought. And it has puzzled poets, philosophers, writers, psychologists and practically everyone else who has tried to understand it. Love has been called a disease, a neurosis, a projection of competitiveness with a parent and the enshrinement of suffering

160

and death. For Freud, it arose from sublimated sexuality; for Harlow, it had its roots in the need for attachment; for Fromm, it was the expression of care, responsibility and respect for another. But despite its elusiveness, love can be measured!

My colleagues and I were interested both in the structure of love and in discovering what leads to success or failure in romantic relationships. We found that love has a basic, stable core; despite the fact that people experience differences in their feelings for the various people they love, from parents to lovers to friends, in each case their love actually has the same components. And in terms of what makes love work, we found that how a man thinks his lover feels about him is much more important than how she actually feels. The same applies to women.

When we investigated the structure of love, the first question Susan Grajek, a former Yale graduate student, and I looked at was the most basic one: What is love, and is it the same thing from one kind of relationship to another? We used two scales: One, called a love scale, was constructed by Zick Rubin, a Brandeis University psychologist; the other was devised by George Levinger and his colleagues at the University of Massachusetts. Levinger's measures the extent to which particular feelings and actions characterize a relationship. Rubin designed his 13-item scale to measure what he believes to be three critical aspects of love: affiliative and dependent need for another, predisposition to help another, and exclusiveness and absorption in the relationship with another.

Consider three examples of statements Rubin used, substituting for the blanks the name of a person you presently love or have loved in the past. For each statement, rate on a one (low) to nine (high) scale the extent to which the statement characterizes your feelings for your present or previous love.

"If I could never be with_____, I would feel miserable." "If_____were feeling badly, my first duty would be to cheer him (her) up." "I feel very possessive toward_____."

The first statement measures affiliative and dependent need, the second, predisposition to help, and the third, exclusiveness and absorption.

VALIDATING THE SCORE

We asked participants to fill out the Rubin and Levinger scales as they applied to their mother, father, sibling closest in age, best friend of the same sex and lover. Thirty-five men and 50 women from the greater New Haven area took part. They ranged in age from 18 to 70 years, with an average age of 32. Although most were Caucasian, they were of a variety of religions, had diverse family incomes and were variously single, married, separated and divorced.

To discover what love is, we applied advanced statistical techniques to our data and used the results to compare two kinds of conceptions, based on past research on human intelligence. Back in 1927, the British psychologist Charles Spearman suggested that underlying all of the intelligent things we do in our everyday lives is a single mental factor, which Spearman called G, or general ability. Spearman was never certain just what this general ability was, but he suggested it might be what he referred to as "mental energy." Opposing Spearman was another British psychologist, Godfrey Thomson, who argued that intelligence is not any one thing, such as mental energy, but, rather, many things, including habits, knowledge, processes and the like. Our current knowledge about intelligence suggests that Thomson, and not Spearman, was on the right track.

We thought these two basic kinds of models might apply to love as well as to intelligence. According to the first, Spearmanian kind of conception, love is a single, undifferentiated and indivisible entity. One cannot decompose love into its aspects, because it has none. Rather, it is a global emotion, or emotional energy, that resists analysis. According to the second, Thomsonian kind of conception, love may feel like a single, undifferentiated emotion, but it is in fact one best understood in terms of a set of separate aspects.

Our data left us with no doubt about which conception was correct: Love may feel, subjectively, like a single emotion, but it is in fact composed of a number of different components. The Thomsonian model is thus the better one for understanding love as well as intelligence.

Although no one questionnaire or even combination of questionnaires is likely to reveal all the components of love, we got a good sense of what some of them are: (1) Promoting the welfare of the loved one. (2) Experiencing happiness with the loved one. (3) High regard for the loved one. (4) Being able to count on the loved one in times of need. (5) Mutual understanding of the loved one. (6) Sharing oneself and one's things with the loved one. (7) Receiving emotional support from the loved one. (8) Giving emotional support to the loved one. (9) Intimate communication with the loved one. (10) Valuing the loved one in one's own life.

These items are not necessarily mutually exclusive, but they do show the variety and depth of the various components of love. Based on this list, we may characterize love as a set of feelings, cognitions and motivations that contribute to communication, sharing and support.

To our surprise, the nature of love proved to be pretty much the same from one close relationship to another. Many things that matter in people's relationship with their father, for example, also matter in their relationship with a lover. Thus, it is not quite correct to say, as people often do, that our love for our parents is completely different from our love for our lover. There is a basic core of love that is constant over different close relationships.

But there are three important qualifications: First, when we asked whom people love and how much, we found that the amounts of love people feel in different close relationships may vary widely. Furthermore, our results differed slightly for men and women. Men loved their lover the most and their sibling closest in age the least. Their best friend of the same sex followed the lover, and their mother and father were in the middle. Women loved their lover and best friend of the same sex about equally. They, too, loved their sibling closest in age the least, with their mother and father in the middle. But whereas men did not show a clear tendency to prefer either their mother or their father, women showed more of a tendency to prefer their mother. These results are good news for lovers and same-sex best friends but bad news for siblings close in age.

Second, the weights or importances of the various aspects of love may differ from one relationship to another. Receiving emotional support or intimate communication may play more of a role in love for a lover than in love for a sibling.

And third, the concomitants of love—what goes along with it—may differ from one relationship to another. Thus, the sexual attraction that accompanies love for a lover is not likely to accompany love for a sibling.

We did not obtain clear evidence for sex differences in the structure of love for men versus women. However, other evidence suggests that there are at least some. George Levinger and his colleagues, for example, investigated what men and women found to be most rewarding in romantic relationships. They discovered that women found disclosure, nurturance, togetherness and commitment, and self-compromise to be more rewarding than men did. Men, in contrast, found personal separateness and autonomy to be more rewarding than women did. There is also evidence from other investigators to suggest that women find love to be a more integral, less separable part of sexual intercourse than men do.

Some people seem to be very loving and caring people, and others don't. This observation led us to question whether some people are just "all-around" lovers. The results were clear: There is a significant "love cluster" within the nuclear family in which one grows up. Loving one member of this family a lot is associated with a tendency to love other members of the family a lot, too. Not loving a member of this family much is associated with a tendency not to love others in the family much, either.

ROMANTIC PREDICTION

These results do not generalize at all outside the nuclear family. How much one loves one's mother predicts how much one loves one's father, but not how much one loves one's lover. So people who haven't come from a loving family may still form loving relationships outside the family—though coming from a loving family doesn't guarantee that you will be successful in love.

Having learned something about the nature of love, we were interested in determining whether we could use love-scale scores to predict and even understand what leads to success or failure in romantic relationships. Because our first study was not directly addressed to this question, Michael Barnes, a Yale graduate student, and I conducted a second study that specifically addressed the role of love in the success of romantic relationships.

In our study, each of the members of 24 couples involved in romantic relationships filled out the love scales of Rubin and Levinger. But they filled them out in four different ways, expressing: (1) Their feelings toward the other member of the couple. (2) Their perceptions of the feelings of the other member of the couple toward them. (3) Their feelings toward an ideal other member of such a couple. (4) Their perceptions of the feelings of an ideal other member of such a couple toward them. These questions dealt with two basic distinctions: the self versus the actual other and the actual other versus an ideal.

The participants, all of whom were students in college or graduate school and none of whom were married, were asked to think in terms of a realistic ideal that would be possible in their lives, rather than in terms of some fantasy or Hollywood ideal that could exist only in movies or other forms of fiction. In addition to filling out the love-scale questionnaires, participants also answered questions regarding their satisfaction and happiness with their present romantic relationship.

BETWEEN REAL AND IDEAL

We compared two different conceptions of how love might affect satisfaction in a romantic relationship. According to the first conception, level of satisfaction is directly related to the amount of love the couple feel: The more they love each other, the more satisfied they will be with their relationship. According to the second and more complex conception, the relation between love and satisfaction is mediated by one's ideal other. In particular, it is the congruence between the real and the ideal other that leads to satisfaction. As the discrepancy between the real and ideal other increases, so does one's dissatisfaction with the relationship.

Consider two couples: Bob and Carol and Ted and Alice. Suppose that Bob loves Carol just as much as Ted loves Alice (at least, according to their scores on the love scales). According to the first conception, this evidence would contribute toward the prediction that, other things being equal, Bob and Ted are equally satisfied with their relationships. But now suppose that Bob, inlike Ted, has an extremely high ideal: He expects much more from Carol than Ted expects from Alice. According to the second conception, Ted will be happier than Bob, because Bob will feel less satisfied.

These two conceptions of what counts in a relationship are not mutually exclusive, and our data show that both matter about equally for the success of the relationship. Thus, it is important to remember that although love contributes to a successful relationship, any relationship can be damaged by unrealistically high ideals. At the other extreme, a relationship that perhaps does not deserve to last may go on indefinitely because of low ideals.

In addition to love and the ideal, we found that both how a person feels about his lover and how he thinks she feels about him matter roughly equally to satisfaction in a relationship. But there are three important qualifications.

First, the correlation between the love-scale scores of the two members of a couple is not, on the average, particularly high. In many relationships, the two members do not love each other equally.

Second, it is a person's *perception* of the way his lover feels about him, rather than the way the lover actually feels, that matters most for one's happiness in a relationship. In other words, relationships may succeed better than one might expect, given their asymmetry, because people sometimes systematically delude themselves about the way their partners feel. And it is this perception of the other's feelings rather than the other's actual feelings that keeps the relationship going.

Third, probably the single most important variable in the success of the relationships we studied was the difference between the way a person would ideally *like* his partner to feel about him and the way he thinks she really does feel about him. We found that this difference is actually more important to the success of a relationship than a person's own feelings: No variable we studied was more damaging to the success of a romantic relationship than perceived under- or overinvolvement by the partner.

Why might this be so? We believe it is because of the ultimate fate of relationships in which one partner is unhappy with the other's level of involvement. If a person perceives his partner to be underinvolved, he may try to bring her closer. If she does not want to come closer, she may react by pulling away. This leads to redoubled efforts to bring her closer, which in turn lead her to move away. Eventually, the relationship does.

All our results suggest that the Rubin and Levinger scales could be useful tools to diagnose whether relationships are succeeding or not. There is one important and sobering fact to keep in mind, though: Scores from a liking scale devised by Zick Rubin were even better predictors of satisfaction in romantic relationships than were scores from the love scales, especially for women. Thus, no matter how much a person loves his partner, the relationship is not likely to work out unless he likes her as well.

AN END TO A MYSTERY?

Despite its complexity, love can be measured and studied by scientific means. With a national divorce rate approaching 50 percent and actually exceeding this figure in some locales, it is more important than ever that we understand what love is, what leads to its maintenance and what leads to its demise. Scientists studying love have the opportunity not only to make a contribution to pure science but to make a contribution to our society. At the very least, the study of love can suggest the cause, if not the cure, for certain kinds of failed relationships.

IV.

MIND AND BODY

Psychological Hardiness

by Maya Pines

The modern world is afflicted by what have been called "diseases of civilization." Maladies like heart disease, seem to be the toll our bodies pay for the pace of life today. Stress takes its toll on the body by activating the fight-or-flight response, a pattern of readiness for trouble that served us well in early evolution, but which modern life advises far too often. An increased heart rate, blood pressure, and metabolism are well and good when there is a bear lurking about, but all too often it is a deadline looming that causes it.

Researchers have shown that the changes of life—getting a new job, marrying or divorcing, moving, and the like—all lead to stress. And the more of such stressors, the less well the body is likely to do. But the picture is not all bad. Some people are resistant to stress in the face of life's hurly-burly; in fact, they seem to thrive on it as a challenge to be met rather than as something overwhelming to avoid. The trait that distinguishes these people, as Maya Pines elaborates in the following article, is hardiness: an openness to change; a feeling of involvement in whatever they're doing; and a sense of control over their lives.

IT'S TRUE, STRESS researchers will tell you, that tax accountants become particularly susceptible to heart attacks around April 15th—the deadline for tax returns. It is also true that air-traffic controllers, who have to make split-second decisions affecting many lives, develop hypertension with four times the frequency of people in other occupations. And it's true that the death of a close relative statistically increases one's own chances of becoming ill or dying soon afterward; in England, for instance, some 5,000 widowers who were studied for six months after the death of their wives had a mortality rate 40 percent higher than the average for men of their age.

Dozens of studies in the past two decades have shown that people who are in high-stress occupations or who have suffered a major setback in their lives run an unusually high risk of disease. Despite the increased risk, however, such disease is not inevitable. As a small group of researchers is now emphasizing, large numbers of people do not fall sick under stress.

Thus, many people work night and day at high-powered jobs without becoming ill, even while others who have seemingly easier occupations develop ulcers, colitis, hypertension, or heart disease. Some people survive even the horrors of a concentration camp, while others cannot cope with everyday problems without falling apart, mentally or physically.

What distinguishes the people who stay healthy? This is one of the most absorbing questions in medical science today. A good heredity surely helps. But investigators in the field of behavioral medicine are only starting to learn how various kinds of behavior, such as the restless striving and impatience of so-called Type A's, are related to such illnesses as hypertension or coronary disease. Though the research is in its infancy, we now have a few clues to the psychological qualities and social circumstances that may account for resilience to stress.

At the University of Chicago, Suzanne C. Kobasa and Salvatore R. Maddi have defined some of the characteristics of what they call "hardiness." Stress-resistant people, they say, have a specific set of attitudes toward life—an openness to change, a feeling of involvement in whatever they are doing, and a sense of control over events. In the jargon of psychological research, they score high on "challenge" (viewing change as a challenge rather than a threat), "commitment" (the opposite of alienation), and "control" (the opposite of powerlessness). These attitudes have a profound effect on health, according to the two psychologists, who have been studying the incidence of life stresses and illnesses among hundreds of business executives, lawyers, army officers, and retired people.

Unlike researchers in psychosomatic medicine in the 1950s, who attributed much illness to patients' inner conflicts, Kobasa and Maddi have been looking at how people interact with specific aspects of their environment. In this sense, they follow in the footsteps of Richard S. Lazarus of the University of California at Berkeley, the psychologist whose 1966 book, *Psychological Stress and the Coping Process,* emphasized that stress resides neither in the person nor in the situation alone, but depends on how the person appraises particular events. (See "Positive Denial: The Case for Not Facing Reality," *Psychology Today,* November 1979.) Kobasa and Maddi have been trying to find out what determines such appraisals—as well as the consequences of these appraisals. Interestingly, their subjects' answers vary somewhat according to the unwritten rules of behavior within different occupations.

Kobasa's work began with a study of 670 middle- and upper-level managers at an Illinois public utility—all of them white Protestant males, college graduates, between 40 and 49 years old, married, with two children. As part of her doctoral dissertation, Kobasa first asked them to describe on checklists all of the stressful life events and illnesses they had experienced in the previous three years. Next she picked out two groups for comparison: 200 executives who scored above average both on stress and on illness, and another 126 with equally high total stress scores who had scored below average on illness. Members of both groups filled out detailed personality questionnaires.

Kobasa had defined the three criteria of hardiness in advance as a working hypothesis; her premises were drawn from existential psychology, whose principal exponents in the United States include Maddi, Rollo May, and Viktor Frankl. Existential psychology postulates that a feeling of engagement and of control over one's life is essential to mental health. Both Maddi and Kobasa practice a form of psychotherapy based on it.

When Kobasa analyzed the Illinois utility managers' answers in 1977, she found that the high-stress/low-illness men stood out in all three categories of hardiness: they were much more actively involved in their work and social lives than those who became sick under stress; they were more oriented to challenge; and they felt more in control of events. Those were exciting findings. As Kobasa explained, "The mechanism whereby stressful life events produce illness is presumably physiological. Yet whatever this physiological response is, the personality characteristics of hardiness may cut into it, decreasing the likelihood of breakdown into illness."

Nevertheless, this study was open to question. Might not the executives' negative view of themselves and their lives be a *result* rather than the *cause* of the illness? "What we were seeing was just the tip of the iceberg," recalls Maddi, who was Kobasa's thesis adviser. To get more reliable answers, various groups of persons would have to be studied *before* they became ill and then followed for a few years to see what happened to them.

Maddi joined forces with Kobasa in a longitudinal project of this sort. He was deeply interested in the problem because he felt that much of the advice being given to people on the basis of existing stress research was misleading. He had been particularly upset by an article appearing in a women's magazine in 1972 that reported on the widely used stress scale developed by psychiatrists Thomas Holmes and Richard Rahe called the Schedule of Recent Life Events. Used with their Social Readjustment Rating Scale, the Holmes-Rahe test measures and gives specific weight to all the recent changes in a person's life—and assumes that any major change is stressful. Marriage, for example, rates 50 points on their scale, halfway up the scale from 0 to 100. The most severe stress of all, the death of a spouse, rates 100. The magazine published a checklist with which readers could add up their own stress scores. What incensed Maddi was the advice that came with it.

"It said that if your stress score is above 200, you have a 60 percent probability of being ill within the following year," Maddi recalls angrily. "And if your score is above 300, you have an 80 percent chance of falling sick. So if you want to stay healthy, avoid further stress. Don't even drive on the Los Angeles freeways, and don't have a confrontation with your spouse, because it might kill you!"

This baleful view of change contradicted some of Maddi's own research, which focused on the beneficial effects of novelty and surprise. He had not studied extreme circumstances, such as a death in the family or being sent to a concentration camp. But he had evidence that minor changes in people's routines were stimulating and led to growth. Maddi continues to believe that whether novelty is good or bad for a person depends on how it is experienced. He remains adamantly opposed to the theory that stress should be avoided whenever possible.

In this view, he would be supported by the father of stress research, Hans Selye, who has argued that certain kinds of stress—which he calls "eustress"—are good for people. Selye, who practically invented the concept of stress about 40 years ago, has described the body's physical response to it in numerous experiments. But since then, he has pointed out that the racing pulse, the quickened breathing, and the accelerated heart rate that betray stress also occur during times of great joy. A certain amount of stress is essential to well-being, though people's requirements will vary, Selye argues. In a 1978 interview ("On the Real Benefits of Eustress," *Psychology Today*, March 1978), Selye suggested that there are two main types of human beings: "race horses," who are only happy with a vigorous, fast-paced lifestyle, and "turtles," who need peace, quiet, and a tranquil environment. The trick is to find the level of stress that suits one best, he said.

Longitudinal studies of stress and disease are very rare. Most studies rely almost entirely on subjects' recollections of events and illnesses that occurred in the past. The few studies that look forward generally focus on college students and follow up on them for only a few weeks—hardly enough time to allow much stress to develop, let alone a related illness (according to Kobasa and Maddi, such illnesses often follow stress after a six-month lag). Furthermore, these studies seldom try to relate personality traits to the stress and disease, as Kobasa and Maddi did.

In their longitudinal study, Kobasa and Maddi collected information on 259 executives at three different times over a period of two years. They first analyzed the men's personalities and hardiness, based on questionnaires that pulled together a number of items which they had developed, plus some items from other scales relating to challenge, commitment, and control. They then asked the men to fill out a version of the Holmes-Rahe test and another questionnaire that asked for information on serious illnesses. To score high on the illness survey, a person would have to report far more serious illnesses than headaches or colds. A cold rated only 20 points, and even six colds a year would add up to only 120 points. By contrast, an ulcer rated 500 points, and a heart attack 855 points.

The results at the end of two years showed clearly that people whose attitudes toward life could be rated high on challenge, commitment, and control remained healthier than the others. Despite a high score on stressful life events, they had a total illness rating of only 510 for two years, compared with an illness rating of 1,080 for men who scored low on hardiness. "You see the striking degree to which a personality of the hardy type protects people who are under stress," says Maddi. "It could decrease your chance of being ill by 50 percent."

The healthier group's attitude towards change (challenge) appeared to be their most important protective factor, closely followed by commitment. When a man loses his job, for example, he can see it either as a catastrophe—an irreplaceable loss that shows he is unworthy and predicts his downfall—or as an experience that falls within the range of risks he accepted when he took the job. In some cases, he may even view it as an opportunity to find a new career that is better suited to his abilities. Similarly, when an elderly couple is forced to sell their home because it has become too expensive and too difficult to keep, they can view the change either as a tragedy or as a chance to find housing that is safer and perhaps closer to their children.

To rate people on challenge, Kobasa and Maddi asked them to what extent they agreed with statements such as, "Boredom is fatal," "A satisfying life is a series of problems; when one is solved, one moves on to the next problem," or, "I would be willing to give up some financial security to be able to change from one job to another if something interesting came along." People who strongly agreed with those statements would rate high on the challenge scale. However, those who agreed with the following statements would rate low: "I don't believe in sticking to something when there is little chance of success," or, "If a job is dangerous, that makes it all the better." The first of these two statements reflects a lack of persistence in the face of challenge. The second represents what Kobasa calls "adventurousness," a form of excessive risk-taking that is typical of people who cannot feel really involved in anything unless it is extreme—for example, a fascist movement. Those who score high on challenge are willing to take some risks, but not excessive risks, she explains.

Kobasa points out that such differences in cognitive appraisal can make an enormous difference in how people respond to events. Those who score high on challenge are much more likely to transform events to their advantage and thus reduce their level of stress. In contrast, people who are low in hardiness may try avoidance tactics—for example, distracting themselves by watching more TV, drinking too much, taking tranquilizers or other drugs, or sleeping more. These are self-defeating tactics, since the real source of stress does not go away. Instead, says Kobasa, "it remains in the mind unassimilated and unaltered, a likely subject matter for endless rumination and subconscious preoccupation"—and it continues to exert its debilitating effects.

The healthy group also rated high on commitment, meaning—as Kobasa and Maddi define the word—that they *engaged* life rather than hanging back on the fringes of it. On Kobasa's tests, the hardy men strongly disagreed with statements such as, "Most of life is wasted in meaningless activity," or, "I am better off when I keep to myself." They took an active role in their work and family lives and believed that their activities were both interesting and important. The executives in the healthy group also believed they could have a real impact on their surroundings. They disagreed with such statements as, "No matter how hard you work, you never really seem to reach your goals," or, "This world is run by a few people in power, and there's not much the little guy can do about it." This gave the healthy executives a high score on control, the third aspect of hardiness.

In order to see whether the same psychological characteristics are equally protective for other kinds of people, Kobasa has also conducted similar studies of 157 lawyers and 75 army captains—all white Protestant males, college graduates, and married with two children, just like the business executives. She is now following up on 2,000 women patients reached through their gynecologists, as well as a group of men who are early retirees.

To her surprise, in the sample of lawyers there was no relationship whatever between stressful events and physical illness. The men who fell sick were often those who had scored lowest on stress, and vice versa. Some of the lawyers did show a relationship between high stress and a variety of psychiatric symptoms: they had trouble sleeping, suffered anxiety, or became severely depressed. Nevertheless, out of the 157 lawyers who had stress scores above 300 (which Holmes and Rahe would call evidence of a major life crisis), 24 reported no psychiatric illness. In line with Kobasa's previous findings, these 24 lawyers were distinguished by higher scores on the commitment scale.

In trying to explain why the lawyers did not become physically ill under stress while the business executives did, Kobasa examined the two groups' contrasting views of stress. Lawyers tend to believe that they perform best under pressure. Their whole training—as advocates, adversaries, and cross-examiners—conditions them to produce, confront, and deal with stress. And despite all the stresses they are exposed to, they are reputed to lead very long, productive lives. The myth that lawyers thrive under stress seems to become a self-fulfilling prophecy.

Business executives, on the other hand, are constantly told that stress can kill them. As Kobasa puts it, the up-and-coming executive who is felled by a heart attack before the age of 50 is described as "the classical stress victim." Unfortunately, she says, "many business corporations, in their eagerness to set up stress-management programs, gyms on their top floors, and cardiac units in the medical department, seem to be buying into this negative, narrow view of stress. The executive is told that stress is harmful and that attempts will be made to reduce it; but in the meantime, use biofeedback or the exercise machine to ready your body for the assault." According to Kobasa, the executive's social group thus provides little support for a view of stress as positive or controllable. While a lawyer handling a difficult case might be congratulated for it by colleagues ("Gee, it must be really exciting to work on; it'll move you up in the firm"), a business executive who feels under pressure may receive only sympathy or be advised to work out frustrations in the gym.

Another professional difference came to light in Kobasa's study of army officers. In response to stress, these officers fell ill, mentally or physically, far more frequently than the business executives. Kobasa speculates that this might be because the army is a total institution, from which there is little escape; for military officers, the stresses that occur at work cannot easily be isolated from the rest of their lives. She also found that the army officers scored lower on commitment than either the business executives or the lawyers.

One aspect of hardiness that had proved particularly protective for the business executives—openness to change and challenge—actually led to more physical illness among the army officers. Again, Kobasa can only speculate on the reason. In the post-Vietnam army, she suggests, there is no room for people who have a taste for novelty or challenge. "It may be that to want interesting experiences is to want what the peacetime army is not providing right now,'' she adds. In this environment, those who seek only security appear to be healthier.

Such differences suggest complexities in the question of what produces stress resistance. As Hans Selye was the first to point out, many factors affect one's reaction to stress: physiological predispositions, early childhood experiences, personality, and social resources. Kobasa's findings imply that specific aspects of personality interact with specific aspects of the social environment in many ways, leading to more or less resilence. For that reason, researchers need to know a great deal more about the expectations and social pressures within different groups.

Meanwhile, other investigators have been studying the role of social supports such as family, friends, colleagues, and wider networks in protecting people from illness. The strength of these supports is closely tied in with one's personality and commitment. According to some studies, the most potent protection of all may be the closeness of a spouse.

Recently 10,000 married men who were 40 years of age or older were followed for five years in Israel. The researchers, Jack H. Medalie and Uri Goldbourt, wanted to find out how new cases of angina pectoris—a form of heart attack—develop. They assessed each man's risk factors for heart disease and then asked, among other items on a questionnaire, ''Does your wife show you her love?'' The answer turned out to have enormous predictive power. Among high-risk men—men who showed elevated blood cholesterol, electrocardiographic abnormalities, and high levels of anxiety—fewer of those who had loving and supportive wives developed angina pectoris than did those whose wives were colder (52 per 1,000 versus 93 per 1,000). It remains unclear, however, to what extent such love and support depend on the husband's personality characteristics.

Another Israeli researcher, Brooklyn-born Aaron Antonovsky, a professor of medical sociology at Ben-Gurion University of the Negev, became interested in resistance to disease as a result of his work with survivors of Nazi concentration camps. Originally, he was only trying to find out how 1,150 women of different ethnic origins had adapted to menopause. In the course of this study, he happened to include the following question: "During World War II, were you in a concentration camp?" Of the 287 Central European women who participated in the study, 77 said yes. This presented Antonovsky with an unusual, randomly selected subgroup of women whom he could compare with controls.

Not surprisingly, he found that the concentration-camp survivors, as a group, were more poorly adapted than the others on all his measures of physical and emotional health. What struck him, however, was another observation: a number of women among the concentration-camp survivors were well adapted by any standard, even though their proportion was relatively small. "Despite having lived through the most inconceivably inhuman experience," Antonovsky wrote, "some women were reasonably healthy and happy, had raised families, worked, had friends, and were involved in community activities."

Whence their strength? he asked. And what about the countless members of minorities or immigrants who have survived atrocious conditions in many countries? What about the poor everywhere? "Despite the fact that the poor are screwed at every step of the way, they are not all sick and dying," he noted. In fact, the human condition is inherently stressful. Stress cannot be avoided by human beings ("the bugs are smarter," he comments). Then how do any of us manage to stay healthy?

To answer this question, Antonovsky shifted his research focus from specific stressors to what he called "generalized resistance resources"—characteristics of the person, the group, or the environment that can encourage more effective tension management. Knowledge and intelligence offer such a resource, he believes, for they allow people to see many ways of dealing with their difficulties—and to choose, when possible, the most effective means. A strong ego identity is another vital resource, he postulates.

And so is commitment to a stable and continuing social network.

Antonovsky cites a nine-year study of 7,000 persons in Alameda County, California, which showed that people with many social ties—such as marriage, close friends and relatives, church membership, and other group associations—have far lower mortality rates than others. The study, by Lisa Berkman, an epidemiologist now at Yale University, found that even men in their fifties who seemed to be at high risk because of a very low socioeconomic status, but who scored high on an index of social networks, lived far longer than high-status men with low social-network scores.

Similarly, the social support provided by life in a kibbutz seems to protect children against the anxiety that one would expect as a result of prolonged bombardment. In 1975, at a time of heavy Arab shelling in certain parts of the country, an Israeli researcher compared the anxiety levels of children in several kibbutz and urban communities, in both bombed and tranquil areas. Although urban children who had lived through prolonged bombardment had higher anxiety levels than those from urban areas who had been spared, the kibbutz children did not show any such difference: their anxiety levels were low whether or not their kibbutz had been shelled. The researchers reported that at times of shelling, the kibbutz children were calmly led to shelters that were familiar to them, where educational programs and social life went on pretty much as usual. On the other hand, the urban children, accustomed to living in family units, were suddenly taken to alien and somewhat disordered community shelters; their daily routine was upset. Their higher anxiety level could be explained by the disruption of their normal social network.

In extreme cases, the loss of one's social ties can kill, Antonovsky points out. The phenomenon of voodoo death among tribes in Australia, Central Africa, and the Caribbean is probably the best illustration. When the tribe decides to punish one of its members for breaking a taboo, a witch doctor points a magic bone at him and recites some incantations which place him under a spell of death. ''The man who discovers that he is being 'boned' is a pitiable sight," wrote an explorer in Australia, as quoted by the Harvard physiologist Walter Cannon. "He sways backwards and falls to the ground . . . he writhes as if in mortal agony and, covering his face with his hands, begins to moan. After a while he becomes very composed and crawls to his wurley [hut]. From this time onward he sickens and frets . . . his death is only a matter of a comparatively short time."

In Cannon's view, the primary factor in the victim's disintegration is the withdrawal of tribal support. Once the bone is pointed, his fellow tribesmen give him up for dead—and in his isolation, he has no alternative but to die. His heart becomes exhausted by overstimulation, his blood pressure drops calamitously, and his vital functions cease. Much the same appears to happen to some old people in this country when they are consigned to dismal nursing homes or back wards of hospitals, abandoned by the rest of the members of their "tribe."

A different approach to social ties, stress, and personality comes from the eminent Harvard psychologist David C. McClelland. People establish social ties for a variety of reasons, McClelland points out. Some are driven by a deep need for friendship, while others want prestige and power. McClelland and his associates have been studying the need for power for the past 30 years. Recently, they have examined its links to various kinds of stress and to illness.

The people who are most vulnerable to illness under stress, McClelland has found, are those who have a strong drive for power coupled with a high degree of inhibition about expressing it. Such persons "control their assertiveness in a socialized way and make good managers of people," McClelland says. But when they encounter difficulties, they become good candidates for hypertension and heart attacks. McClelland compares them to monkeys that were both enraged and restrained in an experiment by two British researchers; the monkeys developed heart disease as a result. "The equivalent at the personality level would appear to be a strong disposition to act assertively which is simultaneously checked by an inner desire for control and restraint,'' McClelland writes.

Last year, McClelland and John B. Jemmott III, compared the effects of various types of stress on 82 male and female college students who were rated according to their need for power, their degree of inhibition in expressing this need openly, their need for friendship (called "affiliation"), and their need for achievement. First, the students were given projective tests in which they wrote stories about six pictures that were presented to them (one shows a ship captain explaining something to someone, another a man and a woman seated at a table in a nightclub). These stories were then coded, according to criteria developed by McClelland, for the frequency with which they contained "power thoughts" (of having impact on others through aggression, persuasion, or helping, or of seeking prestige and recognition); "achievement thoughts" (of performing better or of unique accomplishments); "affiliative thoughts" (of establishing, maintaining, or repairing friendly relations with others); or evidence of inhibition, such as the frequency of the word "not," which McClelland has found to be a powerful indicator of restraint. (He believes his scoring methods are statistically reliable and permit him to measure such characteristics "objectively, much as one would identify leukocytes in a blood sample, to avoid the self-serving biases that distort the self-reports of motivations obtained from questionnaires.")

Next, the students filled out a Schedule of Life Change events for the previous six months, a checklist of mood states, and an illness inventory. The researchers then classified the life-change events according to the type of stress they represented: power/achievement stress (events that challenged or threatened the student's ability to perform powerfully or to impress others), affiliative stress (such as loss of a loved one), or other changes (such as a change in residence).

When all the information was analyzed, it turned out that the students' health or illness depended largely on whether the kinds of stress they had been exposed to impinged on their basic motivations. For example, a high degree of power/achievement stress had disastrous effects on students who scored high both in need for power and in inhibition. When students were motivated more by a need for affiliation, however, the same high degree of power/achievement stress was *not* associated with severe illness. "Generally speaking, when the stress is related to the dominant motive disposition in the individual, it is more likely to be associated with illness," McClelland concluded. He also found that students who were high in need for power but not too inhibited about expressing it seemed relatively protected against power/achievement stress: their illness score was less than half that of students who could not express their power urge openly. The less-inhibited students may have been much like the business tycoon who said, "I don't *get* ulcers; I *give* them."

According to McClelland, men who have a strong need for power are generally "more argumentative and aggressive; they engage more often in competitive sports; they are sexually more active; they accumulate prestige supplies, like fancy clothes and cars; and they tend to join organizations and ally themselves with others who have influence." This sounds suspiciously like the hard-driving, hostile, and aggressive Type A's who began to make headlines a few years ago. The Type-A pattern was popularized by cardiologists Meyer Friedman, and Ray H. Rosenman. In their 1974 book, *Type-A Behavior and Your Heart*, they reported on an eight-year study which showed that men with a Type-A pattern were twice as likely as the less-aggressive Type B's to develop coronary heart disease. McClelland has concluded that "the kind of behavior that has been described as Type A looks very much like that of persons who are high in the need for power, whose power motivation is inhibited, and who are also under power stress"—in other words, those he has found to be at greatest risk of stress-related illnesses.

McClelland is now running several experiments to find out how these men differ physiologically in their reaction to stress. One indication may come from an increase in the level of catecholamines and other hormones released by the sympathetic nervous system of Type A's under stress.

Another clue may be that some of McClelland's subjects have smaller numbers of certain white cells in their blood—the NK (natural killer) cells that are part of the immune system—and therefore may be more prone to infections and tumors.

Meanwhile, Kobasa and Maddi have started to analyze the actual health records of the executives in their study, so they need not rely entirely on self-reports of illness. The public utility involved gives its managers a free medical exam every year, including some 40 lab tests, and the two psychologists are now working with physicians from the University of Chicago Medical School and the company's medical department to sort out this treasure trove of records.

As behavioral scientists begin to ally themselves with physicians, both groups are becoming more aware of the intricacy of the processes that lead to health or disease. Much of the information about the effects of stress in the existing research literature is still fragmentary—or even contradictory. Depending on circumstances, for example, fear can make one's heart beat either faster or slower (as when the heart "stands still"). Even more surprisingly, some kinds of stress will make breast cancers grow in mice, but the same stresses will slow down or actually prevent the growth of breast cancers in rats.

Eventually, with more research, we may be able to mitigate some of the dangerous effects of stress. Meditation techniques and biofeedback appear to help some people. Behavioral methods can, within limits, assist in breaking certain habits that lead to stress. For instance, Type-A individuals have been taught to allot more time to each activity in their lives, thus slowing down their pace and reducing tension. But these approaches are palliatives that do not deal with the basic causes of stress—or with the way stress is appraised by different people.

More fundamental kinds of reeducation are also possible, Maddi and Kobasa believe. They place their confidence in existential psychotherapy. Whether this form of therapy, however sophisticated, can give people the sense of challenge, commitment, and control that they may need in order to maintain their physical and mental health remains to be proved. It is obviously far more difficult to change one's underlying character structure than to learn a few behavioral techniques. Nevertheless, Maddi remains optimistic. He hopes to show that people of all ages can be taught hardiness. "People's attitudes and outlooks are largely learned from experience," he maintains, and "therefore, they can be altered."

Right Brain, Left Brain: Fact and Fiction

by Jerre Levy

While there has been considerable research on the brain and its hemispheres in recent years, there have also been considerable misunderstandings in the popular realm. In "Right Brain, Left Brain: Fact and Fiction," Chicago bio-psychologist Jerre Levy tries to clear up some widespread misconceptions.

For example, people are not "left-brained" or "right-brained," contrary to popular belief. People use both sides of the brain all the time. There is no "on-off" switch; both lights burn simultaneously. Levy also maintains that the idea that the right brain is the source of creativity is a myth. It is not true that the left hemisphere controls logic and language and that the right solely controls intuition and creativity. Moreover, readers in education may wish to take special note: Levy finds that it is therefore impossible to educate one hemisphere at a time in a normal brain.

"I GUESS I'M MOSTLY a right-brain person . . . my left side doesn't work long enough for me to figure it out," concludes a character in a *Frank and Ernest* cartoon. "It's tough being a left-brained person . . . in a right-brained world," moans a youngster in the cartoon *Wee Pals*, after perusing a tome on the "psychology of consciousness."

The notion that we are "left brained" or "right brained" has become entrenched in the popular culture. And, based on a misinterpretation of the facts, a pop psychology myth has evolved, asserting that the left hemisphere of the brain controls logic and language, while the right controls creativity and intuition. One best-selling book even claimed to teach people how to draw better by training the right brain and bypassing the left. According to the myth, people differ in their styles of thought, depending on which half of the brain is dominant. Unfortunately, this myth is often represented as scientific fact. It is not.

As a researcher who has spent essentially her whole career studying how the two hemispheres relate to one another and to behavior, I feel obliged to set the record straight on what is known scientifically about the roles of the hemispheres. As it turns out, the brain's actual organization is every bit as interesting as the myth and suggests a far more holistic view of humankind.

People's fascination with relating mental function to brain organization goes back at least to Hippocrates. But it was René Descartes, in the 17th century, who came up with the notable and influential notion that the brain must act as a unified whole to yield a unified mental world. His specific mental mapping was wrong (he concluded that the pineal gland—now known to regulate biological rhythms in response to cycles of light and dark—was the seat of the soul, or mind). But his basic premise was on the right track and remained dominant until the latter half of the 19th century, when discoveries then reduced humankind to a half-brained species.

During the 1860s and 1870s, Paul Broca, a French neurologist, and Karl Wernicke, a German neurologist, reported that damage to the left cerebral hemisphere produced severe disorders of language, but that comparable damage to the right hemisphere did not. Neurology was never to be the same.

Despite their generally similar anatomies, the left and right cerebral hemispheres evidently had very different functions. Language appeared to be solely a property of the left side; the right hemisphere, apparently, was mute. The scientific world generalized this to conclude that the left hemisphere was dominant not only for language but for all psychological processes. The right hemisphere was seen as a mere relay station. Since each half of the brain is connected to and receives direct input from the opposite side of the body, the right hemisphere was needed to tell the left hemisphere what was happening on the left side of space and to relay messages to muscles on the body's left side. But the right hemisphere was only an unthinking automaton. From pre-19th century whole-brained creatures, we had become half-brained.

From the beginning, there were serious difficulties with the idea that the left hemisphere was the seat of humanity and that the right hemisphere played no role in thinking. In the 1880s, John Hughlings Jackson, a renowned English neurologist, described a patient with right-hemisphere damage who showed selective losses in certain aspects of visual perception—losses that did not appear with similar damage of the left hemisphere. He suggested that the right hemisphere might be just as specialized for visual perception as the left hemisphere was for language.

From the 1930s on, reports began to confirm Hughlings Jackson's findings. Patients with right-side damage had difficulties in drawing, using colored blocks to copy designs, reading and drawing maps, discriminating faces and in a variety of other visual and spatial tasks. These disorders were much less prevalent or serious in patients with left-hemisphere damage.

The investigators, quite aware of the implications of their findings, proposed that although the left hemisphere was specialized for language, the right hemisphere was specialized for many nonlinguistic processes. Nonetheless, these were voices in the wilderness, and their views hardly swayed the general neurological community. Until 1962, the prevalent view was that people had half a thinking brain.

Beginning in the early 1960s, Nobel Prize winner Roger W. Sperry and his colleagues and students demonstrated certain unusual characteristics in patients who, to control intractable epileptic seizures, had undergone complete surgical division of the corpus callosum, the connecting bridge between the two sides of the brain. These patients, like split-brain animals that Sperry had studied, couldn't communicate between the cerebral hemispheres. An object placed in the right hand (left hemisphere) could be named readily, but one placed in the left hand (nonverbal right hemisphere) could be neither named nor described. But these same patients could point to a picture of the object the left hand had felt. In other words, the right hemisphere knew what it felt, even if it could not speak.

Outside the laboratory, the split-brain patients were remarkably normal, and within the laboratory, each cerebral hemisphere seemed to be able to perceive, think and govern behavior, even though the two sides were out of contact. In later split-brain studies, a variety of tasks were devised to examine the specialized functions of each hemisphere. These showed that the right hemisphere was superior to the left in spatial tasks but was mute and deficient in verbal tasks such as decoding complex syntax, short-term verbal memory and phonetic analysis. In brief, the split-brain studies fully confirmed the inferences drawn from the earlier investigations of patients with damage to one hemisphere.

These findings were further expanded by psychologist Doreen Kimura and others, who developed behavioral methods to study how functions of the hemispheres differed in normal people. These involved presenting visual stimuli rapidly to either the left or right visual fields (and the opposite hemispheres). Normal right-handers were more accurate or faster in identifying words or nonsense syllables in the right visual field (left hemisphere) and in identifying or recognizing faces, facial expressions of emotion, line slopes or dot locations in the left visual field (right hemisphere).

Another method was "dichotic listening," in which two different sounds were presented simultaneously to the two ears. The right ear (left hemisphere) was better at identifying nonsense syllables, while the left ear (right hemisphere) excelled at identifying certain nonverbal sounds such as piano melodies or dog barks.

By 1970 or soon thereafter, the reign of the left brain was essentially ended. The large majority of researchers concluded that each side of the brain was a highly special-

ized organ of thought, with the right hemisphere predomi-
nant in a set of functions that complemented those of the
left. Observations of patients with damage to one side of
the brain, of split-brain patients and of normal individuals
yielded consistent findings. There could no longer be any
reasonable doubt: The right hemisphere, too, was a fully
human and highly complex organ of thought.

It was not long before the new discoveries found their
way into the popular media and into the educational community. Some mythmakers sought to sell the idea that
human beings had neither the whole and unified brain
described by Descartes, nor the half brain of Broca and
Wernicke, but rather two brains, each devoted to its own
tasks and operating essentially independently of the other.
The right hemisphere was in control when an artist painted
a portrait, but the left hemisphere was in control when the
novelist wrote a book. Logic was the property of the left
hemisphere, whereas creativity and intuition were properties of the right. Further, these two brains did not really
work together in the same person. Instead, some people
thought primarily with the right hemisphere, while others
thought primarily with the left. Finally, given the presumed absolute differences between hemispheres, it was
claimed that special subject matters and teaching strategies
had to be developed to educate one hemisphere at a time,
and that the standard school curriculums only educated the
"logical" left hemisphere.

Notice that the new two-brain myth was based on two
quite separate types of scientific findings. First was the
fact that split-brain patients showed few obvious symptoms
of their surgery in everyday life and far greater integrity of
behavior than would be seen if two regions within a hemisphere had been surgically disconnected. Thus, it was
assumed that each hemisphere could be considered to be
an independent brain.

Second, a great deal of research had demonstrated that
each hemisphere had its own functional "expertise," and
that the two halves were complementary. Since language
was the specialty of the left hemisphere, some people
concluded that any verbal activity, such as writing a novel,

depended solely on processes of the left hemisphere. Similarly, since visual and spatial functions were the specialties of the right hemisphere, some people inferred that any visuospatial activity, such as painting portraits, must depend solely on processes of that hemisphere. Even if thought and language were no longer synonymous, at least logic and language seemed to be. Since intuitions, by definition, are not accessible to verbal explanation, and since intuition and creativity seemed closely related, they were assigned to the right hemisphere.

Based, then, on the presumed independent functions of the two hemispheres, and on the fact that they differed in their specializations, the final leap was that different activities and psychological demands engaged different hemispheres while the opposite side of the brain merely idled along in some unconscious state.

The two-brain myth was founded on an erroneous premise: that since each hemisphere was specialized, each must function as an independent brain. But in fact, just the opposite is true. To the extent that regions are differentiated in the brain, they must integrate their activities. Indeed, it is precisely that integration that gives rise to behavior and mental processes greater than and different from each region's special contribution. Thus, since the central premise of the mythmakers is wrong, so are all the inferences derived from it.

What does the scientific evidence actually say? First, it says that the two hemispheres are so similar that when they are disconnected by split-brain surgery, each can function remarkably well, although quite imperfectly.

Second, it says that superimposed on this similarity are differences in the specialized abilities of each side. These differences are seen in the contrasting contributions each hemisphere makes to all cognitive activities. When a person reads a story, the right hemisphere may play a special role in decoding visual information, maintaining an integrated story structure, appreciating humor and emotional content, deriving meaning from past associations and understanding metaphor. At the same time, the left hemisphere plays a special role in understanding syntax, translating written words into their phonetic representations and deriving meaning from complex relations among word concepts and syntax. But there is no activity in which only one hemisphere is involved or to which only one hemisphere makes a contribution.

Third, logic is not confined to the left hemisphere. Patients with right-hemisphere damage show more major logical disorders than do patients with left-hemisphere damage. Some whose right hemisphere is damaged will deny that their left arm is their own, even when the physician demonstrates its connection to the rest of the body. Though paralyzed on the left side of the body, such patients will often make grandiose plans that are impossible because of paralysis and will be unable to see their lack of logic.

Fourth, there is no evidence that either creativity or intuition is an exclusive property of the right hemisphere. Indeed, real creativity and intuition, whatever they may entail, almost certainly depend on an intimate collaboration between hemispheres. For example, one major French painter continued to paint with the same style and skill after suffering a left-hemisphere stroke and loss of language. Creativity can remain even after right-hemisphere damage. Another painter, Lovis Corinth, after suffering right-hemisphere damage, continued to paint with a high level of skill, his style more expressive and bolder than before. In the musical realm, researcher Harold Gordon found that in highly talented professional musicians, both hemispheres were equally skilled in discriminating musical chords. Further, when researchers Steven Gaede, Oscar Parsons and James Bertera compared people with high and low musical aptitude for hemispheric asymmetries, high aptitude was associated with equal capacities of the two sides of the brain.

Fifth, since the two hemispheres do not function independently, and since each hemisphere contributes its special capacities to all cognitive activities, it is quite impossible to educate one hemisphere at a time in a normal brain. The right hemisphere is educated as much as the left in a literature class, and the left hemisphere is educated as much as the right in music and painting classes.

Finally, what of individual differences? There is both psychological and physiological evidence that people vary in the relative balance of activation of the two hemispheres. Further, there is a significant correlation between which hemisphere is more active and the relative degree of verbal or spatial skills. But there is no evidence that people are purely "left brained" or "right brained." Not even those with the most extremely asymmetrical activation between hemispheres think only with the more activated side. Rather, there is a continuum. The left hemisphere is more active in some people, to varying degrees, and verbal functioning is promoted to varying degrees. Similarly, in those with a more active right hemisphere, spatial abilities are favored. While activation patterns and cognitive patterns are correlated, the relationship is very far from perfect. This means that differences in activation of the hemispheres are but one of many factors affecting the way we think.

In sum, the popular myths are misinterpretations and wishes, not the observations of scientists. Normal people have not half a brain nor two brains but one gloriously differentiated brain, with each hemisphere contributing its specialized abilities. Descartes was, essentially, right: We have a single brain that generates a single mental self.

Seeing

by R. L. Gregory

In this concise article on vision, R. L. Gregory reminds us of the early roots of the study of perception in the tradition of gestalt psychology. In that tradition it was believed that an object could not be reduced to its separate elements alone: its overall configuration is what mattered most—the whole is greater than its parts. Thus, a triangle was more than three equally straight, individual lines; it was the unique relation-ship formed by those lines.

The gestalt perspective also suggested that every percep-tion required a "figure" and "ground"; i.e., a foreground and a backdrop. The juxtaposition of the two formed the impres-sion registered by the seeing eye. For example, the sky-scrapers of Manhattan, in conjunction with a sunset sky, create the silhoutted skyline we observe.

In explaining vision, Gregory uses some perceptual illu-sions to show that the eye is far more than a passive observer or receiver. On the contrary, the eye actively se-lects and filters what eventually reaches consciousness. A probing, active eye is at work in making sense of the visual world.

WE ARE SO familiar with seeing, that it takes a leap of imagination to realise that there are problems to be solved. But consider it. We are given tiny distorted upside-down images in the eyes, and we see separate solid objects in surrounding space. From the patterns of stimulation on the retinas we perceive the world of objects. This is nothing short of a miracle.

The eye is often described as like a camera, but it is the quite uncamera-like features of perception which are most interesting. The task of eye and brain is quite different from either a photographic or a television camera converting objects merely into images. There is a temptation, which must be avoided, to say that the eyes produce pictures in the brain. A picture in the brain suggests the need of some kind of internal eye to see it—but this would need a further eye to see *its* picture . . . and so on in an endless regress of eyes and pictures. This is absurd. What the eyes do is to feed the brain with information coded into neural activity—chains of electrical impulses—which by their code and the patterns of brain activity, represent objects. We may take an analogy from written language: the letters and words on this page have certain meanings, to those who know the language. They affect the reader's brain appropriately, but they are not pictures. When we look at something, the pattern of neural activity represents the object and to the brain *is* the object. No internal picture is involved.

Gestalt psychologists point to several important phenomena. They saw very clearly that there is a problem in how the mosaic of retinal stimulation gives rise to perception of objects. They particularly stressed the tendency for the perceptual system to group things into simple units. This is seen in an array of dots (Figure 1-1). Here the dots are in fact equally spaced, but there is a tendency to see, to "organise," the columns and rows as though there are separate objects. This is worth pondering, for in this example we have the essential problem of perception. We can see in ourselves the groping towards organising the sensory data into objects. If the brain were not continually on the look-out for objects, the cartoonist would have a hard time. But, in fact, all he has to do is present a few lines to the eye and we see a face, complete with an expression. The few lines are all that is required for the eye—the brain does the rest: seeking objects and finding them whenever possible. Sometimes we see objects which are not there: faces-in-the-fire, or the Man in the Moon.

Figure 1-2 is a joke figure which brings out the point clearly. Just a set of meaningless lines? No—it is a washerwoman with her bucket! Now look again: the lines are subtly different, almost solid—they are objects.

The seeing of objects involves many sources of information beyond those meeting the eye when we look at an object. It generally involves knowledge of the object derived from previous experience, and this experience is not limited to vision but may include the other senses; touch, taste, smell, hearing and perhaps also temperature or pain. Objects are far more than patterns of stimulation: objects have pasts and futures; when we know its past or can guess its future, an object transcends experience and becomes an embodiment of knowledge and expectation. Without this phenomenon, life of even the simplest kind is impossible.

1-1. This array of equally spaced dots is seen as continually changing patterns of rows and squares. We see something of the active organising power of the visual system while looking at this figure.

Although we are concerned with how we see the world of objects, it is important to consider the sensory processes giving perception—what they are, how they work and when they fail to work properly. It is by coming to understand these underlying processes that we can understand how we perceive objects.

There are many familiar so-called "ambiguous figures,"

which illustrate very clearly how the same pattern of stimulation at the eye can give rise to different perceptions, and how the perception of objects goes beyond sensation. The most common ambiguous figures are of two kinds: figures which alternate as "object" or "ground," and those which spontaneously change their position in depth. Figure 1-3 shows a figure which alternates in figure and ground—sometimes the black part appears as a face, the white being neutral background, and at others the black is insignificant and the white surround dominates and seems to represent an object.

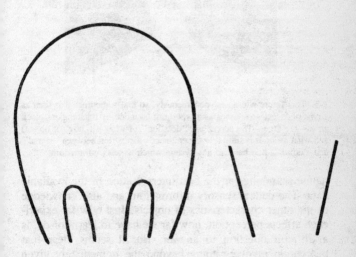

1-2. A joke figure—what is it? When you see it as an object, not merely meaningless lines, it will suddenly appear almost solid—an *object*, not a *pattern*.

The well-known Necker cube (Figure 1-4) shows a figure alternating in depth. Sometimes the face marked with the "o" lies in front, sometimes at the back—it jumps suddenly from the one position to the other. Perception is not determined simply by the stimulus patterns; rather it is a dy-

1-3. This figure alternates spontaneously, so that sometimes it is seen as a pair of faces, sometimes as a white urn bounded by meaningless black areas—the faces. The perceptual "decision" of what is figure (or object) and what ground, is similar to the engineer's distinction between "signal" and "noise." It is basic to any system which handles information.

namic searching for the best interpretation of the available data. The data is sensory information, and also knowledge of the other characteristics of objects. Just how far experience affects perception, how far we have to learn to see, is a difficult question to answer. But it seems clear that perception involves going beyond the immediately given evidence of the senses. The senses do not give us a picture of the world directly; rather they provide evidence for checking hypotheses about what lies before us. Indeed, we may say that a perceived object *is* a hypothesis, suggested and tested by sensory data. The Necker cube is a pattern which contains no clue as to which of two alternative hypotheses is correct: the perceptual system entertains first one then the other hypothesis, and never comes to a conclusion, for there is no best answer. Sometimes the eye and brain come to wrong conclusions, and then we suffer hallucinations or illusions. When a perceptual hypothesis—a perception—is wrong we are misled, as we are misled in science when we see the world distorted by a false theory. Perceiving and thinking are not independent: "I see what you mean" is not a puerile pun, but indicates a connection which is very real.

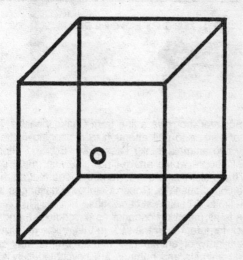

1-4. This figure alternates in depth: the face of the cube marked by the small circle sometimes appearing as the *front*, sometimes as the *back* face. We can think of these ways of seeing the figure as perceptual "hypotheses." The visual system entertains alternative hypotheses, and never settles for one solution. This process goes on throughout normal perception, but generally there is a unique solution.

Has Not an Animal Organs, Dimensions, Senses, Affections, Passions?

by Robert Solomon

Robert Solomon borrows a line from Shakespeare's *The Merchant of Venice* to call attention to a nagging issue in psychology: Do animals think? Lassie, Mr. Ed, and Flipper aside, most people would answer no. Likewise, most psychologists have dismissed out of hand the idea that animals might have consciousness. Robert Solomon challenges that view of the limits on animals' capacities.

Solomon is as much philosopher as psychologist, and he has a knack for integrating the two. In this article he argues that the similarity of animal and human brains may well indicate that animals and humans are psychologically similar too. Solomon tells us that we need greater empathy with the animal world in order to study it more accurately. Animals may suffer like humans do, he suggests, and animal consciousness may be far more sophisticated than we have assumed.

FROM FABLES AND fantasies, we have become accustomed to ants and elephants and creatures of all kinds who talk and tell us what is on their minds. They scheme, brood, rationalize, resent their superiors. They become morally indignant, proud, furious. They fall in love, often with members of other species. (Kermit the Frog and Miss Piggy are our latest *ménage à bête*.) Ants warn grasshoppers of the perilous winter; ducklings are embarrassed about their looks; young elephants complain to crows about the size of their ears. Even those of us who try to be hardheaded in such matters find ourselves, on occasion, telling buoyant and often tedious tales about the intelligence and cunning of our cat, who has the craftiness of a con artist, or the love of our dog, whose devotion puts ancient Greek heroes and Christian saints to shame.

The scientific community, by contrast, puts less stock in the animal mind. Three centuries ago, Descartes declared that animals are mere "machines," without minds or intelligence and devoid of reason and will. The American behaviorist John Watson revolutionized not only the science of animal behavior but human psychology, too, by denouncing "anthropomorphism" wherever it proposed benign but unjustifiable empathy in place of more rigorous methods. B. F. Skinner reduced mainstream American psychology to systematic correlations between stimulus and response, with no intervening mental way stations. College sophomores may have protested, "Where is consciousness?" but the proscription of nonexplanatory and unconfirmable concepts remained the first rule for the scientific study of animals.

There has always been a hint of absurdity in the unwillingness of humane behaviorists, who fondle, pamper, and converse with their pets at home (and sometimes in the lab), to ascribe the most basic mental properties to their experimental subjects. Fifty years of strict adherence to behaviorist methods have proved that behaviorism is just as limited, scientifically, as the anthropomorphism it replaced. H. S. Terrace, one of Skinner's most eminent students, points out that even in the classic behaviorist experiments with rats and pigeons, it is necessary to postulate something between stimulus and response: memory, for instance, or some form of "representation," or "inner" function. Even the philosophical behaviorist W. V. O. Quine, Skinner's longtime colleague and defender at Harvard, now accepts the necessity of understanding the stimulus as some form of active perception, not merely passive neurophysiological reception.

Contemporary neurological studies have demonstrated a clear continuity between animal and human brain structures and functions that makes it utterly unreasonable to deny to animals at least some of the psychological features that we ascribe to ourselves. Jerre Levy, a University of Chicago neurophysiologist, has concluded from this research that "we have no reason to suppose that there are any unique properties of the human organ of thought." Indeed, Levy observes, much medical research on animals *assumes* the continuity of consciousness from one species to another.

These days, scientists are once again becoming wary of *a priori* or dogmatic limitations on the range of their investigations and conclusions, whether imposed in the name of science or of sentimentality. And speaking of sentimentality, scientific agnosticism concerning the existence of consciousness in animals is intolerably at odds with the recently renewed concern about animal suffering and animal rights, which are supported by many scientists themselves. "The welfare of animals must depend on *understanding* animal suffering," writes biologist Peter Medawar, "and one does not come to this understanding intuitively." Accordingly, it is not surprising that the existence of animal consciousness has again become an open scientific question.

THE DAHLEM CONFERENCE: A NEW OPENING

A year ago, just across the street from the Berlin Zoo, a large group of distinguished scientists came together under the auspices of the much-respected Dahlem Konferenzen. The Dahlem Conferences have traditionally been oriented toward the biological sciences, attracting from around the world leading researchers in such fields as molecular genetics and neurology, to formulate "state of the art" reports and to frame new vistas for investigation. More recently, the conferences have adopted a sometimes philosophical stance; a few years ago, for instance, they took a critical look at sociobiology.

In 1981, the purpose of the conference was not only to

bring together the current research in one area but also, and more important, to establish the legitimacy of the field itself—in this case, the scientific study of animal minds. The exact title of the conference was "Animal Mind— Human Mind," and its purpose, prominently announced below the familiar *Nicht Rauchen* signs on the wall of every meeting room, was to reintroduce the once *verboten* concepts of "experience" and "consciousness" into the study of animal behavior. Indeed, Donald Griffin of Rockefeller University in New York City stated the question in a particularly scandalous way: "What is it like to *be* an animal of a particular species?" The old idea of empathy had been welcomed back into scientific psychology.

Among the 50 or so conferees were evolutionary biologists, neurologists, animal behaviorists, psychologists, and philosophers. The experimental psychologists and biologists who came were interested in such varied subjects as bees, birds, dolphins, and college undergraduates. The presence of many participants in the recent "ape language" controversies guaranteed at least one lively discussion. Terrace, teacher of the chimp Nim, was there. So was Levy, one of the pioneers in right brain/left brain experimentation. Hans Kummer, Carolyn Ristau, and E. S. Savage-Rumbaugh were the other resident experts on apes. C. G. Beer and Peter Marler, the confidants of gulls and song birds respectively, were there. Theodore Bullock from San Diego, sometimes in his dolphin T-shirt, represented the Delphinidae. James Gould, the Princeton ethologist, dominated much of the argumentation with accounts of his bee experiments. Philosophers Daniel Dennett, author of *Brainstorms*, and Jerry Fodor, who teaches at the Massachusetts Institute of Technology, kept the larger issues in view.

With such a broad spectrum of interests, there was little likelihood of reaching a consensus. Nevertheless, one could at least be confident that the various issues would be argued. Of course, the old academic wounds were much in evidence. Despite the best efforts of the observer-inmates at the zoo, who provided much of the informal entertainment for the conference, the arguments often put the believers in animal minds on the defensive. Skeptics ignored the evidence of the animals' own antics in favor of the too-familiar philosophical arguments about the "unconfirmability" of all claims about animal minds.

Griffin, the conference director, set the tone for the unusual discussions to follow by noting in his opening remarks "how little we really know about animal minds"—in part, he said, because "scientists have so long ruled out *a priori* the possibility that mental experiences could occur in animals." And yet, perhaps surprisingly, rather clear agreement on the main point was apparent by the end of the conference: that it makes sense to talk about the minds of animals and to investigate, in a scientific context, precisely what kind of mind this or that animal has.

THE QUESTION OF ANIMAL SUFFERING

Consider for a painful moment the behavior of a puppy whose paw has just been slammed in the screen door. It is difficult to take seriously any theory or methodological principle that rules out explaining that behavior in terms of the *feeling* of pain. The question becomes less clear, however, as we climb down the phylogenetic ladder. Does a lobster feel pain as it is dropped into the pot of boiling water? Does the inadequately swatted wasp feel pain as it chases us out of the room? Does the bisected worm feel pain, and if so, in both halves? Or are such questions beyond the domain of science?

It would surely be folly to say so. But scientific discussions of the basic features—raw feelings and sensations—of what we might tentatively call consciousness have too long fallen into one of two equally unacceptable patterns. Either all mentalistic terms have been forbidden as nonexplanatory, or, as many people have too easily assumed, whatever squirms or reacts feels pain, just as we do. If the question is whether or not an animal is suffering in a particular situation (*the* dominant question in discussions of animal rights), the first way of thinking is totally unsatisfactory. It is tantamount to the demand that no concern for animal well-being can have scientific justification. The second way of thinking, though perhaps acceptable in Aesop and Walt Disney, is no better. How do we *know* whether an animal has a feeling, and how do we know *what* it is feeling?

The current outcry against the use of animals in unnecessary experiments and against the alleged brutality of the conditions under which animals are mass-produced for food presupposes the potential of animals for suffering. Peter Singer's epochal treatise on *Animal Liberation,* for example, indicted what he called the "concentration-camp methods" of cosmetics manufacturers, who squirt chemicals into the eyes of rabbits until they go blind, and of poultry farmers, who keep chicks cooped up in cages no larger than their bodies. But do we know what constitutes suffering for a chicken?

"Scientists are accused of using 'torture' and 'concentration camp methods,' " writes Marian Dawkins of Oxford University, a participant in the Dahlem Conference. "Their critics must therefore know how to judge when an animal is suffering." Mere intuition is not always dependable; Dawkins argues that there are conditions under which chickens actually *prefer* small cages. "We have to *find out* about animal suffering, species by species," he concludes. Or as Julian Huxley wryly put it, "The tapeworm's peptic Nirvana is not for me."

The existence of animal feeling on this basic level, though we can never "observe" the feeling itself, can be tested by experiment. Animals cannot report their pains and preferences, but, Dawkins insists, they can "vote with their feet." Pigs can be taught to use light switches, and by using them can choose their ambience. Hens can choose cages, bees trees, and paramecia their chemical homes. Such studies at least establish the existence of pain and of preferences.

One might well object that the demonstration that an animal feels something certainly does not warrant use of the term "consciousness." This point led to the most often repeated conclusion of the Dahlem Conference: that the traditional question of whether or not a creature is conscious has to be rejected in favor of a broader question about gradations or levels of consciousness. The all-or-nothing question only reinforces the old disputes, Bullock argued. Virtually every animal, he said, has a mind (though perhaps not consciousness) of some degree of complexity. It responds to its environment through sequences of more or less complex behavior, sometimes learning, sometimes calculating, sometimes even thinking. But whether we mean by mind simply the ability to experience sensory input or pain, or the ability to learn and adapt, it becomes clear that we are now talking about degrees of development within the realm of minds.

At the end of the conference, Bullock conducted a survey to find out how the conferees rated the capacity for suffering and the intelligence of 40-odd creatures, from human infants and chimps down to earthworms and paramecia. In one sense, the results reflected the obvious: Ratings decreased as the list descended and biological scale. Yet the survey also reflected a new attitude among scientists: There was no precipitous drop-off in ratings from one species to another. Cats scored slightly higher than jackals, mice slightly higher than crows, starfish slightly higher than anemones. Thus it was clear that "conscious or not" was no longer the issue.

WHAT IS CONSCIOUSNESS?

The language of mind, unlike the concrete terminology of neurology, is riddled with vague and value-laden terms. To say of a creature that it has a cerebellum is not to pay it a compliment, but to say of someone or something that it is "intelligent" certainly is. We use "having a mind" as a term of praise. (It brings to mind the professor who responded to an athletic-scholarship student's query about his I.Q.: "Why, I didn't know that you *had* an I.Q.") Both "consciousness" and "sensitivity" are desirable attributes as well as psychological descriptions. It is therefore extremely important to recognize the *ethical* edge of these terms, and to be exceedingly cautious in defining them.

There was a kind of absurdity to many of the definitions that conferees proposed. One discussion group used the characterization of consciousness suggested by David Premack, the ape-language researcher. who defined it as the ability to make a true-false judgment. Reaching such a judgment, however, is an extremely high-level reflective and linguistic operation that might well be argued to be within the province of only some human beings. Simple sensitivity was generally rejected as inadequate for consciousness, as was the ability to learn or even to carry out complex calculations.

What too often emerged as a criterion for consciousness was the ability to reflect and articulate the possession of some concept of selfhood and of what we would call "self-consciouness." The effect of setting such high standards for consciousness was to give the animal mind only token recognition, and to save all of the high-level attributes of mind, especially consciousness, for human beings, and, perhaps, a couple of apes.

To take the levels-of-consciousness theme seriously, however, is to take seriously not only the presence of a minimal mind but a wide variety of mental abilities and processes. "What is it like to be a bat?" asked philosopher Thomas Nagel of New York University, who had taken part in the Dahlem sociobiology conference. Even at the most basic level of consciousness, it is the empathetic query "What is it like *to be* an *X*?" that marks off the realm of mind and consciousness.

There is consciousness in the sense of organized sensory perception, a rather passive process, and consciousness in the more developed sense of organizing sensory perception, which requires active mental functioning. There is simple pattern recognition, and then there are the far more sophisticated processes of comparison and generalization. There are many levels of learning that include memory and mental representations. Then there is the very high-level process of articulating those representations, a process that divides again into many levels. They range from the ability to use single words or signs, to the ability to produce distinctive speech, to the ability to employ words or signs with broad semantic meaning (as opposed to more context-bound utterances), to the ability to combine words in a syntax, to the ability to employ syntactic transformations, and finally to the ability to use a metalanguage (literally, a language about language) in which one can not only express one's representations but also talk about the relationships between representations and language, including the use of such metalinguistic terms as true and false.

Between full-scale reflection and simpler communicative consciousness lie other dimensions of mind, including the capacity for interpersonal intrigue. Robert Seyfarth, then at Rockefeller University, who observes monkeys in the wild, told fellow conferees about a monkey that intentionally deceived its peers by giving the "leopard warning cry" (ordinarily used by monkeys to give notice of the presence of an enemy) as a means of breaking up a fight. Koko the gorilla is often reported to deceive the human beings who talk to her. Even dogs and cats sometimes behave as if they had at least rudimentary awareness of the idea of deception, which involves knowing what others believe and how they can be fooled.

With such a range of linguistic levels, the heated debates over whether or not the likes of Nim and Koko actually speak a language strike us as somewhat medieval. Language, too, admits of gradations. We might well balk at the claim that a parrot knows Spanish. But there is certainly some sense in which a dolphin or a gorilla speaks a language while dogs and cats do not, and a further sense in which dogs and cats can at least understand language while fish and clams do not.

Neither is self-consciousness a single concept, with an all-or-none manifestation only in species that have some concept of self. Some animals display interesting behavior in front of a mirror, others do not. (Chimps do, dogs don't.) Noticing one's reflection suggests a sense of self, but so, too, does the recognition of one's own smell, or possessing a sense of one's territory.

Biologist Lewis Thomas has argued that even sponges and bacteria might have such a limited sense of self-identity, an idea that leads him to the somewhat suspect thesis that individual self-identity is one of the more pervasive aspects of nature. We do not need to confuse the chemical self-consciousness of single-celled animals with the identity crisis of American adolescents, however, to recognize that there is more than one kind of self-consciousness and a ladder of levels upon which the many creatures with minds distribute themselves. Socrates insisted that "the unexamined life is not worth living," but this is an unfair criterion of self-consciousness to apply to a squirrel.

INTELLIGENCE vs. FEELING

The conferees always came back to the unavoidable question: Granted that an animal is behaving in such and such a manner, how can we know that it feels anything? A basic distinction emerged between what some members of the conference summarized quasi-poetically as "sapience and sentience," or intelligence and feeling. Some participants suggested that the former was clearly within the domain of science, while the latter was not. Virtually everyone agreed that sapience and sentience are not the same, and that they present researchers with different issues. Even remarkable intelligence is not enough to establish the existence of consciousness in the "sentient" sense, a few argued. Indeed, it was even argued that the one renders the other unnecessary.

The elaborate forages, flights, and filial dances of bees provide one of the awesome examples of intelligence and communication in lower species. Gould explained the work done some years ago by Karl von Frisch to demonstrate that bees make very complex calculations of the shortest distance between hive and flower, no matter what obstacles lie between and no matter how circuitous the route they must take. Gould also described his own recent findings. When he moved flowers whose location bees had previously learned to communicate to their sisters, bees returning to their hive at first gave what had become a false description of the flowers' location. But they quickly learned to compensate for their error.

The intelligence of these bees is beyond dispute, but what of consciousness? It is hard, if not impossible, to empathize with a bee, to believe in the consciousness of a species so far away in "the great chain of cuddliness," as one conferee called it. In any case, the intelligence of bees does not provide an argument for bee consciousness, as Gould himself acknowledged.

One might argue that bee perceptions require at least sensations of a reasonable level of sophistication, but the reply is that any theory of information-processing is sufficient to explain their behavior without postulating the existence of consciousness. One might also argue that the learning capacity of bees, although limited, points to a form of intelligence that cannot be attributed to mere mechanism. In this case, the reply is that even computers can be built to adapt themselves to changes. Indeed, that is what a bee is: a remarkably concise and precise organic computer. The slightest deviation from the bee's hard-wired routines results in utter chaos. A drop of oleic acid placed on a healthy, living bee triggers dead-bee removal activity on the part of its sisters, who are oblivious to its frantic struggle.

The assumption in this argument, which unfortunately permeated much of the conference discussion, was that mechanism and consciousness are in opposition; that if behavior can be explained mechanistically (for example, in terms of information-processing and familiar computer operations), the behaving organism is therefore not conscious. Part of the argument was evolutionary: It was said that an organism programmed to its environment does not *need* consciousness, which is essentially a device that allows increased adaptability. The larger part of the argument was an argument that goes back to Descartes: If it is mechanism, it cannot be conscious. (The other half of the

Cartesian argument, "If it is conscious, it can't be a mechanism," was notably omitted.)

But even the first half of the Cartesian argument fails. There is no longer much reason to think that we—as paragons of consciousness—might not also be explainable, some day soon, in terms of computerlike mechanisms. Indeed, the argument can even be turned around. Dennett, co-editor of *The Mind's I,* suggested that one might properly attribute mind (though not consciousness) to computers and thermostats, which display "intelligence" in the mechanistic sense.

Intelligence can be measured, and there can be no intelligible doubts about the operational correctness of such questions as "Can an animal learn to do X in Y situation?" If it can, it is to some degree intelligent.

But there is a difference between intelligence and sentience, and establishing one seems to have only minimally to do with establishing the other. Whatever the intelligence of a bee or an octopus, the issue of what it experiences is an open question. Indeed, at what point would we be willing to ascribe even the most rudimentary feelings or experiences to a computer, no matter how superior its intelligence?

There is intelligence, and then there is sentience. The second without the first seems unlikely; the first without the second, whether in a computer or in a bee, is not worthy of the name "consciousness," or, for that matter, the less provocative (perhaps just shorter) word "mind." Information-processing plus sensitivity, whatever the sophistication of the mechanisms involved, are the basic ingredients of both animal and human minds.

THE NEW LANGUAGE OF ANIMAL PSYCHOLOGY

However attractive, the distinction between intelligence and feeling only temporarily clarifies some issues, and then it further muddles them. The distinction reintroduces, though covertly, the old separation of those features of animal behavior that admit of observation and experimentation, and those that do not. Given that separation, feeling seems to become the residuum of science—that which is left over, unexplained, after all the more testable results are in. But this is not really the case. Feelings, while not directly observable, are nonetheless demonstrable, usually beyond any reasonable doubt. And feelings, if they are of any complexity, are not easily distinguishable from what we are calling intelligence. Whether or not feelings are learned, they are almost always influenced by learning.

A too-sharp contrast of intelligence and feeling leads too easily to the old behaviorist theory that only testable and measurable behavior counts and that those mysterious "inner" feelings have no standing as far as science is concerned. Rejecting that too-sharp contrast in turn underscores the importance of those new developments in psychology that currently parade under the banner of cognitive science. Unlike behaviorism, cognitive science accepts the need to refer to inner aspects of animal minds to explain all but the simplest reflex behavior.

But the "inner aspect" is no longer considered to be anything so ineffable as a "feeling"; it is a demonstrable "representation," which may be said to be either a function of the nervous system or a function of the mind, depending on one's viewpoint. In either interpretation, it is a function, the series of links between the contingencies of the animal's environment and the animal's behavior. Accordingly, the view thus defended is often called "functionalism," and the various functions are at least sometimes, notably in ourselves, products of conscious awareness as well as operative steps in a logical and perhaps programmable sequence of inferences and reactions.

What is a representation? Jerry Fodor, the MIT philosopher, argued at the conference that virtually all psychological explanation requires talk of representations, and that only sometimes can these be viewed as internal images, such as our own imaginings. We postulate a representation, a kind of flight plan, in Gould's bees. We postulate a representation, another kind of map, in Terrace's pigeons and in Koko the gorilla, whose representations include (at least) the dictionary for hundreds of signs and their references. To ask whether these representations are essentially conscious is to miss the point, in fact two points. First, consciousness is a multi-leveled conception. Second, the consciousness of the representations, in the sense of self-awareness, is a quite different question from the functioning of the representations; they may function in the absence of self-awareness, and often do. Postulating a certain representation does not require that an animal actually feel much of anything, but neither does it rule out feeling.

Discovering or postulating the nature of representations and how they are processed is a matter susceptible to experimental investigation. The representations of bees can be tested by detailed observation and by manipulation of the situations in which bees respond in predictable ways; the adaptability of bee intelligence can be tested by changing circumstances until the "bee computer" breaks down.

In some animals, information-processing can be extremely sophisticated while adaptability is limited. Young birds, according to Peter Marler, need to hear only a brief fragment of their characteristic song to learn it. Without that short sample, however, the bird does not learn the song at all, so the song is not purely instinctive. Within that species song, however, there is also individual variation, such that every bird's song is clearly distinguishable from that of other birds of the same species. The representation is relatively simple, in this case, but the processing and adaptability are more sophisticated.

In most mammals, representations and their processing and adaptability are much more complex than in birds, most dramatically so when symbols and language are involved. It is a matter of fascinating debate where such representations begin: with the varied communications of monkeys, with the "language" of birds and bees, or with the more basic communication that, it might be argued, takes place even in the microbial world, even within a single cell. Here again, the only answer worth investigation rather than argument would seem to be that there is a hierarchy of symbols and languages, some more sophisticated than others. We can investigate the language of gulls calling out to each other over the cliffs of Dover, and the sign-language conversations between Francine Patterson and Koko, without falling into the often nasty debates over what counts as a language and what does not.

It is not the existence of consciousness but the nature of conscious experience that remains the open question. Granted that some insects have remarkable ability to communicate, and granted that they must sense something if they are to process any information at all, we can still ask: Do they feel confusion when lost, or patriotic when the hive is attacked? Gulls display remarkable ability to discriminate one another's calls, according to C. G. Beer of Rutgers. But does it make sense to suppose that they are glad to see each other? When my dog displays his "hangdog" look as I pack my suitcase for a trip, am I justified in saying that he is depressed? To reject that question *a priori* is no longer justifiable—which does not mean (as Watson and Skinner feared) that we are thereby bound to believe everything reported by Aesop and Disney. To open the question is not to give up one's experimental criteria or what we are used to calling (when it is convenient) our common sense.

THE GREAT CHAIN OF CONSCIOUSNESS

Several years ago, Cambridge philosopher G. M. E. Anscombe was asked about the implications for our concept of human uniqueness if apes were taught to talk. "They'll up the ante," she replied. Indeed, Justin Leiber, the philosopher who organized the "Apes and Language" conference in Houston last year, referred to the dispute over primate intelligence as a religious debate, concerned as much with the self-image of the human species as with the evidence about primates. The distinction between the human and the nonhuman has been basic to Western thought ever since the Greeks. We insist on maintaining the distinction in an absolute and non-negotiable way, but no sooner do we congratulate ourselves on one or another unique human quality than some beast or bird mocks us by displaying that very quality. Thus the defensive predominance of method over anecdote: The interesting cases are too often ruled out before they can even be considered.

The view that mind and consciousness, like intelligence, are graded phenomena, different for different species, changes all of this, and underlies the twin conclusions of the Berlin conference: that significant questions about animal mind and consciousness can be asked, and that traditional methodology more often rules out than answers these questions.

Animal psychologists once dismissed out of hand the idea that animal minds, animal consciousness, and animal experience might be part of science. Now, that idea has become their basic premise, the starting point for much of their work. The question now is one of degree. The old—and, it is to be hoped, moribund—question about the validity of ascribing consciousness to creatures other than ourselves can be replaced with hundreds of more precise experimental questions about the sensitivity, intelligence, and experience of animals. With this recognition of continuity from species to species can also emerge a renewed appreciation of differences. We need not ask whether animals have intelligence, or language, or emotions, but rather what intelligence, what kind of language, and which emotions. However, the answers to such questions will not come easily. If they come at all, it will be only after far more observation, experimentation, and conceptual clarification than the past few decades of science or centuries of storytelling, have required of us.

The True Speed Trip: Schizophrenia

by Solomon Snyder

Solomon Snyder is an expert on the biochemistry of mental illness, a highly significant area of medical and psychological research. With regard to schizophrenia itself, Solomon's work has offered hope that someday a chemical key to the dread disease will be found.

In "The True Speed Trip," Solomon focuses on amphetamine psychosis—a state of hallucinations and delusions that mirrors schizophrenia but is induced artificially, through the ingestion of the drug amphetamine, or "speed." Researchers believe that by studying this pharmacological psychosis we can learn a great deal about the mysterious biochemistry of the malady it imitates.

One unique feature of amphetamine psychosis is compulsive, stereotyped behavior that the victim repeats hour after hour—a scenario resembling a brand of schizophrenia called catatonia. Snyder also discusses some very vivid hallucinations induced by speed—patients' images of extraterrestrial rays and paranoid scenes of murder and torment. Thus, as he concludes, amphetamine psychosis may actually be the best available chemical analog of schizophrenia we know of. Science, it seems, can find compelling data in the most unexpected places!

THE PATIENT HAS just been admitted to the hospital emergency room, so violent that it took three strong men to bring him in.

From relatives and from bits of the patient's incoherent ramblings, the admitting psychiatrist begins piecing together an account. Yesterday John felt that others were looking at him in a peculiar way. He had walked the streets all night and spent this morning looking for gold in the gravel paths of the city park. This afternoon he heard voices talking about him. Hostile, secretive persons were looking at him; he was sure they were planning to kill him.

In an interview, the psychiatrist concludes that John suffers from auditory hallucinations and that he has delusions of persecution, and volatile, inappropriate emotions. The diagnosis is simple: an obvious case of paranoid schizophrenia.

But there is a hooker. John is not schizophrenic at all. After a few hours his wife arrives at the hospital and tells the psychiatrist that John has been injecting methamphetamine into his veins for the past three months. John is a speed-freak, an amphetamine addict, and is suffering the principal hazard of the habit.

Key. For years researchers have been trying to find a chemical key to schizophrenia. The first quest is for a drug that will make normal persons act, temporarily, in the peculiar ways that schizophrenic patients act. Such a drug could provide an important lead to the causes of schizophrenia. And if the drug also will make animals behave schizophrenically, investigators will be able to manipulate schizophrenia in their laboratories. They can explore how environmental, chemical and genetic factors influence schizophrenic behavior, and they can investigate a wealth of possible cures. A growing number of scientists believe that this approach is likely to pay off in the search for a cure for schizophrenia.

Amphetamine offers promise to be this key drug, because it produces patients like John who can trick even experienced clinicians into erroneous diagnoses of schizophrenia. But other chemicals also are under serious study in the search. LSD is the best known psychotomimetic—psychosis-mimicking—drug; LSD, mescaline, psilocybin and other drugs produce effects similar to psychosis. Alcohol is another; an alcoholic in withdrawal undergoes delirium tremens—d.t.s—an agitated state fraught with frequent, frightening hallucinations. And many drunks have heard nonexistent voices and seen occasional elephants of unusual colors. Marijuana and its concentrate, hashish, taken in sufficient quantity, can produce hallucinations. And the United States Army, with somewhat different motives, has investigated several highly secret chemicals related to atropine, minute doses of which produce a delirious, psychoticlike state.

Daze. Most of these drugs yield only imperfect approximations of schizophrenia: drugged patients usually become disoriented and confused—often they cannot say who they are, where they are, or what time of day it is, or what month. The true schizophrenic patient, on the other hand, is likely to be well oriented as to person, place and time. Most drug-produced disorientation resembles the symptoms of brain damage—from accident, stroke, brain tumor, vitamin deficiency, or hormonal imbalance—more than it resembles schizophrenia. Amphetamines provide a much better chemical analog to schizophrenia—speed-freaks are invariably well oriented, perhaps even more when they are under the influence than when they are not drugged.

After recovering from a psychotic episode, an amphetamine user usually retains a detailed memory of the whole experience, as do most patients recovering from schizophrenia. By contrast, the other drugs—possibly excepting the psychedelics—deaden the mental faculties so that a patient may have partial or total amnesia that covers the episode.

See. Another important difference is that in drug-induced psychosis, hallucinations or perceptual distortions are primarily visual; in true schizophrenia they are almost always auditory.

When a schizophrenic patient does report visual hallucinations, it is usually during the early stages, after an acute onset. This was true in the cases of amphetamine psychosis reported by Phillip H. Connell in London: visual hallucinations occurred primarily in patients whose psychoses developed acutely after a few large doses of amphetamine. The patients who had escalated dosage gradually over several months tended to have mostly auditory hallucinations. Another telling link is that the drug therapy most effective for schizophrenia is the one that is most effective for amphetamine psychosis. A barbiturate or sedative may be helpful for a number of drug states, but phenothiazine tranquilizers are uniquely effective in amphetamine psychosis and schizophrenia.

For all of these reasons, it appears that amphetamine psychosis is the best chemical model of true schizophrenia, at least of the paranoid type.

Pills. The average patient with amphetamine psychosis started taking the drug in pill form. Most pills on the market contain five or 10 milligrams of active drug, and are called pep pills or diet pills, depending on the user's purpose. Tolerance for amphetamine builds up rapidly; the pill-popping addict must take more and more pills at shorter and shorter intervals to reach the same high—sometimes more than 100 pills a day. But the typical amphetamine addict tires of pills quickly and begins mainlining: he injects the drug directly into veins, with perhaps 100 or 200 milligrams of methamphetamine—crystal—in each injection, or hit.

Even before he withdraws the needle he feels an intense buzzing euphoria, called a rush, that users sometimes liken to an orgasm of the whole body. After this, the addict will be elated and hyperactive for several hours, with no desire for food. He may eventually shoot up every three or four hours, on a five- or six-day run, until he crashes, exhausted, to sleep for two to four days. He awakens with a ravenous hunger; after he has eaten as much as he can hold, he goes into profound depression, he seeks the only known cure: more amphetamine.

F.B.I. Signs of amphetamine psychosis first develop while the speed-freak is under the influence of the drug (they are thus unlike delirium tremens, a withdrawal psychosis). The harbinger is vague fear and suspicion—*What was that? I heard something. Is somebody trying to get me?*

Soon the paranoia centers around a specific delusion—for example, that the FBI is out to get him. An amphetamine party may begin with everyone very elated and talkative, and may end with each person stationed silently at a window, peeking through the curtains for signs of the police.

Acting on his delusions, the speed-freak may become violent—*to get them before they get me*. It is in this sense that the slogan SPEED KILLS is most accurate: more persons die from senseless and brutal violence associated with amphetamine delusions than from overdoses of the drug itself.

Bag. Another unique feature of amphetamine psychosis is compulsive, stereotyped behavior that the victim repeats hour after hour, apparently without fatigue or boredom. A woman sorted out her handbag over and over for several hours. A man at a table constantly rearranged his knife and spoon. A teen-ager counted cornflakes all evening. While a user is busy at this major repetitive behavior, he may also grind this teeth, lick his lips, or constantly shift his eyes from side to side.

Drugged laboratory animals behave similarly. Under small doses of amphetamine, they become hyperactive and vigilant; with greater doses, they develop repetitive, stereotyped behavior. And Roy Pickens and his colleagues have found that when laboratory rats can dose themselves with amphetamines by pressing a bar, they follow a pattern of intake and abstinence, run and crash, that is similar to the pattern of the human amphetamine user.

Why. Some theorists believe that lack of sleep may cause amphetamine psychosis, not any ingredient of the drug itself. We know that often persons who go without sleep for long periods develop bizarre, psychoticlike behavior. Others speculate that amphetamine's overstimulation of the senses brings on the psychosis. Still others argue that the intense emotional arousal in the amphetamine experience simply triggers a latent psychosis that any stress could have provoked.

The best way to resolve these questions was to produce

amphetamine psychosis in human beings—deliberately drive people crazy— and carefully follow the sequence of events.

The first person to essay such an experiment was a physician, John Griffith at Vanderbilt University. He recruited four men in their late 20s and early 30s who already were amphetamine addicts but who had never shown signs of amphetamine psychosis, or any tendencies toward schizophrenia. They were all mildly to moderately psychopathic, a condition that is readily distinguishable from schizophrenia. Griffith relentlessly dosed each man with dextroamphetamine—10 milligrams, orally, every hour of the day and night—until he developed signs of amphetamine psychosis. Griffith carefully monitored each man's physiological and psychological symptoms throughout the experiment.

Cling. Each man exhibited unequivocal psychosis within two to five days, and the psychotic symptoms followed the same sequence in each. After the first doses of amphetamine he showed the usual euphoria, excitement and hyperactivity. During this time he was lucid, in good contact with his surroundings, normally boyish and warm. But by the fifth or sixth dose, he had changed: he became quiet, depressed, uninterested in amusement—a hypochondriac who clung dependently to Griffith.

This pattern was not ordinary amphetamine behavior, probably because the subjects were tested in solitude in a controlled hospital environment. On his own, an amphetamine addict would probably increase his dosage before such symptoms developed, and social variables undoubtedly would color the experience. For example, his interactions with other amphetamine users probably would keep him hyperactive longer than Griffith's subjects were.

Signs. The first patient developed psychotic signs after about 24 hours; the last after 120 hours (five days). In each case the subject began peculiar behavior about eight hours before the explicit psychotic symptoms appeared. He became taciturn, and refused to talk about his thoughts or feelings. He asked guarded questions about the room, the experiment, or unusual noises, but backed off if anyone asked why he wanted the information. In retrospect, the patients recalled that it was at about this time that paranoid ideas first entered their minds. For a while they could recognize that the ideas were unfounded, chemical delusions—familiar and expected side-effects of the drug. Later the ideas were not so easy to dismiss.

The florid psychosis commenced abruptly in each man. After being stony-faced and silent for about eight hours, he began discussing his thoughts openly and sharply, though he remained cold and aloof. His paranoid ideas became more elaborate and organized, and he believed them. One man believed he was the target of rays from a "giant oscillator." Another maintained that his wife planned to kill him. Strikingly unlike patients with other forms of drug-psychosis, these subjects could not be comforted easily and they were not at all suggestible. The psychosis dissipated within eight hours of the drug cut-off in three of the subjects; the fourth remained somewhat paranoid for another three days.

Out. Griffith's experiment answers some questions about possible alternative explanations of drug-induced psychosis. First of all, the psychosis cannot be attributed simply to sleep deprivation, because two of the men became psychotic after losing only one night's sleep, which alone is not long enough to produce psychotic symptoms.

Nor can the psychosis be attributed to intense stimulation and arousal—the men never appeared to be overstimulated—in fact, after the first few hours they all appeared to be depressed.

Griffith also was careful to rule out pre-drug personality as a significant factor; he selected subjects who had never shown schizophrenic tendencies either in a drugged state or undrugged.

Order. The amphetamine psychosis that Griffith observed is a good imitation of schizophrenia, probably the best of the drug-induced states. But it isn't perfect; there are differences, the most salient being that Griffith's subjects showed no signs of formal, schizophrenic thought disorder. This is the bizarre mental process that produces crazy associations and meandering, contradictory, hard-to-follow speech [see "Schizophrenia: Carnival Mirror of Coherence," by Donald Bannister, *P.T.*, January 1971]. Other researchers confirm Griffith's finding: amphetamine addicts rarely display thought disorder.

This lack would seem to destroy any systematic analogy between amphetamine psychosis and schizophrenia, for many psychiatrists consider thought disorder to be the vital element of schizophrenia [see "The Shattered Language of Schizophrenia," by Brendan A. Maher, *P.T.*, November 1968]. But the issue is not so simple. Doctrinaire diagnosis aside, thought disorder does not invariably accompany schizophrenia. Acute schizophrenics show much less thought disorder than chronic schizophrenics do; and paranoid schizophrenics, with their tight and ordered delusional systems, may show no thought disorder at all. In this connection it is encouraging to note that the amphetamine psychosis usually is both acute and paranoid, and thus resembles the types of schizophrenia with least thought disorder.

Brain. From Griffith's research and from clinical experience, it seems safe to say that large doses of amphetamines will almost invariably produce psychosis similar to acute, paranoid schizophrenia. The clinical picture is not identical to schizophrenia, however, perhaps because amphetamine's grab-bag of side-effects (arousal, sleeplessness, loss of appetite, stereotyped behavior, etc.) may complicate matters. To find out which components of the amphetamine experience are most responsible for the psychosis, we must study the brain to find how nerves, tissues and brain chemicals respond when amphetamine is added to the system.

An obvious clue is that the chemical structure of amphetamine closely resembles the structures of dopamine and norepinephrine, two chemicals that occur naturally in the brain. Dopamine and norepinephrine are found at the brain's synapses, the points at which branches of one neuron come close to, but do not quite touch, the sensitive portions of another neuron.

Fire. When a nerve impulse in a neuron reaches a synapse, it triggers the release of chemicals—dopamine or norepinephrine, among others—out of the nerve endings. These wash up against the next neuron and trigger it to renew the nerve impulse and send it on its way to the next neuron link in the chain.

It is through these brain chemicals that one neuron thus communicates with the next, and this neuronal conversation underlies all information-processing, thoughts, plans, and perceptions in the brain. Whether the neurotransmitter is dopamine, norepinephrine or some other chemical, it must be inactivated after it has done its job. Otherwise it would continue to stimulate the second neuron and make it continue firing. Some transmitters are inactivated by other chemicals that neutralize them. Dopamine and norepinephrine are inactivated by being transported back into the nerve endings that released them. Julius Axelrod, who discovered this mechanism, called it "reuptake," and won a Nobel Prize in 1970 for his discovery.

One of the ways amphetamine enters the picture is by inhibiting the reuptake mechanism: small pools of used dopamine or norepinephrine build up at the synapses, thereby causing nerves that are sensitive to dopamine and norepinephrine to fire erratically, repeatedly, and without stimulation from other neurons. The resulting behavior depends on whether the stimulated nerves are in dopamine pathways or norepinephrine pathways.

Image. Which pathways are responsible for which symptoms? We get help in answering this question because amphetamine can be broken down into two mirror-image forms that have different effects on behavior and on the brain's transmitter chemicals. One type rotates polarized light to the right, and is called dextroamphetamine; the left-handed form is levoamphetamine, borrowing *dextro* from Latin to indicate *right* and *levo* to indicate *left*.

It has long been known that dextroamphetamine is by far the more potent of the two forms in stimulating the central nervous system. Smith Kline & French puts out a pill form of dextroamphetamine, under the trade name Dexedrine.

Joseph Coyle, Kenneth Taylor and I have found that

dextroamphetamine is 10 times more powerful than levoamphetamine in inhibiting the reuptake mechanism in norepinephrine nerves. When dextroamphetamine is present in a system, there will be more norepinephrine at brain synapses, the nerves triggered by norepinephrine will fire more often than usual, and the behaviors that are governed by these norepinephrine tracts will be exaggerated. And all of these effects will be dramatically more pronounced with dextroamphetamine than they are with levoamphetamine.

In dopamine tracts, on the other hand, dextroamphetamine and levoamphetamine tend to be equally effective: dextroamphetamine produces a slightly greater pileup of dopamine at the synapses than levoamphetamine does, but the difference is nowhere near the order of 10 to one. This suggests that if a given symptom of amphetamine intake appears about as often with dextroamphetamine as with levoamphetamine, that behavior is probably mediated by the dopamine neurons. If a behavior occurs much more readily with dextroamphetamine than with levoamphetamine, the behavior probably is governed by tracts of norepinephrine neurons.

Rats. Kenneth Taylor and I recently studied two typical amphetamine effects—motor activity and stereotyped behavior—in laboratory rats. With relatively small doses the animals appeared to be excited, running about their cages furiously, and this effect was exactly 10 times more pronounced under dextroamphetamine than it was under levoamphetamine. This perfectly parallels the 10-fold advantage that dextroamphetamine has in producing excess norepinephrine, and it strongly suggests that the central-stimulant and heightened-activity effects are probably produced when amphetamine comes in contact with the norepinephrine neurons of the brain.

With somewhat larger doses of amphetamine, animals begin stereotyped behavior similar to the compulsive, repetitive behavior of speed-freaks. Rats tend to stay in one corner of the cage, to sniff and lick repeatedly, and to gnaw incessantly on any available object, such as the bars of the cage. We found that the two forms of amphetamine were fairly close in their ability to produce stereotyped gnawing in rats. This suggests that the brain's dopamine tracts are responsible for repetitious, stereotyped behavior in amphetamine users. Other investigators have reached the same conclusion by showing that, when dopamine areas of the rat brain are cut out, amphetamine does not produce stereotyped behavior as readily as it usually does.

After hearing about our successful experiments with animals, Burton Angrist and Samuel Gershon at New York University asked the next logical question: how do dextroamphetamine and levoamphetamine compare in producing amphetamine psychosis in human beings? They studied three former amphetamine addicts, volunteers, putting them through the 10-milligram-per-hour regimen that Griffith followed. Each subject went through three separate sessions; once with dextroamphetamine, once with levoamphetamine, and once with a mixture of the two.

Both drugs and the mix produced psychosis in each man and none was markedly more powerful than any other. (Dextroamphetamine was slightly faster than the other preparations, levoamphetamine was the slowest, and the mixture, as might be expected, was intermediate.)

Maps. This finding suggests that amphetamine psychosis is produced by excessive activity in the dopamine tracts of the brain, while such other amphetamine effects as hyperactivity and euphoria originate in the norepinephrine tracts. With a chemical stain developed by a group of Swedish researchers, it has recently become possible to map dopamine and norepinephrine pathways through the brain. We have learned, for example, that some prominent dopamine tracts end in areas of the brain's limbic system that regulate a variety of emotional behaviors. The largest dopamine tract has become famous in its own right: it leads to an area that coordinates body movements, and if the tract is damaged so that there is a deficiency of dopamine, the patient is likely to suffer from Parkinson's disease. L-dopa, the drug that is converted to dopamine in the brain, has been hailed as a miraculous treatment for Parkinson's disease.

The major norepinephrine tracts start in the brain stem and ascend through the medial forebrain bundle—the pleasure center. Animals will work very hard to get electrical stimulation in this area, which likely has an important role in the euphoric high of amphetamine use. The norepinephrine tracts also extend into other parts of the hypothalamus, perhaps into the so-called satiety center which, when stimulated, makes a food-deprived animal stop eating.

Several pharmacologists have found that phenothiazine tranquilizers produce improvements in schizophrenic patients by blocking the dopamine receptors in the brain. This fits nicely with our idea that amphetamine produces psychosis by increasing the amount of dopamine around dopamine-sensitive cells. Phenothiazine alleviates symptoms by working in the opposite direction: it makes the dopamine-sensitive neurons less sensitive.

Systems. Amphetamine-induced psychosis seems to be the best available chemical imitation of schizophrenia. But there remains one nagging difficulty: the amphetamine illness resembles paranoid schizophrenia, not catatonic schizophrenia, undifferentiated schizophrenia, or other forms of the disorder. I don't think this means that paranoid schizophrenia is a different disease from other types. I think that if amphetamine were to act solely on dopamine neurons and had no effect on norepinephrine neurons, the result might be the classic, undifferentiated form of schizophrenia, or a form with characteristics determined only by the personality of the patient. But norepinephrine stimulation adds another set of symptoms to the clinical picture—hyperactivity, sleeplessness, and loss of appetite. The alerting effect may make the patient try to find an intellectual framework for the strange feelings that come over him. He searches for explanations and meanings, and this leads to the elaborate system of delusions that is the essence of paranoia. In short, the basic amphetamine psychosis may arise through the brain's dopamine mechanisms, but the specific paranoid solution comes from the contribution of norepinephrine systems.

Investigators are now trying to improve upon amphetamine, to find a drug that will stimulate dopamine systems but not norepinephrine systems. If my reasoning is accurate, such a drug would produce a pure schizophrenia indistinguishable from the disorder that is observed in mental-hospital wards. The drug would be a boon. It would give specific direction to the search for the cause of natural schizophrenia, and would allow investigators to manipulate schizophrenic symptoms in the laboratory and study, in animals, a vast range of possible cures.

The Right Way to Use a Lie Detector

by David T. Lykken

When people take a lie detector test, the changes in their breathing, heart rate, and sweating can tell the polygrapher when they are lying. But, as David Lykken points out, innocent people also may appear guilty when doubt and fear increase their anxiety, abetted by incriminating questions. These emotions can make anyone look guilty. Thus, says Lykken, lie detectors can lie.

But the picture of lie detection use needn't be that bleak. Lykken discusses a rapid, newer technique that points policemen toward the guilty—and assigns guilt to less than one in ten million innocent individuals. While the author importunes employers on the whole not to use lie detection, he makes an important exception. The device may be pertinent in the selection of police candidates, who can include psychopaths and other dangerous types. And Lykken clarifies the ethical issues raised by the use of polygraphs in contemporary society.

THE LIE-DETECTION business is booming. Millions of people each year are subjected to polygraph tests, and most are not criminal suspects. Some are industrial or business employees, some are job applicants, others are applying for compensation for injuries suffered on the job or in the war. To keep up with the demands for service, more than 3,000 professional polygraphers ply their trade in business and industry alone, and at least a dozen schools are train-

ing new examiners. Polygraphy may soon bring in more
dollars per year than any other area of applied psychology;
what is more, lie detection is having an increasing social
impact.

Not only is the polygraph spreading, it is gaining dangerous clout in our criminal-justice system. Judges are
lifting restrictions on admitting test results as evidence in
criminal trials. In many states, if both the prosecution and
the defense agree, a polygrapher may examine a suspect,
and then testify about the test results in court. Whereas
other expert witnesses help juries by clarifying facts, the
polygrapher testifies essentially about the suspect's guilt or
innocence. He does so by stating his opinion about whether
or not the suspect lied when he denied his guilt. Deciding
guilt or innocense is supposed to be the jury's job.

Psychologists are critical of lie detectors for other reasons. They believe that measuring and interpreting bodily
changes to detect someone's emotional reactions is a job
for trained clinicians, and few polygraphers have any psychological training. They also contest the validity of the
tests, and believe they infringe upon civil rights. Some feel
the whole enterprise should be scrapped. I disagree.

When lie-detector tests are designed, administered and
evaluated properly, they may be one of the most valid
psychological tools we possess. But their purview has
become too broad; they do not belong in business, industry, or court trials. Their proper use is in police interrogation. In fact, I believe that the police use the polygraph too
infrequently because they don't know how to use it effectively. If used wisely, polygraphy can greatly facilitate
police work. To explain why I encourage law-enforcement
officials to use polygraphy, while frowning on its use by
others, I must first outline the fundamentals of the technique, which incidentally, demands considerable psychological insight and skill on the part of the polygrapher.

Detecting Lies, Uncovering Guilt. A polygraph
can be used in two ways; to detect lies or to find out
whether someone knows something. To uncover a liar, an
examiner simply hooks the person up to the machine and

asks him a question: "Did you kill John Doe?" The polygraper evaluates the subject's answer by comparing the accompanying changes in his breathing, heart rate, and skin resistance with his physiological responses to irrelevant questions that also are supposed to produce emotional responses. When a person lies, his autonomic responses are stronger than when he tells the truth. Most polygraphic examinations are lie-detector tests.

But the police fail to take advantage of the polygraph's second function; they fail to use it in what I call the guilty-knowledge test. By recording physiological responses to information that only the police and the guilty party could know, a polygrapher can identify the guilty suspect. Because he lacks guilty knowledge, an innocent suspect has no basis for responding differently to details of the crime than to fictitious details used as control items. The guilty suspect, because he does recognize the details, tends to react differently to the relevant than to the control items. Thus he betrays his guilty knowledge.

One way to demonstrate the value of the polygraph is to describe the course of an actual criminal investigation and show how the polygraph might have prevented an injustice.

Several years ago in New York, a bass player was arrested and charged with armed robbery. He was accused of holding up a number of Manhattan liquor stores and a loan company. The prosecution's case was based entirely on the fact that each victim positively identified the musician as the man who had threatened them with a gun and taken their money.

After two years of court delays, a mistrial, and a second trial, the court found the bass player guilty as charged. Just before he was transferred to prison, another man who looked remarkably similar to the musician, was arrested for armed robbery. He confessed to the previous crimes.

The High Costs of a Mistake. The bass player finally was exonerated. But he had lost his job, his home, his life savings, and his wife, who had been committed to a mental hospital because she could not withstand the emotional strain produced by her husband's predicament.

Now let us suppose that our protagonist had taken a lie-detector test soon after his arrest. While he answered questions such as, "Did you rob the Friendly Loan Company?," the examiner would compare his autonomic responses to this question with his reactions to irrelevant questions. Based on this comparison, he would assess the subject's veracity and report: "deception indicated," "deception not indicated," or "indeterminate."

Let's assume that the polygrapher came to the correct conclusion and ruled, "deception not indicated." This might have led the police to reexamine their evidence against him, and to try harder to corroborate his alibis. But in this case, with an array of positive eyewitness identifications, passing the test might not have convinced the police the musician was innocent.

Suppose, however, that the polygrapher had been more sophisticated. He realized that the guilty-knowledge test would be more useful than a lie-detection test in this case and, with the help of investigating officers, he prepared a test along these lines:

ITEM ONE: The man we're looking for held up a loan office in Manhattan. If you're the guilty party, you will recognize the name of that loan company. I'm going to name a few loan companies that have offices in the vicinity; you just sit there and repeat the names after me. Was it the Ideal Loan Company? . . . the Continental Loan Company? . . . the Guarantee Loan Company? . . . The Friendly Loan Company? . . . or the Fidelity Loan Company?

ITEM TWO: Before showing his gun, the robber pretended that he wanted to take out a loan for a certain purpose. If you're the guilty man, you will know whether that purpose was to buy a car, to pay doctor bills, to pay for a vacation trip, to buy a color TV, or to get a present for his wife. I'm going to name each of these five possibilities in order, and I want you to sit quietly and just repeat what I say.

If the bass player had committed the crimes he would have reacted more dramatically to the true alternatives than to the false ones. And if he were innocent, there would have been only one chance in five on each item that his strongest autonomic response would have been to the guilty alternative.

The examiner would have found that the musician knew little about the crimes. He would have reported his findings to the police, and they might have released the suspect and then resumed their search for the offender.

One Chance in a Million. With 10 guilty-knowledge items of this type, there is only about one chance in 10 million that an innocent suspect will react strongly to the "correct" alternative in all 10 items. And if a suspect shows guilty knowledge on as many as six out of 10 items, the chances that he is innocent are only one in 1,000.

Unfortunately, police departments don't use the polygraph in this way because they fail to understand the difference between guilty knowledge and the lie-detector test. However, I must point out that the guilty-knowledge test cannot be used in all cases. The police have to have enough privileged information to design a test. But even in well publicized cases, it often would be possible to dig up enough details of the crime that only the culprit would know.

The basic assumption of the guilty-knowlege test is straightforward; when an offender recognizes details of his crime, he responds autonomically. The assumptions underlying lie detection are not so straightforward.

Both guilty and innocent suspects may react strongly to a question such as "Did you do it?" Incriminating questions make everyone anxious. Moreover, the magnitude of a suspect's response may depend on factors that have nothing to do with guilt or innocence. Highly emotional but innocent individuals who fear the consequences of flunking a lie-detector test may react to incriminating questions more strongly than unreactive but guilty suspects who are not so fearful. In addition, the lie tests' validity is greatly affected by the subjects' confidence in the test procedure. When they have faith in the technique, guilty suspects react strongly to their own lies because they "know" the test detects lies; innocent persons react less to incriminating questions because they "know" the test correctly assesses the fact that they are telling the truth.

But when suspects do not believe the test is valid, there is a good chance their responses will be affected by their doubts and fears. It is possible that an innocent man, who is terrified that he will go to prison if he flunks the test, will fail the examination, while a psychopathic killer who cares little about the test will pass it.

The same emotional influences that affect a suspect's replies in the lie-detector test can also affect his responses to correct alternatives on the guilt-knowledge test, but in the latter case they also color his responses to the four incorrect choices for each item. By subtracting a suspect's average score on the four incorrect alternatives from his score on the correct choice in each item, the tester can judge whether or not the suspect responded significantly more to the correct answer. In this manner he can rule out the effects of sheer emotionality.

Although the guilty-knowledge test can distinguish guilt from innocence more accurately than the lie-detector test can, I am not suggesting that the latter is invalid. On the contrary, if skillfully administered, the lie test may be one of the most accurate psycholgical test procedures ever developed. The important question, however, is whether or not the test is as infallible as professional polygraphers claim it is. I believe it is not.

When polygraphers estimate that the test is 95 percent or more accurate, we should be skeptical. An examiner cannot know how many of his verdicts were correct and how many were not. Even though courts may find a suspect who has flunked a test guilty, this verdict hardly proves that the examination was infallible. Besides, I know of no polygrapher who even pretends to keep track of the disposition of all cases involving the suspects he has questioned. Polygraphers simply don't know how often their decisions agree with the outcome of cases. Nevertheless, at least one highly experienced polygrapher testified before at least one state legislature that he had conducted more than 20,000 polygraph interrogations and that he had "never once been proved to have made a mistake." We should be wary of these testimonials.

Even laboratory studies cannot adequately measure the

validity of lie-detector tests. Experiments involving mock crimes usually show lie-detector tests are accurate about 70 to 85 percent of the time. Professional polygraphers themselves are critical of laboratory data. They insist, and reasonably, that results might be altogether different in real police investigations. While they believe the polygraph is more accurate in real life, I believe that moving from the laboratory into the real world might also lower the test's validity. Although a guilty suspect may be more apprehensive than a college sophomore facing a mock trial, an innocent suspect may be more anxious in life than in the laboratory. Thus he might appear more guilty than the culprit in a real criminal investigation.

Testing the Test in the Army. It is also difficult to design an experiment to test the validity of lie-detector tests given during police investigations. So far, only one such field study that meets reasonable scientific standards has been published. P. J. Bersh collected records of military criminal investigations. He removed the polygraphic record from each file, and then had four attorneys in the Judge Advocate General's office independently evaluate each case. He asked them to eliminate cases in which there was insufficient evidence, and to arrive at guilty or innocent verdicts in the rest of them.

In 92.4 percent of the 157 cases in which the verdict was unanimous, the judges' decisions agreed with the polygrapher's verdict. In the 59 cases where three of the four judges agreed, test records agreed with their decisions 74.6 percent of the time. But we don't know how many times the verdict was split two to two, and we don't know how many cases the judges threw out for lack of evidence. And most important, none of these findings tells us anything definitive about the lie-detector test itself. Unless the polygraph charts are scored by someone who did not administer the test, the examiner's subjective opinion of the suspect and his other knowledge of the case can influence his decision.

Clearly we have no way to verify the professional claims that the ''mechanical'' lie-detector is accurate 90 or more percent of the time. But Bersh's study does indicate that the "human" lie detector, if he is as well trained and skillful as these Army examiners, can, given additional evidence, evaluate nine out of 10 suspects correctly. Any method that assesses guilt and innocence this accurately is an important investigative tool. When a polygrapher says "guilty," the police should concentrate on finding physical evidence to prove the suspect's guilt; when the examiner says "innocent," the law should look for evidence to prove the subject's innocence. As long as the police view results of lie-detector tests as tentative and advisory rather than as conclusive, the lie detector can make an important and legitimate social contribution.

Looking for Thieving Employees. In recent years, the use of polygraphy has spread far beyond the confines of criminal investigation. Faced with "intramural" theft amounting to some six billion dollars each year, the managers of business and industry have turned to lie detection to root out deceptive employees. Some companies screen workers annually, others require prospective employees to pass lie-detector tests before they will hire them.

Just as the guilty-knowledge test differs from a lie-detector test, so employee screening differs from the use of polygraphy in criminal investigations. These differences make it clear why polygraphy is inappropriate in the world of work.

The first difference has to do with what happens to an innocent suspect who flunks a lie-detector test. In criminal investigations, police officers must have other evidence to back up a polygrapher's decision before they bring a case to trial. But when an employee fails the lie-detector test, he may be immediately fired, and a job applicant who flunks loses any chance at the job. The Constitution protects a criminal suspect from going to prison for failing a lie-detector test, but nothing protects a man from losing gainful employment for the same reason. A recent occurrence in a Minneapolis advertising agency illustrates how innocent people are hurt by this practice.

One day someone stole a $6,000 movie camera from a

locked cabinet. Because the lock was intact, the company assumed an employee had taken the camera. Investigators asked the four men who had keys to the cabinet to take lie-dector tests, and all agreed to be tested. One of them clearly failed. He was a young, black, account executive who was doing so well with the company that management refused to accept the verdict and sent him back to be reexamined by another polygrapher. Again he failed. The company had him tested a third time and, for the third time, the verdict was "probable deception."

Just as the company president was about to fire this apparent thief, a fifth worker confessed to the crime. Except for this lucky turn of events, the promising young executive would have lost his job. He would have been out on the street, saddled with the fact that he had been fired for dishonesty, with little hope of finding work in his profession.

Innocent individuals are more likely to fail lie-detector tests in personnel screening than in criminal investigations because employers routinely screen all workers while the police restrict the test to prime suspects. If we assume that the test is valid 90 percent of the time, the mathematics of the situation go something like this.

Criminal investigators will give the test only to likely suspects. If as many as half of them are actually guilty, then nine out of 10 who fail the test will indeed be liars. But the base rate for lying in the employee-screening situation will be much lower than in police work, certainly much lower than 50 percent.

Suppose 50 of a company's 1,000 employees are pilferers. The lie detector will assess 45 (90 percent) of them as guilty. It will also correctly identify 855 (90 percent) of the 950 innocent workers. But the remaining 95 (10 percent) will fail the test. This means that more than two out of three of the 140 persons who flunk the test will be innocent. It is plain that too many innocent persons suffer when lie-detector tests are used to screen employees. I believe the practice should be outlawed.

Any professional polygrapher who reads these words will be gnashing his teeth as he thinks of all those shame-faced individuals who have confessed under the pressure of a lie-detector examination. But we cannot use elicited confessions and ignore all others who fail the test, but don't confess. If we could, I might feel differently about the whole thing. Unfortunately it wouldn't work. Once guilty employees got wind of the fact that no one fails the test unless he confesses, they would no longer confess.

Screening Police Officers. There is one exception, however, to my belief that lie detectors should be ousted from employee screening. Because of the great attraction police work has for the psychopath and other dangerous types, polygraphic screening of applicants for jobs on the police force or for other sensitive occupations may be in the public interest.

Two years ago I testified before the Minnesota Legislature in support of a bill that would prohibit employers from requiring or even requesting employees or prospective employees to take polygraphic examinations. The bill became law, but the law is ineffective. Employers continue to screen applicants because the present law is difficult to enforce. The most effective course of action might be for legislatures to proscribe the sale of lie-detector services for employee screening. It is much easier to police a few sellers then the myriad offending employers.

In answer to those who claim that the practice is necessary to curb mounting employee pilferage, I say this: stealing is the employer's problem. The fact that theft exists does not justify the violation of an employee's civil rights. Rising theft indicates that something is seriously wrong with employer-employee relations in this country. I suggest most workers would not steal if they felt involved in the company's success or failure, or if they had any pride in their own contributions. As survey researcher Daniel Yankelovich pointed out [see "Turbulence in the Working World: Angry Workers, Happy Grads," PT, December], when employers treat employees like cogs in a machine, employees retaliate.

Management must humanize the work place, structure jobs so employees feel they are a valued part of the organization, and reward workers' contributions. We should take lie-detector tests away from business, and let managers live with financial losses. When they are no longer willing to put up with employee theft, they may change oppressive work conditions.

Unfortunately, few people are aware of the expanding use of lie detectors. Fewer still understand the fundamentals of the art. Perhaps once the public has the facts concerning the uses and misuses of lie detectors, they will force legislatures and industry to evaluate the burgeoning practice of polygraphy.

V.

ADJUSTING

Risky Assumptions

by Paul Slovic, Baruch Fischoff, and Sarah Lichtenstein

Paul Slovic and his colleagues specialize in problems of judgment, decision-making and risk-taking. In "Risky Assumptions," they share with us some of their expertise on social policy and risk: choices about nuclear power and handguns, among other issues.

In their investigations Slovic et al. asked people to guess the frequency and risk of death from a formidable array of hazardous situations and circumstances—e.g., pesticides, earthquakes, antibiotics. On the whole, people guessed wrong: They exaggerated some fears and downplayed others.

Yet experts, Slovic and his colleagues are quick to point out, are not much more accurate. By trying to explain how both professional and lay perceptions of dangers can be so distorted, the authors alert us to some common dangers in decision-making. They caution against overconfidence on the one hand, and groundless fears on the other, whether it is regarding the risks of nuclear power or home appliances.

WHY DO SOME communities vigorously oppose the siting of a nuclear reactor or liquified natural gas terminal in their vicinity despite expert assurances that these technologies are safe? Why, on the other hand, do expert warnings about earthquake faults or the dangers of large dams go unheeded? Making sense of such reactions falls to the psychological study of perceived risk. Some of the findings are ripe for application by policymakers and utilities officials, and also by individuals trying to deal with their personal fears.

We have recently completed a number of studies that asked people to judge the frequency and risk of death from a large number of hazardous activities, substances, and technologies, ranging from nuclear power to power lawn-mowers. We found that people greatly overestimated the frequency of deaths from such dramatic, sensational causes as accidents, homicides, cancer, botulism, and tornadoes—and underestimated the frequency of death from unspectacular causes that claim one victim at a time and are common in nonfatal form—diabetes, stroke, tuberculosis, asthma, and emphysema. Accidents were judged to cause as many deaths as diseases; diseases actually take about 15 times as many lives. Homicides were judged to be about five times as frequent as suicides; suicides are actually 30 percent more frequent. Death from asthma was judged to occur only slightly more often than death from botulism; asthma is actually responsible for more than 900 times as many deaths.

Participants in our studies were college students and members of the League of Women Voters in Eugene, Oregon. In one experiment, we told them the annual death toll for motor vehicle accidents in the United States (50,000) and asked them to estimate the frequency of 40 other causes of death. In another, we gave participants pairs of causes of death and asked them to choose which cause in each pair was more frequent.

The errors of estimation we found seemed to reflect the working of a mental shortcut or "heuristic" that people commonly use when they judge the likelihood of risky events. The psychologists Daniel Kahneman and Amos Tversky have identified one heuristic of special importance, "availability," whereby people judge an event as likely or frequent if instances of it are easy to imagine or recall. Since frequent events are generally easier to imagine and recall than rare ones, availability is often an appropriate cue. However, availability is also affected by numerous factors unrelated to the real frequency of occurrence, such as how dramatic or sensational an event is. A recent disaster or a vivid film, such as *Jaws* or *The China Syndrome*, could inflate judgments of the likelihood of similar events.

In another study, we asked participants to rank the overall *risk* of dying from 30 activities or technologies on a list including, this time, nuclear power. We also obtained estimates from 15 experts across the country who are professionally involved in assessing risks, including a geographer, an environmental policy analyst, an economist, a lawyer, a biologist, a biochemist, and a government regulator of hazardous materials. Forty participating members of the League of Women Voters agreed closly with the experts in ranking some hazards, like power lawnmowers, as low in risk, and others, like handguns and motor vehicles, as high. But they ranked nuclear power as much more dangerous than the experts did (again, a dramatic issue), and thought x-rays, contraceptives, and nonnuclear electric power safer. In fact,the lethal potential of technologies such as nuclear power plants is in dispute even among experts, with technical estimates based on uncertain inferences about processes that are not always well understood.

The tendency of people to overestimate the frequency of dramatic or sensational events is compounded by similar biases in the news media. In collaboration with our colleague Barbara Combs, we examined reports of causes of death for six months of 1975 in two small newspapers on opposite coasts of the United States: the Eugene, Oregon *Register Guard* and the New Bedford, Massachusetts *Standard Times*. Reports of deaths involving diseases were relatively infrequent and received less space than reports of deaths from violent, often catastrophic, and more newsworthy events such as tornadoes, fires, drownings, homicides, and accidents, which were reported disproportionately often. For instance, even though diseases take about 100 times as many lives as homicides do, the papers carried about three times as many articles about homicides as they did about deaths involving diseases.

* * *

One pernicious aspect of heuristics is that people are often very confident about the judgments they base on them. In a follow-up to our study on causes of death, we asked participants for the odds that they were incorrect in choosing the more frequently lethal event in several pairs. For example, if they thought botulism killed more frequently than asthma, we asked them to estimate the odds on their being wrong. The participants frequently—25 percent of the time—said the odds against their judgment being wrong were 100 to 1 or greater. If they had given correct odds, such people in fact would have been wrong once in 100 times or less; instead, they were wrong about 1 out of every 8 times; thus they should have given themselves odds of 7 to 1. About 30 percent gave odds greater than 50 to 1 to the incorrect assertion that homicides outnumber suicides.

The psychological basis for this overconfidence seems to be people's insensitivity to the tenuousness of the assumptions on which they base their judgments. In this case, they may have assumed that frequent media reports of homicide and suicide accurately reflected the actual rates. Such overconfidence, of course, can keep us from realizing how little we know and how much additional information we need about the risks we face.

Another important and potentially tragic form of overconfidence is people's tendency to consider themselves personally immune to many hazards whose risks to others they would acknowledge readily. In a report titled "Are We All Among the Better Drivers?" Ola Svenson, a Swedish psychologist, showed that most people tend to rate themselves as among the most skillful and the safest drivers in the population. This effect does not seem to be limited just to driving. A recent study by Arno Rethans, a professor of marketing at Penn State, found that people rated their own risks from each of 29 hazardous consumer products like knives and hammers as lower than risks those products posed to others. Ninety-seven percent of Rethans's respondents thought they would be either average or above average in their ability to avoid bicycle and power lawnmower accidents—which is highly improbable. A study by Neil Weinstein, a psychologist at Rutgers University, found people to be unrealistically optimistic in evaluating the chances that good and bad life events would happen to them, such as living past 80 or having a heart attack.

We believe that several factors contribute to determining when such optimism comes into play. First, people tend to underestimate personal risks if they think hazards are under their control. Second, the hazards they underrate tend to be familiar ones in which risks are so low that personal experience of them is overwhelmingly benign. Automobile driving is a prime example. Although poor drivers may drive too fast or tailgate, they make trip after trip without mishap, "proving" to themselves their exceptional skill and caution. Moreover, indirect experience, via the media, shows them that when accidents do happen, they happen to others. Misleading experiences encourage erroneous conclusions; they can help rationalize a refusal to take protective action, such as wearing seat belts.

A corollary of being influenced by the information that is available is that one ignores the information that is unavailable: out of sight is out of mind. For this reason, experts also seem subject to overconfidence, particularly when they try to assess the risks of potentially catastrophic hazards that are rare or for which direct experience is lacking, such as nuclear-reactor accidents. If they cannot imagine important causes of possible problems, such causes will be omitted from their analysis—with no cue that the basis of their estimate is faulty until an actual problem occurs. (See "Post-Freudian Slips," *PT*, April 1980.)

In another of our experiments, we showed 15 professional automobile mechanics a diagram outlining various types of mechanical failures that could keep a car from starting. When we deliberately left out many important problems, most of the experts failed to notice their absence. Other sources of bias in expert judgement are:

☐ Overconfidence in current scientific knowledge. For example, experts failed to recognize the harmful effects of x-rays until their use had become widespread and largely uncontrolled.

☐ Insensitivity to how technological systems function

as a whole. The DC-10 crashed in two early flights because its designers had not realized that accidental decompression of the cargo compartment would destroy vital parts of the plane's control system.

☐ Failure to anticipate human responses to safety measures. The partial flood protection afforded by dams and levees gives people a false sense of security and promotes development on flood plains. When a rare flood exceeds the capacity of the dam, however, damage can be considerably greater than it might have been had the flood plain not been "protected."

☐ Human errors. Due to inadequate training, operating procedures, and control room design, operators at Three Mile Island misdiagnosed the problems of the reactor and took inappropriate corrective actions. A minor incident thus became a major accident.

Nowhere are the issues of perceived risk more salient or the stakes higher than in the controversy over nuclear power. Though a number of commentators have speculated that people's strong fears of nuclear power stem from a belief that death from radiation is somehow more horrible than death from other causes, our studies of members of the League of Women Voters indicate that, instead, their fears appear to derive from concern over how many deaths are likely. Their mental images of a nuclear accident include the specter of hundreds of thousands, even millions, of immediate deaths, accompanied by incalculable and irreversible damage to the environment. These images bear little resemblance to the views of industry officials (and most technical experts), who expect redundant safety and containment systems to prevent almost all reactor accidents and limit the damage of those that do occur.

Industry proponents attribute this perception gap to public irrationality—"emotionalism that threatens technological progress." Increasingly, they call for programs to "educate" us about "real" nuclear power risks.

We question this attribution of irrationality, and we doubt that its proposed remedy, education, will easily succeed. For although people's fears may be exaggerated, they are not divorced from reality. People are aware of experts' serious mistakes in the past and of the experts' own disagreements about the risks of nuclear power. Hence, to be believed, any balanced presentation of information has to convey the uncertainty and disagreement that characterizes expert opinion. The immediate impact of such education is illustrated by the Swedish government's massive campaign in 1974 to inform people about nuclear power and other energy sources. More than 80,000 people listened to at least 10 hours of instruction sponsored by the Ministries of Education and Industry. Yet according to Dorothy Nelkin, a sociologist at Cornell, the most significant effect of this was to increase public confusion and uncertainty: people could not resolve conflicting technical views.

Then, too, education can also encourage people to imagine risks they might never have thought about otherwise. An engineer might argue for the safety of disposing of nuclear wastes in a salt bed, for example, by pointing out the improbability of each of the several ways radioactivity could accidentally be released. Rather than reassure the audience, the presentation might lead them to think, "I didn't realize there were that many things that could go wrong."

Another barrier to educational attempts is that people's beliefs change slowly and are extraordinarily resistant to new information. Research in social psychology has often demonstrated that once formed, people's initial impressions tend to structure the way they interpret subsequent information. They give full weight to evidence that is consistent with their initial beliefs while dismissing contrary evidence as unrealiable, erroneous, or unrepresentative. Whereas opponents of nuclear power believe the accident at Three Mile Island "proved" how dangerous reactors are, proponents felt that it confirmed their faith in the effectiveness of the multiple safety and containment systems.

Since even well-informed citizens have difficulty in judging risk accurately, and the cognitive functioning of experts appears to be basically like that of everyone else, it seems clear that no one person or profession knows how to get the right answers. The best we can hope to do is to keep the particular kinds of mistakes to which each of us is prone to a minimum by being more aware of our tendency to make mistakes.

For nonexperts, the challenge is to be sensitive to the circumstances that might seriously distort judgments of risk and to be open to new evidence that may alter our current views. Experts need to recognize their own cognitive limitations, to sympathize with the concerns of the public, and to understand how people come to those concerns. As both groups get better at perceiving risks, society may be able to move on to the harder task of deciding which risks are worth running.

The Perfectionist's Script for Self-defeat

by David D. Burns

Reaching for the proverbial stars, perfectionists clutch at empty air. Obsessive-compulsives, the technical label for perfectionists, are especially given to troubled relationships, moodiness, and generalized malaise. They drive themselves to achieve perfection, working doggedly toward a receding goal. Surprisingly, their propensity for work may not be advantageous; they often achieve less than others. So writes David Burns, a psychiatrist who has studied the obstacles to happiness in the hues of perfectionists.

Burns presents some startling observations. For example, he uncovers the surprising statistic that insurance agents with perfectionistic habits actually earn $15,000 a year less than other agents. Perfectionistic dieters are particularly prone to self-destructive behavior. One dieter interviewed by Burns felt so guilty after tasting some ice cream that she ate the whole quart!

Burns also provides some psychological understanding of the perfectionistic syndrome. Perfectionists are especially sensitive to disapproval, owing to early rejections, and this inhibits both their performance at work and intimacy with lovers. They have difficulty in taking some needed risks and thus are tentative with their creative energy, which also hampers their work performance. But all is not hopeless for the thousands among us who have perfectionistic tendencies to one degree or another. Burns concludes with some suggestions for change and growth. The burdens of perfectionism can be eased, Burns seems to say, but usually with the help of a therapist.

A HIGHLY SUCCESSFUL BUT chronically depressed academician recently told me, "Without my perfectionism, I'd be just an inadequate and basically mediocre person. Who wants to be average?" Like many people, this man sees his perfectionism as the painful price he must pay for success. He acknowledges that his relentless standards are stressful and somewhat unreasonable, but he believes they drive him to levels of excellence and productivity he could never attain otherwise.

This attitude is remarkably widespread. Indeed, it amounts to a cultural phenomenon and is reinforced by language patterns, the media, and religious beliefs. Many athletes and coaches live by the maxim No Pain, No Gain, reflecting their conviction that significant gains in strength and endurance occur only when athletes push themselves beyond their natural limits to the point of agony. In complimenting a friend on a good golf shot or a pleasant dinner party, people feel constrained to say "Superb!" or "It was a *perfect* evening!" A recently published advertisement for a camera urged in bold print, "Experience the Sense of Perfection." The text went on, "If you have ever taken a luxury sports car through a tight turn, you know the feeling."

The implied promise is that perfectionism brings rewards. Are these rewards real, or is the promise false and the allure based on illusion? Just what in fact are the costs and benefits of perfectionism?

Before trying to answer the question, I want to make clear what I mean by perfectionism. I do *not* mean the healthy pursuit of excellence by men and women who take genuine pleasure in striving to meet high standards. Without concern for quality, life would seem shallow and true accomplishment would be rare. The perfectionists I am talking about are those whose standards are high beyond reach or reason, people who strain compulsively and unremittingly toward impossible goals and who measure their own worth entirely in terms of productivity and accomplishment. For these people, the drive to excel can only be self-defeating.

Evidence is mounting that the price this kind of perfectionist pays for the habit includes not only decreased productivity but also impaired health, poor self-control, troubled personal relationships, and low self-esteem. The perfectionist also appears to be vulnerable to a number of potentially serious mood disorders, including depression, performance anxiety, test anxiety, social anxiety, writer's block, and obsessive-compulsive illness. In studies conducted at the University of Pennsylvania Mood Clinic (also known as the Center for Cognitive Therapy), we observed a high incidence of perfectionistic attitudes in people suffering from depressive illness. While that does not prove that there is a causal relationship between perfectionism and depression, our clinical research suggests that perfectionism may be one of the key psychological factors predisposing certain people to painful mood swings. Perfectionistic individuals, we find, are likely to respond to the perception of failure or inadequacy with a precipitous loss in self-esteem that can trigger episodes of severe depression and anxiety.

In order to evaluate the proposition that these represent extreme cases and that a little perfectionism can help a person achieve high levels of success, I recently administered a questionnaire that measures perfectionistic attitudes to a group of 34 highly successful insurance agents at the Philadelphia Million Dollar Forum. The salaries of the group ranged from $29,000 a year to more than $250,000. Eighteen of the agents proved to have perfectionistic "cognitive styles" (ways of thinking), while 16 were nonperfectionistic. I also administered a second questionnaire that assesses the tendency to measure personal worth and self-esteem by success and productivity. I anticipated that the highest salaries would be earned by those who were perfectionistic and most likely to evaluate their self-esteem in terms of sales.

The results were surprising. The average earnings of the perfectionists were not significantly greater than those of the nonperfectionists. In fact, the trend was in the opposite direction; the perfectionists who linked self-worth and achievement earned an average of $15,000 a year less than the nonperfectionists did. Apparently the salesmen who were striving for perfection were actually paying a price in dollars for their mental habit.

Actually, the findings at the Million Dollar Forum were not so unusual. Studies of highly successful athletes have documented an absence of perfectionistic cognitive styles. In one study, Michael Mahoney and his collaborators at Penn State University described attitudinal characteristics that differentiated "elite" male gymnasts who qualified for Olympic competition from less successful athletes who failed to qualify. The researchers found that the elite group tended to underemphasize the importance of past performance failures, while the athletes who failed to qualify were more likely to rouse themselves into near-panic states during competition through mental images of self-doubt and impending tragedy. Andrew W. Meyers and his collaborators at Memphis State University recently confirmed a number of Mahoney's findings in their study of highly successful racquetball players. The Meyers group found that the less-skilled players reported greater difficulty in recovering from mistakes and were more likely to set perfectionistic standards.

Perfectionism also takes a heavy toll within our educational system. I recently conducted a study of the dropout phenomenon at the University of Pennsylvania Law School, in collaboration with Vice-Dean Phyllis Beck. We studied and treated 25 students, 80 percent of them in their first year of law school, who sought counseling because of a high degree of stress. Many of them expressed an urge to leave school, and most were suffering from depression or anxiety.

Among a majority of students in this group, we observed an entrenched, perfectionistic thinking pattern. The law school has highly competitive entrance requirements, so these students had been used to perceiving themselves at or near the top of their class during high school and college. In spite of their rational understanding that law school lumped them together with the cream of the crop, they nevertheless had great difficulty in accepting any personal role that meant being less than No. 1.

PERFECTIONIST FEARS AND SYMPTOMS

When such students begin to realize that their performance will place them somewhere in the middle of the pack, they react with frustration, anger, depression, and panic. Because their previous experiences have left them psychologically unprepared for an "average" role, they are prone to perceive themselves, unrealistically, as second-rate losers. Their self-respect plummets, and they experience a strong desire to withdraw from painful circumstances. The disturbance can become so intense that they may contemplate and even attempt suicide. (The high suicide rate among some professional groups, such as physicians, is perhaps explained in part by the perfectionistic thinking patterns that are believed to be common among them.)

The dropout phenomenon occurs most frequently in students who have been excellent performers in school. Students who have performed unevenly or poorly in the past rarely complain about their grades. They apparently have learned to cope with middling or poor performance by using methods that protect their personal identity and esteem from wounding self-criticism.

In addition to being victimized by impaired productivity and emotional disturbances, the perfectionist may also be at risk of impaired health. During the mid-1970s, reports by Meyer Friedman and Ray H. Rosenman of increased coronary disease in people exhibiting Type-A behavior attracted considerable attention. The Type-A person has been described as highly competitive, excessively achievement-oriented, impatient, easily frustrated and angered, time-pressured, and preoccupied with deadlines. A number of investigators have reported a high incidence of perfectionistic beliefs in such people.

Finally, it appears that many perfectionists are plagued by loneliness and disturbances in personal relationships. Because the perfectionists fear and anticipate rejection when they are judged as imperfect, they tend to react defensively to criticism. Their response usually frustrates and alienates others and may bring about the very disapproval perfectionists most fear. This reinforces their irrational belief that they must be perfect to be accepted.

Because of their fear of appearing foolish or inadequate, perfectionists may have a disclosure phobia that causes them to resist sharing their inner thoughts and feelings. They believe that their human foibles will not be acceptable to others, and their excessive sensitivity to real or imagined disapproval inhibits intimate communication, further depriving them of the warmth and unconditional acceptance they crave but cannot earn through accomplishment.

When perfectionists apply their excessively high standards to others and are inevitably disappointed, they react with annoyance. Typically, the object of the perfectionist's judgmental attitude reacts with resentment, the perfectionist becomes more demanding, and both parties end up exasperated.

Recently investigators have been asking why the perfectionist is so vulnerable to emotional turmoil and impaired productivity. It appears that a variety of factors may undermine the perfectionist's motivation and sense of competence. These factors include illogical and distorted thinking patterns, self-defeating strategies for self-management, and the fact that the perfectionist generally experiences more punishment than reward.

THE MECHANISM OF IMPAIRMENT

Perhaps the most common mental distortion found among perfectionists is all-or-nothing thinking. They evaluate their experiences in a dichotomous manner, seeing things as either all-black or all-white; intermediate shades of gray do not seem to exist. That outlook is epitomized by the straight-A student who receives a B on an examination and concludes, "Now I am a total failure." Dichotomous thinking causes the perfectionist to fear mistakes and to overreact to them.

A second system of mental distortion commonly observed in perfectionists derives from overgeneralization: they tend to jump to the dogmatic conclusion that a negative event will be repeated endlessly. When perfectionists make mistakes, they tell themselves, "I'm always goofing up. I'll never get this right." Because of such over-generalized thinking, perfectionists perceive themselves as having a very narrow margin of safety.

A third distortion system that plagues perfectionists involves "should" statements. Many therapists, including Karen Horney, have emphasized the tyranny of "should" systems. When perfectionists fall short of a goal (for example, by overeating on a weekend), they are not likely to ask themselves "How can I learn from this?" with a compassionate attitude of self-acceptance. Instead, they harangue themselves, saying, "I *shouldn't* have goofed up! I *ought to* to do better! I *mustn't* do that again!" Such statements create feelings of frustration and guilt that, ironically, cause them to get stuck on the error. They become trapped by nonproductive, self-critical ruminations that lead to depression and an unrealistically negative self-image. Consistent with that, in a study conducted at UCLA, Constance L. Hammen and Susan Krantz reported that depressed women had more self-critical thoughts than nondepressed women did, and that real life success failed to reduce self-criticism.

The perfectionists' dichotomous thinking and moralistic self-evaluations contribute to their psychological distress and cause them to adopt strategies for personal growth and self-management that are naive and self-defeating. Michael Mahoney has described a saint-or-sinner syndrome that contributes to the failure of the perfectionist's efforts at self-control in activities like eating, smoking, and drinking. When perfectionists embark on a diet, they tell themselves they must either be *off* or *on* the diet, which is defined in strict terms. The first time the perfectionist lapses from the rigorous routine, the period of sainthood ends and the chance for perfect dieting is viewed as lost forever. This ushers in an ensuing period of "sin," characterized by guilt, moralistic self-deprecation, and binges. One dieting physician ate a tablespoon of ice cream and scolded herself by saying, "I shouldn't have done that!

I'm a pig." These ideas so upset her that she went on to eat an entire quart of ice cream.

Research has underscored just how ineffective self-punishment can be in facilitating personal growth or modifying habits. Mahoney and his collaborators found that self-reward was far more effective in helping dieters lose weight. In fact, a group who were taught to follow a system of self-punishment when they went off their diets did not lose significantly more weight than did a no-treatment control group. Because the perfectionist pursues this pernicious strategy for self-control in a wide variety of activities, he or she experiences an uncontrollable roller-coaster effect characterized by emotional lability, extreme fluctuation in motivation, and inconsistent effort.

Albert Bandura at Stanford University has recently hypothesized that the probability that a person will perform any behavior necessary to bring about a desired result depends, first, upon the perception that the behavior will in fact produce the desired result (this is termed "outcome efficacy"), and, second, upon the person's being capable of performing the necessary behavior (this is termed "self-efficacy"). The perfectionist's mind-set undermines both types of efficacy: the chance that a desired outcome can be achieved is inversely proportional to the stringency of the standard used to measure it. Stated simply, the higher the standard of success, the less likely it is that a successful result will be perceived as a probable outcome. Thus, the perfectionist minimizes outcome efficacy by setting over-ambitious and nearly inaccessible goals.

Because of a compulsive drive to achieve a flawless product, he or she also has trouble sensing when the point of diminishing returns has been reached and when a task should be considered complete. As a perfectionistic academician confessed, "I spent three years writing one superb paper that I would rate as 99 percent excellent. It was emotionally exhausting. During the same time, a less-talented associate wrote five papers. I would rate each of them as only about 80 percent excellent. Overall, he ended up with 400 achievement units [five times 80 percent], whereas I ended up with only 99 [one times 99 percent].

He got much more recognition overall, even though he didn't do any one thing that was particularly brilliant.'' (Of course, it can be argued that one superb paper is worth more than five lesser papers and that the academician might have chosen to explore the reasons why he found it emotionally exhausting, rather than gratifying, to carry out a task that was evidently not beyond his abilities.)

Perfectionists also perceive themselves as inefficient because they tend to imagine that successful people achieve personal goals with minimal effort, few errors, maximal self-confidence, and little, if any, emotional distress. Because of this fantasy, perfectionists are likely to view their own quite human coping efforts as inadequate. As they dwell on their shortcomings, they tend to feel inferior and underrewarded, robbing themselves of satisfaction and further undermining their motivation.

Because perfectionists see themselves as inefficient and are likely to fall short of their unreachable aims, they are plagued by a sense of helplessness to achieve desired goals. This effect may explain the extreme motivational paralysis we observe in perfectionistic patients during periods of depression. It is reminiscent of the "learned helplessness" noted by Martin Seligman in dogs subjected to stressful shocks that they were unable to control. Seligman observed that when experimental conditions were changed so that the dogs had only to cross a low hurdle to escape the pain, they repeatedly failed to move. He then proposed a learned-helplessness hypothesis to explain this passivity and has documented the phenomenon in many species, including man. (See *Psychology Today*, June 1969.)

There has been little systematic research on the origins of perfectionism as a cognitive style or characteristic way of thinking. Freud proposed that obsessive-compulsive tendencies result from the need to repress unacceptable hostile impulses, but there has been little, if any, convincing experimental data to support his theory. Treatment strategies that urge the patient to "get the anger out" by expressing aggressive feelings are rarely, if ever, successful. More recent theorists, including Harry Stack Sullivan, have viewed perfectionism as a way of dealing with feelings of insecurity and uncertainty that result from growing up in an unloving household. In his recent book, *Treatment of the Obsessive Personality*, Leon Salzman of Georgetown University Medical School has argued that the perfectionist's tender impulses are at the core of the difficulty; the problem is not the hostile impulses, but rather the need to be loved and accepted.

LEARNING TO BE PERFECTIONISTIC

I believe that perfectionism may be in part learned from a child's interactions with perfectionistic parents. This is the way I see the process working: a child is regularly rewarded with love and approval for outstanding performance; when the parents react to the child's mistakes and failures with anxiety and disappointment, the child is likely to interpret that as punishment or rejection. The perfectionistic parent often feels frustrated and threatened when a child is having difficulties in schoolwork or in relationships with peers. Because the parent is unrealistically self-critical, he or she personalizes the child's difficulties by thinking, "This shows what a bad mother (or father) I am." Because the parent's self-esteem is contingent on the child's success, the parent puts great pressure on the child to avoid failure. Consequently, when the troubled child turns to the parent for reassurance or guidance, the parent reacts with irritation, not love, and the child is flooded with shame.

The child begins to anticipate that mistakes will lead to a loss of acceptance. Because the child bases a sense of self-esteem on the parent's approval, the child begins to fear mistakes and to avoid failure. This leads to emotional constriction and fear of any experience or adventure in which the outcome is not guaranteed. The child becomes anxious and upset about making mistakes, which further reinforces the perfectionistic parent's belief that failure is dangerous and undesirable. Essentially, the parent and child are locked into a kind of *folie-à-deux*.

Once the child has adopted a perfectionistic mind-set, I

believe it perpetuates itself easily. Whenever the child performs in an outstanding manner, he or she repeats an internal message of the following type: "I did *perfectly* on this. This shows I'm okay; I deserve to feel good." It is easy to imagine that the positive feelings created by the inner dialogue powerfully reinforce the perfectionism. In contrast, when the child makes an error or goofs up, the automatic response is a succession of self-punishing negative thoughts: "Oh no, I goofed up. I *shouldn't* have made that mistake. This is terrible! How could I be so stupid?" That kind of thinking results in guilt, anxiety, and frustration, further reinforcing the belief that mistakes are unacceptable.

I believe that perfectionistic attitudes and their emotional consequences reinforce each other. Since powerful positive and negative emotional effects probably occur many times every day as a child grows up, it is not difficult to comprehend the power that perfectionism exerts and the rigidity with which many people adhere to it.

As perfectionistic children grow up, the ratio of reward to punishment begins to shift in an unfavorable direction because they find it increasingly difficult to live up to the unrealistic standards they have learned to set. As they enter high school and move on to college and graduate school, the competition stiffens, and the level of work becomes increasingly sophisticated. The gap between expectation and actual performance widens, and perfectionistic students now begin to experience stress and an aversion to learning. They also become vulnerable to painful mood swings and loss of self-esteem, sometimes at a tragically young age.

One might think that the increasing pain and decreasing reward would tend to extinguish the perfectionistic habit as a child gets older, but in point of fact, the opposite may occur. Many behavior-modification studies, among them one by B. F. Skinner, have suggested that intermittent reinforcement (infrequent and unpredictable reward) can actually intensify a conditioned behavior and prevent its extinction. That may explain the stubborn and illogical insistence with which many perfectionists cling to their self-defeating attitudes in spite of the suffering they experience.

Conditioning may be only part of the story. The clinical psychologist Albert Ellis has speculated that human beings may be born with an innate tendency to engage in certain self-defeating thinking patterns, among them perfectionism, but there is little, if any, systematic research to prove or disprove his hypothesis.

In addition to possible contributions from heredity and upbringing, we cannot rule out the potential influence of culture in developing perfectionistic attitudes. It can be readily observed, as I suggested earlier, in religious doctrine, advertising, literature, education systems, and language.

The causes and effects of perfectionism cannot be studied scientifically unless perfectionism can be measured. In collaboration with our research group, Arlene Weissman recently completed reliability and validity studies on a Dysfunctional Attitude Scale (DAS) that measures a number of self-defeating attitudes commonly seen in people who suffer from clinical depression and anxiety. I have modified a portion of the DAS to create the Perfectionism Scale. The total score on the test can range between +20 and −20. Scores between 0 and 20 indicate increasing degrees of perfectionism, while negative scores indicate a nonperfectionistic mind-set.

The Perfectionism Scale can be used in correlational studies to answer any number of interesting research questions. For example, is there more perfectionism in people who suffer from writer's block, or is there more of it in people with performance anxiety and depression? Does a training program that reduces perfectionistic thinking patterns result in improved productivity, self-control, and mood?

In addition, the Perfectionism Scale can be used to sort out the relative role of genetics, upbringing, and cultural influence in the development of perfectionism. For instance, if the incidence of perfectionism in the children of perfectionistic parents is *not* significantly higher than that observed among the children of nonperfectionistic parents, that would imply a negligible contribution from genetic factors as well as from parental influence. In contrast, if perfectionistic parents do have an increased incidence of perfectionistic children, systematic genetic studies—perhaps studies of identical twins reared apart—would be needed to evaluate the relative contributions from heredity and parental interaction. None of this research has yet been done.

THE TREATMENT OF PERFECTIONISM

Of course, there is nothing inherently pathological about setting high standards for oneself, and those who do so selectively are not necessarily unhappy or unproductive. But people who are habitual perfectionists can often profit from treatment. The approach I use is called cognitive behavior therapy, which relies on trying to change certain cognitive processes: the perceptions, beliefs, or wishes that make a patient anxious or depressed. An account of how this kind of therapy works for some perfectionists sheds a good deal of light on the nature of perfectionism and on the thinking processes of people whose lives are dominated by it.

Therapists find they can readily elicit self-defeating perfectionistic attitudes with gentle Socratic questioning. During his first therapy session, a troubled first-year law student named Fred confessed, "When the professor calls on me, I'll probably goof up." I explored the meaning of this with him:

    David: Suppose you did goof up in class, Fred. Why would that be particularly upsetting? What would that mean to you?

    Fred: Well, then I would make a fool of myself.

    David: Suppose you did make a fool of yourself? Why would that be upsetting to you?

    Fred: Because then everyone would look down on me for it.

    David: Suppose people did look down on you, what then?

Fred: Then I would feel miserable.

David: Why is that? Why is it that you would feel miserable if people were looking down on you?

Fred: Well, that would mean I wouldn't be a worthwhile person. Furthermore, it might ruin my career. I'd get bad grades, I'd flunk out, and I might never become an attorney.

David: And what then? What would that mean to you?

Fred: That would mean I had failed at something I've wanted all my life.

David: And then what would that mean to you?

Fred: Life would be empty. It would mean I was a failure. It would mean I was worthless.

In this brief dialogue, Fred revealed the perfectionistic orientation that causes his difficulties. He believes it would be terrible for him to be disapproved of, to make a mistake, or to fail at achieving a personal goal. Because of his tendency to overgeneralize, he has convinced himself that if one person looks down on him, then everybody will. It is as if he feared that the word "reject" would suddenly be stamped on his forehead in capital letters for everyone to see. Fred seems to have a sense of self-esteem that is contingent upon approval or success. He believes that his achievements have to be outstanding or else they will be no good at all. If his cravings for perfection, approval, and success are not satisfied, Fred senses that he will be an unloved nothing, because he has no true support from within. Because he wants to be totally competent and confident, he cannot accept his own humanity or cope effectively with the daily realities he encounters as a struggling, insecure law student.

Many perfectionists have complained that traditional treatment methods are unsatisfactory. A first-year law student named Jennifer had been treated during high school and college for episodes of depression and anxiety but had not been helped. She explained, "My therapist told me that my problem was perfectionism. She said I had impossible expectations, and I made excessive demands on myself.

She traced the origins of my problem to my relationship with my mother. My mother is very compulsive and can find 16 things wrong with an incredibly clean room. The therapist suggested that if I would stop being so perfectionistic, I'd feel better, but she never told me how to go about doing that. I'd like to get over my perfectionism. But how do I proceed?''

Jennifer was aware that simply understanding the nature of her problem or even tracing its childhood origins was not especially helpful. Just as a stutterer doesn't stop stuttering because he realizes he has a speech problem, most perfectionists find that insight into the nature of their difficulties is not sufficient for change. At the University of Pennsylvania Mood Clinic, we have developed a step-by-step attitude-retraining program focusing on the motivational, cognitive, and interpersonal aspects of perfectionism. While it might seem paradoxical to treat perfectionists, who tend to be overly rigid, with a structured treatment program, we have found that this usually brings about a more relaxed outlook, spontaneity, and an improvement in mood more readily than does nondirective, supportive therapy that emphasizes emotional ventilation.

CHANGING OLD HABITS OF THOUGHT

As a first step in treating perfectionists, we urge them to make a list of the advantages and disadvantages of attempting to be perfect. As clients balance the costs against the benefits, they frequently become aware for the first time that perfectionism is not to their advantage. That awareness enhances their motivation to work toward giving it up. Until the perfectionist has arrived at that conclusion, we find it fruitless to treat the disorder. Jennifer was able to list only one advantage of perfectionism: ''It can produce fine work. I'll try hard to come up with an excellent result.'' She listed six disadvantages: ''One, it makes me so tight and nervous I can't produce fine work or even adequate work at times. Two, I am often unwilling to risk the mistakes necessary to come up with a creative piece of work. Three, my perfectionism inhibits me from trying new things and making discoveries because I am so preoccupied with being 'safe.' Thus, my world becomes narrow and somewhat boring, and I lose out on the opportunity for new challenges. Four, it makes me self-critical and takes the joy out of life. Five, I can't ever relax because I'll always find something that isn't perfect. Six, it makes me intolerant of others because I am constantly aware of the errors people make, and I end up being perceived as a fault-finder." It did not take long for Jennifer to conclude that her life would be more rewarding and productive without perfectionism.

Many perfectionists believe they can't experience substantial satisfaction from any activity unless they perform in an outstanding manner. They may find out differently—and thus win a degree of freedom from their perfectionism—if they make out a form called the "Pleasure-Predicting Sheet." I begin by asking a patient to schedule a series of activities with a potential for personal growth, satisfaction, or pleasure, and to predict how satisfying each of them will be, using a figure between 0 and 100. After each activity has been completed, the patient records how satisfying it actually was and estimates how well he or she performed. A depressed physician who completed the form had complained of feeling frustrated and unrewarded for many years, despite his substantial academic accomplishments. He was surprised to learn that he could experience greater personal satisfaction in doing a below-average job of fixing a broken pipe that flooded his kitchen than in giving an outstanding lecture to a group of medical students. The discovery helped him realize that excellent performance was neither necessary nor sufficient for satisfaction. In fact, he was shocked to observe that many activities he did in an "average" or "below-average" way were among the most rewarding. As a result, he began to think about activities in terms of their potential for making him feel rewarded. He reported that that helped him to feel more relaxed and gave him the courage to initiate a number of potentially exciting professional projects about which he had procrastinated for years, because he had feared an imperfect outcome.

It can be quite important for a perfectionist to reprogram the distorted all-or-nothing thinking that gave birth to the mental habit of perfectionism. As a first step in this cognitive tune-up, I ask perfectionists to spend a day investigating whether or not the world can be evaluated in a meaningful way using all-or-nothing categories. As they notice people and things, they are to ask themselves, "Are the walls in this room totally clean, or do they have at least some dirt?" They might also ask, "Is that person totally handsome? Or totally ugly? Or somewhere in between?" The exercise usually demonstrates the irrationality of dichotomous thinking. As one client reported, "I found out that the universe simply does not divide itself into two categories, all-good versus all-bad."

Once clients become aware of a dichotomous cognition, they are to substitute a more realistic thought. If a client thinks, "This barbecue was a total flop because I overcooked the steaks," the next step is to substitute: "It's not the best meal I've cooked, but it's certainly adequate."

Another technique many find helpful is to keep a daily written record of self-critical cognitions. These are called "automatic thoughts" because they flood the perfectionist's mind involuntarily and seem highly plausible to the person who thinks them, even though they might seem quite irrational to an outside observer. As the client writes down each automatic thought, he or she pinpoints the form of mental distortion it contains and substitutes a more objective and self-enhancing thought. These are called "rational responses."

For example, at 4:30 one afternoon a college student felt panic because he began to dwell on the shortcomings of a paper that was due by 5:00. He had a powerful urge to request an extension so he could revise it and get it "just right." Once in the past he had become so consumed by a similar compulsion that he ended up dropping out of school for an entire year to work on a paper. This time he decided to resist the impulse and recorded the following automatic thoughts that upset him after he had turned in the paper:

"The professor will surely notice all the typos. He'll think the paper is poorly thought out. He'll feel that I didn't care about it. He'll see what an irresponsible student I am. I'll probably end up with a D or an F." First the student observed that he was engaged in all-or-nothing thinking and that he was jumping to conclusions unwarranted by the facts. Then he wrote down the following rational responses: "The professor will notice the typos, but he will read the whole paper and will probably notice that there are some fairly good sections. It is unlikely that he will feel I am an irresponsible student just because one paper is imperfect. Since I usually get A's, it is unlikely that I'll get a D or an F even though this paper could have been improved somewhat." These responses reduced his anxiety to bearable levels until he got the paper back—marked with an A- and a number of compliments.

The positive feedback further put the lie to his belief that his work had to be flawless to be acceptable. Suppose, however, that he had not received a good grade. One of the catastrophes that perfectionists dread is rejection. Many of them are convinced that others will think less of them if they are not successful, and they have never questioned that belief. They usually react with skepticism to a therapist's suggestion that they design an experiment to test that belief objectively, and they are very often startled by the results. One of Philadelphia's top attorneys complained of stress at work because of a constant preoccupation with the idea that his associates would think less of him if he made a mistake or lost a case. He agreed to ask several of them about it and was surprised when they reported that they felt *better* about him when he goofed up. They said it was a relief to learn that he could be human.

Of course, there was no guarantee that the feedback he received from his peers would be positive. Since he might have encountered another perfectionist who did, in fact, think less of him when he made a mistake, we turned this contingency to his advantage by training him in verbal judo—techniques for responding to criticism. Several approaches are useful. One is empathy, or learning to see the world through the critic's eyes instead of responding defensively. Another is inquiry. When the criticism involves a vague, pejorative label ("You're a real jerk"), a person can prompt the critic to respond in a more specific and objective way ("Just what did I do or say that struck you as jerky?"). Disarming is also a helpful technique. The idea is to take the wind out of a critic's sails by finding a grain of truth in the criticism, even if it seems largely unfair and untrue.

These methods are practiced by role-playing during therapy sessions. The therapist plays the role of the critic and abuses the client with the most hurtful insults he or she can think up. When the client falters or becomes upset or defensive, they reverse roles so the therapist can demonstrate an effective response. The process continues until the patient can learn to feel calm and self-respecting in light of the worst imaginable criticisms.

Most perfectionists assume that setting the highest personal standards will result in an optimal performance and satisfaction but have never questioned or tested that assumption. They nearly always attribute their success in life to perfectionism, and the suggestion that they might have been successful in spite of their high standards and not because of them strikes them initially as unrealistic. The therapist suggests that standards can be thought of as imaginary abstractions people create to motivate themselves and proposes that the client might want to experiment creatively with various standards to see which work out best. In any given activity a person might aim for "perfect," "good," "above average," "average," "below average," or "adequate."

Most perfectionists express dread when a therapist proposes that they aim for any outcome other than "the best." If a therapist suggests they aim for "average" as an experiment, the typical reaction is disgust. A therapist can then explain that it is statistically inevitable that a person's performance at any task will be below his own average half the time and above his average the other half. It can therefore be argued that it is fruitless to aim to be "the best" at all times. In fact, a person's "best" performance at any activity is possible only once in a lifetime, which means that aiming for the best virtually guarantees failure. In contrast, if goals are modest, the probability that they will be reached and even surpassed is high.

Setting lower goals proved to be a useful strategy for a perfectionist high school principal who had difficulty adhering to his daily jogging routine. At the completion of every run he had been in the habit of telling himself that he would try to run a little farther and faster the next day. Although that motivated him to better and better performances initially, after a few weeks the running became so strenuous and exhausting that he gave it up entirely for a month or two. Then he started again, repeating the pattern. Because his efforts lacked consistency, he failed to make progressive gains over the long haul.

In order to overcome his pattern, he made it his aim to run only a quarter of a mile instead of the five to ten miles he was accustomed to. He was instructed that he could run farther than that if he chose to, but that he should consider his jogging 100 percent successful for the day as soon as he had covered one-quarter mile. Anything beyond that would be gravy—optional running for pure pleasure. He also agreed that every subsequent day he was to aim to run one-half the distance he had run the day before. He reported that as a result of these modest goals, his aversion and anxiety disappeared, he began to enjoy running much more, and he was able to adhere to his exercise program consistently.

The same strategy, he reported, improved his outlook and productivity at work. He found it surprising that the lower he set his standards, the greater his output became and the more satisfaction he experienced. In writing for educational journals, he had been stymied by writer's block. He would tell himself "This has to be outstanding" every time he sat down to prepare a draft. Then he would daydream or obsess over the first sentence and eventually give up in disgust. When, instead, he told himself, "I'll just crank out a below-average draft and have it typed up," he found that his resistance to writing diminished, and he was able to improve his output substantially. It struck him as odd that as he began to aim to make his writing increasingly "average," other people seemed increasingly impressed. Eventually, he gave up his perfectionism entirely and became addicted, he said to the idea of being average.

Insights into Self-deception

by Daniel Goleman

Self-deception is an ancient malady; Greek tragedies used it as a plot device, and philosophers have long argued over its roots. Freud made self-deception—in the form of psychological defenses—a mainstay of his analysis of the mind and how it works. With the advent of modern techniques for studying the mind, though, a new understanding of the anatomy of self-deception has emerged. Self-deception, the new view holds, is a natural outgrowth of how the mind is organized.

The unconscious mind, cognitive scientists have come to see, is vastly important in mental life. Their view of the unconscious is even broader than Freud's: Most of the mind's workings, they say, goes on outside awareness, and awareness is a small part of the mind as a whole. And it is in the unconscious that self-deception operates.

By synchronizing self-deceptions, Daniel Goleman argues, people are able to share blind-spots, areas of experience that they tacitly agree not to notice, and not to notice that they do not notice. In this article he describes how self-deception is rooted in the brain and mind. And he describes how the rules for orchestrating attention in this way are learned in childhood, in one's family, and then operate to some degree in virtually every other group one belongs to through life—even at the national level.

THE WOMAN SPOKE about her father only after being reassured she would not be identified, because, in his time, the man had been famous. Even now, some 25 years after his death, the woman's voice was halting as she talked about her father's alcoholism and about how her family had somehow managed not to know how troubled he was:

"After my father died, we would find bottles of liquor hidden around the house, behind books, in the backs of closets. And, looking back, I can remember how poppa was always 'taking a nap,' as my mother would say. Sometimes he would get very loud and angry with my mother and push her around. She'd tell my little sister and me that he was 'in a mood,' and, without another word, she'd take us by the hand outdoors for a walk.

"He was an alcoholic, but somehow we stayed oblivious to it all. Once, after I was grown and married myself, I got up the nerve to ask my mother about it all. She denied it out-and-out." To this day, her mother has refused to admit the truth about her husband's drinking.

Family therapists have described this sort of denial and cover-up as "the game of happy family." It is just one aspect of the larger phenomenon of human self-deception, the nature of which is only now beginning to be understood by cognitive psychologists. The scientists' work explains how and why people lie to themselves. And patterns emerge from the scientific evidence that would seem to indicate that, just as individuals and families deceive themselves, so do larger groups of people, so do whole societies. The new research reveals a natural bent toward self-deception so great that the need for counterbalancing forces within the mind and society as a whole—forces such as insight and respect for truth—becomes more apparent than ever.

The theme of buried secrets is so familiar and ancient in literature that it attests to the universality of the experience. The story of Oedipus revolves around such secrets. Willy Loman's tragic fall in "Death of a Salesman" testifies to the explosive potential of family secrets unmasked. Ibsen called this sort of secret a "vital lie," a myth that stands in place of a disturbing reality.

To acknowledge that it is commonplace for people to lie to themselves is not to understand why or how unpleasant truths can be buried so effectively. Freud explained it by proposing a range of psychological defenses, but his speculations came long before the detailed mapping of the mind's mechanics by cognitive psychologists, researchers who study how the mind perceives, processes and remembers information. Working in the laboratory with new techniques for measuring perception and memory, researchers have been able to sketch a scientific model of the mind, one that shows how and why self-deception can operate with such ease.

Among the major discoveries that have contributed to the modern understanding of the mind's architecture, and the place of self-deception in that design, are the following:

There is now firm scientific evidence that the unconscious mind plays an immensely potent role in mental life. The evidence includes the startling phenomenon known as "unconscious reading," in which, as psychologists at Cambridge University in England have shown, a person unconsciously registers the meaning of words that are presented to him in such a way that he has no conscious awareness of having seen them at all. The premise that *most* mental processes go on prior to awareness—and may never reach awareness at all—has now come into widespread acceptance among cognitive scientists.

Recently, psychologists at the University of Wisconsin have obtained evidence—for the first time ever—that suggests there is a specific mechanism in brain function associated with the psychological defense of repression. The transfer of information from one half of the brain to the other, they have found, is the point at which upsetting emotional experience may be blocked from awareness.

Self-deception itself is coming to be seen in a more positive light by psychologists, who find that it can serve people well as a psychological basis for self-confidence and hope. Researchers at the University of California at Berkeley have found that, in certain medical situations, those patients who deny the seriousness of medical risk fare better than those who dwell on it. This is not to say that self-deception is always to the good. But it may be that people fall prey to self-deception with such ease precisely because it has an appropriate, even essential, place in the ecology of mind.

Although researchers are exploring self-deception by probing deep into the mechanics of the mind, the phenomenon itself can easily be observed in everyday life and at several levels of human activity. The roots of self-deception seem to lie in the mind's ability to allay anxiety by distorting awareness. Denial soothes. Freud saw that the mind, with remarkable alacrity, can deny a range of facts it would rather avoid and then not seem to know that it has done so.

At a dinner party, for example, a young woman commented on how close she was to her family, how loving family members had always been. She then went on to report, as evidence of their closeness, "When I disagreed with my mother she threw whatever was nearest at me. Once it happened to be a knife and I needed 10 stitches in my leg. A few years later my father tried to choke me when I began dating a boy he didn't like. They really are very concerned about me," she added, in all seriousness.

While the self-deception here is obvious, it often takes much more subtle forms, such as those that psychoanalysts track—defense mechanisms like denial and repression. All such mental maneuvers are part of a psychological calculus in which painful truths and soothing denials are the main variables. In the game of happy family, for instance, the rules call for twists of attention to bolster the pretense that nothing is wrong. Such psychological charades require that family members orchestrate their attention in an exquisitely coordinated self-deception.

As the Scottish psychiatrist R. D. Laing put it, "I have never come across a family that does not draw a line somewhere as to what may be put into words, and what words it may be put into." The line directs attention *here* and away from *there*. The rule works best when family members are not aware it exists at all but simply respect it automatically. In Dr. Laing's words, "If you obey these rules, you will not know that they exist."

Synchronized denial can take place in groups of all

kinds. We slip so easily into group membership, as Freud saw, because we have learned the art of belonging as children in our families. The unspoken pact in the family is repeated in every other group we will join in life. Part of the price of membership, of being valued as part of a group, is to honor the implicit rules of shared attention and shared denial.

Such orchestrated self-deceptions were at work, for example, among the group that planned the Bay of Pigs invasion. Irving L. Janis, a psychologist at Yale University, studied in detail how the plans were laid for that fiasco. It was a textbook case of the collective defenses that Janis has called "groupthink."

Essentially, when groupthink is at work, group members hobble their seeking of information in order to preserve a cozy unamimity. Loyalty to the group requires that no one raise embarrassing questions, nor attack weak arguments, nor counter soft-headed thinking with hard facts. "The more amiable the esprit de corps among the members of a policy-making group," Janis has observed, "the greater is the danger that independent critical thinking will be replaced by groupthink."

Looking back, Arthur Schlesinger Jr., who was then on the White House staff, observed how the meetings in which the Bay of Pigs plan took shape went on "in a curious atmosphere of assumed consensus." Yet, he suspects that had a single person voiced a strong objection, President Kennedy would have canceled the plan. No one spoke up. In a post-mortem, Theodore Sorenson, who had been special counsel to President Kennedy, concluded that "doubts were entertained but never pressed, partly out of a fear of being labeled 'soft' or undaring in the eyes of their colleagues." The rationalization, erroneous, as it turned out, that there would be a mass uprising against Castro once the invasion began, kept the group from contemplating such devastating information as the fact that Castro's army outnumbered the invading force by more than 140 to one.

The same dynamics that shunt discomforting facts from attention in groups operate in society at large. When some aspects of the shared reality are troubling, a semblance of cozy calm can be maintained by an unspoken agreement to deny the pertinent facts, to ignore key questions.

Take the case of Argentina in the late 1970's. While the military junta was in control there, the unaskable question within the society was: "What happened to the 10,000 or so political dissenters who mysteriously disappeared?" When the democratic regime took over in 1983, the unaskable question was the first to be asked. The answer, of course, pointed the finger of guilt at the junta itself.

To understand such self-deceit, whether individual or shared, cognitive psychologists focus on the mechanisms of the mind. A key element in the mind's architecture is rather dramatically represented by the phenomenon known as "blindsight." Certain functionally blind people—sightless as the result of stroke or brain injury rather than damage to the eye—have the uncanny ability to reach with accuracy for an object placed in front of them, even though, before they reach, they can not say where it is, or whether it is there at all. If asked to reach for the object, they will say it is impossible, since they cannot see it. But if they can be persuaded to try, they will find it with a sureness that amazes even themselves.

Blindsight is such a startling ability that some experts refuse to believe it can happen. Its authenticity is still hotly debated among cognitive scientists, some of whom are uncomfortable with the implication that only part of the mind can be aware of something. They argue that blindsight must be due to some form of cheating or sloppy research. One of those who defends blindsight is Anthony Marcel, a psychologist at Cambridge University. Marcel is more comfortable with blindsight than are some of his colleagues partly because he has done other experimental work that shows in normal people the mental capacity that seems most jarring in blindsight: That one part of the mind can know something, while the part that supposedly knows what is going on—awareness—remains oblivious.

Marcel had been doing studies of how people read when he chanced upon a strange effect. In his experiments, he would rapidly flash words on a screen, displaying them in a visual context so confusing they could not be read. When he asked his subjects to guess at the words that they thought they hadn't read, he was struck by a pattern of "clever mistakes." Often, the subjects would guess a word with a closely related meaning: "Day," for instance, might have been the word on the screen, and "night," the subject's guess.

Intrigued, Marcel began to flash words in such a way that observers did not even know that any describable image had been presented. Then he would project a pair of words and ask his subjects to guess which of the words meant or looked the same as the one they had not been able to perceive. He found that people guessed right more often than could be predicted by chance.

The results of these and subsequent studies involving the perception of words from strings of letters—Marcel calls these "unconscious reading"—make sense only if we adopt a rather radical premise in terms of how we normally think about the mind: Much consequential mental activity goes on outside awareness.

The whole process of recognition, sorting and selection takes a fraction of a second. Emanuel Donchin of the University of Illinois, a leading researcher in the field of cognitive psychophysiology, has done a great many studies using the evoked potential, a sophisticated brain-wave measure, to track the timing of the mind's operations. "In our research, we find that the mind recognizes a word within the first 150 milliseconds of seeing it," says Donchin. "But nothing shows up in awareness, as the subject reports it, for another 100 milliseconds or so, if it shows up at all."

At any given moment, then, most of what impinges on the senses, and most of the thoughts or memories that might come to mind as a result, never do come to mind. A huge amount of mental effort goes into sorting through and selecting a slim thread of consciousness from an immense array of mental candidates for awareness. The evidence is that the vast majority of possible thoughts and perceptions that might enter awareness are blocked from consciousness. There is a filter at work, and an intelligent one at that.

There are compelling reasons for this arrangement in the design of the mind. Awareness would be far too cluttered were the flow of information not vastly reduced by the time it arrived. If too much gets through, awareness is swamped by irrelevant information, as happens, in different forms, during anxiety attacks and in schizophrenia.

"Awareness is a limited capacity system," Donchin explains. "We don't know—and don't need to know— about most of the stuff the mind does. I have no idea how I search memory or get grammatically correct sentences out of my mouth. It's hard enough to handle the little that reaches awareness. We'd be in terrible shape if everything were conscious."

The existence of an intelligent filter raises the question of just what intelligence guides the filter's operations. The answer seems to be that what enters through the senses gets a thorough, automatic scan by memory itself. There are several kinds of memory, and this crucial gatekeeper's task seems to be performed, in part, by "semantic" memory, the repository of meanings and knowledge about the world. Semantic memory filters experience so that those messages that reach awareness are primarily those that have pertinence to current mental activity.

Donald A. Norman, a cognitive psychologist at the University of California at San Diego, who was one of the first to propose this design of the mind, argues that perception is a matter of degree. The judgment of relevancy is orchestrated by "schemas," the term psychologists use for the packets in which the mind organizes and stores information. All the contents of the mind are sorted into schemas; a train of association in thought is a road map through loosely connected schemas.

Schemas and attention interact in an intricate dance. Attention to one facet of experience—it is lunchtime, say, and you are hungry—activates other relevant schemas— thoughts of nearby restaurants, say, or of what is at hand in the refrigerator. The schemas, in turn, guide attention.

If you walk down the street with these schemas active, your focus will be on the restaurants, not the other kinds of shops on the street; if you go to the refrigerator, your attention will fix on the cold cuts, not on the roast for the evening meal. Schemas choose this and not that; they determine the scope of attention. The interplay between attention and schemas puts them at the heart of the matter of self-deception. Schemas not only determine what we will notice: They also can determine what we do *not* notice.

Ulric Neisser, a psychologist at Emory University who wrote "Cognitive Psychology," the volume that put the discipline on the intellectual map, makes the point with an elegant, straightforward demonstration. He made a video-tape of four young men playing basketball. The tape lasts just one minute. About midway, an attractive young woman carrying a large white umbrella saunters through the game. She is on the screen for four seconds.

Neisser showed the tape to visitors to his laboratory, who were asked to press a key whenever the basketball was passed between players. When Neisser asked after-ward if they had seen anything unusual, very few mentioned the woman with the white umbrella. They had not noticed her; the schema guiding their viewing fixed attention on the ball. When Neisser then replayed the tape, they were astonished to see the woman.

I once asked Neisser whether there might be schemas that, in effect, say "do not notice that."

"Yes," said he, "I'm sure there are, at several levels. It probably starts from cases like the woman with the umbrella. People don't shift their attention from the task at hand. But the mechanism would be much the same when you have a pretty good suspicion of what's over there if you were to look, and you'd rather not deal with it. And you don't look; you don't shift your attention. You have a diversionary schema that keeps you looking at something else instead."

This kind of schema has a special potency in the mind: It operates on attention like a magician misdirecting his audience. Just such a mechanism seems to have been at work in a classic study conducted by Lester Luborsky, a psychologist at the University of Pennsylvania School of Medicine. Luborsky used a special camera to track people's eye movements while they looked at pictures. His apparatus allowed him to tell precisely where their gaze fell at each moment.

Some people gave a remarkable performance. When he had them look at pictures that were partly sexual in content, they were able to avoid letting their gaze stray even once to the sexual part of those pictures, though, presumably, their peripheral vision could detect it. Thus, when they looked at a drawing of the outline of a woman's breasts, beyond which there was a man reading a paper, their eye did not fix on the woman at all, but focused only the man and his paper. Later, when asked to describe the picture, they had no recall of the sexual aspects; as it turned out, these people were particularly anxious about sexual matters.

"I think there's a lot of this kind of repression in everyday life," says Neisser, "lots of limits and avoidance in thinking about or looking at things. We all do that. There may be some painful experience in your life which, when you start to think about, you simply decide at some level not to pursue. So you avoid using your recall strategies. You could probably get pretty skilled at it, at not remembering what's painful."

In what may be the most telling results to date on the roots of self-deception, a team of researchers have pinpointed a brain mechanism associated with at least one defensive maneuver, a prospect Freud himself envisioned and then abandoned because of the primitive state of the brain sciences of his time.

The first step in this breakthrough was accomplished by Daniel A. Weinberger, now a psychologist at Stanford University, while he was still a graduate student at Yale. Weinberger was able to show that certain people, whom he called "repressors," consistently denied being anxious. In research on stress, he contended, they were being misclassified as being very low in anxiety, when, in fact, they displayed all the physical and behavioral signs of tension.

Weinberger presented college students identified as repressors with sexual or aggressive phrases. He would confront them, for instance, with "the prostitute slept with the
student," or "his roommate kicked him in the stomach."
He then asked them to free-associate from the phrases and
found that their repression was obvious. Unlike other students who did the same task, the repressors offered associations that downplayed or avoided altogether the sexual or
hostile tone of the phrases. At the same time, measure-
ments of their heart rate, perspiration and forehead muscle
tension revealed that they were, in fact, agitated.

There is, of course, the question of how conscious the
repressors were of their self-deception: Were they lying
about their feelings, or actually unaware of them?

An answer to that question has been suggested by Richard J. Davidson, a psychologist at the University of Wisconsin who has been a collaborator of Weinberger, and
who carried the investigation one crucial step further. Davidson, working with Jonathan Perl and Clifford Saron of
the State University of New York at Purchase, and using
an ingenious technique, has been able to show that repressors suffer from a faulty transfer of information from one
half of the brain to the other.

Davidson's experiments employed a device that, by means
of a precise arrangement of lenses, projects a word so that
it is seen by only that part of the retina that sends signals
to the right hemisphere. Then the brain passes the information to the left. In a right-handed person, this means that
the right hemisphere, which can register the meaning of
words, must transfer the information to the speech center
in the left before the person can speak that meaning.

Davidson had repressors free-associate to negative emotional words, many of which were sexual or hostile in
meaning. When he presented these words to the right
hemisphere, he found that a significant time elapsed before
the subjects could utter their responses. Among those who
study brain response, this slower reaction time is interpreted to mean that there is a deficiency in the transfer of
information, in this case from the right to the left hemisphere. Of most significance was the specificity of the lag:

It was for the negative words—which presumably posed a psychological threat—not for neutral or positive words. And the lag showed up only when the words were presented to the right hemisphere, not when shown to the left.

These findings take on special significance in light of the fact that the right hemisphere is strongly believed to be a center for emotions, such as fear and anxiety. Thus, in theory, when repressors experience anxiety, their emotional center in the right brain sends that information to the verbal center in the left over the same faulty circuits. In short, the entire pattern suggests that the repressor's denial of his anxiety is associated with deficient brain function centering on the transfer of information from the right to the left hemisphere. The findings suggest that the repressor is not lying about his lack of agitation, but is actually less aware of it than are most people. The same mechanism, Davidson believes, may operate whenever people repress threatening information.

A range of research suggests a decidedly positive role for certain kinds of self-deceit. For example, in research at a hospital near San Francisco, Richard S. Lazarus of the University of California at Berkeley found that patients who avoided thinking about the surgery they were facing fared better afterward. Lazarus's colleague, Frances Cohen, interviewed patients about to undergo elective surgery, such as for gall bladder problems. Some patients, they found, were extremely vigilant about what would happen—and what might go wrong—during surgery, even reading medical texts to discover fine details of the procedure. Others completely ignored such facts, relying instead on faith that things would go right.

The avoiders, the researchers found, recovered more quickly after the surgery, and with fewer complications. In a similar study, researchers at the University of North Carolina have found that those patients who similarly avoided thinking about forthcoming dental surgery showed more rapid healing afterward.

Avoiding what is painful, to a great extent, seems to

serve a positive function. There is a growing body of research evidence that shows there to be a pervasive mental tendency for people to ignore or forget unpleasant facts about themselves and to highlight and remember more easily the pleasant ones. The result is an illusory glow of positivity. When people become depressed, the illusion that things are better than a neutral weighing of facts might suggest disappears. Hope, the crucial mainstay in the face of all adversity, depends to a great extent on the same illusion. In short, self-deception, to a point, has a decidedly positive place in the human psyche.

Nevertheless, Lazarus is quick to point out that the context makes all the difference. "You shouldn't assume denial is *necessarily* good," he observes. "The presurgical patients had nothing to gain from their vigilance. Take, by contrast, the case of a diabetic; he's got to monitor his sugar levels constantly. If he denies his problem, he's in great trouble."

If there is a lesson to be drawn from the new research, it is the urgent need for compelling antidotes to self-deception. The more we understand how natural a part self-deceit plays in mental life, the more we can admit the almost gravitational pull toward putting out of mind unpleasant facts. And yet, as in the case of the diabetic cited by Richard Lazarus, there is often danger in giving in to denial, whether that denial is individual or collective.

Psychotherapy seeks to heal by exposing, not suppressing, hidden truths, and the therapist's stance is no different from that of the investigative reporter, the ombudsman, the grand jury or the whistle-blower. Each bespeaks a willingness to rock the boat, to bring into the open those facts that have been hidden in the service of keeping things comfortable.

We live in an age, we say, when information has taken on an import and urgency unparalleled in history. A mark of democracy, we maintain, is that information flows freely. It is totalitarian authority that must choke off alternative views and suppress contrary facts: Censorship seems the social equivalent of a defense mechanism.

Now that cognitive psychology is showing how easily our civilization can be put at risk by burying our awareness of painful truths, we may come to cherish truth and insight, more than ever before, as the purest of goods.

The Two Faces of Power

by David C. McClelland

David McClelland of Harvard, who is best known for his seminal work on the need to achieve, has also studied the need for power. His work is based on observations from a wide range of people, world leaders as well as ordinary citizens.

Power, McClelland proposes, is two-sided. He distinguishes between a "socialized" version, which underlies leadership, and a more hedonistic form of power, "dominance power." The leadership motive indicates a desire to apply power for the benefit of others; it respects the integrity of other people rather than seeing them as mere pawns of the power holder. In sharp contrast, dominance power is characterized by the thirst for victory over one's adversaries and the subjegation of others. Historically, we know this form of power as dictatorship—and the infamous figures of Mussolini and Hitler come to mind.

According to McClelland, such power can exist in the individual outside of public life as well—the tyrant in one's family or one's office. In its more mundane forms the need for power is simply the urge to do things that will make an impact on or influence other people. "The Two Faces of Power" is as pertinent to political science as it is to psychology.

FOR OVER TWENTY years I have been studying a particular human motive—the need to Achieve, the need to do something better than it has been done before. As my investigation advanced, it became clear that the need to Achieve, technically *n* Achievement, was one of the keys to economic growth, because men who are concerned with doing things better have become active entrepreneurs and have created the growing business firms which are the foundation stones of a developing economy. [McClelland 1961]. Some of these heroic entrepreneurs might be regarded as leaders in the restricted sense that their activities established the economic base for the rise of a new type of civilization, but they were seldom leaders of men. The reason for this is simple: *n* Achievement is a one-man game which need never involve other people.

Boys who are high in *n* Achievement like to build things or to make things with their hands, presumably because they can tell easily and directly whether they have done a good job. A boy who is trying to build as tall a tower as possible out of blocks can measure very precisely how well he has done. He is in no way dependent on someone else to tell him how good his performance is. So in the pure case, the man with high *n* Achievement is not dependent on the judgment of others; he is concerned with improving his own performance. As an ideal type, he is most easily conceived of as a salesman or an owner-manager of a small business, in a position to watch carefully whether or not his performance is improving.

While studying such men and their role in economic development, I ran head on into problems of leadership, power, and social influence which *n* Achievement clearly did not prepare a man to cope with. As a one-man firm grows larger, it obviously requires some division of function and some organizational structure. Organizational structure involves relationships among people, and sooner or later someone in the organization, if it is to survive, must pay attention to getting people to work together, or to dividing up the tasks to be performed, or to supervising the work of others. Yet it is fairly clear that a high need to Achieve does not equip a man to deal effectively with managing human relationships. For instance, a salesman with high *n* Achievement does not necessarily make a good sales manager. As a manager, his task is not to sell, but to inspire others to sell, which involves a different set of personal goals and different strategies for reaching them.

I shall not forget the moment when I learned that the president of one of the most successful *achievement*-oriented firms we had been studying scored exactly zero in *n* Achievement! Up to that point I had fallen into the easy assumption that a man with a high need to Achieve does better work, gets promoted faster, and ultimately ends up as president of a company. How then was it possible for a man to be head of an obviously achieving company and yet score so low in *n* Achievement? At the time I was tempted to dismiss the finding as a statistical error, but there is now little doubt that it was a dramatic way of calling attention to the fact that stimulating achievement motivation in others requires a different motive and a different set of skills than wanting achievement satisfaction for oneself. In short, the man with high *n* Achievement seldom can act alone, even though he might like to. He is caught up in an organizational context in which he is managed, controlled, or directed by others. And thus to understand better what happens to him, we must shift our attention to those who are managing him, to those who are concerned about organizational relationships—to the leaders of men. Since managers are primarily concerned with influencing others, it seems obvious that they should be characterized by a high need for Power, and that by studying the power motive we can learn something about the way effective managerial leaders work.

There is one striking difference between the two motivation systems which is apparent from the outset. In general, in American society at least, individuals are proud of having a high need to Achieve, but dislike being told they have a high need for Power. It is a fine thing to be concerned about doing things well (*n* Achievement) or making friends (*n* Affiliation), but it is reprehensible to be concerned about having influence over others (*n* Power). The vocabulary behavioral scientists use to describe power relations is strongly negative in tone. If one opens *The Authoritarian Personality* [Adorno, Frenkel-Brunswick, Levinson & Stanford 1950], one of the major works deal-

ing with people who are concerned with power, one finds
these people depicted as harsh, sadistic, fascist, Machia-
vellian, prejudiced, and neurotic. Ultimately, many claim,
the concern for power leads to Nazi-type dictatorships, to
the slaughter of innocent Jews, to political terror, police
states, brainwashing, and the exploitation of helpless masses
who have lost their freedom. Even less political terms for
power than these have a distinctively negative flavor—
dominance-submission, competition, zero sum game (if I
win, you lose). It is small wonder that people do not
particularly like being told they have a high need for
Power.

Yet surely this negative face of power is only part of the
story. Power must have a positive face too. After all,
people cannot help influencing one another. Organizations
cannot function without some kind of authority relationships. Surely it is necessary and desirable for some people
to concern themselves with management, with working out
influence relationships that make it possible to achieve the
goals of the group. A man who is consciously concerned
with the development of proper channels of influence is
surely better able to contribute to group goals than a man
who neglects or represses power problems and lets the
working relationships of men grow up unsupervised by
men. Our problem, then, is to try to discern and understand two faces of power. When is power bad and when is
it good? Why is it often perceived as dangerous? Which
aspects of power are viewed favorably, and which unfa-
vorably? When is it proper, and when improper, to exercise influence? And finally, are there different kinds of
power motivation?

It will not be possible to answer all of these questions
definitively, but the findings of recent research on the
power motive as it functions in human beings will help us
understand the two faces of power somewhat better.

There are two faces of power. One is turned toward
seeking to win out over active adversaries. Life tends to be
seen as a "zero-sum game" in which "if I win, you lose" or
"I lose, if you win." The imagery is that of the "law of
the jungle" in which the strongest survive by destroying

their adversaries. The thoughts of this face of power are aroused by drinking alcohol or, more socially, by putting a person in a personal dominance situation in which he is threatened. At the level of action, a personal power concern is associated with heavy drinking, gambling, having more aggressive impulses, and collecting "prestige supplies" like a convertible. People with this personalized power concern are more apt to speed, have accidents, and get into physical fights. If these primitive and personalized power-seeking characteristics were possessed by political officeholders, especially in the sphere of international relations, the consequences would be ominous.

The other face of the power motive is more socialized. It is aroused by the possibility of winning an election. At the fantasy level it expresses itself in thoughts of exercising power for the benefit of others and by feelings of greater ambivalence about holding power—doubts of personal strength, the realization that most victories must be carefully planned in advance, and that every victory means a loss for someone. In terms of activities, people concerned with the more socialized aspect of power join more organizations and are more apt to become officers in them. They also are more apt to join in organized informal sports, even as adults.

We have made some progress in distinguishing two aspects of the power motive, but what exactly is the difference between the way the two are exercised? Again a clue came from a very unexpected source. It is traditional in the literature of social psychology and political science to describe a leader as someone who is able to evoke feelings of obedience or loyal submission in his followers. A leader is sometimes said to have charisma if, when he makes a speech, for example, the members of his audience are swept off their feet and feel that they must submit to his overwhelming authority and power. In the extreme case they are like iron filings that have been polarized by a powerful magnet. The leader is recognized as supernatural or superhuman; his followers feel submissive, loyal, devoted, and obedient to his will. Certainly this is the most common description of what happened at mass meetings addressed by Hitler or Lenin. As great demagogues they established their power over the masses which followed loyally and obediently.

Winter wished to find out exactly, by experiment, what kinds of thoughts the members of an audience had when exposed to a charismatic leader [1967]. He wanted to find out if the common analysis of what was going on in the minds of the audience was in fact accurate. So he exposed groups of business school students to a film of John F. Kennedy's Inaugural Address as President of the United States some time after he had been assassinated. There was no doubt that this film was a highly moving and effective presentation of a charismatic leader for such an audience at that time. After the film was over he asked them to write imaginative stories as usual, and contrasted the themes of their stories with those written by a comparable group of students after they had seen a film explaining some aspects of modern architecture. Contrary to expectation, he did not find that the students exposed to the Kennedy film thought more afterwards about submission, following, obedience, or loyalty. Instead the frequency of power themes in their stories increased. They were apparently strengthened and uplifted by the experience. They felt more powerful, rather than less powerful and submissive. This suggests that the traditional way of explaining the influence which a leader has on his followers has not been entirely correct. He does not force them to submit and follow him by the sheer overwhelming magic of his personality and persuasive powers. This is in fact to interpret effective leadership in terms of the kind of personalized power syndrome described above, and leadership has been discredited in this country precisely because social scientists have often used this personal power image to explain how the leader gets his effects. In fact, he is influential by strengthening and inspiriting his audience.

The leader arouses confidence in his followers. The followers feel better able to accomplish whatever goals he and they share. There has been much discussion of whether the leader's ideas about what will inspire his followers come from God, from himself, or from some intuitive

sense of what the people need and want. But whatever the
source of the leader's ideas, he cannot inspire his people
unless he expresses vivid goals and aims which in some
sense they want. Of course, the more he is meeting their
needs, the less "persuasive" he has to be, but in no case
does it make much sense to speak as if his role is to force
submission. Rather it is to strengthen and uplift, to make
people feel like origins, not pawns of the socio-political
system. His message is not so much: "Do as I say because
I am strong and know best. You are children with no wills
of your own and must follow me because I know better,"
but rather "Here are the goals which are true and right and
which we share. Here is how we can reach them. You are
strong and capable. You can accomplish these goals." His
role is to clarify which goals the group should achieve and
then to create confidence in its members that they can
achieve them. The negative or personal face of power is
characterized by the dominance-submission mode: if I win,
you lose. It is *primitive* in the sense that the strategies
employed are adopted early in life, before the child is
sufficiently socialized to learn more subtle techniques of
influence. In fantasy it expresses itself in thoughts of
conquering opponents. In real life it leads to fairly simple
direct means of feeling powerful—drinking heavily, ac-
quiring "prestige supplies," and being aggressive. It does
not lead to effective social leadership for the simple reason
that a person whose power drive is fixated at this level
tends to treat other people as pawns rather than as origins.
And people who feel that they are pawns tend to be
passive and useless to the leader who is getting his childish
satisfaction from dominating them. Slaves are the poorest,
most inefficient form of labor ever devised by man. If a
leader wants to have far-reaching influence, he must make
his followers feel powerful and able to accomplish things
on their own.

The positive or socialized face of power is characterized
by a concern for group goals, for finding those goals that
will move men, for helping the group to formulate them,
for taking some initiative in providing members of the
group with the means of achieving such goals, and for

giving group members the feeling of strength and competence they need to work hard for such goals. In fantasy it leads to a concern with exercising influence *for* others, with planning, and with the ambivalent bitter-sweet meaning of many so-called "victories." In real life, it leads to an interest in informal sports, politics, and holding office. It functions in a way that makes members of a group feel like origins rather than pawns. Even the most dictatorial leader has not succeeded if he has not instilled in at least some of his followers a sense of power and the strength to pursue the goals he has set. This is often hard for outside observers to believe, because they do not experience the situation as it is experienced by the group members. One of the characteristics of the outsider, who notices only the success or failure of an influence attempt, is that he tends to convert what is a positive face of power into its negative version. He believes that the leader must have "dominated" because he was so effective, whereas in fact direct domination could never have produced so large an effect.

There is, however, a certain realistic basis for the frequent misperception of the nature of leadership. In real life the actual leader balances on a knife edge between expressing personal dominance and exercising the more socialized type of leadership. He may show first one face of power, then the other. The reason for this lies in the simple fact that even if he is a socialized leader, he must take initiative in helping the group he leads to form its goals. How much initiative he should take, how persuasive he should attempt to be, and at what point his clear enthusiasm for certain goals becomes personal authoritarian insistence that those goals are the right ones whatever the members of the group may think, are all questions calculated to frustrate the well-intentioned leader. If he takes no initiative, he is no leader. If he takes too much, he becomes a dictator, particularly if he tries to curtail the process by which members of the group participate in shaping group goals. There is a particular danger for the man who has demonstrated his competence in shaping group goals and in inspiring group members to pursue them. In time both he and they may assume that he knows best, and he may almost imperceptibly change from a democratic to an authoritarian leader.

There are, of course, safeguards against slipping from the more socialized to the less socialized expressions of power. One is psychological: the leader must thoroughly learn the lesson that his role is not to dominate and treat people like pawns, but to give strength to others and to make them feel like origins of ideas and of the courses of their lives. If they are to be truly strong, he must continually consult them and be aware of their wishes and desires. *A firm faith in people as origins prevents the development of the kind of cynicism that so often characterizes authoritarian leaders.* A second safeguard is social: democracy provides a system whereby the group can expel the leader from office if it feels that he is no longer properly representing its interests.

Self-actualizing and Beyond

by Abraham Maslow

Among theories of personality, Abraham Maslow's represent the "humanistic" approach—a perspective that places great weight on human values and a growth-oriented approach to living. Maslow's views emphasize human potential, and the human-potential movement was largely inspired by his thought. Indeed, he inspired a whole array of brands of psychotherapy very different from the behaviorist and psychoanalytic kinds that had dominated therapy before. Under the banner of "existential-humanistic" therapies, these approaches focus on helping the client achieve his or her personal fulfillment or "self-actualization."

In "Self-Actualizing and Beyond," Maslow reflects on the meaning of his famous concept and takes the reader through a lucid step-by-step explanation. In so doing, he tries to counter some common misconceptions. Maslow explains that the actual phenonenon is not a sudden realization, or even a revelation, but a gradual process of change and growth. By demystifying the concept, Maslow places self-actualization in the more accessible context of normal personality development, rather than as the sole possession of the psychologically privileged.

MY INVESTIGATIONS ON self-actualization were not planned to be research and did not start out as research. They started out as the effort of a young intellectual to try to understand two of his teachers whom he loved, adored, and admired and who were very, very wonderful people. It was a kind of high-IQ devotion. I could not be content simply to adore, but sought to understand why these two people were so different from the run-of-the-mill people in the world. These two people were Ruth Benedict and Max Wertheimer. They were my teachers after I came with a Ph.D. from the West to New York City, and they were most remarkable human beings. My training in psychology equipped me not at all for understanding them. It was as if they were not quite people but something more than people. My own investigation began as a prescientific or nonscientific activity. I made descriptions and notes on Max Wertheimer, and I made notes on Ruth Benedict. When I tried to understand them, think about them, and write about them in my journal and my notes, I realized in one wonderful moment that their two patterns could be generalized. I was talking about a kind of person, not about two noncomparable individuals. There was wonderful excitement in that. I tried to see whether this pattern could be found elsewhere, and I did find it elsewhere, in one person after another.

By ordinary standards of laboratory research, i.e., of rigorous and controlled research, this simply was not research at all. My generalizations grew out of *my* selection of certain kinds of people. Obviously, other judges are needed. So far, one man has selected perhaps two dozen people whom he liked or admired very much and thought were wonderful people and then tried to figure them out and found that he was able to describe a syndrome—the kind of pattern that seemed to fit all of them. These were people only from Western cultures, people selected with all kinds of built-in biases. Unreliable as it is, that was the only operational definition of self-actualizing people as I described them in my first publication on the subject.

The people I selected for my investigation were older people, people who had lived much of their lives out and were visibly successful. We do not yet know about the applicability of the findings to young people. We do not know what self-actualization means in other cultures, although studies of self-actualization in China and in India are now in process. We do not know what the findings of these new studies will be, but of one thing I have no doubt: When you select out for careful study very fine and healthy people, strong people, creative people, saintly people, sagacious people—in fact, exactly the kind of people I picked out—then you get a different view of mankind. You are asking how tall can people grow, what can a human being become?

Being-Values. Self-actualizing people are, without one single exception, involved in a cause outside their own skin, in something outside of themselves. They are devoted, working at something, something which is very precious to them—some calling or vocation in the old sense, the priestly sense. They are working at something which fate has called them to somehow and which they work at and which they love, so that the work-joy dichotomy in them disappears. One devotes his life to the law, another to justice, another to beauty or truth. All, in one way or another devote their lives to the search for what I have called the "being" values ("B" for short), the ultimate values which are intrinsic, which cannot be reduced to anything more ultimate. There are about fourteen of these B-Values, including the truth and beauty and goodness of the ancients and perfection, simplicity, comprehensiveness, and several more.

Metaneeds and Metapathologies. The existence of these B-Values adds a whole set of complications to the structure of self-actualization. These B-Values behave like needs. I have called them *metaneeds*. Their deprivation breeds certain kinds of pathologies which have not yet been adequately described but which I call *metapathologies*—the sicknesses of the soul which come, for example, from living among liars all the time and not trusting anyone. Just as we need counselors to help people with the simpler problems of unmet needs, so we may need *metacounselors* to help with the soul-sicknesses that grow from the unfufilled metaneeds. In certain definable and empirical ways, it is necessary for man to live in beauty rather than ugliness, as it is necessary for him to have food for an aching belly or rest for a weary body. In fact, I would go so far as to claim that these B-Values are the meaning of life for most people, but many people don't even recognize that they have these metaneeds. Part of the counselors' job may be to make them aware of these needs in themselves, just as the classical psychoanalyst made his patients aware of their instinctoid basic needs. Ultimately, perhaps some professionals shall come to think of themselves as philosophical or religious counselors.

Some of us try to help our counselees move and grow toward self-actualization. These people are often all wrapped up in value problems. Many are youngsters who are, in principle, very wonderful people, though in actuality they often seem to be little more than snotty kids. Nevertheless, I assume (in the face of all behavioral evidence sometimes) that they are, in the classical sense, idealistic. I assume that they are looking for values and that they would love to have something to devote themselves to, to be patriotic about, to worship, adore, love. These youngsters are making choices from moment to moment of going forward or retrogressing, moving away from or moving toward self-actualization. What can counselors, or metacounselors, tell them about becoming more fully themselves?

BEHAVIORS LEADING TO SELF-ACTUALIZATION

What does one do when he self-actualizes? Does he grit his teeth and squeeze? What does self-actualization mean in terms of actual behavior, actual procedure?

First, self-actualization means experiencing fully, vividly, selflessly, with full concentration and total absorption. It means experiencing without the self-consciousness of the adolescent. At this moment of experiencing, the person is wholly and fully human. This is a self-actualizing moment. This is a moment when the self is actualizing itself. As indiviudals, we all experience such moments occasionally. As counselors, we can help clients to experience them more often. We can encourage them to become totally absorbed in something and to forget their poses and their defenses and their shyness—to go at it "whole-hog." From the outside, we can see that this can be a very sweet moment. In those youngsters who are trying to be very tough and cynical and sophisticated, we can see the recovery of some of the guilelessness of childhood; some of the innocence and sweetness of the face can come back as they devote themselves fully to a moment and throw themselves fully into the experiencing of it. The key word for this is "selflessly," and our youngsters suffer from too little selflessness and too much self-consciousness, self-awareness.

Second, let us think of life as a process of choices, one after another. At each point there is a progression choice and a regression choice. There may be a movement toward defense, toward safety, toward being afraid; but over on the other side, there is the growth choice. To make the growth choice instead of the fear choice a dozen times a day is to move a dozen times a day toward self-actualization. *Self-actualization is an ongoing process*; it means making each of the many single choices about whether to lie or be honest, whether to steal or not to steal at a particular point, and it means to make each of these choices as a growth choice. This is movement toward self-actualization.

Third, to talk of self-actualization implies that there is a self to be actualized. A human being is not a *tabula rasa*, not a lump of clay or Plasticine. He is something which is already there, at least a "cartilaginous" structure of some kind. A human being is, at minimum, his temperament, his biochemical balances, and so on. There is a self, and what I have sometimes referred to as "listening to the impulse voices" means letting the self emerge. Most of us, most of the time (and especially does this apply to children, young people), listen not to ourselves but to Mommy's introjected voice or Daddy's voice or to the voice of the Establishment, of the Elders, of authority, or of tradition.

As a simple first step toward self-actualization, I sometimes suggest to my students that when they are given a glass of wine and asked how they like it, they try a different way of responding. First, I suggest that they *not* look at the label on the bottle. Thus they will not use it to get any cue about whether or not they *should* like it. Next, I recommend that they close their eyes if possible and that they "make a hush." Now they are ready to look within themselves and try to shut out the noise of the world so that they may savor the wine on their tongues and look to the "Supreme Court" inside themselves. Then, and only then, they may come out and say, "I like it" or "I don't like it." A statement so arrived at is different from the usual kind of phoniness that we all indulge in. At a party recently, I caught myself looking at the label on a bottle and assuring my hostess that she had indeed selected a very good Scotch. But then I stopped myself: What was I saying? I know little about Scotches. All I knew was what the advertisements said. I had no idea whether this one was good or not; yet this is the kind of thing we all do. Refusing to do it is part of the ongoing process of actualizing oneself. Does *your* belly hurt? Or does it feel good? Does this taste good on *your* tongue? Do *you* like lettuce?

Fourth, when in doubt, be honest rather than not. I am covered by that phrase "when in doubt," so that we need not argue too much about diplomacy. Frequently, when we are in doubt we are not honest. Clients are not honest much of the time. They are playing games and posing. They do not take easily to the suggestion to be honest. Looking within oneself for many of the answers implies taking responsibility. That is in itself a great step toward actualization. This matter of responsibility has been little studied. It doesn't turn up in our textbooks, for who can investigate responsibility in white rats? Yet it is an almost tangible part of psychotherapy. In psychotherapy, one can see it, can feel it, can know the moment of responsibility. Then there is a clear knowing of what it feels like. This is one of the great steps. Each time one takes responsibility, this is an actualizing of the self.

Fifth, we have talked so far of experiencing without self-awareness, of making the growth choice rather than the fear choice, of listening to the impulse voices, and of being honest and taking responsibility. All these are steps toward self-actualization, and all of them guarantee better life choices. A person who does each of these little things each time the choice point comes will find that they add up to better choices about what is constitutionally right for him. He comes to know what his destiny is, who his wife or husband will be, what his mission in life will be. One cannot choose wisely for a life unless he dares to listen to himself, *his own self*, at each moment in life, and to say calmly, "No, I don't like such and such."

The art world, in my opinion, has been captured by a small group of opinion- and taste-makers about whom I feel suspicious. That is an *ad hominem* judgment, but it seems fair enough for people who set themselves up as able to say, "You like what I like or else you are a fool." We must teach people to listen to their own tastes. Most people don't do it. When standing in a gallery before a puzzling painting, one rarely hears, "That is a puzzling painting." We had a dance program at Brandeis University not too long ago—a weird thing altogether, with electronic music, tapes, and people doing surrealistic and Dada things. When the lights went up everybody looked stunned, and nobody knew what to say. In that kind of situation most people will make some smart chatter instead of saying, "I would like to think about this." Making an honest statement involves daring to be different, unpopular, nonconformist. If clients, young or old, cannot be taught about being prepared to be unpopular, counselors might just as well give up right now. To be courageous rather than afraid is another version of the same thing.

Sixth, self-actualization is not only an end state but also the process of actualizing one's potentialities at any time, in any amount. It is, for example, a matter of becoming smarter by studying if one is an intelligent person. Self-actualization means using one's intelligence. It does not mean doing some far-out thing necessarily, but it may mean going through an arduous and demanding period of preparation in order to realize one's possibilities. Self-actualization can consist of finger exercises at a piano keyboard. Self-actualization means working to do well the thing that one wants to do. To become a second-rate physician is not a good path to self-actualization. One wants to be first-rate or as good as he can be.

Seventh, peak experiences are transient moments of self-actualization. They are moments of ecstasy which cannot be bought, cannot be guaranteed, cannot even be sought. One must be, as C. S. Lewis wrote, "surprised by joy." But one can set up the conditions so that peak experiences are more likely, or one can perversely set up the conditions so that they are less likely. Breaking up an illusion, getting rid of a false notion, learning what one is not good at, learning what one's potentialities are *not*—these are also part of discovering what one is in fact.

Practially everyone does have peak experiences, but not everyone knows it. Some people wave these small mystical experiences aside. Helping people to recognize these little moments of ecstasy when they happen is one of the jobs of the counselor or metacounselor. Yet, how does one's psyche, with nothing external in the world to point at—there is no blackboard there—look into another person's secret psyche and then try to communicate? We have to work out a new way of communication. I think that kind of communication may be more of a model for teaching, and counseling, for helping adults to become as fully developed as they can be, than the kind we are used to when we see teachers writing on the board. If I love Beethoven and I hear something in a quartet that you don't, how do I teach you to hear? The noises are there, obviously. But I hear something very, very beautiful, and you look blank. You hear the sounds. How do I get you to hear the beauty? That is more our problem in teaching than making you learn the ABC's or demonstrating arithmetic on the board or pointing to a dissection of a frog.

Eighth, finding out who one is, what he is, what he likes, what he doesn't like, what is good for him and what bad, where he is going and what his mission is—opening oneself up to himself—means the exposure of psychopathology. It means identifying defenses, and after defenses have been identified, it means finding the courage to give them up. This is painful because defenses are erected against something which is unpleasant. But giving up the defenses is worthwhile. If the psychoanalytic literature has taught us nothing else, it has taught us that repression is not a good way of solving problems.

Resacralizing. Resacralizing means being willing, once again, to see a person "under the aspect of eternity," as Spinoza says, or to see him in the medieval Christian unitive perception, that is, being able to see the sacred, the eternal, the symbolic. It is to see Woman with a capital "W" and everything which that implies, even when one looks at a particular woman. Another example: One goes to medical school and dissects a brain. Certainly something is lost if the medical student isn't awed but, without the unitive perception, sees the brain only as one concrete thing. Open to resacralization, one sees a brain as a sacred object also, sees its symbolic value, sees it as a figure of speech, sees it in its poetic aspects.

Put all these points together, and we see that self-actualization is not a matter of one great moment. It is not true that on Thursday at four o'clock the trumpet blows and one steps into the pantheon forever and altogether. Self-actualization is a matter of degree, or little accessions accumulated one by one. Too often our clients are inclined to wait for some kind of inspiration to strike so that they can say, "At 3:23 on this Thursday I became self-actualized!" People selected as self-actualizing subjects, people who fit the criteria, go about it in these little ways: They listen to their own voices; they take responsibility; they are honest; and they work hard. They find out who they are and what they are, not only in terms of their mission in life, but also in terms of the way their feet hurt when they wear such and such a pair of shoes and whether they do or do not like eggplant or stay up all night if they drink too much beer. All this is what the real self means. They find their own biological natures, their congenital natures, which are irreversible or difficult to change.

VI.

PROBLEMS

Coleman, D. & Heller, D. *The Pleasures of Psychology*. New American Library, NY, 1986

College Blues

by Aaron T. Beck and Jeffrey Young

Contrary to what the creators of *Animal House* may have had us believe, college is a very serious time in a person's life: It is where adolescence and adulthood meet. Sometimes this confluence can be painless and reasonably smooth. However, some transitions in college are not so easy; the student may find himself or herself depressed and directionless. Since college can be a very stressful time, when crucial decisions about career and relationships begin to take shape, such difficulties are far from uncommon. This is the subject of "College Blues."

Aaron Beck and Jeffrey Young are both well schooled in the dilemmas of college-age populations, since both have worked extensively with students on the campus of the University of Pennsylvania. Moreover, Beck is one of the leading authorities in America on the nature of depression.

In the following piece, Beck and Young observe that depression is common on college campuses—much as we would like to think otherwise. Students often fail to recognize or locate the source of their difficulties. Is it home, classes, an ill-fated relationship, loneliness? The origin of a problem is sometimes difficult to discern, and so the college student may prolong the depression as a result. Beck and Young describe how to spot the depression, and pinpoint the common misperceptions that worsen it.

OVER THE NEXT nine months, as many as 78 percent of the 7,500,800 students enrolled in American colleges may suffer some symptoms of depression—roughly a quarter of the student population at any one time. These figures come from recent studies, such as the one conducted by Joan Oliver, Leo Croghan, and Norman Katz at four unnamed universities, and are echoed by our clinical experience. We cannot be sure how they relate to the depression rate for the population as a whole, because funds have been lacking for definitive studies. Those estimates that do exist are based on very limited samples that are not representative of the entire country. But the incidence of student depression seems quite high, with depression the leading psychiatric disorder on our college campuses.

Triggered by traditional student pressures—including failure to meet personal academic standards, the need to define goals for life and career, and the lack of support systems to fend off loneliness—the depression will be mild or subclinical for about a third of the students who get the campus blues. But for 46 percent of them, however, the depression will be intense enough to warrant professional help. Campus depression will play a role in as many as 500 suicides, which are 50 percent more frequent among college students than among nonstudents of the same age.

Despite the amount of depression around them, however, depressed students often perceive themselves to be alone. One result is that they often have trouble evaluating the seriousness of their problems and whether or not they should consult a psychiatrist or psychologist.

In our work for the past six years at the Mood Clinic of the University of Pennsylvania Hospital's Center for Cognitive Therapy—and in 20 years of previous research—we have found that it is often difficult for students to distinguish, for example, between a temporary feeling of sadness and full-blown clinical depression. Frequently, they decide not to seek professional help, which is one reason that statistics on depression in both the college population and the general population are thin.

The confusion is understandable. A student who is just "low" and one who is clinically depressed might both describe themselves as blue, unhappy, empty, sad, and lonely. Both may have difficulty falling asleep at night, feel fatigued, or lose their appetites. The difference between them lies in the number, intensity, and duration of their symptoms: while merely in a sad mood, for example, an individual may have to exert extra effort to get started at something, while depressed patients often cannot work at all, even when others prod them.

For those students who do decide to approach mental-health clinics for help, the senior author has developed the Beck Depression Inventory to help diagnose their level of depression. Students are asked to fill out a 21-item survey—now used at several clinics and colleges around the country—choosing from among four statements in each category to describe the intensity of their condition. The results then indicate to both therapist and student just how debilitating the student's symptoms are.

The basis of our treatment for depression is an application to students of cognitive therapy [*Psychology Today*, January 1977]. It grows from our finding that students' misperceptions of the world, of the stresses that surround them, may be as important a cause of depression as the stresses are.

Students do not hallucinate their problems—they cope with the real stresses of academic and social adjustment—but they inflate the importance of temporary setbacks and misjudge the severity of rejections; in short, they misperceive their problems. Students who grieve over their lack of friends, for example, may have real problems in social adjustment, yet they usually turn out to have at least some caring and supportive friends. They may also severely overestimate academic difficulties—on the basis of one mediocre grade.

Not all students suffer from mere misperception, of course; their distortions of reality may mask other problems, such as a deep fear of new situations. As we apply cognitive therapy to college students, correcting the errors in thinking and social behavior of those who are lonely and depressed, such phobias, once uncovered, can reveal themselves in treatment.

STRESS AND TRANSITION

College students may be especially prone to psychological problems because they encounter so many new situations that potentially can be misperceived. They experience simultaneously all the transitions that are major stresses in adulthood: all at once, they lose family, friends, and familiar surroundings, with college supplying no ready-made substitutes. They lose their high school "job"—simple student status—and must substitute a career choice with long-term consequences. Going to college may even mean a shift in social or class status. These pressures war with each other for students' time and attention; and, if their competing goals are not balanced successfully, the students are likely to feel deprived.

Students who cannot make career decisions, for example, may feel they are working hard, but to no purpose; those who allot too much time to study may feel that their future is assured at the price of getting no pleasure from their present lives; students who engage in many extracurricular activities but have not developed an intimate relationship may feel the lack of someone they can confide in. Students who concentrate on one goal to the exclusion of other people and other pursuits may find that they are left without necessary support systems in the event of disillusionment.

Carl's problems were typical of those growing primarily out of academic pressures. He was a 17-year-old freshman at an Ivy League university several hours away from his hometown. He had been a popular student in high school—a member of the student council and the tennis team—and had a close circle of friends. He had also worked hard and obtained high grades. Carl knew he wanted to become a doctor, and wanted to guarantee his admission to medical school as soon as possible.

Carl decided before starting college that if he was going to compete successfully, he would have to devote all his time to studying. By the end of his first week at college, he was spending virtually every waking hour at classes, in the library, or shut in his room alone. Carl knew many of the other students in his dormitory by name, but felt that he could not spare too much time for socializing because he might lose his "competitive edge." He decided not to continue with his tennis because he simply could not spare the time required for team practice every afternoon.

When Carl received a C on his chemistry midterm exam, he felt his world crumbling. He believed that he had lost any chance for admission to medical school and that, to make matters worse, nobody else really cared what happened to him. Carl soon developed a severe depression.

Many students like Carl enter college with a past record of successes both academic and social. Although they recognize, rationally, that the selective college-admissions process may throw them together with others from the top 10 or 20 percent of high school students, nonetheless, they still expect to excel. Never having learned to cope with failure, they attach inordinate importance to each disappointing grade, letting it blot out the memory of other successes. They may come to think they have overestimated their academic potential and will never measure up.

The dissatisfaction and self-reproach may lead to clinical depression that will begin to interfere with their actual performance, creating a vicious spiral: as students misinterpret their academic difficulties as evidence of intellectual deficiencies rather than emotional stress, they become still less able to do well academically, and get still sadder and less motivated.

Students, of course, have worried about grades forever— or at least since college ceased to be the province of Fitzgerald's prep-school princes with their "Gentleman's C's." But as competition for admission to graduate and professional schools becomes more intense, it becomes more and more likely that mediocre grades *can*, in fact, spell the difference between success and failure; these lapses can break the carefully planned chain that in theory, at least, leads a student from college to professional school to career.

Intensifying this tightrope pressure still further is what we call "obligated success": students on scholarships, for example, may feel an extra obligation to do well in order to justify their special treatment. As college costs increasingly pinch middle-class families, more and more students feel the pressure of obligated success because of their parents' financial sacrifice. This feeling of responsibility to the family—to live out the parents' ambitions or live up to their expectations—may hit especially hard if a student is away from home and family for the first time.

Some students caught in the cycle of "failure" and self-torment decide to leave school, feeling that they are simply "not cut out for college." A study of dropouts by David Luecke and James McClure at Washington University showed that one-third had suffered serious depression just before leaving school, and a majority had not sought out professional help.

Similarly, a recent study at University of Pennsylvania Law School conducted by vice-dean Phyllis Beck and psychiatrist David Burns found that a high proportion of law students who consulted the administration about dropping out of school were also suffering from depression or anxiety.

Here, however, dropping out was dramatically reduced by a system for identifying and treating depression. Students who complained that they did not have the intellectual "equipment," had lost their interest in law, or had made some terrible mistake in choosing law as a profession were helped through guidance and psychotherapy to recognize and vanquish their underlying depression, and could then acknowledge that they did, in fact, have the interest and qualifications to continue in school.

OUT OF THE NEST

Other stressful collegiate situations are primarily social. Jill was the youngest child in a large family, and was always pampered as "the baby." Her older brothers and sisters lavished attention on her. Although everyone else in the family had household responsibilities, Jill was encouraged to "just enjoy herself." When she had problems, she would turn to someone else in the family for help and reassurance. In junior high school, Jill found a circle of older girl friends who "adopted" her, tutored her in her academic work, and told her how to act with boys. During three years of high school, Jill came to depend on Mark, her boyfriend, for praise and affection. When she entered college and left him and her family, she was fearful about what would happen to her.

Jill soon felt overwhelmed by college. Unable to manage her time, she began to fall behind in her course work. Nor was she making friends. She waited for other students to come over and introduce themselves, but they all seemed too busy. After a month, she met Ron. They became very close, and she once again felt secure. But later, when he broke off with her, Jill became depressed. Feeling that she could no longer cope with all the problems in her life, she would sit alone most of the day and cry.

Jill's case demonstrates how students can be devastated by the loss of social support systems. Many high school students have a circle of friends to "party" with; a good friend to confide in; a parent to turn to in times of crisis; and an intimate boyfriend or girlfriend to love. When they enter college, these supports are gone and freshmen have to develop new relationships as substitutes. This may take months or even years, and during the process, students almost inevitably experience loneliness.

The process of transition was especially difficult for Jill, who had moved from an environment in which other people took care of her to one in which she had to function independently. Unfortunately, like many college freshmen, Jill had never learned to be self-sufficient. Accustomed to having others initiate relationships, Jill had never had to seek out friends. But in college, her passivity left her isolated.

We have seen a number of students who, like Jill, have been popular in the precollege years and who "suddenly" develop fears of going to classes, attending social functions, and making new acquaintances. In most of these cases, we have found that the underlying problem was a lifelong fear of going into new environments. In high school, these students generally were able to compensate for their phobia (which therefore went unrecognized) by having a friend along at all times. Deprived of these social supports after entering college, such students would tend to avoid classes and social events. As they progressively withdrew, and fell further behind in their schoolwork, they were deprived of the types of satisfactions to which they had been accustomed, and fell into the cycle of depression.

Jill's underlying social fears were set off by one of the most common triggers for depression: the breakup of an intimate relationship. Here again, misperceptions made the problems worse. College students often do not know how to adjust to a lover's rejection. Deprived of intimacy, companionship, and support, students magnify the long-term importance of the loss. Instead of thinking realistically, "I'm going to miss him, but I'll get over it," they think, "No one cares what happens to me and no one ever will." The distorted interpretation of rejection is often responsible for excruciating feelings of loneliness, which are often the first link in a chain leading to clinical depression.

DYNAMICS OF LONELINESS

Loneliness is a major cause of depression, but it can also be a problem on its own or in combination with other emotional states. Loneliness arises from the perceived absence of a desired relationship; and although some forms of relationships can compensate for the lack of others, relationships are certainly not interchangeable. Through a recent study of students at the University of Pennsylvania, the junior author pinpointed several distinct forms of loneliness, each reflecting a particular kind of relationship. Using the Young Loneliness Inventory (modeled on the Beck Depression Inventory), we have identified four types of loneliness:

1. *Exclusion* reflects the belief that one is not part of a group of people to which one would like to belong. This is the feeling students report at a large party when everyone else seems to be having a good time and they feel left out,

or the feeling of wanting to belong to a particular dorm clique but not being accepted by its members.

2. *Feeling unloved* may be the most painful form of loneliness, perhaps because the feeling of being loved provides us with a basic sense of security and stability. Students beginning college often miss parents or intimate boyfriends or girlfriends who, in high school, cared about their welfare and could be depended upon during periods of crisis. Naturally, they turn to new relationships, but problems can develop if they rely too heavily on the new relationships to validate their self-worth. Donald, a 22-year-old college junior who visited the Mood Clinic, started out by telling us, "I have never done anything right. I have always let everybody down." He had started to feel depressed, lonely, and suicidal, he said, when his year-long relationship with his girlfriend became punctuated by quarrels.

His opinion of himself had been based on the notion that he had to achieve a degree of academic success in order to be regarded as worthwhile. Both his parents were successful scientists and, although they did not directly set high standards for him, he felt that they expected a great deal of him and could not accept his academic shortcomings. As long as Elaine loved him, he said, "it meant that she loved me for myself. I didn't have to be anything." He could feel totally accepted, regardless of how well he performed. When he and Elaine quarreled, his tendency to evaluate himself harshly became greatly intensified; their relationship could no longer protect him against his savage self-criticisms.

3. *Constriction* is the feeling that one's thoughts and feelings are bottled up inside. Depressed students often report that there is no one they can talk to about their private concerns. Our experience dovetails with a study at Boston University, which found that students who had attempted suicide were much more likely to feel that they did not have confidantes than did students who had suicidal thoughts but had not made an actual attempt. This study used only women, but constriction loneliness may be more of a problem among men. A survey at UCLA dem-

onstrated that students of either sex were generally intolerant of male students' expressing depression, yet showed
sympathy for women who expressed the same feelings.
This may explain why women seeking help at student
mental-health clinics outnumber men two to one. Male
students may be more reluctant to either acknowledge their
depression or talk to others about it because of a fear of
social intolerance and disparagement that appears to be
realistic.

4. *Alienation* is a form of loneliness in which one feels
that he or she is completely different from other poeple.
Some college students who feel they do not share the
values and interests of their peers experience pervasive
loneliness. A black high school student who grew up in the
inner city and enters a college with primarily white, upper-
middle-class students, for example, is likely to feel left
out. Unless he finds other students ''like him,'' he may
come to feel increasingly depressed and isolated. We have
seen the same alienation among female students at for-
merly all-male institutions that have gone coed. Another
variation afflicts students who are either dramatically more
conservative or more liberal than other students they know.
Many college students from conservative backgrounds felt
severe alienation during the late 1960s, at a time when
many of their fellow students were involved in political
protest.

DIAGNOSING LONELINESS

These four types of loneliness can affect students with
varying frequency, intensity, and duration. These dimensions of students' symptom levels help us in turn to distinguish chronically lonely, situationally lonely, and transiently
lonely students.

Chronic loneliness evolves when an individual is not
able to establish satisfactory interpersonal relationships over
a period of years. These students, like Jill, may have a
phobia about initiating relationships with other people or
they may be unable to sustain friendships at a deep level of

intimacy for a long-enough period of time. Some of the chronically lonely come to us feeling bitter about people in general and express beliefs like "You can't trust other people" or "People only care about themselves." Their beliefs then sustain their pattern of social isolation.

A second category consists of students who are lonely because of changes in their life situations. Most college freshmen initially fall into this category as they try to develop new social contacts to replace the old. Situational loneliness may also involve more serious changes, such as the death of a parent. In this case, a brief period of grieving and depression can be considered normal as the individual learns to accept the loss of a lifelong attachment.

Transient loneliness is probably the most common of the three diagnostic categories and refers to the everyday, garden variety of loneliness, the periodic passing mood that usually disappears as soon as someone comes to talk with us.

Students often fall into this kind of loneliness when they exaggerate the importance of a minor event (such as a quarrel with a friend) and take it as a sign that all of their relationships are deficient; in fact, transiently lonely people can see a day or two later that most of their friendships were actually satisfactory all along.

The process of exaggerating the importance of unpleasant events is called "cognitive distortion." A study we completed last year at the University of Pennsylvania illustrates how these distortions can work to increase loneliness. One hundred and three freshmen and sophomores completed questionnaires: one-third were instructed to answer the questions when they felt happy, one-third when they were sad, and one-third when they were lonely.

Students in sad and lonely moods painted a distinctly more desolate picture of their relationships than did students who were feeling good. They were more likely to report that they had no one to depend on and no one who really cared about them or loved them at school. Lonely students stated more often that there was a group of people who did not like them as much as they would have wanted. They were also more likely to question whether anyone understood them, describing themselves as outsiders who bottled up their feelings. Furthermore, lonely students were more likely to attribute these problems to personal inadequacies and to feel disappointed in themselves. Overall, these students were more pessimistic about the future and less content with their lives.

But the lonely students' feeling that they were living isolated lives, devoid of relationships, was a distortion of reality. Although the lonely students generally agreed with the statement that "there's no one here at school I can really depend on," when asked to list and rate *specific* friends, students who were in lonely moods listed the same number of close friends as did the happy students. Moreover, they were just as likely as the happy group to report that the close friends they listed really cared about them.

TREATING DEPRESSION AND LONELINESS

The techniques we use at the Center for Cognitive Therapy emphasize three primary goals: relieving the student's primary symptoms of depression, changing the unrealistic thoughts responsible for the student's negative view of life, and teaching the student new skills for adapting to schoolwork and to relationships. We have found that most students can overcome depression and loneliness relatively quickly, without having to probe into childhood experiences.

Before students can begin actively working to change their thinking or learn new skills, they often need some relief from the most distressing symptoms of depression, especially sadness and fatigue. Because most depressed students report sleeping much of the time and remaining inactive, we encourage them to use a Daily Activity Schedule, planning activities to fill up every hour of the day. We help them select activities that provide them either with a sense of pleasure or a feeling of accomplishment. These seemingly simple activities, such as going to movies with a friend or taking notes in class, are often sufficient to demonstrate to the students that they are not totally incompetent and have not lost the ability to enjoy themselves. To help give students "mental space," we may also intervene with administration or faculty to arrange makeup examinations or postpone paper deadlines, temporarily removing some academic pressure.

One approach we use is to have students fill out a Dysfunctional Thought Record each day. Each time a student experiences an unpleasant emotion such as sadness, he describes the situation, and the underlying irrational thought. With the help of the therapist, he then writes a rational response to the upsetting thought. For example, a student who thinks, "No one loves me," and then feels lonely, could supply the response "Just because my girlfriend left me doesn't mean no one loves me."

As we work with students to correct their misconceptions, we also employ a variety of other behavioral techniques going beyond traditional therapeutic roles. For example, we teach students like Jill better methods for studying and scheduling time efficiently. We school them in making important decisions, rehearsing the process of formulating a problem, thinking of solutions, and deciding which alternative will best fulfill their needs.

For students with social phobias, we employ several behavioral methods for anxiety management. Most of these methods involve graduated exposure to the feared situation. In some cases, students are taught ways to relax while imagining the feared situation or actually confronting it. Lonely students might also be trained to develop and maintain close friendships. This is often done through role-playing, in which the student and therapist rehearse real-life situations in the office. The therapist serves as a director, coaching the student in skills to improve his or her performance in such situations as initiating a conversation with a new acquaintance or handling a problem with a close friend.

For the student experiencing situational loneliness, in crisis because of the abrupt loss of important relationships, treatment is directed, first, at offering support and reassurance so that the student's loneliness does not intensify because he or she has no one to communicate with. We next initiate a preventive approach to help the student anticipate, recognize, and combat such common cognitive distortions as thinking, "I'll never meet anyone." Finally, the therapist advises the student on places and strategies for making new friends. Many students, surprisingly, have never thought of the laundromat or the vending machines at the library as places to meet people.

Techniques like these can be employed not only by clinicians—although in the case of serious depression we urge students to consult professionals—but also by campus paraprofessionals: upper-class "big brothers" or "big sisters," housemasters, and resident counselors. "Faculty friend" programs at such places as Princeton and Vanderbilt Universities have also proven useful in helping students to cope with psychological, as well as academic, problems.

With recent budget cuts at many universities reducing the availability of mental-health professionals, these paraprofessional alternatives take on added importance. Many students who are reluctant to consult psychologists or psychiatrists, thinking of it as too drastic a step, can be helped through early counseling by faculty or peers.

In fact, one study at Yale University by Andrew Slaby showed that of freshmen seeking counseling help over a five-week period, only 17 percent went to the mental-health service; the others consulted deans, chaplains, and freshmen counselors.

The magnitude of the college depression problem is such, however, that the real remedies can only be institutional. It is unlikely that as a society, we will reconsider the practice of placing heavy pressures of career choice and competition on young men and women, but if such pressures are expected, students can be cushioned against their impact. High schools must provide better training in study techniques, and even in social skills, warning students what to expect from college in terms of competition and isolation. Increased use of independent study projects in high schools, still extremely limited, would help college-bound students get their sea legs before they set off into the academic storm. Colleges, in turn, should strengthen their orientation and transition programs, providing easy access to counselors for all types of problems, real or illusory. Recognizing and treating college depression on an institutional level may be the best hope for curbing the prevalence of this widespread disorder, whose every sufferer feels alone.

Mark Twain's Separation Anxiety

by Robert Sears

If you ever have had fantasies of being Huck Finn or experiencing freedom along the river, then this next selection is for you. Robert Sears is a distinguished authority on child development from Stanford, who also has a personal fascination with Samuel Clemens. Sears's psychological background and personal interest come together in his essay, "Mark Twain's Separation Anxiety."

Separation anxiety normally occurs when a young child feels upset at being apart from his parents. To the extent that it persists into adulthood, it represents a psychological problem. Such seems to have been the case with Samuel Clemens.

Sears measures the famous author's separation anxiety through his letters and novels—an unorthodox but creative source of data. He has also done his homework by researching Samuel Clemens's early history and the events of his later life. The result is an intriguing look at the links between the literary work and the life of the person most of us know as Mark Twain.

IF YOU HAVE read *The Adventures of Tom Sawyer*, you may remember the time Aunt Polly punishes Tom for breaking a sugar bowl. Unjustly, as it turns out, for she had been in the kitchen at the time and is unaware of the real culprit. Tom protests:

" 'Hold on, now, what 'er you belting *me* for?—Sid broke it!'

"Aunt Polly paused, perplexed, and Tom looked for healing pity. But when she got her tongue again, she only said:

" '*Umf!* Well, you didn't get a lick amiss, I reckon. You been into some audacious mischief when I wasn't around, like enough.'

"Then her conscience reproached her, and she yearned to say something kind and loving; but she judged that this would be construed into a confession that she had been in the wrong, and discipline forbade that. . . .

"Tom brooded and pictured himself lying sick unto death and his aunt bending over him beseeching one little forgiving word, but he would turn his face to the wall and die with that word unsaid."

That episode expresses in fictional form Mark Twain's powerful and pervasive separation anxiety—the fear of losing love. It is just one of 23 such episodes that suggest that theme in the first two-thirds of *Tom Sawyer*.

By measuring separation anxiety in Twain's letters and novels, I have been able to match the peaks and valleys of his suppressed feelings with the events of his adult life, in order to discover some of the causes of his anxiety. I chose nine of Twain's novels and one short piece to analyze; they were written fairly evenly over the course of his adult lifetime and have been quite accurately dated as to time of composition. With the help of Deborah Lapidus and Christine Cozzens, I divided the works into a total of 615 discrete episodes, short segments that constitute autonomous chunks of the narrative. We then scored each of the episodes for presence or absence of loss of love. While our method ignores, by its nature, those themes of loss of love that extend throughout a novel—the betrayal represented by the Duke and the Dauphin in *The Adventures of Huckleberry Finn*, for example—it opens continuous narratives to reliable measurement in a way that can be compared with figures for similar expressions in the letters.

For biographical purposes, these data are quite valuable. That makes them important for history, too. History hangs on people—on their impulses, their values, their loves, and their hates. The more we can know about how personal attributes came about in the writers who have molded our thoughts, the better we can understand those writers and the society they helped to create.

A major problem in constructing a life history is trying to discover the subject's enduring motives. A person can express some motives openly under some circumstances, but others are under varying degrees of external or internal control and may not be verbalized. Psychoanalysts long ago discovered that a patient's fantasies—particularly when compared with his or her other, reality-based, communications—provide clues both to those unexpressed motives and to the events that trigger them.

In a clinical setting, the psychologist can probe fantasies by giving projective tests or by examining reported dreams and daydreams. The biographer, as a substitute for testing, can examine the raw data of his subject's writings. In Mark Twain's case, I selected loss of love as a category because I felt sure that his early experiences of loss must have left some mark on him that would influence his adult writing. We have no projective tests for Mark Twain, but we have both his voluminous published correspondence (his reality-based communications) and the fictional expressions of his novels. Working with those two sets of data, together with the substantial information we have about the external events of his life, we can trace the course of Twain's separation anxiety from its origin in his early childhood through its partial suppression and transformation in middle age to its unabashed and tragic overt expression in later years.

Born in 1835, Samuel Clemens was a premature infant, the fifth of six children. His father was a cold and remote man; he had to get most of his love from his mother, an affectionate but peppery woman (like Aunt Polly) who evidently mixed love with rejection. Sam's attachment and dependency must have been strengthened by the extra attention he received intermittently during his frequent illnesses. Hence, his feelings of love were ambivalent; he experienced both love and the fear of its withdrawal.

His fear of separation was reinforced by several early losses. A brother and sister died before he was 10 years old; his father when he was 12. His younger brother, Henry, was killed in a steamboat explosion when Sam was 22. Then, within a few months of Twain's marriage to Olivia Langdon, his father-in-law died of cancer. Two years later, their first child, Langdon, died at 18 months.

Twain and Olivia had three other children, all girls. Susy, the eldest, died suddenly in her late 20s of meningitis, and shortly after that, Jean, the youngest of the three, became epileptic. Olivia developed crippling heart trouble and died in 1904. Twain himself died in 1910 after severe financial reverses.

Fortunately for our purposes, Mark Twain wrote seven of the nine novels we examined in spurts; a great deal is known about when he composed certain sections. Twain wrote the first 18 chapters of *Tom Sawyer*, for example, during the summer of 1874; he then put the manuscript aside until the following spring, and finished it on July 5, 1875. The first *Tom Sawyer* stint contained 55 of the episodes we examined; the second, 26. Twain's letters to his wife were written during the same span of time, beginning with their courtship in 1868 and ending just before Olivia's death in 1904. Each of the letters and each of the episodes from the novels was scored in the same way.

In the letters, Twain expressed fewest loss-of-love feelings in 1870, the year of his marriage to Olivia. Twenty percent of his earlier courting letters—in 1868 and 1869—contained loss references. None of those related to a realistic source, such as death; all were of the "suffering lover" type. After his marriage, the frequency of loss expressions was sharply reduced and remained low until the 1890s, when actual losses of friends, as well as his own impending old age, brought a new peak.

Looking only at those letters, we can derive a seemingly reasonable hypothesis: Sam Clemens' childhood experiences—such as the early loss of his father—established in him a propensity for separation fears, mainly about the death of loved ones. He generalized those fears to other types of loss, especially in relation to his newly loved Olivia. With marriage and maturity, the fears disappeared—until real losses by death evoked them again. The biographical evidence supports this interpretation.

Since most of Mark Twain's separation anxiety *not* connected with actual death disappeared from the letters after 1872, when he appeared no longer to be a suffering lover, one might infer (in view of his earlier openness of expression) that his anxiety had disappeared. But it is just here that the novels reveal a quite different state of affairs. Within the seemingly innocuous period of 1873 to 1885 there were two massive upsurges in Twain's fictional expression of loss of love. The first began in the late winter of 1873 with *The Gilded Age*, and reached its zenith the following summer with the first stint of *Tom Sawyer*. Frequency decreased through 1875 and 1876, only to climb sharply in the following eight years, years that comprised both stints on *The Prince and the Pauper* and the last three stints on *Huckleberry Finn*.

Those two peaks, associated with no open expression in letters, demonstrate that Twain's separation anxiety could be drawn from sources other than the realistic one of death, actual or impending. Were it not for those clues from the novels, there would be no reason to search for explanation of loss feelings during the first five years of Twain's marriage or in the following decade. That is the very reason such analysis is useful: fictional expression is under less conscious control than are direct communications such as letters.

What induced such a high frequency of loss fantasy in Twain during those years? Could it be ascribed to the subject matter of *Tom Sawyer* and *Huckleberry Finn*? Mark Twain was writing about childhood—his own. The writing brought back his own feelings about loss and death, and such loss became a central theme.

More to the point, however, is the question of why Twain chose boyhood as his subject. The choice is not difficult to understand. In both men and women—especially in late maturers—the sudden intimacy of marriage quite commonly initiates regressive fantasy. There is clear evidence that it did so for Mark Twain. On the fourth day after his marriage—he was almost 35 at the time—he wrote a long, ecstatic letter to Will Bowen (fictionalized as one of Tom Sawyer's gang), reminiscing effusively about the events of their boyhood. The welling up of those memories led him, during that first year, to express the loss-of-love theme in an incomplete work, *Boy's Manuscript*, and no doubt set the stage for *Tom Sawyer*, which he finished a few years later.

But what caused the subsequent variation in the strength of Twain's loss-of-love feelings? Neither marriage nor the death of Olivia's father can account for the later peaks. Something else must have happened in that first year of marriage—something that *was* repeated. Indeed, something did: Olivia became pregnant. The peaks of loss fantasy in 1874 and 1880 coincided with Olivia's pregnancies with her last two daughters, Clara and Jean.

The incident of the broken sugar bowl from *Tom Sawyer* was written during Olivia's pregnancy with Clara. An instance from her pregnancy with Jean can be found in *Huckleberry Finn* at the end of the Shepherdson-Grangerford feud episode: "When I got down out of the tree," says Huck, "I crept along down the river bank a piece, and found the two bodies laying in the edge of the water, and tugged them till I got them ashore; then I covered up their faces and got away as quick as I could. I cried a little when I was covering up Buck's face, for he was mighty good to me."

My interpretation is that the impending (and actual) births of the children represented a threat to the love—and dependency—relation between Twain and Olivia. There is evidence that Jean was an unexpected and unwanted child, and that is borne out by our analysis. After Clara was a couple of years old, Twain's loss fantasies decreased (in the second writing spurt of *Tom Sawyer* and the first of *Huckleberry Finn*)—only to build up again in the first stint of *The Prince and the Pauper* (early 1878), and then rise further in the startling feud episodes of *Huckleberry Finn* and the second stint of *The Prince and the Pauper*.

The only high point that does not coincide with a known pregnancy is that of the first stint of *The Prince and the Pauper* early in 1878. However, Twain wrote those episodes immediately after his mid-December Whittier's Birthday speech in Boston, a slightly tasteless performance before an august gathering of the Boston literary establishment, which brought him some realistic loss of love. It seems possible that the event was responsible for the high frequency in 1878. It is too bad (and annoying to the biographer) that Twain wrote no novel during his wife's pregnancy with Susy. Hence, that opportunity for testing our generalization was lost.

Twain's final surge of loss fantasies began in 1889 when he was 54 years old and reaching the age at which sources of loss and bereavement were very real indeed. Once again, his fictional expression paralleled his open expression of grief and sympathy in letters. In the last part of *A Connecticut Yankee in King Arthur's Court*, in 1889, we have a transparent example: "The parting—ah, yes that was hard. As I was devouring the child with last kisses, it brisked up and jabbered out its vocabulary " and so on, into a perfect welter of grief about father-daughter separation.

By this analysis of his novels, then, we have confirmed that Mark Twain had a strong predisposition toward separation anxiety, which appeared in his fiction as well as in his social communication. We have discovered, moreover, that his wife's pregnancies appear to have served to stimulate his anxiety. Those are significant biographical findings in themselves. They also give promise of making more understandable the astonishing relationship Mark Twain had with his daughters as they grew into middle childhood and adolescence. Never was any father so utterly possessive and loving as was Mark Twain. Was it a case of protesting too much after his earlier fears and implied rejection?

Some students of literature object to any analytic method that breaks up an author's work as our episodic analysis does. If we were dealing with problems of literary criticism, that might or might not be a relevant objection, but we are not. All we are doing here is providing equivalent units for measurement.

Again, some may say it works well enough with Mark Twain, who has always been described as "episodic," but what about with other authors? In fact, both episodic and content analysis work equally well with such diverse stylists as Dumas, Hemingway, Orwell, Hesse, and Steinbeck. The content categories for understanding different personalities will differ widely, of course, but the basic method need not. In Orwell, for example, loss of love is very scanty, but a deep sense of revulsion toward bodily functions is reflected in repeated, obsessive references to them, in episode after episode.

But no one method of analyzing fantasy—or reality— need be used alone. A full-scale psychobiography will only be made possible by combining many methods. Here, I have described one that can be used in that part of the task that seeks to match fantasy against reality in the search for a man's enduring motives and the life events that awaken them.

Crazy Talk

by Elaine Chaika

One of the most bizarre signs of schizophrenia is its garbled speech. In "Crazy Talk," linguist Elaine Chaika looks at how schizophrenic speech becomes so crazy.

As Chaika observes, the strangeness of schizophrenic speech tends to draw attention to the schizophrenic rather than to provide a camouflage for his ideas, as some schizophrenic patients seem to believe they are doing. Speech quality also seems to correspond to other schizophrenic activities. The author tells how one linguist could tell whether his patient had neglected medication by how far his speech had deteriorated. Chaika finds that schizophrenics are victims of sidetracking; they veer off on extreme and barely related tangents. Distracted by chance associations, the schizophrenic cannot follow a single train of thought, and garbled sentences are the result.

Chaika suggests that studying this process may help us unscramble puzzles about schizophrenic thought, and also teach us about the nature of language itself and how it sometimes breaks down.

"MY MOTHER'S NAME was Bill . . . and coo? St. Valentine's Day is the start of the breedin' season of the birds. All buzzards can coo. I'd like to see it pronounced buzzards rightly. They work hard. So do parakeets."

Who would say such strange things, and why? The who is easy to answer. Some schizophrenics talk this way, but

332

not all. And even among those who do, the odd speech comes and goes with the illness.

The question of why has been hotly debated for decades and has received a variety of answers. We are all creatures of our training. Psychiatrists are trained to look at behavior as being governed by suppressed desires or problems. Behavioral psychologists are trained to look at humans in terms of stimulus and response. And linguists, like me, are trained to examine language in terms of levels of production and failures to apply linguistic rules, an approach that I believe has a special contribution to make in understanding schizophrenic speech. But first, let's look at other explanations.

The psychiatric resident who introduced me to the vagaries of schizophrenic speech subscribed to an idea that no longer has much support, Bateson's Double Bind theory. The schizophrenic's mother hates her child, the theory holds, but cannot accept the idea. When the child protests, the mother not only insists that she does love him or her but punishes the child for saying that she doesn't. Or the child attempts to kiss the mother, who subtly rebuffs him and then later says, "Why don't you ever kiss me?" The child is caught in a double bind, unable to resolve or escape the contradictory demands, and never learns to communicate properly.

There are several problems with this interpretation. For one thing, children do not learn to speak solely from their parents, but also from playmates, teachers and other adults. Furthermore, there is little solid evidence that many adult schizophrenics were caught in a double bind as children or, for that matter, that many normal people were not.

Some clinical psychologists and psychiatrists suggest that the strange speech helps schizophrenics avoid the therapeutic situation. A related theory is that schizophrenics speak strangely to express and at the same time hide socially unacceptable feelings, such as homosexual tendencies.

If we adopt these explanations, we are still left with a mystery. Normal language skills allow us to think one thing and say something else or nothing at all. Why would schizophrenics choose to produce such bizarre speech to avoid therapy or hide feelings? Its very strangeness draws attention, not the best situation for someone wanting to hide ideas or avoid a situation.

There is also the question of why schizophrenics speak this way only during their psychotic episodes. It seems reasonable to assume that the speech is a symptom of the illness rather than a learned response. What we really need to establish is how or why the illness causes the peculiar speech.

David V. Forrest and other psychiatrists suggest that these strange utterances are poetic. Schizophrenics use strange, even bizarre, speech to describe what it is to be schizophrenic. Forrest maintains that all speech is metaphorical, and that the psychiatrist's task is to interpret its deep meaning. For example, we all know about Freudian slips. If someone says "no" instead of "yes," a Freudian analyst would say that the person subconsciously really meant no. Psychiatrists look for this kind of meaning everywhere. Schizophrenic speech, more complex than a simple slip, requires even more skillful interpretation.

Forrest illustrates his point by citing the patient who said: "Doctor, I have pains in my chest and hope and wonder if my box is broken and heart is beaten for my soul and salvation and heaven, Amen."

This means, Forrest says, "Doctor, I am heartbroken and hopeless and I pray you will save me."

Why didn't the patient just come out and say so? Because, according to Forrest, poetic speech is more powerful, more moving. He is telling what it is like to be schizophrenic. He is indulging in poetry.

To test the idea that schizophrenic speech is really poetic language, let us analyze another example, this one reported by a psychologist who had asked the patient to identify a color chip:

"Looks like clay. Sounds like gray. Take you for a roll in the hay. Hay day. Mayday. Help. I need help."

This certainly rhymes and we associate poetry with rhyme. But in most poetry, rhyme and imagery are subordinate to meaning. In the above example, the first phrase in the sequence is correct; the chip was clay-colored. The rest of the rhyming, however, is an out-of-control associating of words that happen to end with the same final sounds. There seems no other reason for "sounds like gray." "Roll in the hay" is yet another chance rhyme. "Hay day" and "Mayday" continue the rhyme, and perhaps share the meaning of "fun" with the preceding phrase. Finally, "Help!" is what "Mayday" means.

Perhaps the patient really did feel in need of help, but it seems unlikely that the entire sequence was deliberately chosen to lead to "Help!" If it were, we would then have the problem of explaining why someone would ask for help in such a bizarre fashion.

Poetic rhymes and imagery ordinarily don't show this almost random going from one word or phrase to another. The words, bizarre or otherwise, are chosen with final sounds that are alike but which fulfill the larger meaning of the poem. Robert Frost's humorous *The Span of Life* is a good example:

> *"The old dog barks backward*
> *without getting up,*
> *I can remember when he was a*
> *pup."*

The unusual choice of wording gives an image of a dog barking backward in time, as well as of turning his head to bark at something behind him. Both the rhyme and word choice fit in with the second line, which reinforces the idea that he is now an old dog. The deviation from normal speech is based on meaning, not chance similarity between words.

Our everyday language skills let us create sentences and comprehend the words of others, linguist Noam Chomsky has shown, even when we never before have seen or heard those words in that order. We understand even complex poetry by using the same skills. But we don't understand schizephrenics' poetry, because they don't follow the same rules of language.

There is yet another difference between normal and schizophrenic creativity. If we have trouble understanding normal speech, the speaker can rephrase it until we do.

"The schizophrenic," according to Forrest, "gets in trouble by trying to press on others the private linguistic connections he or she has found as the order of things they should accept; social manners demand more reactivity of viewpoint than that." We can accept this assumption, or we can assume that schizophrenics don't explain further because they don't realize that what they said is not what they thought they said.

My own training and experiences lead me to accept the second explanation. To give just one example, I observed one patient, who exhibited especially severe speech disruption during psychotic episodes, as he watched a videotape of himself speaking in this disoriented way. Astonished, he said that he had never realized he spoke like that, and that it was no wonder people couldn't understand him. He had heard himself on audio tapes before, but explained, "I thought they were distorted."

We all monitor our speech as we talk; that's how we usually catch our slips of the tongue. Even if we occasionally miss one, we agree when someone points it out. If you're setting up a lunch date with a friend and say, "I'll meet you on the corner just after lunch," she might respond, "You mean 'before?' " To which you would probably answer, "Oh, yeah, sorry, 'before.' " Schizophrenics don't seem to monitor their speech in this way. They don't acknowledge their speech errors, either by correcting themselves or by agreeing when others correct them.

The psychologist who reported the "looks like clay" example explained it in behaviorist terms, saying the patient was trying to avoid a response that was wrong, hence punishable, by trying out a variety of responses. The problem with this explanation is that the first statement, "Looks like clay," is the most accurate. And the more the patient speaks, the more incorrect and bizarre his speech becomes. Even if we could prove that the patient was afraid he would be punished for a mistake, we would then still have to explain why he went on to say more and more wrong (punishable) things.

To linguists, these and other features of schizophrenic speech share a bond. When I compare it to normally structured speech, it seems clear that there is something wrong with the schizophrenics' verbal productions. Closer examination makes it evident that the deviations result from one basic process gone awry: retrieval of words and grammar.

A linguist is trained to look at language in terms of levels of production. Eugene Nida, a pioneer in modern linguistics, told me that what struck him most about a schizophrenic friend's speech was that it appeared to be disrupted at different levels, singly or in combination. He could almost tell how many days his friend had neglected his medication by noticing to which level his speech had disintegrated.

The lowest level consists of sounds that are put together by rules into syllables. For instance, in English we have the sounds "m," "b," "w" and "a," but we cannot form a syllable "mbwa," although one can be formed in Swahili. Sounds and syllables form morphemes, the smallest units of language which have meaning. "Dis" is a morpheme in English. So is "temper." We combine morphemes to form words, words to form sentences and sentences to form discourses such as jokes, conversations, sermons, reports and books.

Nida found that his friend's speech disintegration proceeded from the top down. Rules of organized discourse were the first affected, then rules for sentences, as he started to chain words on the basis of associations rather than sense. This was followed by inappropriate choice of words and, finally, gibberish, as even the minimum ability to form words broke down. The progression seems to be generally true of schizophrenic speech dysfunction, although many patients cycle through the levels more than once in a single monologue.

Disintegration takes place when schizophrenics get sidetracked, so to speak. They may speak a coherent phrase or even a sentence, but then a word triggers another that rhymes or shares some meaning with it and they are off on a tack that has no relation to the original thought. Normal people control which words they choose to say what they want; schizophrenics lose this control and cycle through their mental dictionaries, producing associational chains or rhymes. As they lose control still further, they fail to match sounds to words or words to grammar, producing the gibberish or word salad I will discuss later.

Psychologists have advanced several other theories for schizophrenic speech based on the way people associate words. Some claim that schizophrenics "pigeonhole" the meanings of words rigidly. Psychologists Loren and Jean Chapman, for example, have found that schizophrenics tend to use the most dominant meaning of a word, the one most people ascribe to it in word-association tests. An opposing theory says that the meanings of words have become weakened for schizophrenics so that they associate words erroneously.

Neither of these contradictory theories explains schizo-phrenic speech very well. The fact that the erroneous associating takes place at all is what is deviant about such speech. The pathology lies in the fact that sentences are produced on the basis of associations between words that just happen to sound alike or share some meaning.

In normal speech, we select words according to the topic at hand, not random association. For instance, we wouldn't start to talk about cats and then in mid speech start to talk about dogs just because we associate the word "cats" with the word "dogs." We inhibit such random associations.

Here is a longer example, in which a schizophrenic is talking about her medication:

"Speeds up your metabolism. Makes your life shorter. Makes your heart bong. Tranquilizes you if you've got the metabolism I have. I have distemper just like cats do, 'cause that's what we all are, felines. Siamese cat balls. They stand out. I had a cat, a Manx, still around some-where. His name is GI Joe: He's black and white. I had a little goldfish too like a clown. Happy Halloween down."

First she talks of the effects of the medicine. Then she erroneously picks the word "distemper" to refer to her mental illness, perhaps because "dis" means not and "tem-per" refers to mind. Also, women in our society are often referred to as if they were felines: cats, pussies, kittens.

The apparent pun on cat balls (fur balls in their stomachs, or testicles) may be motivated by the sexual connotations of these terms. Next she goes from cats as humans to cats as pets, then leaps to a goldfish as a pet. Next, "clown" used to describe the fish evokes another association with clowns: "Halloween," when children dress up as clowns. Then she gives the chance rhyme of "down" to "clown."

Examples like this have caused some observers to suggest that schizophrenics suffer from a filtering defect. They simply cannot screen out inappropriate matters. This certainly explains the associational character of the examples given so far. But schizophrenic speech abounds in other kinds of peculiarities. Among those that filtering doesn't explain are gibberish and word salad.

In the following examples of gibberish, a schizophrenic was explaining to me a videotape he had just seen about a little girl who wanted ice cream. The gibberish is in brackets.

". . . a little girl. She's uh, she's on her own. She's so [weh] she gets her [ous ow] after she ask her own father if she can go out for ice cream and he says uh answers her [shi] dunno and get ice cream for herself and [es] pass by [sh wu] and so it happened they're all happy . . ."

Stretches of gibberish like this mimic the structure of English so well and blend in so smoothly with the rest of the narrative that at first listeners may think they have simply failed to catch what was said. I always go over passages of schizophrenic gibberish dozens of times and then have colleagues listen to them many times before conceding that the patient didn't say words. The example above was English gibberish, but still gibberish.

Another patient, describing his neighborhood, produced this word salad, a string of words put together without any recognizable grammatical frame. Poor filtering can't explain:

". . . when I'm not sure it's possible about the way I could read people mind about people's society attitude plot spirit . . . their thought of how I read think."

Another important feature of schizophrenic speech that filtering doesn't explain is perseveration, a major reason schizophrenic speech becomes more disorganized as it goes along. Once an intrusion of sound or meaning occurs, the schizophrenic perseveres along the new tack rather than going back to the original topic.

The strange rhyming in the "looks like clay . . ." sequence is caused by persevering first in rhymes with "clay" and then with the meaning of "Mayday." The mention of "St. Valentine's Day" after "bill and coo" is a perseveration of the meaning of love. This gets compounded with the image of birds in "bill and coo," explaining the following sequence about parakeets and buzzards.

Schizophrenic speech also features repetition, a form of perseveration. For example, the patient who described his neighborhood kept returning to this sequence of words and phrases:

". . . will I see Paradise will I not see Paradise
should I answer should I not answer."

He would lead into it in many ways, such as:

". . . so I think I could read their mind as they drive by in the car sh-will I see Paradise . . ."

Sometimes he would pick up the refrain in the middle, as in:

". . . I just correct for them for having me feel better about myself not answer will I should I answer should I not answer . . ."

From a linguistic point of view, schizophrenic speech is caused by an impairment, usually temporary, in the ability to control language on one level or more. This results in errors ranging from small intrusions to complete gibberish. The intrusions resemble the kinds of associations one finds among normal people in tests of word association and in slips of the tongue. The difference is that in schizophrenics, the slips are far more severe. Schizophrenics also combine slips with perseveration down the path opened by their association of words.

Gibberish and word salad, symptoms that show the most complete disintegration of language, are rare today. The drugs, such as Thorazine, that are used to treat schizophrenics lessen many psychotic symptoms, including disordered speech. While no one knows precisely why the drugs have this result, many researchers believe one key is their effect on the neurotransmitter dopamine.

How we view the weird speech of some schizophrenics affects how we treat them. If the speech is a way of avoiding therapy, patients must be persuaded or conditioned to accept therapy. If schizophrenics are merely being poetic or creative, then we must analyze every utterance to uncover its true meaning. If, as I think, schizophrenics who speak weirdly do so because of a linguistic problem caused by a biochemical imbalance, then the solution is biochemical. Find the proper medication and you alleviate the source of the problem.

On Being Sane
in Insane Places

by David Rosenhan

The dividing line between sanity and madness is one of
the perennial debates in psychology. R. D. Laing, in writing
on the politics of experience, and Thomas Szasz, in calling
mental illness a "myth," were two of the early challengers of
the traditional concept of mental illness. Szasz sounded a
call to arms when he wrote: "... the notion of mental
illness has outlived whatever usefullness it may have had.
The concept of mental illness thus serves mainly to obscure
the everyday fact that life for most people is a continuous
struggle, not for biological survival, but for a 'place in the
sun,' 'peace of mind,' or some other meaning or value."

While David Rosenhan writes within the conventional view
of mental illness, his contribution needs to be understood in
the context of Szasz's statement. For Rosenhan takes the
position that mental deviance reflects a departure from social
and legal norms, not just psychological ones. The way
a person is diagnosed determines deviance, Rosenhan
suggests, and this renders the notion of abnormality as much
a sociological occurrence as a purely psychological one.

In the article that follows, Rosenhan describes his innova-
tive field experiment in a psychiatric institution: He and other
mentally normal researchers were themselves admitted to
mental hospitals to test whether "normal" individuals could be
recognized by the psychiatric staff. The study was the inspiration for Rosenhan's emphasis on labeling theory as a key
factor in understanding mental illness, and it caused the professional community to question its standards for diagnosis.

IF SANITY AND insanity exist, how shall we know them?

The question is neither capricious nor itself insane. However much we may be personally convinced that we can tell the normal from the abnormal, the evidence is simply not compelling. It is commonplace, for example, to read about murder trials wherein eminent psychiatrists for the defense are contradicted by equally eminent psychiatrists for the prosecution on the matter of the defendant's sanity. What is viewed as normal in one culture may be seen as quite aberrant in another. Thus, notions of normality and abnormality may not be quite as accurate as people believe they are.

To raise questions regarding normality and abnormality is in no way to question the fact that some behaviors are deviant or odd. Murder is deviant. So too are hallucinations. Nor does raising such questions deny the existence of the personal anguish that is often associated with "mental illness." Anxiety and depression exist. Psychological suffering exists. But normality and abnormality, sanity, and the diagnoses that flow from them may be less substantive than many believe them to be.

At its heart, the question of whether the sane can be distinguished from the insane reduces to a simple matter: whether the salient characteristics that lead to diagnostic judgments reside in the patients themselves, or in the environments and contexts in which observers find them.

Gains can be made in deciding between these alternative views by admitting normal people (i.e., those who do not have, and have never suffered serious psychiatric symptoms) to psychiatric hospitals and determining whether and how they were discovered to be sane. If the sanity of such pseudopatients were always detected, we would have prima facie evidence that a sane individual can be distinguished from the insane context in which he is found. Normality (and presumably abnormality) is sufficiently distinct that it can be recognized wherever it occurs for it is carried within the person. If on the other hand, the sanity of the pseudopatients were never discovered, serious difficulties would arise for those who support traditional modes of psychiatric diagnosis. Given that the hospital staff was not incompetent, that the pseudopatient had been behaving as sanely as he had outside of the hospital, and that it had never been previously suggested that he belonged in a psychiatric hospital, such an unlikely outcome would support the view that psychiatric diagnosis betrays little about the patient but much about the environment in which an observer finds him.

This paper describes such an experiment. Eight sane people gained secret admission to twelve different hospitals. Their diagnostic experiences constitute the data of the first part of this paper. The remainder of the paper is devoted to a description of their experiences in psychiatric institutions. Too few psychiatrists and psychologists, even those who have worked in such hospitals, know what the experience is like. They rarely talk about it with former patients, perhaps because they distrust information coming from the previously insane. Those who have worked in psychiatric hospitals are likely to have adapted so thoroughly to the settings that they are insensitive to the impact of that experience. And while there have been occasional reports of researchers who submitted themselves to psychiatric hospitalization (7), these researchers have commonly remained in the hospitals for short periods of time, often with the knowledge of the hospital staff. It is difficult to know the extent to which they were treated like patients or like research colleagues. Nevertheless, their reports about the inside of the psychiatric hospital have been valuable. This article extends those efforts.

PSEUDOPATIENTS AND THEIR SETTINGS

The eight pseudopatients were a varied group. One was a psychology graduate student in his twenties. The remaining seven were older and "established." Among them were three psychologists, a pediatrician, a psychiatrist, a painter and a housewife. Three pseudopatients were women, five were men. All of them employed pseudonyms, lest their alleged diagnoses embarrass them later in life. Those who were in mental health professions alleged another occupation in order to avoid the special attentions that might be accorded by staff, as a matter of courtesy or caution, to ailing colleagues. With the exception of myself (I was the first pseudopatient and my presence was known to the hospital administrator and chief psychologist, and so far as I can tell, to them alone), the presence of pseudopatients and the nature of the research program was not known to the hospital staffs.

The settings were similarly varied. In order to generalize our findings, we sought admission into a spectrum of hospitals. The twelve hospitals in the sample were located in five different states on the East and West coasts. Some were old and shabby, some were quite new. Some were research oriented, others not. Some had good staff-patient ratios, others were quite understaffed. Only one was a strictly private hospital. All of the others were supported by state or federal funds or, in one instance, by university funds.

After calling the hospital for an appointment, the researcher arrived at the Admissions Office complaining that he had been hearing voices. Asked what the voices said, he replied that they were often unclear, but so far as he could tell they said "empty," "hollow," and "thud." The voices were unfamiliar and were of the same sex as the pseudopatient. The choice of these symptoms was occasioned by their apparent similarity to existential symptoms. Such symptoms are alleged to arise from painful concerns about the perceived meaninglessness of one's life. It is as if the hallucinating person were saying, "My life is empty and hollow." The choice of these symptoms was also determined by the *absence* of a single report of existential psychoses in the literature.

Beyond alleging the symptoms and falsifying name, vocation, and employment, no further alterations of person, history, or circumstances were made. The significant events of the researcher's life history were presented as in fact they had occurred. Relationships with parents and siblings, with spouse and children, at work and in school, consistent with the aforementioned exceptions, were described as they were or had been. Frustrations and upsets were described along with joys and satisfactions. These facts are important to remember. If anything, they strongly biased the subsequent results in favor of detecting sanity since none of their histories or current behaviors were seriously pathological in any way.

Immediately upon admission to the psychiatric ward, the pseudopatient ceased simulating *any* symptoms of abnormality. In some cases there was a brief period of mild nervousness and anxiety, since none of the researchers really believed that they would be admitted so easily. Indeed, their shared fear was that they would be immediately exposed as frauds and greatly embarrassed. Moreover, many of them had never visited a psychiatric ward, and even those who had nevertheless had some genuine fears about what might happen to them. Their nervousness then, was quite appropriate to the novelty of the hospital setting and it abated rapidly.

But apart from that short-lived nervousness, the pseudopatient behaved on the ward as he "normally" behaved. The pseudopatient spoke to patients and staff as he might ordinarily. Because there is uncommonly little to do on a psychiatric ward, he attempted to engage others in conversation. When asked by staff how he was feeling, he indicated that he was fine, that he no longer experienced symptoms. He responded to instructions from attendants, to calls for medication (which was not swallowed) and to dining-hall instructions. Beyond such activities as were available to him on the admissions ward, he spent his time writing down his observations about the ward, its patients, and the staff. Initially these notes were written "secretly," but as it soon became clear that no one much cared, they were subsequently written on standard tablets of paper in such public places as the dayroom. No secret was made of these activities.

The pseudopatient, very much as a true psychiatric patient, entered a hospital with no foreknowledge of when he would be discharged. Each was told that he would have to get out by his own devices, essentially by convincing the staff that he was sane. The psychological stresses associated with hospitalization were considerable, and all but one of them desired to be discharged almost immediately after being admitted. They were, therefore, motivated not only to behave sanely but to be paragons of cooperation. That their behavior was in no way disruptive is confirmed by nursing reports which have been obtained on most of the patients. These reports uniformly indicate that the pseudopatients were "friendly," "cooperative," and "exhibited no abnormal indications."

THE NORMAL ARE NOT DETECTABLY SANE

Despite their public "show" of sanity, the pseudopatients were never detected. Admitted in the main with a diagnosis of schizophrenia, each was discharged with a diagnosis of schizophrenia "in remission." The label "in remission" should in no way be dismissed as a formality, for at no time during any hospitalization had any question been raised about any pseudopatient's simulation. Nor are there any indications in the hospital records that the pseudopatient's status was suspect. Rather, the evidence is strong that once labeled schizophrenic, the pseudopatient was stuck with that label. If the pseudodpatient was to be discharged he must naturally be "in remission"; but he was not sane nor, in the institution's view, had he ever been sane.

The uniform failure to recognize sanity cannot be attributed to the quality of the hospitals, for although there were considerable variations among them, several are considered excellent. Nor can it be alleged that there was simply not enough time to observe the pseudopatients. Length of hospitalization ranged from seven to fifty-two days, with an average of nineteen days. As we shall see, they were not in fact carefully observed, but this failure clearly speaks more to traditions within psychiatric hospitals than to lack of opportunity.

Finally, it cannot be said that the failure to recognize the pseudopatients' sanity was due to the fact that they were not behaving sanely. While there was clearly some tension present in all of us, daily visitors could detect no serious

behavioral consequences. Nor indeed could other patients!
It was quite common for the patients to "detect" our
sanity. During the first three hospitalizations, when accurate counts were kept, 35 of a total of 118 patients on the
admissions ward voiced their suspicions, some vigorously.
"You're not crazy. You're a journalist, or a professor"
(referring to the continual note-taking). "You're checking
up on the hospital." While most of the patients were
reassured by our insistence that we had been sick before
we came in but were fine now, some continued to believe
that we were sane throughout our hospitalization. The fact
that they often recognized normality when staff did not
raises important questions.

THE UTILITY OF FALSE POSITIVES

Failure to detect sanity during the course of hospitalization may be due to the fact that physicians operate with a
strong bias toward what statisticians call the Type II error.
This is to say that physicians are more inclined to call a
healthy person sick (a false positive: Type II) than a sick
person healthy (a false negative: Type I). The reasons for
this are not hard to find: It is clearly more dangerous to
misdiagnose illness than health. Better to err on the side of
caution, to suspect illness even among the healthy.

But what holds for medicine does not hold equally well
for psychiatry. Medical illnesses, while unfortunate, are
not commonly pejorative. Psychiatric diagnoses, on the
contrary, carry with them personal, legal, and social stig-
mas (12). It was therefore important to see whether the
tendency toward diagnosing the sane insane could be reversed. The following experiment was arranged at a research and teaching hospital whose staff had heard these
findings but doubted that such an error could occur in their
hospital. The staff was informed that at some time during
the following 3 months, one or more pseudopatients would
attempt to be admitted into the psychiatric hospital. Each
staff member was asked to rate each patient who presented
himself at admissions or on the ward according to the

likelihood that the patient was a pseudopatient. A 10-point scale was used, with a 1 and 2 reflecting high confidence that the patient was a pseudopatient.

Judgment were obtained on 193 patients who were admitted for psychiatric treatment. All staff who had had sustained contact with or primary responsibility for the patient—attendants, nurses, psychiatrists, physicians, and psychologists—were asked to make judgments. Forty-one patients were alleged, with high confidence, to be pseudopatients by at least one member of the staff. Twenty-three were considered suspect by at least one psychiatrist. Nineteen were suspected by one psychiatrist *and* one other staff member. Actually, no genuine pseudopatient (at least from my group) presented himself during this period.

The experiment is instructive. It indicates that the tendency to designate sane people as insane can be reversed when the stakes (in this case, prestige and diagnostic acumen) are high. But what can be said of the 19 people who were suspected of being "sane" by one psychiatrist and another staff member? Were these people truly "sane," or was it rather the case that in the course of avoiding the type 2 error the staff tended to make more errors of the first sort—calling the crazy "sane"? There is no way of knowing. But one thing is certain: any diagnostic process that lends itself so readily to massive errors of this sort cannot be a very reliable one.

THE STICKINESS OF PSYCHODIAGNOSTIC LABELS

Beyond the tendency to call the healthy sick—a tendency that accounts better for diagnostic behavior on admission than it does for such behavior after a lengthy period of exposure—the data speak to the massive role of labeling in psychiatric assessment. Having once been labeled schizophrenic, there is nothing the pseudopatient can do to overcome the tag. The tag profoundly colors others' perception of him and his behavior.

THE EXPERIENCE OF PSYCHIATRIC HOSPITALIZATION

The term "mental illness" is of recent origin. It was coined by people who were humane in their inclinations, and who wanted very much to raise the station of, and sympathies towards, the psychologically disturbed from that of witches and "crazies" to one that was akin to the physically ill. And they were at least partially successful, for the treatment of these people *has* improved considerably over the years. But while treatment has improved, it is doubtful that people really regard the mentally ill in the same way that they view the physically ill. A broken leg is something one recovers from, but mental illness allegedly endures forever. A broken leg does not threaten the observer, but a crazy schizophrenic? There is by now a host of evidence that indicates that attitudes towards the mentally ill are characterized by fear, hostility, aloofness, suspicion, and dread. The mentally ill are society's lepers.

That such attitudes infect the general population is perhaps not surprising, only upsetting. But that they affect the professionals—attendants, nurses, physicians, psychologists and social workers—who treat and deal with the mentally ill is more disconcerting, both because such attitudes are self-evidently pernicious, and because they are unwitting. Most mental health professionals would insist that they are sympathetic towards the mentally ill, that they are neither avoidant nor hostile. But it is more likely the case that an exquisite ambivalence characterizes their relations with psychiatric patients such that their avowed impulses are only part of the whole attitude picture. Negative attitudes are there too, and can easily be detected. Such attitudes should not surprise us. They are the natural offspring of the labels patients wear and the places in which they are found.

POWERLESSNESS AND DEPERSONALIZATION

Eye-contact and verbal contact reflect concern and individuation: their absence, avoidance and depersonalization. The statistical data do not do justice to the rich daily encounters that grew up around matters of depersonalization and avoidance. We have records of patients who were beaten by staff for the sin of having initiated verbal contact. During my own experience, for example, one patient was beaten in the presence of other patients for having approached an attendant and told him, "I like you." Occasionally, punishment meted out to patients for misdemeanors seemed so excessive that it could not be justified by the most radical interpretations of psychiatric canon. Nevertheless, they appeared to go unquestioned. Tempers were often short. A patient who had not heard a call for medication would be roundly excoriated, and the morning attendants would often wake all of us with "Come on, you m-----f-----s, out of bed!"

Neither anecdotal nor "hard" data can convey the overwhelming sense of powerlessness which invades the individual as he is continually exposed to the depersonalization of the psychiatric hospital. It hardly matters *which* psychiatric hospital—the excellent public ones and the very plush private hospital were better than the rural and shabby ones in this regard, but again, the features that psychiatric hospitals had in common overwhelmed by far their apparent differences.

Powerlessness was evident everywhere. The patient is deprived of many of his legal rights by dint of his psychiatric commitment. He is shorn of credibility by virtue of his psychiatric label. His freedom of movement is restricted. He cannot initiate contact with the staff, but may only respond to such overtures as they make. Personal privacy is minimal. Patient quarters and possessions can be entered and examined by any staff member, for whatever reason. His personal history and anguish is available to any staff member (often including the "grey lady" and "candy striper" volunteer) who chooses to read his folder, regardless of their therapeutic relationship to him. His personal hygiene and waste evacuation are often monitored. The water closets may have no doors.

At times, depersonalization reached such proportions that pseudopatients had the sense that they were invisible, or at least unworthy of account. Upon being admitted, I and other pseudopatients took our initial physical examinations in a semi-public room where staff members went about their own business, as if we were not there.

SUMMARY AND CONCLUSIONS

It is clear that we cannot distinguish the sane from the insane in psychiatric hospitals. The hospital itself imposes a special environment in which the meanings of behavior can easily be misunderstood. The consequences to patients of hospitalization in such an environment—the powerlessness, depersonalization, segregation, mortification and self-labeling—seem undoubtedly countertherapeutic.

I do not, even now, comprehend the fullness of this problem sufficiently to perceive solutions. But two matters seem of some promise. The first concerns the proliferation of community mental health facilities, of crisis intervention centers, of the human potential movement, and of behavior therapies that, for all their problems, tend to avoid psychiatric labels, to focus on specific problems and behaviors, and to retain the individual in a relatively nonpejorative environment. Clearly, to the extent that we refrain from sending the distressed to insane places, our impressions of them are less likely to be distorted. (The risk of distorted perceptions, it seems to me, is always present since we are much more sensitive to an individual's behaviors and verbalizations than we are to the subtle contextual stimuli that often promote them. At issue here is a matter of magnitude. And as we have seen, the magnitude of distortion is exceedingly high in the extreme context that is a psychiatric hospital).

The second matter that might prove promising speaks to the need to increase the sensitivity of mental health workers and researchers to the *Catch 22* position of psychiatric patients. Simply reading materials in this area will be of help to some such workers and researchers. For others, directly experiencing the impact of psychiatric hospitalization will be of enormous use. Clearly, further research into the social psychology of such total institutions will both facilitate treatment and deepen understanding .

We were pseudopatients in the psychiatric setting, and our reactions were distinctly negative. We do not pretend to describe the subjective experiences of true patients. Theirs may be different from ours, particularly with the passage of time and the necessary process of adaptation to one's environment. But we can and do speak to the relatively more objective indicies of treatment within the hospital. It could be a mistake, and a very unfortunate one, to consider that what happened to us derived from malice or stupidity on the part of the staff. Quite the contrary, our overwhelming impression of them was of people who really cared, who were committed and who were uncommonly intelligent. Where they failed, as they sometimes did painfully, it would be more accurate to attribute those failures to the environment in which they, too, found themselves, than to personal callousness. In a more benign environment, one that was less attached to global diagnosis, their behaviors and judgments might have been more benign and effective.

VII.

GROUPS

Can We All Be Better Than Average?

Can We All Be Better Than Average?

by David Myers and Jack Ridl

Much as we may try to minimize them, comparison and competition seem to be part of everyday life. We are constantly checking out the neighbors' latest home renovations, concerned with who got the largest raise at work or whose dress cost the most. And, in making these comparisons, we all like to think we are above average. But what does that say about the law of averages?

David Myers and Jack Ridl examine the self-serving and ego-serving biases that help us believe we are above average. They observe, for example, that most people attribute their successes to their own ability and effort but blame their failures on bad luck. Myers, a psychologist, is an expert on group influence; his colleague, Ridl, teaches English and has a particular interest in thought processes that cause or avoid emotional distress, including this universal, self-serving bias.

HARRY IS A better-than-average golfer; his wife, Jean, a better-than-average tennis player. Harry may spend more time searching in the rough than he does strolling the fairways, and Jean may have a serve that would bring down a weather balloon. Yet, ask Harry to comment on his golf game, or Jean on her serve, and both will bashfully admit: "Oh, I guess I'd have to say, 'better than average.' "

Believing ourselves better-than-average observers of the

ways and wiles of human nature, we were not surprised to
find in some recent studies evidence that average people
see themselves as "better than average." Social psychology, it seems, is dusting off the old story of human pride.
As William Saroyan put it: "Every man is a good man in a
bad world—as he himself knows."

Many experiments disclose a self-serving bias in the
way we perceive events. We explain our positive behavior
in terms of our dispositions ("I helped that blind man
because I am a considerate person") while we attribute
nasty remarks or inconsiderate behavior to external factors
("I was angry because everything was going wrong").
This enables us to take credit for our good acts and find
scapegoats for our bad.

People assigned the roles of teachers or therapists in
experiments tend to take credit for any positive outcome,
but blame failure on the person being helped. The
pseudoclinician surmises, "I helped Mrs. X get better,
but, despite all my help, Mr. Y got worse." Generally
speaking, people attribute their successes mostly to ability
and effort, but blame their failures on bad luck or other
outside factors.

Games that combine skill and chance may be popular
because they permit similar rationalizing. Winners at bridge,
for example, can easily attribute their success to skill,
while losers can mutter, "Four points, four lousy points
was all I had, a king and a jack." Or when we win at a
word game, for example, it is because of our verbal dex-
terity; when we lose, it is because "who could get any-
where with a q but no u?" In experiments that pit two or
more people against others, winners usually take personal
credit for their victories but hold their partners responsible
when they lose, following a tradition established by Adam:
"The woman whom thou gavest to be with me, she gave
me of the tree, and I did eat."

Even college professors—obviously, much better than
average folk—are not immune. When we are frustrated in
our attempts to write and publish, we blame the situation:
"With these horrible teaching loads and inadequate resources, you can't be a productive scholar." When fortu-

nate circumstances do enable us to publish, we are inclined to ignore them and take personal credit for our having overcome great difficulties.

Students are equally vain. Anthony Greenwald, a psychologist at Ohio State University, asked students who had just received their grades on an examination to judge how well the exam measured their knowledge. Students who did well typically saw the exam as a good measure of their competence, while students who did poorly felt it was a poor test of their knowledge. Faculty members must share the blame for the students' delusions about competence. For their grandiose self-perceptions are no doubt based, in part, on the recent trend toward grade-inflation. The C grade has gone the way of grammar. The lament uttered among today's students is not, "An F? I had better buckle down or try something else." Instead, one hears, "He gave me a B-? B-! B- is average. At the least, I'm better than average."

The self-serving bias would be less troubling if we were equally generous in our perception of others. But researchers have found that we are inclined to attribute others' failures to their dispositions. We often hear, or say, "Doesn't surprise me at all that John made those remarks. He's hostile. Personally, I can't stand such people." John may have made "those remarks" not because he is hostile, but because he depises corruption. The tendency to chastise John for his temper while excusing our own often leads to social conflict. Bill attributes Mary's actions to her nasty disposition, but sees his own toughness as "certainly reasonable, given the stress I'm under." Mary, of course, perceives the situation as being precisely the reverse.

No generalization has been more firmly established during the last two decades of social-psychological research than this: our attitudes both shape our behavior and are shaped by it. Every time we act, we amplify the idea underlying the act. For example, people who are induced by a researcher to say something they are unsure of will generally begin to believe their "little lies," especially if they feel they had some choice in what they said. Likewise, harming an innocent victim—by muttering a cutting comment or delivering electric shocks—typically leads aggressors to derogate their victims, thus justifying their own actions, at least to some extent. Such acts corrode the conscience of those who perform them; they soon become not people playing a part, but the part itself. Action and attitude feed one another, sometimes to the point of moral numbness.

The French psychologist Jean-Paul Codol conducted 20 experiments on the self-serving bias of the French with people ranging from 12-year-olds to adults. The perceived superiority of the self was omnipresent, regardless of those involved or the experimental methods used. In one case, Codol had each person in a group of four give three estimates of the length of a rod. After they all had given their estimates, the experimenter measured the rod and announced its correct length. Rating their performances later, most individuals—regardless of their real accuracy— proclaimed themselves at or near the top of their group. In other experiments, Codol found that the more people admired a particular trait, such as honesty or creativity, the more likely they were to see themselves as more honest or creative then other people.

We can almost hear readers saying, "But, of course, those were Frenchmen, and you know the French!" The phenomenon is not uniquely French, however. Americans are just as likely to accept and recall more positive than negative information about themselves and to see themselves as better than average. Research indicates that, compared with ourselves, most of us see our friends, neighbors, coworkers, and classmates as a sorry lot. They are weaker ethically ("I was shocked to hear that Betty . . ."), more intolerant ("I admit I have my prejudices, but I couldn't believe it when Carl said . . ."), and less intelligent ("I'm no genius, mind you, but even a moron could . . ."). We even think our peers are likely to die sooner than we are. C. R. Snyder, a psychologist at the University of Kansas, reports that college students view themselves as likely to outlive by 10 years their actuarially predicted age of death. It has been said that Freud's favorite joke was about the man who told his wife, "If one of us should die first, I think I would go live in Paris."

You can demonstrate the self-serving bias for yourself, if you like. Have people anonymously compare themselves with others on a variety of socially desirable traits by filling in a blank: for example, "My hunch is that about —% of the others in the group are more sympathetic than I am." You will find that the percentage is usually a modest one. Bias operates more freely in assessing attitudes and character traits, such as sympathy, responsibility, and considerateness, rather than in more objective matters, such as a person's income or height.

Consciously, at least, a "superiority complex" pervades most self-comparisons, although it may, in many cases, be merely a cover for deeper insecurities. But rarely are we willing to proclaim our perceived superiorities publicly, since we know that others (who harbor similar self-perceptions) are unlikely to be charmed.

Most of us, moreover, have already learned that self-put downs are a useful technique for eliciting "strokes" from others. We know that a remark like "Every time I see Carol in that beautiful dress, I wish I weren't so ordinary-looking" will elicit a comforting "Now Jane, don't say you're plain. You have gorgeous hair and your ponytail will soon be back in style."

Experiments conducted by psychologist Baruch Fischhoff and colleagues at Decision Research in Eugene, Oregon, indicate there is also a pervasive "intellectual conceit" to our judgments of our knowledge. We boast that we knew all along how a given experiment or historical event would turn out, despite the fact that, in many cases, the results were unexpected. Thus, we seldom feel surprised by the results of psychological research or of current events. "I knew the Yankees would win last year. I could have told you in July that they would pull it out."

Such statements are not lies, but self-deceptions that may be personally useful. Some sociobiologists have even suggested that self-deception may be a trait that has been bred into us through natural selection: cheaters, for example, may give a more convincing display of honesty if they believe in their honesty. Similarly, thinking positively about one's abilities and traits may provide the self-confidence conducive to success.

This egocentric bias is not always adaptive, however. In a series of nine experiments, Barry Schlenker, a psychologist at the University of Florida, showed how egocentric bias can disrupt a group of people working together on a task. After completing each task, the group was told whether or not it had been successful. The feedback was random, bearing no relation to how well or poorly the group had actually done.

Yet in every study, the members of successful groups claimed more responsibility for the group's performance than did members of failing groups. The same self-congratulatory tendency surfaced when people evaluated their contributions to the group. Unless their self-conceit could be debunked by public exposure, most people presented themselves as contributing more to the group's success than others did when the results were good; few of them said they did less.

Such self-deception can cause trouble in a group by leading its members to expect greater-than-average rewards (pay or otherwise) when their organization does well, and less-than-average blame when it doesn't. If most individuals in a group believe they are underpaid and underappreciated, disharmony and envy are likely.

Michael Ross and Fiore Sicoly at the University of Waterloo, in Ontario, observed a similar phenomenon when only two people were involved. In one experiment, they interrupted conversing pairs in cafeterias and lounges and asked each person to estimate how much he or she had spoken during the conversation. Each reported having spoken, on the average, 59 percent of the time. In other studies, the investigators found that married persons usually saw themselves as taking more responsibility for activities such as cleaning the house and caring for the children than did their spouses. Ross and Sicoly believe that the bias is partly due to the greater ease with which we recall things *we* have done, compared with what we've seen others do. That we tend to remember our positively valued acts better than negatively valued ones suggests that there are self-serving motivations involved as well.

Such biased self-assessments can distort judgments in business as well, as psychologist Laurie Larwood of Claremont University has demonstrated. When corporation presidents predict more growth for their firms than for the competition, and production managers similarly overpredict performance, their overoptimism can be disastrous. If those who deal in the stock market or in commodities see their business intuition as superior to their competitors', they may be in for some rude awakenings.

Many educational administrators have the same biases. Although the number of college-age Americans will shrink nearly 25 percent between 1979 and the early 1990s, few college officials are making plans to deal with the probable decline in admissions. They figure, rightly, that even in a time of decline, not all colleges will shrink. And since their schools are better than average, they have little doubt that their institutions will be among the few that do not suffer.

We are vulnerable to the consequences of the self-serving bias. Larwood found that Los Angeles residents felt they were healthier than average and that the greater this perception, the less likely they were to avail themselves of a public inoculation program. She also surveyed homes in a Northeastern city and found that most poeple professed to be more concerned than others about assuring clean air and water and believed they used less electricity than other city residents. Average citizens were, self-proclaimed, better-than-average citizens. As Larwood observed, if most poeple "are merely the average persons that they must be statistically, but behave as though they are superior, their goals and expectations must inevitably conflict. Too much will be produced, not enough people will get inoculations, and each of us will continue to use our (more than) fair share of resources."

The better-than-average phenomenon affects our perception not only of ourselves, but also of our groups. Codol found, as have some American researchers, that people see their own groups as superior to other, comparable groups. The children in each of several school classrooms, for instance, were likely to see their class as surpassing others in desirable characteristics such as friendliness or cooperativeness. Psychologist Irving Janis of Yale University noted that one source of international conflict is the tendency of each side to believe in the moral superiority of its acts. Americans say that the United States builds missile bases near the Russian border in Turkey to protect the free world from communism, while the Soviet Union puts missiles in Cuba to threaten our security. The Soviets, of course, see the motivation behind the bases as exactly the opposite.

Modern research on self-serving perceptions confirms some ancient wisdom. The tragic flaw portrayed in Greek drama was *hubris*, or extreme pride. Like the subjects of our experiments, the Greek tragic figures did not self-consciously choose evil, but rather thought too highly of themselves (they were better than average), with consequent disaster. Human evil is described as such by its victims, not its perpetrators. Søren Kierkegaard lamented that becoming aware of our own sin is like trying to see our own eyeballs.

The true end of humility is not self-contempt (which still leaves people concerned with themselves). To paraphrase the English novelist and essayist C. S. Lewis, humility does not consist in handsome people trying to believe they are ugly, and clever people trying to believe they are fools. When we hear a Nobel laureate respond to an interviewer with, "Well, Ted, yes, I was surprised, pleased even, when I heard the news. Actually, I'd have to consider myself no more than a better-than-average nuclear bio-organic microecological physical chemist," we may wonder where that leaves those of us who have a hard time following a recipe for pound cake.

But when Muhammad Ali announced that he was the greatest, there was a sense in which his pronouncement did not violate the spirit of humility. False modesty can actually lead to an ironic pride in one's better-than-average humility. (Perhaps some readers are by now congratulating themselves on being unusually free of the inflated self-perception this article describes.)

True humility is more like self-forgetfulness than false modesty. It leaves people free to rejoice in their special talents and, with the same honesty, recognize their neighbor's. Both the neighbor's talents and one's own are recognized as gifts and, like one's height, are not fit subjects for either inordinate pride or self-deprecation. Ali's self-preoccupation did violate this aspect of humility, for in that ideal state there is neither vain-glory nor false modesty, only honest self-acceptance.

As we have seen, true humility is a state not easily attained. The self-serving bias is the social psychologist's modern rendition of the forever underappreciated truth about human pride. "There is," said C. S. Lewis, "no fault which we are more unconscious of in ourselves. . . . If anyone would like to acquire humility, I can, I think, tell him the first step. The first step is to realize that one is proud. And a biggish step, too."

Beauty and the Best

by Ellen Berscheid and
Elaine Walster

Jacqueline Bisset and Jaclyn Smith, Robert Redford and Roger Moore are four of the "beautiful" people, who exemplify an often overlooked but fascinating area for psychological study, one that tells us much about what we value as individuals and as a society. In the study of beauty, psychological questions arise again and again: Are attractive people really better off? Are beautiful people happier? Psychologists Ellen Berscheid and Elaine Walster offer a most intriguing reponse to these questions.

Most people assume the best about attractive people precisely because of their looks. From grammar school to retirement, there is very little disagreement about who is considered beautiful. Berscheid and Walster find that beauty has more impact than might be expected. Its influence may start very early, with special attention from a teacher, and continue through life. Physical attractiveness may even influence which students make the honor roll in school. However, the picture is not all wine and roses. The more attractive a woman had been in college, one study found, the less satisfied and happy she was twenty-five years later. Beauty, then, has its liabilities too.

A BILLION-DOLLAR COSMETICS industry testifies that the severity of the sentence may depend upon the quality of the skin. We can cold-cream it, suntan it, bleach it, lift it, and paint it—but we cannot shed it. And, unless we are willing to adopt the tactics of the Oregon State student who enclosed himself in a large black bag, our physical appearance is our most obvious personal characteristic.

For the past few years we have investigated the impact of one aspect of appearance—physical attractiveness—upon relationships between persons. Our initial interest in attractiveness was negligible. We shared the democratic belief that appearance is a superficial and peripheral characteristic with little influence on our lives. Elliot Aronson has suggested that social scientists have avoided investigating the social impact of physical attractiveness for fear they might learn just how powerful it is. It may be, however, that we have simply given too much credence to collective assertions that internal attributes are more important determinants of who wins or loses our affections than external appearance is.

Impact. The results of our research suggest that beauty not only has a more important impact upon our lives than we previously suspected, but its influence may begin startlingly early.

Nursery-school teachers often insist that all children are beautiful, yet they can, when they are asked, rank their pupils by appearance. The children themselves appear to behave in accordance with the adult ranking.

This finding resulted from a study of nursery-school records. Some schools collect information on how students view each other. A teacher will ask a child to select from photographs of his classmates the person he likes most and the person he likes least. The teacher also asks such questions as, *Who is teacher's pet?*, *Who is always causing trouble in the class?*, and *Who is most likely to hit other kids?*

The children in our nursery-school sample ranged in age from four to six. We thought that the older nursery-school children, who had had more time to learn the cultural stereotypes associated with appearance, might be more influenced by their classmates' attractiveness than the younger children. To examine this hypothesis, we divided the sample into two age groups. We then studied the chil-

dren's reactions to their classmates who had been judged
to be attractive or unattractive by adults.

We found that boys who had been judged by adults to
be relatively unattractive were not as well liked by their
classmates as the more attractive boys. This was true
regardless of the age of the boy. In contrast, the unattractive
girls in the younger group were more popular than the
attractive girls. With age, however, the unattractive girls
declined in popularity, while the attractive girls gained favor
with their classmates.

Fight. We also examined how the children described
their classmates' behavior. We found that unattractive boys
were more likely to be described by their classmates as
aggressive and antisocial than were attractive boys. Children
said that the less-attractive boys were more likely to
fight a lot, hit other students, and yell at the teacher.

The nursery-school children also thought that their
unattractive peers, regardless of sex, were less independent
than attractive children. They were seen to be afraid,
unlikely to enjoy doing things alone, and as needing help
from others.

When the children were asked to name the one person in
their class who scared them, they were more likely to
nominate an unattractive classmate than an attractive one.

Type. The available data did not reveal whether the
unattractive children actually did misbehave more than the
attractive children. We do not know if the students' opinions
of their classmates were based on factual observation
of the behavior, or on adherence to social stereotypes.

It is possible that physical-appearance stereotypes have
already been absorbed at this early age. We know that
nursery-school children can differentiate among various
body types and prefer some to others. For example, fat
bodies are already disliked at this age. If a child assumes
that nice children are handsome and naughty ones are
unattractive, he may notice only those episodes that fit this
image.

Whether or not attractive and unattractive children really
do behave differently, their classmates think they do and

they doubtless act accordingly. Physical attractiveness thus may become a major factor in the social development of the child. It could affect his self-concept and his first social relationships.

Bias. What if the children's reports of behavioral differences are not the result of distorted perception to fit their stereotype, but are accurate descriptions of their classmates' behavior? What if unattractive nursery-school boys are indeed more aggressive and hostile than handsome boys? Research suggests that such differences might be caused by discriminatory treatment at the hands of parents, teachers, and babysitters.

A study by Karen Dion indicates that adults may have a stereotyped image of the moral character of attractive and unattractive children. She found that this image may affect the way adults handle a matter such as discipline for misconduct.

Dion asked young women to examine reports of disturbances created by schoolchildren. To each report she attached a paper that gave a child's name and age, and a photograph that other adults had judged to be attractive, or unattractive. The women believed that the descriptions came from teachers' journals reporting classroom and playground disturbances. Dion asked each woman to evaluate the disturbance and to estimate how the child behaved on a typical day.

Dion hypothesized that the women would interpret the same incident differently depending on whether the naughty child was attractive, or unattractive. The data supported her hypothesis. When the supposed misconduct was very mild in nature, the women did not distinguish between the everyday behavior of unattractive and attractive children. When the disturbance was severe, however, the women assumed that the unattractive boys and girls were chronically antisocial in their everyday behavior.

Cruelty. One young woman made this comment after reading about an attractive girl who had supposedly thrown rocks at a sleeping dog: "She appears to be a perfectly charming little girl, well-mannered, basically unselfish. It seems that she can adapt well among children her age and make a good impression. . . . She plays well with everyone, but like anyone else, a bad day can occur. Her cruelty . . . need not be taken too seriously."

When a less-attractive girl committed the identical act, another young woman concluded: "I think the child would be quite bratty and would be a problem to teachers. . . . She would probably try to pick a fight with other children her own age. . . . She would be a brat at home. . . . All in all, she would be a real problem."

To a significant degree, the young women expressed the ominous expectation that the unattractive child would be more likely to commit a similar disturbance in the future. To a lesser, nonsignificant degree the women suspected the unattractive child of having misbehaved in the past.

Who. These findings suggest that in cases in which there is some question about who started the classroom disturbance, who broke the vase, or who stole the money (and with children it always seems that there is the question of *who did it?*) adults are likely to identify an unattractive child as the culprit. The women in Dion's study also believed that unattractive children were characteristically more dishonest than their attractive classmates.

Thus, if an unattractive child protests his innocence, his pleas may fall on deaf ears. The long march to the principal's office starts early, and physical unattractiveness may be a silent companion for the marcher. Often the only possible justice is blind justice.

Grades. Contrary to the popular belief that "beauty and brains don't mix," there is evidence that physical attractiveness may even influence which students make the honor roll. In collaboration with Margaret Clifford, we asked 400 fifth-grade teachers to examine a child's report card. The report card itemized the student's absences during the school year, his grades (for six grade periods) in reading, language, arithmetic, social studies, science, art, music, and physical education. It also reported his performance in healthful living, his personal development, and his work habits and attitudes.

Pasted in the corner of the report card was a photograph of a child, one of six boys and girls who previously had been judged to be relatively attractive, or one of six boys and girls judged to be less attractive.

Future. We asked the teachers to evaluate the student's I.Q., his parents' attitudes toward school, his future educational accomplishment, and his social status with his peers. We predicted that the child's appearance would influence the teacher's evaluation of the child's intellectual potential, despite the fact that the report cards were identical in content. It did.

The teachers assumed that the attractive girl or boy had a higher I.Q., would go to college, and that his parents were more interested in his education. Teachers also assumed that the attractive student related to his or her classmates better than did the unattractive student.

Prophecy. Other researchers have shown that a student is likely to behave in the way a teacher expects him to behave. Robert Rosenthal and Lenore Jacobson gave an I.Q. test to students in grades one through six. They told teachers that the test identified children who were likely to show marked intellectual improvement within the year. The researchers then, at random, chose 20 percent of the children and announced that test scores had identified these children as the special students.

A year later, Rosenthal and Jacobson gave the same I.Q. test to the same children—all of them. The results of the second test revealed that the supposed bloomers showed more improvement in I.Q. than the other youngsters did. The gains were most pronounced for first-and second-graders. Rosenthal and Jacobson speculated that teachers probably were more encouraging and friendly toward those children identified as bloomers. Their expectations acted as a self-fulfilling prophecy.

These studies suggest that physical attractiveness in young children may result in adult evaluations that elicit special attention. In turn, special attention may confirm teacher predictions of individual accomplishment.

Dating. The preceding findings, which indicate that a child's physical attractiveness may affect a variety of his early social and educational experiences, were somewhat unexpected. That beauty affects one's social relationships during the adolescent dating years comes as less of a surprise. What is disconcerting, however, is the apparently overwhelming importance of appearance in opposite-sex dating.

Physical attractiveness may be the single most important factor in determining popularity among college-age adults. In a series of studies of blind dates, we found that the more physically attractive the date, the more he or she was liked. We failed to find additional factors that might predict how well a person would be liked. Students with exceptional personality features or intelligence levels were not liked more than individuals who were less well endowed.

Match. In these studies of the factors that influence courtship, we tested the hypothesis that persons of similar levels of social desirability tend to pair off in courtship and marriage. Erving Goffman described this matching process in 1952: "A proposal of marriage in our society tends to be a way in which a man sums up his social attributes and suggests to a woman that hers are not so much better as to preclude a merger or a partnership in these matters." To test the matching hypothesis we sponsored a computer dance for college students. We obtained a rough estimate of each student's social attributes from scores on personality, social skill, and intelligence tests. In addition, we rated each student's physical appearance at the time he or she purchased a ticket.

The participants assumed that the computer would select their dates on the basis of shared interests. But we paired the students on a random basis, with only one restriction— the cardinal rule of dating that the man be taller than the woman.

Gap. At intermission we handed out a questionnaire to determine how the students liked their dates. If the matching hypothesis is true, we would expect that students paired with dates from their own levels of social desirability would like each other more than those paired with dates from levels inferior or superior to their own. The results did not confirm the hypothesis. The most important determinant of how much each person liked his or her date, how much he or she wanted to see the partner again, and (it was determined later) how often the men actually did ask their computer partners for subsequent dates, was simply how attractive the date was. Blind dates seem to be blind to everything but appearance.

Subsequent blind-date studies, however, did provide some support for the hypothesis that persons of similar social-desirability levels pair off. Although a person strongly prefers a date who is physically attractive, within this general tendency he or she does seek a person who is closer to his or her own attractiveness, rather than a person who is a great deal more or less attractive. Apparently, even in affairs of the heart, a person is aware of a credibility gap.

We thought at first that the blind-date studies had exaggerated the importance of physical attractiveness as a determinant of popularity for, after all, blind-date situations do not allow the dates much opportunity to get to know one another. Subsequent evidence indicated, however, that the importance of beauty probably had not been exaggerated.

In one study, for example, Polaroid pictures of a sample of college girls were rated for attractiveness. This rough index of each girl's beauty was compared to each girl's report of the number of dates she had had within the past year. We found an unexpectedly high correlation (+ .61) between physical attractiveness and the woman's actual social experience. The girls in our sample represented a wide range of personality traits, social skills, intelligence, values and opinions, differences in inclination to date, and so on. Although in natural settings men do have the opportunity to know and appreciate such characteristics, physical attractiveness still had a major bearing on popularity.

Vulgarity. These findings contradict the self-reports of college students. A multitude of studies have asked students to list the characteristics they find most desirable in a date or mate ["Is It True What They Say About Harvard Boys?," PT, January]. Males almost always value physical attractiveness more than women, but both sexes claim that it is less important than such sterling characteristics as intelligence, friendliness and sincerity. What accounts for the discrepancy between the reality and the self-report? Many students seem to believe that it is vulgar to judge others by appearance. They prefer to use such attributes as "soul" or warmth as bases for affection. Their apparent disregard for grooming seems to support their charge that it is only to members of the over-30 crowd that appearance matters.

Traits. Young adults may not be as inconsistent as it appears at first glance. There is evidence that students may prefer physically attractive individuals because they unconsciously associate certain positive personality traits (traits which they value) with an attractive appearance. In a study conducted with Dion, we found that students thought good-looking persons were generally more sensitive, kind, interesting, strong, poised, modest, sociable, outgoing and exciting than less-attractive persons. Students also agreed that beautiful persons are more sexually warm and responsive than unattractive persons.

Lure. In addition to estimating the personality characteristics of attractive and unattractive persons, we asked the students to tell us what lay ahead for each individual. They expected that attractive persons would hold better jobs, have more successful marriages and happier and more fulfilling lives in general than less-attractive persons. They reversed their optimism on only one dimension—they did not believe that attractive individuals made better parents than did unattractive ones.

These findings suggest a possible reason for our nearly obsessive pursuit of suitably attractive mates. If we believe that a beautiful person embodies an ideal personality, and that he or she is likely to garner all the world's material benefits and happiness, the substantial lure of beauty is not surprising.

Sex. Is there any truth to these stereotypes? Is it true that attractive persons have better personalities or more successful marriages? It does seem possible that an attractive woman might have a happier marriage than a less-attractive woman. A beautiful woman has a wider range of social activity and consequently has a better chance of meeting a man who has similar interests and values—or any of the factors that appear to lead to stability in marriage.

It also seems possible that physically attractive women are in fact more responsive sexually than less-attractive females. Gilbert Kaats and Keith E. Davis found that good-looking college women were in love more often and had more noncoital sexual experience than girls of medium or low physical attractiveness. They also were more likely to have had sexual intercourse than girls of medium attractiveness. In almost any area of human endeavor, practice makes perfect. It may well be that beautiful women are indeed sexually warmer—not because of any innate difference—but simply because of wider experience.

Reversal. Do attractive coeds actually end up leading happier, more-fulfilling lives than less-attractive coeds? We examined interview data taken from women now in their late 40s and early 50s. We were able to locate early pictures of most of the women by looking through their college yearbooks. A panel of judges from a group of the same age (who presumably were familiar with the standards of beauty that prevailed 25 years ago) rated the pictures. We found that the physical attractiveness of each woman in her early 20s bears a faint but significant relationship to some of the life experiences she reports over two decades later.

Good looks in college seemed to have significant effect on marital adjustment and occupational satisfaction in older women, but the effect was exactly the opposite of what we expected. The more attractive the woman had been in college, the less satisfied, the less happy, and the less well-adjusted she was 25 years later.

Clifford Kirkpatrick and John Cotton have suggested why things do not go well with beautiful-but-aging women:

"Husbands may feel betrayed and disillusioned in various ways and even disgusted with the reliance on charms which have faded with the passing of years." They neglect to mention how aging wives will feel about their once-handsome husbands.

Criterion. Love at first sight is the basis of song and story, but usually we get around to taking a second look. It is possible that time lessens the influence of our stereotyped images of beautiful persons. However, many of our interactions with other persons are once-only, or infrequent. We have limited exposure to job applicants, defendants in jury trials, and political candidates, yet on the basis of initial impressions we make decisions that affect their lives. In the case of political candidates, our decisions also affect our lives.

Our research indicates that physical attractiveness is a crucial standard by which we form our first impressions. There is reason to believe that Richard Nixon lost his first campaign for President at least in part because he did not have a good make-up man, while John Kennedy did not need one. Public figures eventually have to act, however, and handsome is not always as handsome does. Mayor John Lindsay may well have been the most beautiful man in New York, but that apparently didn't solve the problems of subway travel, traffic, crime, or any of the other ills that bedevil New Yorkers.

Beholder. Our research has shown some of the ways we react to attractive persons. We still do not know what variables affect our perception of beauty. If we think that a person has a beautiful personality, do we also see him or her as physically more attractive than we ordinarily would? One study suggests that this may be so. Students took part in discussion groups with other students whose political views ranged from radical to conservative. We later asked the students to judge the physical attractiveness of the group members. We found that students thought that the persons who shared their political views were more physically attractive than those who didn't. Perhaps Republicans no longer think that John Lindsay is as beautiful, now that he is a Democrat.

We should point out that in each study we conducted, we used photographs drawn from relatively homogeneous socioeconomic samples, principally from the middle class. We excluded individuals of exceptional physical beauty and those of unusual unattractiveness, as well as those with noticeable physical handicaps or eyeglasses. Had we included the full range of beauty and ugliness it is possible that the effects of physical attractiveness would have been even more dramatic.

Health. Our research also does not tell us the source of our stereotyped images of beautiful persons. It seems possible that in earlier times physical attractiveness was positively related to physical health. Perhaps it still is. It might be the instinctive nature of any species to want to associate and mate with those who are the healthiest of that species. We may be responding to a biological anachronism, left over from a more primitive age.

Although social scientists have been slow to recognize the implications of our billion-dollar cosmetics industry, manufacturers may be quicker to capitalize upon the additional exploitation possibilities of beauty from early childhood through the adult years. Such exploitation could pour even more of our gross national product into the modification of the skins in which we are all confined—some of us more unhappily than others.

Self-fulfilling Stereotypes

by Mark Snyder

Since the 1960s and the civil rights movement, prejudice and stereotyping have been enduring topics in social psychology. Today there is considerable effort directed toward a better understanding of prejudice because we are keenly aware of its sometimes subtly destructive effects. We are also ever cognizant of how our expectations can influence the way we judge others, as well as the way others interact with us.

Mark Snyder of the University of Minnesota has been studying the psychology of stereotypes. Snyder observes that what we think about a certain group affects how *we* act toward members of that group—and how *they* act too. For example, if we think "their kind" is lazy, pushy, or ignorant, then "they" will probably prove us correct.

The role of expectations has long been a controversial area in education, where teachers' lower expectations of disadvantaged children have sometimes become self-fulfilling prophecies. Here, Snyder extends this line of thinking to adults and the workplace as well. Such self-fulfilling stereotypes, he observes, are at work in job selection. The job issue is a most consequential matter: If we are to be fair, then we have to take into account the subtle bias of self-fulfilling stereotypes.

GORDON ALLPORT, THE Harvard psychologist who wrote a classic work on the nature of prejudice, told a story about a child who had come to believe that people who lived in

Minneapolis were called monopolists. From his father, moreover, he had learned that monopolists were evil folk. It wasn't until many years later, when he discovered his confusion, that his dislike of residents of Minneapolis vanished.

Allport knew, of course, that it was not so easy to wipe out prejudice and erroneous stereotypes. Real prejudice, psychologists like Allport argued, was buried deep in human character, and only a restructuring of education could begin to root it out. Yet many people whom I meet while lecturing seem to believe that stereotypes are simply beliefs or attitudes that change easily with experience. Why do some people express the view that Italians are passionate, blacks are lazy, Jews materialistic, or lesbians mannish in their demeanor? In the popular view, it is because they have not learned enough about the diversity among these groups and have not had enough contact with members of the groups for their stereotypes to be challenged by reality. With more experience, it is presumed, most people of good will are likely to revise their stereotypes.

My research over the past decade convinces me that there is little justification for such optimism—and not only for the reasons given by Allport. While it is true that deep prejudice is often based on the needs of pathological character structure, stereotypes are obviously quite common even among fairly normal individuals. When people first meet others, they cannot help noticing certain highly visible and distinctive characteristics: sex, race, physical appearance, and the like. Despite people's best intentions, their initial impressions of others are shaped by their assumptions about such characteristics.

What is critical, however, is that these assumptions are not merely beliefs or attitudes that exist in a vacuum; they are reinforced by the behavior of both prejudiced people and the targets of their prejudice. In recent years, psychologists have collected considerable laboratory evidence about the processes that strengthen stereotypes and put them beyond the reach of reason and good will.

My own studies initially focused on first encounters between strangers. It did not take long to discover, for example, that people have very different ways of treating those whom they regard as physically attractive and those whom they consider physically unattractive, and that these differences tend to bring out precisely those kinds of behavior that fit with stereotypes about attractiveness.

In an experiment that I conducted with my colleagues Elizabeth Decker Tanke and Ellen Berscheid, pairs of college-age men and women met and became acquainted in telephone conversations. Before the conversations began, each man received a Polaroid snapshot, presumably taken just moments before, of the woman he would soon meet. The photograph, which had actually been prepared before the experiment began, showed either a phsyically attractive woman or a physically unattractive one. By randomly choosing which picture to use for each conversation, we insured that there was no consistent relationship between the attractiveness of the woman in the picture and the attractiveness of the woman in the conversation.

By questioning the men, we learned that even before the conversations began, stereotypes about physical attractiveness came into play. Men who looked forward to talking with physically attractive women said that they expected to meet decidedly sociable, poised, humorous, and socially adept people, while men who thought that they were about to get acquainted with unattractive women fashioned images of rather unsociable, awkward, serious, and socially inept creatures. Moreover, the men proved to have very different styles of getting acquainted with women whom they thought to be attractive and those whom they believed to be unattractive. Shown a photograph of an attractive woman, they behaved with warmth, friendliness, humor, and animation. However, when the woman in the picture was unattractive, the men were cold, uninteresting, and reserved.

These differences in the men's behavior elicited behavior in the women that was consistent with the men's stereotyped assumptions. Women who were believed (unbeknown to them) to be physically attractive behaved in a friendly, likeable, and sociable manner. In sharp contrast, women who were perceived as physically unattractive adopted a cool, aloof, and distant manner. So striking were the differences in the women's behavior that they could be discerned simply by listening to tape recordings of the women's side of the conversations. Clearly, by acting upon their stereotyped beliefs about the women whom they would be meeting, the men had initiated a chain of events that produced *behavioral confirmation* for their beliefs.

Similarly, Susan Andersen and Sandra Bem have shown in an experiment at Stanford University that when the tables are turned—when it is women who have pictures of men they are to meet on the telephone—many women treat the men according to their presumed physical attractiveness, and by so doing encourage the men to confirm their stereotypes. Little wonder, then, that so many people remain convinced that good looks and appealing personalities go hand in hand.

SEX AND RACE

It is experiments such as these that point to a frequently unnoticed power of stereotypes: the power to influence social relationships in ways that create the illusion of reality. In one study, Berna Skrypnek and I arranged for pairs of previously unacquainted students to interact in a situation that permitted us to control the information that each one received about the apparent sex of the other. The two people were seated in separate rooms so that they could neither see nor hear each other. Using a system of signal lights that they operated with switches, they negotiated a division of labor, deciding which member of the pair would perform each of several tasks that differed in sex-role connotations. The tasks varied along the dimensions of masculinity and feminity: sharpen a hunting knife (masculine), polish a pair of shoes (neutral), iron a shirt (feminine).

One member of the team was led to believe that the other was, in one condition of the experiment, male; in the other, female. As we had predicted, the first member's belief about the sex of the partner influenced the outcome of the pair's negotiations. Women whose partners believed them to be men generally chose stereotypically masculine tasks; in contrast, women whose partners believed that they were women usually chose stereotypically feminine tasks. The experiment thus suggests that much sex-role behavior may be the product of other people's stereotyped and often erroneous beliefs.

In a related study at the University of Waterloo, Carl von Baeyer, Debbie Sherk, and Mark Zanna have shown how stereotypes about sex roles operate in job interviews. The researchers arranged to have men conduct simulated job interviews with women supposedly seeking positions as research assistants. The investigators informed half of the women that the men who would interview them held traditional views about the ideal woman, believing her to be very emotional, deferential to her husband, home-oriented, and passive. The rest of the women were told that their interviewer saw the ideal woman as independent, competitive, ambitious, and dominant. When the women arrived for their interviews, the researchers noticed that most of them had dressed to meet the stereotyped expectations of their prospective interviewers. Women who expected to see a traditional interviewer had chosen very feminine-looking makeup, clothes, and accessories. During the interviews (videotaped through a one-way mirror) these women behaved in traditionally feminine ways and gave traditionally feminine answers to questions such as "Do you have plans to include children and marriage with your career plans?"

Once more, then, we see the self-fulfilling nature of stereotypes. Many sex differences, it appears, may result from the images that people create in their attempts to act out accepted sex roles. The implication is that if stereotyped expectations about sex roles shift, behavior may change, too. In fact, statements by people who have undergone sex-change operations have highlighted the power of such expectations in easing adjustment to a new life. As the writer Jan Morris said in recounting the story of her transition from James to Jan: "The more I was treated as a woman, the more woman I became."

The power of stereotypes to cause people to confirm stereotyped expectations can also be seen in interracial relationships. In the first two investigations done at Princeton University by Carl Word, Mark Zanna, and Joel Cooper, white undergraduates interviewed both white and black job applicants. The applicants were actually confederates of the experimenters, trained to behave consistently from interview to interview, no matter how the interviewers acted toward them.

To find out whether or not the white interviewers would behave differently toward white and black job applicants, the researchers secretly videotaped each interview and then studied the tapes. From these, it was apparent that there were substantial differences in the treatment accorded blacks and whites. For one thing, the interviewers' speech deteriorated when they talked to blacks, displaying more errors in grammar and pronunciation. For another, the interviewers spent less time with blacks than with whites and showed less "immediacy," as the researchers called it, in their manner. That is, they were less friendly, less outgoing, and more reserved with blacks.

In the second investigation, white confederates were trained to approximate either the immediate or the nonimmediate interview styles that had been observed in the first investigation as they interviewed white job applicants. A panel of judges who evaluated the tapes agreed that applicants subjected to the nonimmediate styles performed less adequately and were more nervous than job applicants treated in the immediate style. Apparently, then, the blacks in the first study did not have a chance to display their qualifications to the best advantage. Considered together, the two investigations suggest that in interracial encounters, racial stereotypes may constrain behavior in ways that cause both blacks and whites to behave in accordance with those stereotypes.

REWRITING BIOGRAPHY

Having adopted stereotyped ways of thinking about another person, people tend to notice and remember the ways
in which that person seems to fit the stereotype, while
resisting evidence that conradicts the stereotype. In one
investigation that I conducted with Seymour Uranowitz,
student subjects read a biography of a fictitious woman
named Betty K. We constructed the story of her life so that
it would fit the stereotyped images of both lesbians and
heterosexuals. Betty, we wrote, never had a steady boyfriend in high school, but did go out on dates. And although we gave her a steady boyfriend in college, we
specified that he was more of a close friend than anything
else. A week after we had distributed this biography, we
gave our subjects some new information about Betty. We
told some students that she was now living with another
woman in a lesbian relationship; we told others that she
was living with her husband.

To see what impact stereotype about sexuality would
have on how people remembered the facts of Betty's life,
we asked each student to answer a series of questions
about her life history. When we examined their answers,
we found that the students had reconstructed the events of
Betty's past in ways that supported their own stereotyped
beliefs about her sexual orientation. Those who believed
that Betty was lesbian remembered that Betty had never
had a steady boyfriend in high school, but tended to neglect
the fact that she had gone out on many dates in college.
Those who believed that Betty was now a heterosexual
tended to remember that she had formed a steady relationship
with a man in college, but tended to ignore the fact that
this relationship was more of a friendship than a romance.

The students showed not only selective memories but
also a striking facility for interpreting what they remembered
in ways that added fresh support for their stereotypes. One
student who accurately remembered that a supposedly lesbian
Betty never had a steady boyfriend in high school confidently
pointed to that fact as an early sign of her lack of romantic
or sexual interest in men. A student who correclty remem-

bered that a purportedly lesbian Betty often went out on dates in college was sure that these dates were signs of Betty's early attempts to mask her lesbian interests.

Clearly, the students had allowed their preconceptions about lesbians and heterosexuals to dictate the way in which they interpreted and reinterpreted the facts of Betty's life. As long as stereotypes make it easy to bring to mind evidence that supports them and difficult to bring to mind evidence that undermines them, people will cling to erroneous beliefs.

STEREOTYPES IN THE CLASSROOM AND WORK PLACE

The power of one person's beliefs to make other people conform to them has been well demonstrated in real life. Back in the 1960s, as most people well remember, Harvard psychologist Robert Rosenthal and his colleague Lenore Jacobson entered elementary-school classrooms and identified one out of every five pupils in each room as a child who could be expected to show dramatic improvement in intellectual achievement during the school year. What the teachers did not know was that the children had been chosen on a random basis. Nevertheless, something happened in the relationships between teachers and their supposedly gifted pupils that led the children to make clear gains in test performance.

It can also do so on the job. Albert King, now a professor of management at Northern Illinois University, told a welding instructor in a vocational training center that five men in his training program had unusually high aptitude. Although these five had been chosen at random and knew nothing of their designation as high-aptitude workers, they showed substantial changes in performance. They were absent less often than were other workers, learned the basics of the welder's trade in about half the usual time, and scored a full 10 points higher than other trainees on a welding test. Their gains were noticed not only by the researcher and by the welding instructor, but also by other trainees, who singled out the five as their preferred co-workers.

Might not other expectations influence the relationships between supervisors and workers? For example, supervisors who believe that men are better suited to some jobs and women to others may treat their workers (wittingly or unwittingly) in ways that encourage them to perform their jobs in accordance with stereotypes about differences between men and women. These same stereotypes may determine who gets which job in the first place. Perhaps some personnel managers allow stereotypes to influence, subtly or not so subtly, the way in which they interview job candidates, making it likely that candidates who fit the stereotypes show up better than job-seekers who do not fit them.

Unfortunately, problems of this kind are compounded by the fact that members of stigmatized groups often subscribe to stereotypes about themselves. That is what Amerigo Farina and his colleagues at the University of Connecticut found when they measured the impact upon mental patients of believing that others knew their psychiatric history. In Farina's study, each mental patient cooperated with another person in a game requiring teamwork. Half of the patients believed that their partners knew they were patients; the other half believed that their partners thought they were nonpatients. In reality, the nonpatients never knew a thing about anyone's psychiatric history. Nevertheless, simply believing that others were aware of their history led the patients to feel less appreciated, to find the task more difficult, and to perform poorly. In addition, objective observers saw them as more tense, more anxious, and more poorly adjusted than patients who believed that their status was not known. Seemingly, the belief that others perceived them as stigmatized caused them to play the role of stigmatized patients.

CONSEQUENCES FOR SOCIETY

Apparently, good will and education are not sufficient to subvert the power of stereotypes. If people treat others in such a way as to bring out behavior that supports stereotypes, they may never have an opportunity to discover which of their stereotypes are wrong.

I suspect that even if people were to develop doubts about the accuracy of their stereotypes, chances are they would proceed to test them by gathering precisely the evidence that would appear to confirm them.

The experiments I have described help to explain the persistence of stereotypes. But, as is so often the case, solving one puzzle only creates another. If by acting as if false stereotypes were true, people lead others, too, to act as if they were true, why do the stereotypes not come to *be* true? Why, for example, have researchers found so little evidence that attractive people are generally friendly, sociable, and outgoing and that unattractive people are generally shy and aloof?

I think that the explanation goes something like this: Very few among us have the kind of looks that virtually everyone considers either very attractive or very unattractive. Our looks make us rather attractive to some people but somewhat less attractive to other people. When we spend time with those who find us attractive, they will tend to bring out our more sociable sides, but when we are with those who find us less attractive, they will bring out our less sociable sides. Although our actual physical appearance does not change, we present ourselves quite differently to our admirers and to our detractors. For our admirers we become attractive people, and for our detractors we become unattractive. This mixed pattern of behavior will prevent the development of any consistent relationship between physical attractiveness and personality.

Now that I understand some of the powerful forces that work to perpetuate social stereotypes, I can see a new mission for my research. I hope, on the one hand, to find out how to help people see the flaws in their stereotypes. On the other hand, I would like to help the victims of false stereotypes find ways of liberating themselves from the constraints imposed on them by other members of society.

The Dilemma of Obedience

by Stanley Milgram

Since the Nuremberg war trials brought the role of obedience in evil to the center stage of world attention, we have wondered about the relationship between individual conscience and social obedience. How does the individual balance the two, or indeed, should they be balanced?

Trying to study such horrible examples of obedience as exemplified by the Third Reich presented psychologists a troublesome scientific problem: How could such extremes of obedience be recreated in the laboratory setting? The late Stanley Milgram was a key figure in designing such analogs of obedience to external authority. Volunteers for an experiment on learning were induced to administer what they believed were painful shocks to another volunteer—actually a confederate of Milgram's. Many volunteers obeyed a white-coated experimenter who urged them to keep giving shocks despite the screams of pain they heard.

Milgram, describing these controversial experiments, takes the position that obedience is built into the very fabric of social life, since some authority is essential in society. And in a smoothly running society, individuals sometimes violate the guidelines of their conscience in order to comply—a dilemma for a democratic society.

TWO PEOPLE COME to a psychology laboratory to take part in a study of memory and learning. One of them is designated as a "teacher" and the other a "learner." The experimenter explains that the study is concerned with the effects of punishment on learning. The learner is conducted into a room, seated in a chair, his arms strapped to prevent excessive movement, and an electrode attached to his wrist. He is told that he is to learn a list of word pairs; whenever he makes an error, he will receive electric shocks of increasing intensity.

The real focus of the experiment is the teacher. After watching the learner being strapped into place, he is taken into the main experimental room and seated before an impressive shock generator. Its main feature is a horizontal line of thirty switches, ranging from 15 volts to 450 volts, in 15-volt increments. There are also verbal designations which range from SLIGHT SHOCK to DANGER—SEVERE SHOCK. The teacher is told that he is to administer the learning test to the man in the other room. When the learner responds correctly, the teacher moves on to the next item; when the other man gives an incorrect answer, the teacher is to give him an electric shock. He is to start at the lowest shock level (15 volts) and to increase the level each time the man makes an error, going through 30 volts, 45 volts, and so on.

The "teacher" is a genuinely naïve subject who has come to the laboratory to participate in an experiment. The learner, or victim, is an actor who actually receives no shock at all. The point of the experiment is to see how far a person will proceed in a concrete and measurable situation in which he is ordered to inflict increasing pain on a protesting victim. At what point will the subject refuse to obey the experimenter?

Conflict arises when the man receiving the shock begins to indicate that he is experiencing discomfort. At 75 volts, the "learner" grunts. At 120 volts he complains verbally; at 150 he demands to be released from the experiment. His protests continue as the shocks escalate, growing increasingly vehement and emotional. At 285 volts his response can only be described as an agonized scream.

Observers of the experiment agree that its gripping quality is somewhat obscured in print. For the subject, the situation is not a game; conflict is intense and obvious. On one hand, the manifest suffering of the learner presses him to quit. On the other, the experimenter, a legitimate authority to whom the subject feels some commitment, enjoins him to continue. Each time the subject hesitates to administer shock, the experimenter orders him to continue. To extricate himself from the situation, the subject must make a clear break with authority. The aim of this investigation was to find when and how people would defy authority in the face of a clear moral imperative.

There are, of course, enormous differences between carrying out the orders of a commanding officer during times of war and carrying out the orders of an experimenter. Yet the essence of certain relationships remain, for one may ask in a general way: How does a man behave when he is told by a legitimate authority to act against a third individual?

A reader's initial reaction to the experiment may be to wonder why anyone in his right mind would administer even the first shocks. Would he not simply refuse and walk out of the laboratory? But the fact is that no one ever does. Since the subject has come to the laboratory to aid the experimenter, he is quite willing to start off with the procedure. What is surprising is how far ordinary individuals will go in complying with the experimenter's instructions. Despite the fact that many subjects experience stress, despite the fact that many protest to the experimenter, a substantial proportion continue to the last shock on the generator.

Many subjects will obey the experimenter no matter how vehement the pleading of the person being shocked, no matter how painful the shocks seem to be, and no matter how much the victim pleads to be let out. It is the extreme willingness of adults to go to almost any lengths on the command of an authority that constitutes the chief finding of the study and the fact most urgently demanding explanation.

A commonly offered explanation is that those who shocked the victim at the most severe level were monsters, the sadistic fringe of society. But if one considers that almost two-thirds of the participants fall into the category of "obedient" subjects, and that they represented ordinary people drawn from working, managerial, and professional classes, the argument becomes very shaky.

This is, perhaps, the most fundamental lesson of our study: ordinary people, simply doing their jobs, and without any particular hostility on their part, can become agents in a terrible destructive process. Moreover, even when the destructive effects of their work become patently clear, and they are asked to carry out actions incompatible with fundamental standards of morality, relatively few people have the resources needed to resist authority. A variety of inhibitions against disobeying authority come into play and successfully keep the person in his place.

What keeps the person obeying the experimenter? First, there is a set of "binding factors" that lock the subject into the situation. They include such factors as politeness on his part, his desire to uphold his initial promise of aid to the experimenter, and the awkwardness of withdrawal. Second, a number of adjustments in the subject's thinking occur that undermine his resolve to break with the authority. The adjustments help the subject maintain his relationship with the experimenter, while at the same time reducing the strain brought about by the experimental conflict. They are typical of thinking that comes about in obedient persons when they are instructed by authority to act against helpless individuals.

One such mechanism is the tendency of the individual to become so absorbed in the narrow technical aspects of the task that he loses sight of its broader consequences. The film *Dr. Strangelove* brilliantly satirized the absorption of a bomber crew in the exacting technical procedure of dropping nuclear weapons on a country. Similarly, in this experiment, subjects become immersed in the procedures, reading the word pairs with exquisite articulation and pressing the switches with great care. They want to put on a competent performance, but they show an accompanying narrowing of moral concern. The subject entrusts the broader tasks of setting goals and assessing morality to the experimental authority he is serving.

The most common adjustment of thought in the obedient

subject is for him to see himself as not responsible for his own actions. He divests himself of responsibility by attributing all initiative to the experimenter, a legitimate authority. He sees himself not as a person acting in a morally accountable way but as the agent of external authority. In the postexperimental interview, when subjects were asked why they had gone on, a typical reply was: "I wouldn't have done it by myself. I was just doing what I was told." Unable to defy the authority of the experimenter, they attribute all responsibility to him. The disappearance of a sense of responsibility is the most far-reaching consequence of submission to authority.

For decades psychologists have discussed the primitive tendency among men to attribute to inanimate objects and forces the qualities of the human species. A countervailing tendency, however, is that of attributing an impersonal quality to forces that are essentially human in origin and maintenance. Some people treat systems of human origin as if they existed above and beyond any human agent, beyond the control of whim or human feeling. The human element behind agencies and institutions is denied. Thus, when the experimenter says, "The experiment *requires* that you continue," the subject feels this to be an imperative that goes beyond any merely human command. He does not ask the seemingly obvious question, "Whose experiment? Why should the designer be served while the victim suffers?" The wishes of a man—the designer of the experiment—have become part of a schema which exerts on the subject's mind a force that transcends the personal. "It's *got* to go on. It's *got* to go on," repeated one subject. He failed to realize that a man like himself wanted it to go on. For him the human agent had faded from the picture, and "The Experiment" had acquired an impersonal momentum of its own.

The problem of obedience is not wholly psychological. The form and shape of society and the way it is developing have much to do with it. There was a time, perhaps, when men were able to give a fully human response to any situation because they were fully absorbed in it as human beings. But as soon as there was a division of labor among men, things changed. Beyond a certain point, the breaking up of society into people carrying out narrow and very special jobs takes away from the human quality of work and life. A person does not get to see the whole situation but only a small part of it, and is thus unable to act without some kind of over-all direction. He yields to authority but in doing so is alienated from his own actions.

George Orwell caught the essence of the situation when he wrote:

> As I write, highly civilized human beings are flying overhead, trying to kill me. They do not feel any enmity against me as an individual, nor I against them. They are only "doing their duty," as the saying goes. Most of them, I have no doubt, are kind-hearted law abiding men who would never dream of committing murder in private life. On the other hand, if one of them succeeds in blowing me to pieces with a well-placed bomb, he will never sleep any the worse for it.

Groupthink

by Irving Janis

Irving Janis has long been associated with the psychology of "groupthink." Using the concept of groupthink, Janis explains the social psychology of collective decision-making at the national policy level, in the highest circles of government. The pressure for consensus at any cost, he shows, can suppress dissent and disagreement among even the most powerful.

Janis maintains that groupthink operates when each group member accepts the collective assumptions of a group, however one-dimensional and nearsighted they might be. Issues of morality also come into play, as members assume, without careful consideration, that the group has an inherently solid morality, superior to any other. These observations are most disturbing. Groupthink can pave the way to disaster, since it does not allow for sound judgment based on consideration of all possibilities. Janis cites a number of famous examples—Vietnam, the Bay of Pigs, Korea, and Pearl Harbor. While Janis does not suggest that the practice of groupthink is always at work in government, he does suggest that it has real dangers.

"How COULD WE have been so stupid?" President John F. Kennedy asked after he and a close group of advisers had blundered into the Bay of Pigs invasion. For the last two years I have been studying that question, as it applies not only to the Bay of Pigs decision-makers but also to those

who led the United States into such other major fiascos as
the failure to be prepared for the attack on Pearl Harbor,
the Korean War stalemate and the escalation of the Vietnam War.

Stupidity certainly is not the explanation. The men who
participated in making the Bay of Pigs decision, for instance, comprised one of the greatest arrays of intellectual
talent in the history of American government—Dean Rusk,
Robert McNamara, Douglas Dillon, Robert Kennedy,
McGeorge Bundy, Arthur Schlesinger Jr., Allen Dulles
and others.

It also seemed to me that explanations were incomplete
if they concentrated only on disturbances in the behavior
of each individual within a decision-making body: temporary emotional states of elation, fear, or anger that reduced
a man's mental efficiency, for example, or chronic blind
spots arising from a man's social prejudices or idiosyncratic biases.

I preferred to broaden the picture by looking at the
fiascos from the standpoint of group dynamics as it has
been explored over the past three decades, first by the
great social psychologist Kurt Lewin and later in many
experimental situations by myself and other behavioral
scientists. My conclusion after poring over hundreds of
relevant documents—historical reports about formal group
meetings and informal conversations among the members—is
that the groups that committed the fiascos were victims of
what I call "groupthink."

"Groupy." In each case study, I was surprised to discover the extent to which each group displayed the typical
phenomena of social conformity that are regularly encountered in studies of group dynamics among ordinary citizens. For example, some of the phenomena appear to be
completely in line with findings from social-psychological
experiments showing that powerful social pressures are
brought to bear by the members of a cohesive group
whenever a dissident begins to voice his objections to a
group consensus. Other phenomena are reminiscent of the
shared illusions observed in encounter groups and friend-

ship cliques when the members simultaneously reach a peak of "groupy" feelings.

Above all, there are numerous indications pointing to the development of group norms that bolster morale at the expense of critical thinking. One of the most common norms appears to be that of remaining loyal to the group by sticking with the policies to which the group has already committed itself, even when those policies are obviously working out badly and have unintended consequences that disturb the conscience of each member. This one is of the key characteristics of groupthink.

1984. I use the term groupthink as a quick and easy way to refer to the mode of thinking that persons engage in when *concurrence-seeking* becomes so dominant in a cohesive ingroup that it tends to override realistic appraisal of alternative courses of action. Groupthink is a term of the same order as the words in the newspeak vocabulary George Orwell used in his dismaying world of *1984*. In that context, groupthink takes on an invidious connotation. Exactly such a connotation is intended, since the term refers to a deterioration in mental efficiency, reality testing and moral judgments as a result of group pressures.

The symptoms of groupthink arise when the members of decision-making groups become motivated to avoid being too harsh in their judgments of their leaders' or their colleagues' ideas. They adopt a soft line of criticism, even in their own thinking. At their meetings, all the members are amiable and seek complete concurrence on every important issue, with no bickering or conflict to spoil the cozy, "we-feeling" atmosphere.

Kill. Paradoxically, soft-headed groups are often hard-hearted when it comes to dealing with outgroups or enemies. They find it relatively easy to resort to dehumanizing solutions—they will readily authorize bombing attacks that kill large numbers of civilians in the name of the noble cause of persuading an unfriendly government to negotiate at the peace table. They are unlikely to pursue the more difficult and controversial issues that arise when alternatives to a harsh military solution come up for discussion.

Nor are they inclined to raise ethical issues that carry the implication that *this fine group of ours, with its humanitarianism and its high-minded principles, might be capable of adopting a course of action that is inhumane and immoral.*

Norms. There is evidence from a number of social-psychological studies that as the members of a group feel more accepted by the others, which is a central feature of increased group cohesiveness, they display less overt conformity to group norms. Thus we would expect that the more cohesive a group becomes, the less the members will feel constrained to censor what they say out of fear of being socially punished for antagonizing the leader or any of their fellow members.

In contrast, the groupthink type of conformity tends to increase as group cohesiveness increases. Groupthink involves nondeliberate suppression of critical thoughts as a result of internalization of the group's norms, which is quite different from deliberate suppression on the basis of external threats of social punishment. The more cohesive the group, the greater the inner compulsion on the part of each member to avoid creating disunity, which inclines him to believe in the soundness of whatever proposals are promoted by the leader or by a majority of the group's members.

In a cohesive group, the danger is not so much that each individual will fail to reveal his objections to what the others propose but that he will think the proposal is a good one, without attempting to carry out a careful, critical scrutiny of the pros and cons of the alternatives. When groupthink becomes dominant, there also is considerable suppression of deviant thoughts, but it takes the form of each person's deciding that his misgivings are not relevant and should be set aside, that the benefit of the doubt regarding any lingering uncertainties should be given to the group consensus.

Stress. I do not mean to imply that all cohesive groups necessarily suffer from groupthink. All ingroups may have a mild tendency toward groupthink, displaying one or another of the symptoms from time to time, but it need not be so dominant as to influence the quality of the group's final decision. Neither do I mean to imply that there is anything necessarily inefficient or harmful about group decisions in general. On the contrary, a group whose members have properly defined roles, with traditions concerning the procedures to follow in pursuing a critical inquiry, probably is capable of making better decisions than any individual group member working alone.

The problem is that the advantages of having decisions made by groups are often lost because of powerful psychological pressures that arise when the members work closely together, share the same set of values and, above all, face a crisis situation that puts everyone under intense stress.

The main principle of groupthink, which I offer in the spirit of Parkinson's Law, is this: *The more amiability and esprit de corps there is among the members of a policy-making ingroup, the greater the danger that independent critical thinking will be replaced by groupthink, which is likely to result in irrational and dehumanizing actions directed against outgroups.*

Symptoms. In my studies of high-level governmental decision-makers, both civilian and military, I have found eight main symptoms of groupthink.

1. INVULNERABILITY. Most or all of the members of the ingroup share an *illusion* of invulnerability that provides for them some degree of reassurance about obvious dangers and leads them to become over-optimistic and willing to take extraordinary risks. It also causes them to fail to respond to clear warnings of danger.

The Kennedy ingroup, which uncritically accepted the Central Intelligence Agency's disastrous Bay of Pigs plan, operated on the false assumption that they could keep secret the fact that the United States was responsible for the invasion of Cuba. Even after news of the plan began to leak out, their belief remained unshaken. They failed even to consider the danger that awaited them: a worldwide revulsion against the U.S.

A similar attitude appeared among the members of President Lyndon B. Johnson's ingroup, the "Tuesday Cabinet," which kept escalating the Vietnam War despite repeated setbacks and failures. "There was a belief," Bill Moyers commented after he resigned, "that if we indicated a willingness to use our power, they [the North Vietnamese] would get the message and back away from an all-out confrontation. . . . There was a confidence—it was never bragged about, it was just there—that when the chips were really down, the other people would fold."

A most poignant example of an illusion of invulnerability involves the ingroup around Admiral H.E. Kimmel, which failed to prepare for the possibility of a Japanese attack on Pearl Harbor despite repeated warnings. Informed by his intelligence chief that radio contact with Japanese aircraft carriers had been lost, Kimmel joked about it: "What, you don't know where the carriers are? Do you mean to say that they could be rounding Diamond Head (at Honolulu) and you wouldn't know it?" The carriers were in fact moving full-steam toward Kimmel's command post at the time. Laughing together about a danger signal, which labels it as a purely laughing matter, is a characteristic manifestation of groupthink.

2. RATIONALE. As we see, victims of groupthink ignore warnings; they also collectively construct rationalizations in order to discount warnings and other forms of negative feedback that, taken seriously, might lead the group members to reconsider their assumptions each time they recommit themselves to past decisions. Why did the Johnson ingroup avoid reconsidering its escalation policy when time and again the expectations on which they based their decisions turned out to be wrong? James C. Thompson Jr., a Harvard historian who spent five years as an observing participant in both the State Department and the White House, tells us that the policymakers avoided critical discussion of their prior decisions and continually invented new rationalizations so that they could sincerely recommit themselves to defeating the North Vietnamese.

In the fall of 1964, before the bombing of North Vietnam began, some of the policymakers predicted that six weeks of air strikes would induce the North Vietnamese to seek peace talks. When someone asked, "What if they don't?" the answer was that another four weeks certainly would do the trick.

Later, after each setback, the ingroup agreed that by investing just a bit more effort (by stepping up the bomb tonnage a bit, for instance), their course of action would prove to be right. *The Pentagon Papers* bear out these observations.

In *The Limits of Intervention*, Townsend Hoopes, who was acting Secretary of the Air Force under Johnson, says that Walt W. Rostow in particular showed a remarkable capacity for what has been called "instant rationalization." According to Hoopes, Rostow buttressed the group's optimism about being on the road to victory by culling selected scraps of evidence from news reports or, if necessary, by inventing "plausible" forecasts that had no basis in evidence at all.

Admiral Kimmel's group rationalized away their warnings, too. Right up to December 7, 1941, they convinced themselves that the Japanese would never dare attempt a full-scale surprise assault against Hawaii because Japan's leaders would realize that it would precipitate an all-out war which the United States would surely win. They made no attempt to look at the situation through the eyes of the Japanese leaders—another manifestation of groupthink.

3. MORALITY. Victims of groupthink believe unquestioningly in the inherent morality of their ingroup; this belief inclines the members to ignore the ethical or moral consequences of their decisions.

Evidence that this symptom is at work usually is of a negative kind—the things that are left unsaid in group meetings. At least two influential persons had doubts about the morality of the Bay of Pigs adventure. One of them, Arthur Schlesinger Jr., presented his strong objections in a memorandum to President Kennedy and Secretary of State Rusk but suppressed them when he attended meetings of the Kennedy team. The other, Senator J. William Fulbright, was not a member of the group, but the President invited him to express his misgivings in a speech to the policymakers. However, when Fulbright finished speaking the President moved on to other agenda items without asking for reactions of the group.

David Kraslow and Stuart H. Loory, in *The Secret Search for Peace in Vietnam*, report that during 1966 President Johnson's ingroup was concerned primarily with selecting bomb targets in North Vietnam. They based their selections on four factors—the military advantage, the risk to American aircraft and pilots, the danger of forcing other countries into the fighting, and the danger of heavy civilian casualties. At their regular Tuesday luncheons, they weighed these factors the way school teachers grade examination papers, averaging them out. Though evidence on this point is scant, I suspect that the group's ritualistic adherence to a standardized procedure induced the members to feel morally justified in their destructive way of dealing with the Vietnamese people—after all, the danger of heavy civilian casualties from U.S. air strikes was taken into account on their checklists.

4. STEREOTYPES. Victims of groupthink hold stereotyped views of the leaders of enemy groups: they are so evil that genuine attempts at negotiating differences with them are unwarranted, or they are too weak or too stupid to deal effectively with whatever attempts the ingroup makes to defeat their purposes, no matter how risky the attempts are.

Kennedy's groupthinkers believed that Premier Fidel Castro's air force was so ineffectual that obsolete B-26s could knock it out completely in a surprise attack before the invasion began. They also believed that Castro's army was so weak that a small Cuban-exile brigade could establish a well-protected beachhead at the Bay of Pigs. In addition, they believed that Castro was not smart enough to put down any possible internal uprisings in support of the exiles. They were wrong on all three assumptions. Though much of the blame was attributable to faulty intelligence, the point is that none of Kennedy's advisers even questioned the CIA planners about these assumptions.

The Johnson advisers' sloganistic thinking about ''the

Communist apparatus" that was "working all around the world" (as Dean Rusk put it) led them to overlook the powerful nationalistic strivings of the North Vietnamese government and its efforts to ward off Chinese domination. The crudest of all stereotypes used by Johnson's inner circle to justify their policies was the domino theory ("If we don't stop the Reds in South Vietnam, tomorrow they will be in Hawaii and next week they will be in San Francisco," Johnson once said). The group so firmly accepted this stereotype that it became almost impossible for any adviser to introduce a more sophisticated viewpoint.

In the documents on Pearl Harbor, it is clear to see that the Navy commanders stationed in Hawaii had a naive image of Japan as a midget that would not dare to strike a blow against a powerful giant.

5. PRESSURE. Victims of groupthink apply direct pressure to any individual who momentarily expresses doubts about any of the group's shared illusions or who questions the validity of the arguments supporting a policy alternative favored by the majority. This gambit reinforces the concurrence-seeking norm that loyal members are expected to maintain.

President Kennedy probably was more active than anyone else in raising skeptical questions during the Bay of Pigs meetings, and yet he seems to have encouraged the group's docile, uncritical acceptance of defective arguments in favor of the CIA's plan. At every meeting, he allowed the CIA representatives to dominate the discussion. He permitted them to give their immediate refutations in response to each tentative doubt that one of the others expressed, instead of asking whether anyone shared the doubt or wanted to pursue the implications of the new worrisome issue that had just been raised. And at the most crucial meeting, when he was calling on each member to give his vote for or against the plan, he did not call on Arthur Schlesinger, the one man there who was known by the President to have serious misgivings.

Historian Thomson informs us that whenever a member of Johnson's ingroup began to express doubts, the group used subtle social pressures to "domesticate" him. To start with, the dissenter was made to feel at home, provided that he lived up to two restrictions: 1) that he did not voice his doubts to outsiders, which would play into the hands of the opposition; and 2) that he kept his criticisms within the bounds of acceptable deviation, which meant not challenging any of the fundamental assumptions that went into the group's prior commitments. One such "domesticated dissenter" was Bill Moyers. When Moyers arrived at a meeting, Thomson tells us, the President greeted him with, "Well, here comes Mr. Stop-the-Bombing."

6. SELF-CENSORSHIP. Victims of groupthink avoid deviating from what appears to be group consensus; they keep silent about their misgivings and even minimize to themselves the importance of their doubts.

As we have seen, Schlesinger was not at all hesitant about presenting his strong objections to the Bay of Pigs plan in a memorandum to the President and the Secretary of State. But he became keenly aware of his tendency to suppress objections at the White House meetings. "In the months after the Bay of Pigs I bitterly reproached myself for having kept so silent during those crucial discussions in the cabinet room," Schlesinger writes in *A Thousand Days*. "I can only explain my failure to do more than raise a few timid questions by reporting that one's impulse to blow the whistle on this nonsense was simply undone by the circumstances of the discussion."

7. UNANIMITY. Victims of groupthink share an *illusion* of unanimity within the group concerning almost all judgments expressed by members who speak in favor of the majority view. This symptom results partly from the preceding one, whose effects are augmented by the false assumption that any individual who remains silent during any part of the discussion is in full accord with what the others are saying.

When a group of persons who respect each other's opinions arrives at a unanimous view, each member is likely to feel that the belief must be true. This reliance on consensual validation within the group tends to replace individual critical thinking and reality testing, unless there are clear-cut disagreements among the members. In contemplating a course of action such as the invasion of Cuba, it is painful for the members to confront disagreements within their group, particularly if it becomes apparent that there are widely divergent views about whether the preferred course of action is too risky to undertake at all. Such disagreements are likely to arouse anxieties about making a serious error. Once the sense of unanimity is shattered, the members no longer can feel complacently confident about the decision they are inclined to make. Each man must then face the annoying realization that there are troublesome uncertainties and he must diligently seek out the best information he can get in order to decide for himself exactly how serious the risks might be. This is one of the unpleasant consequences of being in a group of hardheaded, critical thinkers.

To avoid such an unpleasant state, the members often become inclined, without quite realizing it, to prevent latent disagreements from surfacing when they are about to initiate a risky course of action. The group leader and the members support each other in playing up the areas of convergence in their thinking, at the expense of fully exploring divergencies that might reveal unsettled issues.

"Our meetings took place in a curious atmosphere of assumed consensus," Schlesinger writes. His additional comments clearly show that, curiously, the consensus was an illusion—an illusion that could be maintained only because the major participants did not reveal their own reasoning or discuss their idiosyncratic assumptions and vague reservations. Evidence from several sources makes it clear that even the three principals—President Kennedy, Rusk and McNamara—had widely differing assumptions about the invasion plan.

8. MINDGUARDS. Victims of groupthink sometimes appoint themselves as mindguards to protect the leader and fellow members from adverse information that might break the complacency they shared about the effectiveness and morality of past decisions. At a large birthday party for his

wife, Attorney General Robert F. Kennedy, who had been constantly informed about the Cuban invasion plan, took Schlesinger aside and asked him why he was opposed. Kennedy listened coldly and said, "You may be right or you may be wrong, but the President has made his mind up. Don't push it any further. Now is the time for everyone to help him all they can."

Rusk also functioned as a highly effective mindguard by failing to transmit to the group the strong objections of three "outsiders" who had learned of the invasion plan—Undersecretary of State Chester Bowles, USIA Director Edward R. Murrow, and Rusk's intelligence chief, Roger Hilsman. Had Rusk done so, their warnings might have reinforced Schlesinger's memorandum and jolted some of Kennedy's ingroup, if not the President himself, into reconsidering the decision.

Products. When a group of executives frequently displays most or all of these interrelated symptoms, a detailed study of their deliberations is likely to reveal a number of immediate consequences. These consequences are, in effect, products of poor decision-making practices because they lead to inadequate solutions to the problems under discussion.

First, the group limits its discussions to a few alternative courses of action (often only two) without an initial survey of all the alternatives that might be worthy of consideration.

Second, the group fails to reexamine the course of action initially preferred by the majority after they learn of risks and drawbacks they had not considered originally.

Third, the members spend little or no time discussing whether there are nonobvious gains they may have overlooked or ways of reducing the seemingly prohibitive costs that made rejected alternatives appear undesirable to them.

Fourth, members make little or no attempt to obtain information from experts within their own organizations who might be able to supply more precise estimates of potential losses and gains.

Fifth, members show positive interest in facts and opinions that support their preferred policy; they tend to ignore facts and opinions that do not.

Sixth, members spend little time deliberating about how the chosen policy might be hindered by bureaucratic inertia, sabotaged by political opponents, or temporarily derailed by common accidents. Consequently, they fail to work out contingency plans to cope with foreseeable setbacks that could endanger the overall success of their chosen course.

Support. The search for an explanation of why groupthink occurs has led me through a quagmire of complicated theoretical issues in the murky area of human motivation. My belief, based on recent social psychological research, is that we can best understand the various symptoms of groupthink as a mutual effort among the group members to maintain self-esteem and emotional equanimity by providing social support to each other, especially at times when they share responsibility for making vital decisions.

Even when no important decision is pending, the typical administrator will begin to doubt the wisdom and morality of his past decisions each time he receives information about setbacks, particularly if the information is accompanied by negative feedback from prominent men who originally had been his supporters. It should not be surprising, therefore, to find that individual members strive to develop unanimity and esprit de corps that will help bolster each other's morale, to create an optimistic outlook about the success of pending decisions, and to reaffirm the positive value of past policies to which all of them are committed.

Pride. Shared illusions of invulnerability, for example, can reduce anxiety about taking risks. Rationalizations help members believe that the risks are really not so bad after all. The assumption of inherent morality helps the members to avoid feelings of shame or guilt. Negative stereotypes function as stress-reducing devices to enhance a sense of moral righteousness as well as pride in a lofty mission.

The mutual enhancement of self-esteem and morale may have functional value in enabling the members to maintain their capacity to take action, but it has maladaptive consequences insofar as concurrence-seeking tendencies interfere with critical, rational capacities and lead to serious errors of judgment.

While I have limited my study to decision-making bodies in government, groupthink symptoms appear in business, industry and any other field where small, cohesive groups make the decisions. It is vital, then, for all sorts of people—and especially group leaders—to know what steps they can take to prevent groupthink.

Remedies. To counterpoint my case studies of the major fiascos, I have also investigated two highly successful group enterprises, the formulation of the Marshall Plan in the Truman Administration and the handling of the Cuban missile crisis by President Kennedy and his advisers. I have found it instructive to examine the steps Kennedy took to change his group's decision-making process. These changes ensured that the mistakes made by his Bay of Pigs ingroup were not repeated by the missile-crisis ingroup, even though the membership of both groups was essentially the same.

The following recommendations for preventing groupthink incorporate many of the good practices I discovered to be characteristic of the Marshall Plan and missile-crisis groups:

1. The leader of a policy-forming group should assign the role of critical evaluator to each member, encouraging the group to give high priority to open airing of objections and doubts. This practice needs to be reinforced by the leader's acceptance of criticism of his own judgments in order to discourage members from soft-pedaling their disagreements and from allowing their striving for concurrence to inhibit critical thinking.

2. When the key members of a hierarchy assign a policy-planning mission to any group within their organization, they should adopt an impartial stance instead of stating preferences and expectations at the beginning. This will encourage open inquiry and impartial probing of a wide range of policy alternatives.

3. The organization routinely should set up several outside policy-planning and evaluation groups to work on the same policy question, each deliberating under a different leader. This can prevent the insulation of an ingroup.

4. At intervals before the group reaches a final consensus, the leader should require each member to discuss the group's deliberations with associates in his own unit of the organization—assuming that those associates can be trusted to adhere to the same security regulations that govern the policy-makers—and then to report back their reactions to the group.

5. The group should invite one or more outside experts to each meeting on a staggered basis and encourage the experts to challenge the views of the core members.

6. At every general meeting of the group, whenever the agenda calls for an evaluation of policy alternatives, at least one member should play devil's advocate, functioning as a good lawyer in challenging the testimony of those who advocate the majority position.

7. Whenever the policy issue involves relations with a rival nation or organization, the group should devote a sizable block of time, perhaps an entire session, to a survey of all warning signals from the rivals and should write alternative scenarios on the rivals' intentions.

8. When the group is surveying policy alternatives for feasibility and effectiveness, it should from time to time divide into two or more subgroups to meet separately, under different chairmen, and then come back together to hammer out differences.

9. After reaching a preliminary consensus about what seems to be the best policy, the group should hold a "second-chance" meeting at which every member expresses as vividly as he can all his residual doubts, and rethinks the entire issue before making a definitive choice.

How. These recommendations have their disadvantages. To encourage the open airing of objections, for instance, might lead to prolonged and costly debates when a rapidly growing crisis requires immediate solution. It also could cause rejection, depression and anger. A leader's failure to set a norm might create cleavage between leader and members that could develop into a disruptive power struggle if the leader looks on the emerging consensus as anathema. Setting up outside evaluation groups might increase the risk of security leakage. Still, inventive executives who know their way around the organizational maze probably can figure out how to apply one or another of the prescriptions successfully, without harmful side effects.

They also could benefit from the advice of outside experts in the administrative and behavioral sciences. Though these experts have much to offer, they have had few chances to work on policy-making machinery within large organizations. As matters now stand, executives innovate only when they need new procedures to avoid repeating serious errors that have deflated their self-images.

In this era of atomic warheads, urban disorganization and ecocatastrophes, it seems to me that policymakers should collaborate with behavioral scientists and give top priority to preventing groupthink and its attendant fiascos.

Prenuclear-age Leaders and the Nuclear Arms Race

by Jerome D. Frank

Since the fateful explosion of the first nuclear bomb some forty years ago, psychologists and psychiatrists were quick to understand the long-range importance of interviewing survivors and assessing psychological impact. Robert Lifton, a psychiatrist, has been a leader in this effort, studying both survivors of the atomic bomb and our collective reactions to the possibility of nuclear annihilation. Lifton has repeatedly emphasized that all of us are susceptible to "psychic numbing"—we block from awareness the sense of dread that nuclear threat may engender.

Jerome Frank of John Hopkins University addresses the tendency toward denial of the nuclear threat, and its consequences on the geopolitical stage. This was originally presented at a Symposium of Physicians for Social Responsibility in 1982, when Frank was moved by the current state of world affairs to address the psychology of the arms race.

Frank's major premise is that national leaders confront the prospect of nuclear war with outdated psychological attitudes. His paper considers the meaning of the word *enemy* as he analyzes the flaws of the policy of nuclear deterrence. But beyond these observations, Frank proceeds to a consideration of peace studies and reflects on the ancient question of how to rid civilization of war—if this is possible. Frank forcefully suggests that it is.

WHAT IS THE basic psychological obstacle to breaking out of the nuclear arms race? I think that national leaders still perceive nuclear weapons as simply larger conventional weapons. In many areas of our life our thinking and behavior are guided by what we tell ourselves about the world, rather than by what the world actually is. A parable may help to illustrate our situation:

> Three umpires were asked, "How do you tell a strike from a ball?" The first said, "I calls them as they are." The second said, "I calls them as I sees them." The third said. "They ain't nothing until I calls them."

And that, I am afraid, is the situation with nuclear weapons, because their magnitude lies totally outside of human experience. The few survivors of Hiroshima and Nagasaki, and a few who actually witnessed atmospheric nuclear tests, are the only people who have directly experienced a nuclear explosion. No national leader today, as far as I know, has actually witnessed a nuclear explosion. These weapons in distant places, poised to wipe us out, do not impinge upon any of the senses. So it takes a constant effort of the imagination to keep them real to us. Our attitude toward nuclear weapons may be like that we felt toward the bogeyman when we were children: he was very scary, but he just wasn't quite real.

Another reason some Americans can speak calmly about contained, "limited" nuclear war may be that no living American has experienced the devastation wrought by any war on our soil; the last time it happened was the Civil War, and no one is around who remembers that. Furthermore, since nuclear weapons are so new we have no appropriate words for them. We are forced to fall back on language designed to describe prenuclear weapons. An example is President Reagan's characterization of a larger nuclear stockpile than that of the Soviets as providing a "margin of safety." That was true of conventional weapons up to a point, but with nuclear weapons, the more you have, the less safe you are.

When the enormous destructive power of nuclear weapons threatens to break into awareness, its impact is weakened by at least two psychological mechanisms. One is the mechanism of denial, which is often talked about. There is another that we do not hear as much about: habituation. Like all living creatures, we humans stop attending to stimuli when they persist unchanged over a long period of time. Survival in the wild required not only the ability to detect any changes in the environment, but also to ignore them if they persist. If an animal kept attending to every stimulus, its capacity to sense new dangers would be swamped. Therefore it just stops attending to them. We do the same thing. The first atomic bomb dropped on Hiroshima created a worldwide shock wave that stimulated intense efforts to ban nuclear weapons. As decades passed without further nuclear explosions, the nuclear threat slipped from attention, with only occasional flurries of concern. They are part of the ground rather than the figure, as psychologists say, and that makes it very difficult to keep them in mind.

Another very serious psychological obstacle to coping with nuclear weapons is simple force of habit, especially as it affects national leaders. Leaders see the world in terms of power; they see every conflict as a win-or-lose situation. In structured societies, struggles for power are guided and constrained by rules, so winners are those who play the game best within the rules.

National leaders see relations between nations in terms of power. They all seek to increase their nation's power or, if it is dominant, hold onto its dominant position. The trouble is, there are no rules in the international realm; and in an anarchic situation, the ultimate test of pwoer has always been the ability to inflict more damage on one's opponents than one's opponents can inflict on you.

When faced with an entirely new, unprecedented problem, we humans try to make it appear like a familiar one and handle it by methods that have worked in the past. So national leaders still cling to the old system of accumulating more weapons all the time, even though they know intellectually that, as Harold Brown, President Carter's Secretary of Defense, said, "Comprehensive military supremacy for either side is a military and economic impossibility.'' Our intellect tells us what we should do, but our emotions often keep us from doing it.

Unfortunately, as long as the world's leaders perceive nuclear weapons as simply larger conventional ones, the country that has a smaller or less technically advanced stockpile will see itself as weaker and will be seen as weaker by its opponents and allies. In actuality the ''weaker'' power can wipe out the ''stronger power, no matter what the stronger power does. Feeling itself to be weaker, however, the country with a smaller stockpile will act as if it actually *were* weaker. It will be more easily intimidated, will act less decisively in crises, and will be in danger of losing its allies and tempting its opponents to seize the inititive. As Admiral Stansfield Turner put it:

> Whatever we do, it must not only correct the actual imbalance of nuclear capability, it must also correct the perception of imbalance. Changing the world's perception that we are falling behind the Soviet Union is as important as not falling behind in fact.

As already noted, ''not falling behind in fact'' does not mean anything. What does mean something is that we have to change the world's perception. The pursuit of security through illusory nuclear superiority is, in reality, more a race for prestige than for actual strength. The nuclear arms race is an especially costly and dangerous form of psychological warfare. As Robert Jay Lifton has pointed out, it is a vain effort to achieve psychological security at the expense of actual security.

Then there is the so-called ''image of the enemy.'' This is universal. All social animals, including humans, feel distrust of a stranger; and when two groups get into a rivalry situation, distrust escalates very rapidly until the rival group conforms to this image of the enemy. The image of the enemy is alway the same, and it readily forms and dissolves, depending on the nature of the relationship between the groups. Enemies are often seen more as demons than humans. This is well illustrated in *Doonesbury* by Gary Trudeau:

> In one sequence BD went to Vietnam and was captured by a communist named Phred. At one point Phred gets a letter and BD asks, "Who's that letter from?" And Phred says, "It's from my mother." BD looks at the reader with a puzzled expression and says, "I never knew commies had mothers."

One trouble with the enemy image is that it creates a self-fulfilling prophecy. It causes enemies to acquire the evil characteristics they attribute to each other. So the enemy image comes to correspond to reality. No nation, ourselves included, would last very long if it did not believe that its enemies were cruel and treacherous and warlike.

The enemy is seen as untrustworthy. As President Reagan said, "the Russians are liars and cheats." I am afraid, in the diplomatic world, everyone is a liar and a cheat. You may remember the characterization of an ambassador: an honest man sent abroad to lie for his country. But who wants to sit down and talk with a liar and a cheat, so the first thing you do is break off communications, as we are doing with the Russians. They've got to be good, they've got to stop the trouble in Poland, they've got to get out of Afghanistan, before we'll talk to them. This ridiculous posture rests on the assumption that reducing nuclear arms is a favor that we are offering to the Russians, instead of realizing that it would be a favor to both sides.

There is at least one documented false feature of our image of the Russians. This is that the facts about the disastrous consequences of a nuclear war are hidden from the Russian people. I have heard over and over again, "Who's telling the Russians?" The fact is that they have probably heard more about the disastrous consequences of nuclear war then we have. The report of the First Congress of the International Physicians for the Prevention of Nuclear War (IPPNW) in March 1981 was published in Russian newspapers with a combined circulation of millions.

Dr. Chazov, the co-chairman of IPPNW and Brezhnev's personal physician, went on an hour-long television program twice, reaching 100 million viewers, to stress the virtual impossibility of anyone surviving a nuclear holocaust.

The worst effect of the enemy image is that it blinds both sides to interests they might have in common. If the Russians stress the horrors of nuclear war, that's a ruse to dissuade us from building more nuclear arms. It is very difficult to entertain the possibility that mutual reduction of nuclear arsenals would benefit both countries.

For deterrence to work, the group to be deterred must make a rational calculation that it would lose more by doing the prohibited act than by refraining from it. Deterrence breaks down if the calculation indicates that defiance would succeed, as when Hitler invaded Poland. Deterrence also fails when tension reaches such a pitch that one of the parties stops calculating.

Deterrence produces great emotional tension, and emotional tension tends to lead people to simplify alternatives. When under pressure, there is nothing harder to do than to do nothing at all; there is a temptation to throw caution to the winds and simply stop calculating.

We can perhaps derive some comfort from remembering that most national leaders would not have reached the top unless they could tolerate stress, but the graveyard of history is littered with the remains of societies whose leaders' judgment failed under stress. As Robert Kennedy wrote in his book on the Cuban missile crisis, even some of the "best and brightest" can reach the breaking point. Kennedy wrote:

. . . some of the [decision makers]) because of the pressure of events, even appeared to lose their judgment and stability.

We have to face a very difficult problem. The human race will never forget how to make nuclear weapons, so the only ultimate assurance of survival is eventually to outlaw war, violence, as a method of solving international conflicts. The problem is, how to get there from here.

Let me first dispose of the biological argument against elimination of war, which is that man is naturally aggressive—as, indeed, he is—and that war is therefore inevitable. This is based on the demonstrable fallacy that one can directly predict any kind of social behavior from a biological propensity. It is perfectly true that in human nervous systems there are programs for violent behavior, but one sees these programs manifested only in people with epilepsy or brain damage, and these patterns of biting, scratching, yelling, and kicking have nothing to do with giving a command or pressing a button to launch a missile. War is an elaborate social institution which has to be learned afresh by every generation. Someone has said, in this sense, war is only 30 years old. To say that because man is biologically aggressive, war is inevitable, is exactly the same as saying that because man is naturally sexual, temple prostitution is inevitable. You cannot jump from the biological to the social. It is well to keep this in mind, because the hopeful side is that social institutions, whatever their source, wither away when they cease to have any useful social function. And nuclear weapons have certainly undermined the usefulness of war for resolving international conflicts.

This process is already underway, although it has received little attention. Since Hiroshima, no war except one that could involve the nuclear powers has been fought to a win: they grind down to an uneasy truce. The one exception is the Vietnam war, in which a tiny nonnuclear power defeated the world's strongest nuclear power. It was not out of humaneness that we did not use nuclear weapons in Vietnam. We dropped napalm, the most horrible conventional weapon that has ever been invented. But there obviously was something in the world situation that prevented us from using nuclear weapons in that situation. We must have realized that the cost to us would have been much greater than any possible gain. So war is already becoming obsolete.

An approach to thinking about how to get rid of war is to study how societies have managed to keep domestic violence under control. Humans within societies are just as violent biologically as those who fight wars. And yet somehow we have learned to keep that violence at a tolerable level, and it is done by peace-keeping institutions with enforcement provisions. The psychological point is that even in a dictatorship, no law can be enforced unless more than 90% of the people obey it voluntarily; that is, these peace-keeping institutions depend on a consensus of the people that it is worth giving up some freedom to be violent, in order to preserve society.

My last major point, is that a very powerful way of breaking down mutual antagonism is to get groups to work together to achieve goals that all want but none can achieve by themselves. We have examples of this in the world right now. The first was the International Geophysical Year. All nations wanted to obtain information about the land masses and the oceans that no nation could get alone, so they very gingerly, for 18 months, put aside all their claims in the Antarctic and created an area with complete inspection. This worked so phenomenally well that the program is now based on a 30-year treaty. And now these scientists are having to create the rudiments of a world government, because they cannot stick to purely scientific questions. Suppose a Frenchman, using American machinery, discovers uranium on soil claimed by Germany. Whose uranium is it? This is a political question, and more and more of these are coming up all the time. This is the hopeful model. The real strength of the United Nations, similarly, is not the General Assembly and the Security Council; it is all the service organizations such as the Economic and Social Council, the World Health Organization, and the World Labor Offices.

People of my age are apt to view with alarm what is going on in the next generation. We cannot quite understand it, and so we assume that almost everything they do is bad. But the next generation is the first or second postnuclear generation. They have been born into a different world than we were. It may not be too much to hope that there will emerge ways of living compatible with survival in the nuclear world.

HELPFUL GUIDES

(0451)

☐ **BORN TO WIN: Transactional Analysis with Gestalt Experiments by Muriel James and Dorothy Jongeward.** This landmark bestseller has convinced millions of readers that they were **Born to Win!** "Enriching, stimulating, rewarding . . . for anyone interested in understanding himself, his relationships with others and his goals."—*Kansas City Times*
(141954—$4.50)*

☐ **UNDERSTANDING YOURSELF by Dr. Christopher Evans.** An interesting collection of questionnaires, tests, quizzes and games, scientifically designed by a team of psychologists to offer a greater self-awareness. Photographs and illustrations included.   (134532—$4.95)

☐ **OVERCOMING PROCRASTINATION by Albert Ellis, Ph.D. and William J. Knaus, Ed.D.** The scientifically proven techniques of Rational-Motive Therapy are applied to procrastination (delaying tactics, frustration, and self-disgust). Examines the causes of procrastination, and the links between procrastination and obesity, drugs, depression, and sexual dysfunction, and other personality and health problems.
(141865—$3.50)*

☐ **THE FEAR OF SUCCESS by Leon Tec, M.D.** In this valuable self-help book, a well-known psychiatrist tells why people do not succeed and what they can do about it. The fear of success is identified and traced from birth, and a diagnostic test and role-playing suggestions are provided to help overcome the problem.   (134419—$3.95)*

*Prices slightly higher in Canada

MENTOR Books of Special Interest

27 million Americans can't read a bedtime story to a child.

It's because 27 million adults in this country simply can't read.

Functional illiteracy has reached one out of five Americans. It robs them of even the simplest of human pleasures, like reading a fairy tale to a child.

You can change all this by joining the fight against illiteracy.

Call the Coalition for Literacy at toll-free **1-800-228-8813** and volunteer.

Volunteer Against Illiteracy. The only degree you need is a degree of caring.